Chaucer and Dante

CHAUCER
AND
DANTE

A Revaluation

By Howard H. Schless

PILGRIM BOOKS

NORMAN, OKLAHOMA

Published by Pilgrim Books
P.O. Box 2399, Norman, Oklahoma 73070
Copyright © 1984 by Pilgrim Books
All rights reserved
ISBN: 0-937664-59-6

Library of Congress Cataloging in Publication Data

Schless, Howard H., 1924–
    Chaucer and Dante: a revaluation.

    Bibliography: p.
    Includes index.
    1. Chaucer, Geoffrey, d. 1400–Sources.   2. Dante
Alighieri, 1265–1321–Influence–Chaucer.   3. Chaucer,
Geoffrey, d. 1400–Knowledge–Italy.   4. Italy in
literature.   I. Title.
PR1912.D3S34   1984   821'.1   84-483
ISBN 0-937664-59-6

Printed and bound in the United States of America

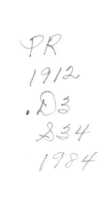
Anne-Ghilaine, Anne-Nicole, Eric Hugh

. . . see that thou lovest that which is lovely

Contents

Preface

No book is ever finished, least of all this one; for while I have endeavored to include all reasonable ascriptions to Dante, I may have omitted a few through judgmental error of their validity, and I have surely overlooked others. In the first category, small though it is, exclusion is certainly arguable; in the second, which I hope is even smaller, it is culpable, and I can only plead, in Dr. Johnson's words, "Ignorance...pure ignorance." And the same conditions apply, though far more blatantly, when I attempt to consider the included ascriptions against the literary background and common knowledge of the period. Here, in the first instance, I have selected from and not surveyed the period, which is an arguable position; in the second instance, my ignorance (in this case, of aspects of the period) cannot be mitigated, even by Johnson's mighty line. Finally, some studies have appeared too late to be included, most notably, the outstanding collection edited by Piero Boitani, entitled *Chaucer and the Italian Trecento* (Cambridge, 1983), especially the insightful studies of Childs on Anglo-Italian contacts, and of Wallace, Windeatt, and Kirkpatrick on Chaucer and Boccaccio. My regret is that I have not been able to profit from such a pertinent book; my concern is that I may have missed some equally important work; my hope is that the present study will offer the reader a foundation for evaluating all that may not have been included.

This book, then, is not, strictly speaking, a census of every suggestion of ascription, nor does it list every scholar who has supported a particular ascription. It does, however, discuss the vast majority of those posited ascriptions, and it discusses them in terms of their strongest argument for inclusion—which is frequently the argument of the first among the proposers, which most often means John Livingston Lowes. This book, which tries to look at Chaucer's use of Dante as objectively and judiciously as possible, will, I hope, serve as a beginning, to be improved and corrected throughout; if it focuses or helps set the tone of further scholarship on the topic, it will have done much.

This book has been difficult to write, not only because of the scope of the subject but also because a revaluation of any sort runs the risk of being charged with adulation on the one hand or skepticism on the other. In addition, the principal aim has been to carry out the study in a broader context, with an investigation of the relevant biographical, critical, and literary problems as they relate to the social and literary background of the period. As I have said, such a study can never hope to be complete, but the admittedly partial solution obtained through what I have called a contextual investigation would seem more valid than an apparently complete solution resulting from a comparison of two or three works *in vacuo*.

The main portion of the book deals with the literary indebtedness of Chaucer to Dante on the basis of an investigation of all the reasonable suggestions of parallels and sources that have been made to date. My work has been aided immeasurably by the doctoral dissertation of J. P. Bethel, "The Influence of Dante on Chaucer's Thought and Expression" (Harvard University, 1927), in the appendix of which are gathered, with brief comments, the more reasonable ascriptions that had been made to Dante up to that time.

To maintain as objective a presentation as possible, the procedure that has been used follows four steps: (1) citation of the ascription, which, when preceded by a *B*, indicates that it comes from Bethel's list and, when preceded by an asterisk, indicates an original ascription by him; (2) parallel citations in full from Chaucer and Dante, with bracketed additions to supply the context where it is otherwise lacking; (3) the Italian and the English translation from the text of Charles S. Singleton for the *Commedia*, that of W. W. Jackson for the *Convivio*, to avoid the real danger of allowing opinion to enter into this phase of the investigation; and (4) discussion of the individual entry. (I have rearranged the order of Bethel's list to conform to the second edition of F. N. Robinson, which has been followed throughout, save for *The Canterbury Tales*, which have been placed between *The Legend of Good Women* and *The Minor Poems*.) It is hoped that this procedure will not only allow an objective presentation of the posited parallels but also serve as a convenient reference by which readers may be able to judge the suggestions more fully and immediately for themselves.

Generally speaking, there seem to be three major bases on which ascriptions can be offered: (1) direct translation or citation, (2) verbal parallelism, and (3) contextual parallelism. With the first of these bases, there is no difficulty, of course, and the combination of the latter two offers reasonably certain evidence of direct borrowing or at least very close parallelism. When the latter two are considered separately, however, it would seem that a verbal or a contextual similarity alone must be supported by some unique feature of word or thought in order not to be merely an analogy. The comparison of two writers *in vacuo* in such cases would appear to be particularly questionable, since under such limited conditions an apparently clear dependence may turn out to be due to a third element – such as a common source or common knowledge – from outside the restricted framework of selective comparison. It is for this reason, among others, that I have made an attempt throughout the book to revaluate the Chaucer-Dante relationship in the light of the social and literary background of the period.

In keeping with editorial practice, I have used standard translations or translated all modern material. Classical and medieval texts are followed by a standard translation where available; where not, I am responsible for translations which have too often sacrificed grace for literalness. Standard translations are indicated by subsequent parenthetical or bracketed location.

Unless otherwise indicated, translations of the Latin classics come from the Loeb Classical Library, located by volume number of the particular poet. Translations of Aquinas's *Summa theologica* are by the Fathers of the English Dominican Province; of *Contra gentiles*, by V. J. Bourke; the translation of John of Salisbury is by J. B. Pike; that of Orosius, by I. W. Raymond. Again, unless otherwise indicated, translations of Dante come from Singleton for the *Commedia*, from W. W. Jackson for the *Convivio*. Translations of Boccaccio come from B. M. McCoy for the *Teseida*, from Griffin and Myrick for the *Filostrato*. The translation of the *Roman de la Rose* is by H. W. Robbins. I wish to acknowledge the assistance of James Mirollo, David Clement, and Mrs. Edmee deM. Schless in the translation of passages from, respectively, Italian, Latin, and French. The kindness is theirs; the faults are mine.

In the "world of books" it is difficult to know where to begin or end one's acknowledgments. I am most deeply indebted to the generous assistance and patient criticism of the late Albert C. Baugh, under whose direction this work was first undertaken. As well, I wish to thank G. L. Haskins, of the University of Pennsylvania Law School, for his kind assistance in matters of medieval law; Sara Lippincott, for her help in astronomical problems; the Reverend Bartholomew Fair, for his unstinting aid in questions of hagiology and canon law; and, above all, the staffs of the libraries of the University of Pennsylvania, Swarthmore College, and Bryn Mawr College, for their constant patience and help. I also take this opportunity of expressing my gratitude to B. J. Whiting, of Harvard University, who introduced me to Chaucer, and to L. F. Solano, of Harvard University, and Eric Auerbach, of Yale University, under whom I studied Dante. Finally, I profess once again my admiration for my colleagues and students, past and present, at Columbia University. Their excellence, their kindness, their brass-knuckles intellectualism have afforded me a lifetime of learning.

New Canaan   HOWARD H. SCHLESS

Abbreviations

Abbreviations of Chaucer's Works

ABC	*An ABC*
Anel	*Anelida and Arcite*
BD	*The Book of the Duchess*
Bo	*Boece*
CkT, CkP	*The Cook's Tale, The Cook's Prologue*
ClT, ClP	*The Clerk's Tale, The Clerk's Prologue*
CT	*The Canterbury Tales*
CYT, CYP	*The Canon's Yeoman's Tale, The Canon's Yeoman's Prologue*
For	*Fortune*
Form Age	*The Former Age*
FranT, FranP	*The Franklin's Tale, The Franklin's Prologue*
FrT, FrP	*The Friar's Tale, The Friar's Prologue*
Gent	*Gentilesse*
GP	*The General Prologue*
HF	*The House of Fame*
KnT	*The Knight's Tale*
Lady	*A Complaint to His Lady*
LGW, LGWP	*The Legend of Good Women, The Legend of Good Women Prologue*
ManT, ManP	*The Manciple's Tale, The Manciple's Prologue*
Mars	*The Complaint of Mars*
MerT	*The Merchant's Tale*
MilT, MilP	*The Miller's Tale, The Miller's Prologue*
MkT, MkP	*The Monk's Tale, The Monk's Prologue*
MLT, MLH, MLP, MLE	*The Man of Law's Tale, Man of Law Headlink, The Man of Law's Prologue, Man of Law Endlink*
NPT, NPP, NPE	*The Nun's Priest's Tale, The Nun's Priest's Prologue, Nun's Priest Endlink*
PardT, PardP	*The Pardoner's Tale, The Pardoner's Prologue*
ParsT, ParsP	*The Parson's Tale, The Parson's Prologue*
PF	*The Parliament of Fowls*
PhyT, Phy-PardL	*The Physician's Tale, Physician-Pardoner Link*
Pity	*The Complaint unto Pity*
PrT, PrP	*The Prioress's Tale, The Prioress's Prologue*
Ret	*Chaucer's Retraction [Retraction]*
Rom	*The Romaunt of the Rose*
Ros	*To Rosemounde*
RvT, RvP	*The Reeve's Tale, The Reeve's Prologue*

Scog	*The Envoy to Scogan*
ShT, Sh-PrL	*The Shipman's Tale, Shipman-Prioress Link*
SNT, SNP	*The Second Nun's Tale, The Second Nun's Prologue*
SqT, SqH, Sq-FranL	*The Squire's Tale, Squire Headlink, Squire-Franklin Link*
Sted	*Lak of Stedfastnesse*
SumT, SumP	*The Summoner's Tale, The Summoner's Prologue*
TC	*Troilus and Criseyde*
Th	*The Tale of Sir Thopas*
Ven	*The Complaint of Venus*
WBT, WBP, WB-FrL	*The Wife of Bath's Tale, The Wife of Bath's Prologue, Wife of Bath-Friar Link*

Abbreviations of Dante's Works

Standard abbreviations have been used: *Inf., Purg., Par.,* for the *cantiche* of the *Commedia; V.N.* for *Vita Nuova,* and *De Mon.* for *De Monarchia.* Other titles have been given more fully.

Journals

ChauR	*Chaucer Review*
ELH	*Journal of English Literary History*
ESt	*Englische Studien*
JEGP	*Journal of English and Germanic Philology*
LeedsSE	*Leeds Studies in English*
MÆ	*Medium Ævum*
MLN	*Modern Language Notes*
MLQ	*Modern Language Quarterly*
MLR	*Modern Language Review*
MP	*Modern Philology*
N&Q	*Notes and Queries*
Neophil	*Neophilologus*
NM	*Neuphilologische Mitteilungen*
PBA	*Proceedings of the British Academy*
PMLA	*PMLA: Publications of the Modern Language Association of America*
PQ	*Philological Quarterly*
RES	*Review of English Studies*
SP	*Studies in Philology*
TSLL	*Texas Studies in Language and Literature*
YES	*Yearbook of English Studies*

Other Abbreviations

EETS, e.s., o.s.	Early English Text Society, extra series, original series
SATF	Société des anciens textes français

Chaucer and Dante

CHAPTER 1

Chaucer and Fourteenth-Century Italy

O DETERMINE with some exactness the relationship of Chaucer and Dante, it becomes necessary to enter almost every aspect of Chaucer scholarship. Biographically, the date at which Chaucer learned Italian is of obvious importance, since it gives automatically an anterior limit to those poems that show the influence of the fourteenth-century (*trecentisti*) poets. Critically, the individual scholar's estimation of the degree and direction of Dante's influence on Chaucer often determines his fundamental view of Chaucer's poetry as a whole. Literarily, the development of Chaucer's use of Dante over almost three decades can help us reconstruct, in part at least, the maturing mind that saw at once the consummate artistry and finally the deep understanding of Dante's writing.

In each of these aspects the almost equal importance of what Lowes (1934) aptly called "the world of affairs" and "the world of books" (the titles of Lowes's second and third chapters) should warn us against considering Chaucer with too narrow a view. Chaucer's use of Dante can be correctly evaluated, one feels, only against the background of medieval thought and reading as a whole, and the effect of Dante upon his writing seems most validly estimated only by keeping constantly in mind the importance of French, Latin, and other Italian writers whom he had read. In like manner the biographical question of the time when Chaucer acquired a knowledge of Italian must be considered not only from the viewpoint of Chaucer's need of it in the world of books but also from a determination of the importance of the language to him in the world of affairs.

In the traditional view of Chaucer's three periods of writing (the French, the Italian, and the English), the anterior time limit of the Italian period is often based on the assumption that Chaucer's knowledge of Italian and his first undoubted trip to Italy are more or less coincidental. The assumption seems, however, to rest on too narrow a view of Chaucer's world, for it tacitly excludes the possibilities, first, that Chaucer could have needed or could have acquired a knowledge of Italian before 1372 and, second, that Dante's work could have arrived in England before Chaucer's possible acquisition of it while he was in Italy on the journey of 1372. The evaluation of these possibilities depends, of course, upon our understanding of the extent and the importance of Italy and the Italians in the English society that Chaucer knew: of the position of the Italians in the English court and in English life, on the one hand, and, on the other, of the degree of social and cultural intercourse that would have been supplied by the English travelers in Italy.

From the start it must be realized that the question of when Chaucer learned Italian seems to be centered principally on the individual scholar's view of Chaucer's literary development rather than on an estimation of his possible need for the language in the world of affairs. Indeed, solely on the basis of probable causality, it would seem that the mission of 1372 indicates an earlier and even close familiarity with Italian.[1] A certain amount of factual support is given this view if we accept Rickert's interpretation (1928:511–12) of the document,[2] discovered by Redstone in 1928,[3] that grants Chaucer permission to go abroad with the rather large sum of ten pounds. Rickert, through a comparison of the amounts granted to others for journeys of known destination, has strongly suggested that Chaucer's trip abroad in 1368 was to Italy; and, if such was the case, it would not be unreasonable to assume that he joined the large and glittering entourage of his former patron, Lionel, Duke of Clarence, whose marriage to Violante Visconti had been celebrated in Milan the previous month. In 1372, however, Chaucer, although still a relatively unknown member of the court, would have had a distinct qualification for the Italian mission if he could have presented a fluency in the language. Without such a knowledge he would hardly have been more than another esquire of the king's chamber whose selection for the trip we would have to ascribe to the plausible coincidence that brought up his name for assignment at the moment that an Italian mission was being formed.[4] Even leaving aside the journey of 1368, it would not have been odd for Chaucer, starting out in his career in the king's service (and eventually entering the customs division of the civil service), to have acquired an early knowledge of Italian, for if Latin was the language of the clerks and French was the language of the courts, then Italian was the language of international business and finance. This is, perhaps, too facile a differentiation, but if taken with some caution, it will serve as a framework both for a review of the position of Italians in the English governmental structure and for a revaluation of the possible reasons that might have led Chaucer to learn Italian at a comparatively early date.

Chaucer could hardly have avoided seeing how important an element the Italian bankers had been in the finance, the customs, and the court of England for well over a century. The reign of the Edwards was one of constant financial difficulties, and, as the Patent Rolls, the Close Rolls, and the Liberate Rolls indicate, the Italian merchants in England were drawn upon heavily and over a long period of time to support the kings' expenses. From 1273, a century before Chaucer's first known Italian journey, until 1316, sixty merchants or groups of merchants were repaid £420,650 by the English court alone (Rhodes 1902:167–68, table Q). Of this rather sizable amount more than 28 percent (£121,941) was disbursed to the Frescobaldi Bianchi, the sum coming principally from the assignment to that Italian house of a very heavy percentage of "the old and new customs on wool &c and the new avoirdupois" (Rhodes, p. 162) and amounting, over a period of five to ten years, to more than 70 percent of the customs in twelve of the larger ports of England.[5] In addition, there are payments from the Irish customs, Exchequer, and

---

[1] Hales, Looten, Lounsbury, Plumptre, Pollard, Flügel, and Torraca believe that Chaucer knew Italian before 1372; Lowes, Tatlock, ten Brink, Kittredge, and Bethel, on the other hand, are opposed to the idea that Chaucer had any knowledge of the language before his journey of 1372. Manly, Rickert, Bennett, and Ruggiers seem inclined to align themselves with the first group.

[2] A concise presentation of the arguments is given by Ruggiers (1968:141–44, 157–58).

[3] The document is in Chancery Warrants, Bills and Privy Seal, C.81/918, no. 16. The text is cited by Rickert (1928:511) as follows: "Soient faitz briefs desous *nostre grant* seal *pur nostre* ame vallet Geffrey Chaucer de passer en port de Douorr' ouesques deux hakeneys vint soldz por ses despenses *et* dis liures en eschange. Donne sous *nostre* priue seal a Wyndesore le xvij iour de Juyl Lan quarante second."

[4] Tout (1929:365–89). He notes (p. 384): "Chamber office, originally the personal service of the king's bedroom, still normally involved close attendance at court and intimate relations with the king. It was, however, usual to employ chamber officers on delicate missions at home and abroad. Such incidents of the duty of an esquire of the chamber gave Chaucer his diplomatic experience in France and Italy, and, perhaps, therefore, his personal acquaintance with Italian poets."

[5] During this period the total customs of the ports concerned amounted to £134,518, of which £97,808 went to the Frescobaldi Bianchi.

Justiciary, the Devonshire mines, and the customs at Winchelsea (Rhodes, p. 162). The Bardi, another house, were no less active, particularly under Edward II, and often "acted as the royal bankers and supplied the King's need of ready money, whether for the Scotch war or for Household expense" (Rhodes, p. 155). In return, they too were assigned the customs or given special trading rights, and at times there were given to them, as to other merchants, gifts and compensations to the amount of £27,133 during the reigns of Edward I and Edward II (Rhodes, pp. 156, 166, table P). Yet despite this disbursement of almost £450,000, the Bardi, the Frescobaldi, and the Riccardi all suffered heavily from their dealings with an English court that constantly anticipated its revenues by farming out the customs. There can be little doubt that the loans that the Italians made were a good deal larger than the disbursements they received. As Rhodes concludes, "The warning of Giovanni Frescobaldi was not without some foundation: 'Nè t'impacciar con uomini di corte'" ["Don't get entangled with men of the court"] (Rhodes, p. 157).[6]

There is a dual purpose in pointing out these early financial transactions, for not only do they tend to establish the traditional importance of the Italians in the English economy, but also the very names involved underline that "it is with the fellow-countrymen and contemporaries of Dante that we are dealing" (Rhodes, p. 138). The merchant companies were almost all from Tuscany—from Florence, Lucca, and Pistoia—and the political wars in which Dante was so closely involved and which divided families into Bianchi and Neri can be seen in the poet's references to the Cerchi (Bianchi) and the Donati (Neri). Since such families as the Frescobaldi and the Bardi were at the very heart of the affairs of their city-states, the extremely topical, political, and personal aspects of the exiled Florentine Alighieri's writing, as well as its being in *lingua volgare*, would have made at least the extremely popular *Commedia* familiar to them all. I believe, therefore, that on this as well as on other grounds, which will be pointed out subsequently, we must treat with caution the argument that Dante's work was unknown in England before Chaucer returned from his Italian journey. The history of the Bardi in Chaucer's own time tends to support this impression as well as demonstrate how integral a part of the English court this Italian group had become.

From the comparatively complete records that are available, it would appear that the failure of the Bardi in the 1340s, while not entirely caused by the English crown's debts of almost £94,000,[7] was certainly accelerated by such large unpaid loans. The government, however, did not repudiate these debts. Over the next forty-five years the Bardi received in direct payments, annuities, and loans a total of £62,525 (Beardwood 1931:8), and, with certain considerations, the rest of the debt was settled by Richard II on October 24, 1391, for the sum of 3,000 marks, that is, £2,000 (Beardwood, p. 9).[8]

---

[6] The monetary basis on which Frescobaldi's remark is founded can be translated into contemporary currency only in the most vague and general way. As Yves Renouard says (1949:253): "It is fruitless to try to establish equivalences between monies of the past and the present, even though one takes into account precisely the quantity of precious metal which goes into the composition of each kind of coinage, because the buying power of the same weight of fine gold varies according to the metal's relative abundance and the possible sources of expenditure; and these last vary with the degree of civilization of the society being considered."

[7] See Beardwood 1931:8. There were four relevant documents: "The letter of 20 April 1345 in which the king promised to pay £50,493. 5 s. 2½ d. at the exchequer of account, the letter of 28 June 1339 granting the Bardi £30,000 in return for their services; a letter of 4 August 1339 in which the king took them under his special protection and bound the Black Prince and eight magnates to honor his obligations, and the letter of 7 November 1348 acknowledging a debt of £13,454. 2 s. 11½ d." According to an earlier estimation by Cook (1919:42), Edward III by 1345 "owed the Bardi 900,000 and the Peruzzi 600,000 gold florins (£135,000 and £90,000 respectively)." Cook's citation here reads: "Giovanni Villani 12.54 (*Rev. Ital. Script.* 13.934); *Dict. Nat. Biog.* 17.57; Coulton, *Chaucer and His England*, p. 126. The rate of interest at this period, owing to debasement of coin, defalcations, repudiations, etc., varied from 20 to 33 percent."

[8] The complete account of the settlement can be found in PRO K.R. Accounts, Various, Foreign Merchants, 127/38, and PRO K.R. Mem. 168, Communia Hill (in Beardwood, app. A).

Further investigation of this settlement shows how closely allied with Chaucer's work were the operations of this Florentine company. Like other companies of alien merchants, it had "varied functions, which were of financial and diplomatic as well as mercantile service to the crown" (Beardwood, pp. 3–4). Following their failure in 1346, the Bardi,

> after ten years of readjustment and diminished activity under the king's protection, reorganized their company in 1357. . . . They seem thereafter to have maintained a sure but inconspicuous position as bankers and merchants, first under the leadership of Philip de Bardi, until his death in 1362 [Sapori 1926:92, n.1], and then under that of his son, Walter de Bardi, who was for many years, under both Edward III and Richard II, the king's moneyer. [Beardwood, p. 5]

Walter de Bardi serves as a case in point in the present argument, for not only does he demonstrate the level to which the Italians rose in the English court, but his services to the crown were employed in areas in which Chaucer had interests. His post as head of the mint was an important one, and had been granted him the year after he took over the society. There are, moreover, other indications of his status at court. Not only did he receive an annuity of 20 pounds from Edward III (Beardwood, p. 6n.), but, as well, he "was sent by the king with Thomas de la Dale of Flanders, to receive from Galeazzo, lord of Milan, the dower of his daughter" (Beardwood, p. 5, n.6), Violante, who was married in the following year to Chaucer's first patron, Lionel, Duke of Clarence. An example of Walter de Bardi's influence can be found in the agreement reached in 1391, and Beardwood seems justified in saying that "Walter de Bardi's position as representative of the company, on the one side, and as an important official of the crown, on the other, may have expedited the settlement" (Beardwood, p. 7).[9]

The position of Walter de Bardi at court was an important one, and the society of the Bardi of Florence was undoubtedly the most important Italian, or indeed foreign, company in England during the fourteenth century (Beardwood, p. 4). They, above all the bankers of Florence, would have known full well the writings of their compatriot, Dante Alighieri, for, to cite Grandgent (1933:xvii):

> Critics have hotly debated the question of whether his Beatrice was a real woman. Boccaccio asserts that she was Beatrice Portinari, daughter of Folco Portinari, a wealthy and public-spirited Florentine who died in 1289; before that date she was married to a rich banker of good family, Simone dei Bardi. There is no valid ground for rejecting this statement.

The testimony of Boccaccio and of Dante's son Pietro has been almost universally accepted.[10] We must, therefore, recognize that the Bardi family[11] would have had particular reason for knowing the *Divina Commedia* thoroughly, and this circumstance should once more make us treat with extreme caution the argument that Dante's work was unknown in England before Chaucer's return from his Italian journey.

---

[9] This is particularly true if we consider that Richard II not only paid the 3,000 marks mentioned above but also "freed Walter de Bardi from certain obligations he had incurred as master of the mint." Walter de Bardi seems to have profited both privately and officially.

[10] The additional authority of Pietro is cited in McKenzie (1922:xix), which continues (pp. xiv–xx): ". . . on the other side there is no evidence, but simply a skepticism, partly inherited from the not quite extinct theory that Beatrice never lived at all."

[11] For an attempt to evolve a genealogy, see Gabotto 1890; see also Randi 1892:5.

The Bardi were not the only Italians with whom Chaucer might well have had some connections before his arrival in Italy in 1372: "Merchants from Turin, particularly Peter and Hugh Provan, were among the king's bankers, as were the societies of the Malbaille, . . . the Leopardi of Asti," and the society of Lucca (Beardwood, pp. 4, 10). While all these groups would have been very much a part of the court and of the civil service of Edward III, particular interest attaches to the Provans. Peter and Hugh held the post of king's bankers, but the latter was also a member of the society of the Malbaille, as was Daniel Provan. It was, one recalls, a certain "Jacobi Provan" who accompanied Chaucer on his mission to Italy in 1372, and it does not seem too absurd to suggest, particularly in light of the possible transactions of the mission (see below), that this Jacobi (or Jacopo) was a member of the family that had served so consistently as bankers to the king. We would, then, have one more function of the Italians at court, one that we can only surmise made use of their international structure and probably involved some sort of liaison, if not actual negotiation, of a financial nature.

Negotiating marriage settlements, settling problems of international trade, and arranging royal loans through foreign banks were some of the Italian merchants' "varied functions, which were of financial and diplomatic as well as mercantile service to the crown" (Beardwood, pp. 3–4). Such court services are in striking parallel to the "delicate missions at home and abroad" (Tout, p. 384) in which esquires of the royal household, such as Chaucer, were regularly employed. Chaucer had been in the king's employ from 1367, first as a yeoman, or *valettus*, and then as an esquire. Encountering the Italians at court would not, it seems, have been an unusual occurrence, and learning to speak or read a language so important would have been quickly accomplished by a mind trained by aural tradition to Latin and French.

Finally, we must realize that Chaucer, after leaving the king's service, would have had ample opportunity to continue to encounter the Italian group in his capacity first as controller of the customs on wools, skins, and hides and later as controller of the petty custom on wine and other merchandise, for outside the court the alien merchants — among whom the Italians were notable — frequently collected the customs in payment of royal debts or underwrote those English magnates to whom these revenues were unsuccessfully farmed out (Beardwood, p. 24, n.1). As merchants they were an extremely important factor in the revenue of the English customs, shipping (principally through London, Boston, Southampton, and Hull) about one-third of the country's chief export, wool, and bringing in about 20 to 25 percent of its chief import, wine (Beardwood, pp. 28–29, 37).[12]

We must realize, however, that the Italian merchant bankers who served as administrative officials and international financiers in Chaucer's time were members of a fairly cultured society. In Italy, whether in Florence or Turin or Lucca, it was these rising mercantile families that became closely associated with the new culture that centered in

---

[12] See also Whitwell 1903:175–233. At the very opening of his article (pp. 176–77) Whitwell points out: "During the whole period [i.e., from the twelfth through the fourteenth centuries], the merchants of Lucca or Florence — better known, in formal documents as well as in speech as 'Lombards' — had a great share in the wool trade and derived great wealth from it, much to the indignation of 'true-born Englishmen' — for whom let John Gower speak: 'In my opinion, in our country one might wonder too much at the Lombards, who are foreigners, what they want to take on by living in our lands, quite openly, quite favored, as though they had been born and brought up among us; but in order to gull us, they put on the appearance of our friends, and beneath that they have set their hearts on robbing us of our silver and gold'" (my translation). Whitwell's citation is *"Mirrour de l'omme*, 25430–25440." Olson (1961:259–63) has made illuminating use of commercial relations between the Lombards and the English.

Lombardy and the north.[13] We should, therefore, be somewhat cautious in thinking of these men merely as minor merchants or petty moneylenders. They had been brought up in the centers of urban culture and were fast becoming the principal patrons of the movement. It would not have been at all strange, considering this background and considering the local interest of the work, for them to have known well one of the most praised and popular works in the *lingua volgare*, the *Commedia*. Certainly the Bardi, whose service to the English court stretches over the whole of the fourteenth century, would in all likelihood have known of that astonishing poem for which Simone dei Bardi's wife had been the very inspiration and keystone. These are the men who were the bankers and minters to the king, who used their vast Continental organization for many an extramercantile purpose, and who handled England's international finances from their sources in the banks of Lombardy, often to their very collection in the customs of London and other ports. At least from 1372, as an esquire, and later, from 1374, as a civil servant, Chaucer was involved in work in which the Italians were active at many levels, and his chances of meeting with these people at court both before and after the earlier date seem to be so strong that their presence and their importance must be taken into account when one is considering the time when he learned Italian or first saw or heard of Dante's work.

The Italian merchants in England were not, however, the sole source from which Chaucer could have obtained a knowledge of Italian or of the *Commedia*; such information could well have come to him from the stream of official and nonofficial travelers who journeyed to Italy regularly. What the chances were of such travelers hearing of the *Commedia* and what kinds of Englishmen would have undertaken such a journey are questions that can best be answered by recalling briefly the cultural status of Italy at the start of its renaissance.

Italy in the fourteenth century stood as the religious, cultural, and commercial hub of Europe, and, proud of its resurgence, it quickly took up, with nationalistic fervor, the *Commedia* of Dante, which was recognized not only for possessing inherent literary greatness but also for having been written in the vulgar tongue. This liberation from Latin formed the basis of the national and nationalistic literature of the succeeding generations of Italian poets, all of whom, as Simone Sismondi puts it, saw Dante as "il sacro fiorentin poeta, / Che nostra lingua a fatto in ciel salire" ["The holy Florentine poet / Who has made our language ascend to heaven"]:

> Florence, which treated him so harshly in his lifetime, now sought for his ashes; men began to study his poem, to write commentaries and eulogies. The lectureship on the Divine Comedy established in Florence in 1373 lasted for an hundred years and was followed by others in different cities. [Kuhns 1904:16][14]

---

[13] Renouard (pp. 195–96) stresses the interaction of these social and cultural movements: "...the Renaissance established itself only because businessmen had already created unconsciously the intellectual and moral climate which was favorable to it. It developed because they constituted a social milieu sufficiently broad and influential, and they had the material means to support its promoters, men of letters and artists, to attempt personally all the expensive experiments. They allowed and brought about the birth of a new form of civilization, and they made it durable. And, in the slow transformation of a century, Florence played the major role because it had acquired predominance over the Tuscan cities of the interior" (my translation). While Renouard is probably correct in stressing the favorable economic milieu which *les hommes d'affaires* had supplied for artistic development, he is on more questionable ground when he concludes the statement above with "because, unlike Milan, it [Florence] was run by businessmen and because the very framework of their businesses, the great companies, imposed upon its citizens a much more rapid intellectual and mental development" (my translation).

[14] Lectures were also established at Bologna, Pisa, Piacenza, and Venice. Cf. Hales (1893:65–69), who cites the following: "'In the year 1350,' says Sismondi, 'Giovanni Visconti, Archbishop and Prince of Milan, engaged a number of learned men in the laborious task of illustrating and explaining the obscure passages of the *Divina Commedia*. Six distinguished scholars, two theologians, two men of science, and two Florentine antiquaries united their talents in this undertaking.'" It was Giovanni Visconti's niece Violante whom Prince Lionel married at Milan in 1368.

The *Commedia* was immediately and astonishingly popular. Within three years of Dante's death the first extant commentary, that of Graziolo de' Bambaglioli, appeared, and by 1340, sixteen years later, Jacopo della Lana and Dante's sons, Jacopo and Pietro, had made their explications. Later famous exegeses appearing before the close of the fourteenth century include those of Boccaccio, Benevenuto da Imola, and Buti.[15] Arthur Livingston estimated that there were "115 commentaries in all before 1500" (Anderson 1944:v). Undoubtedly there was a certain amount of political and social objection to the poem from those groups that Dante had attacked, but the general point here is, of course, that the *Commedia* was a work that almost any person—pilgrim, clerk, or courtier—who traveled in italy in the fourteenth century could hardly have failed to hear discussed.[16]

Of course, one can only attempt to re-create, however inadequately, the contemporary situation with regard to the cultural relations of England and Italy. Not only was there a comparatively active colony of Italians close to the center of English governmental affairs, but, as well, there were relatively large numbers of Englishmen who journeyed to Rome on pilgrimages, as had the Wife of Bath; who studied at the centers of Mediterranean urban culture, as had the Clerk; who went on missions, as had Chaucer; who married for political reasons into one of the ruling families, as had Chaucer's earliest patron, Prince Lionel;[17] or who simply stayed in Italy for many years, as had the English mercenaries under Hawkwood (Cook, pp. 45–47). Hales (1893), after noting the extreme popularity of the *Commedia* in Italy, summarizes the "extensive and continuous" (p. 66) intercourse between Italy and England. This includes English livings held by Italians, pilgrimages, commercial ties, wandering friars, pardoners, and—most important of all—students passing through the universities who "wandered from Oxford to Paris, and into southern France, and to the colleges of Italy, to Bologna, *Mater Studiorum*, and elsewhere" (p. 67).

An instance more specific and relevant to the present subject can be found in the Visconti marriage of Chaucer's patron. If Chaucer had been attached to the household of Prince Lionel in any way during 1366 or 1367,[18] he would almost certainly have undertaken a study of the language in anticipation of ingratiating himself with the intended new mistress and her household. As early as July, 1366, "a formal commission had been issued by Edward III. . . to treat with Galeazzo [Visconti, lord of Milan and Lombardy], concerning a marriage between Lionel and Violante [Galeazzo's daughter]" (Cook 1916b:25). This was probably early in the negotiations, since, "according to a parallel commission, Edmund, Earl of Cambridge, Edward's fifth son, might be substituted for Lionel" (Cook, p. 25), but the overtures made by Galeazzo's relative Amadeo, Count of Savoy (Cook, pp. 25–26), must have been begun earlier that year. By January 19, 1367, there was no question of choice, since Galeazzo had an extraordinarily generous dowry drawn up as

---

[15] See, for example, Grandgent (Dante 1933:xl–xli), who cites "Elisabetta Cavalieri, *La Fortuna di Dante nel Trecento*, 1921."

[16] Pratt (1939:192–93) gives an excellent summary of the Florentines' attitude toward Dante at about the time of Chaucer's visit in 1372–73: "Here the popularity of the *Divina Commedia* was nearing a remarkable climax. The conservative and educated classes, for whom Latin was the elegant and formal language, had harboured an ancient prejudicial hatred towards the statesman-poet. But such men as Boccaccio helped restore Dante's memory in their graces, and the poem increased in fame. Finally, just a few months after Chaucer's visit, a popular petition to the Signoria requested an exposition of Dante's poem. Boccaccio later gave these; but even if Chaucer had attended the lectures themselves, he could hardly have been in Florence at a time more opportune for hearing discussions and enthusiastic praises of the *Commedia*."

[17] For an excellent account of the marriage in all its aspects see Cook 1916b:1–444.

[18] For possible travels during this time of service, see Honoré-Duvergé (1955:2.9–13). Skeat (1912:xi) says that "in October, 1368, his patron, Prince Lionel, died, and it appears that Chaucer's services were consequently transferred to the next brother, John of Gaunt, duke of Lancaster."

the basis for the marriage contract with Lionel (Cook, pp. 27–30).[19] Although it is extremely doubtful that Chaucer was present at the marriage,[20] he may very well have arrived in Milan shortly thereafter. Whether or not he was still associated with Lionel's household is, of course, a moot point. Chaucer's royal position—which began on June 20, 1367—and the description of him there as "dilectus vallectus noster" ["our beloved esquire"] should not, as Manly notes (1926b:29),[21] be taken as indication that Chaucer had been long in Edward's service, since the phraseology of such documents tended to be conventional. Indeed, one is tempted to think of the pension as an indication of a date reasonably close to the time when he entered the king's household, though such an interpretation is admittedly conjectural. If it were true, as the *Cronica de Monferrato* suggests,[22] that Violante and Lionel were in England for a short time, then the name of Chaucer's patron in 1366–67 and the destination of his trip in 1368 might be somewhat less important in the present discussion, for it would be reasonably safe to assume that copies and knowledge of the extremely popular *Commedia* would have been brought along with the household goods. As noted earlier, it was Violante's granduncle Giovanni whom Sismondi mentions as having commissioned research and exegesis of the poem seventeen years before the marriage, and that the popularity of Dante continued to be astonishingly strong through this period is indicated by the public lectures that began to be established throughout Italy five years after the date of the wedding. Granting that Lionel never returned to England, those courtiers who had been in the magnificent entourage and returned to England must surely have heard, heard of, or seen Dante's work while in Milan. Hales feels certain that, even if Chaucer had not been at Prince Lionel's wedding, "it is very difficult to believe that the prince and his friends had, when they returned, nothing to report of Dante; for Italy was then ringing with his fame.... Surely in 1368, if not before, a copy of the *Divine Comedy* reached England" (Hales 1893:69).[23] In any event, the situation in Lionel's household from 1366 to the time of his death presents one more influence that would have led Chaucer to learn Italian before 1372.

Since we lack any explicit confirmation of a date, the positiveness with which Looten (1931) asserts Chaucer's early knowledge of Italian seems somewhat questionable.[24] Against the background of the Italians in England and the regular intercourse that existed between the two countries, we may briefly review those aspects of the 1372 journey that relate to the question of Chaucer's knowledge of Italian. Cook's suggestion (1916b, sec. 10)

---

[19] Cook estimates the total costs at $3,220,335 in 1916 dollars, and this does not include the jewels and plate that were Violante's personal property. It will be recalled that this was the mission upon which the king's moneyer, Walter de Bardi, had been sent.

[20] Cf. Speght's remark in 1598 in support of this idea and the summary of arguments in its favor, compiled by Cook (1916a:161–240, esp. pp. 182–89). The Redstone document referred to above (n.3) makes it virtually impossible for Chaucer to have been at the wedding in Milan in mid-June and yet ready to depart for the Continent again by July 17.

[21] Manly (1926) supports the views of Rickert and Moore on this point.

[22] Cf. Cook (1916b:107 n.1), who cites the *Cronica di Monferrato* of Galeatto del Carretto in *Monumenta Historiae Patriae*, p. 1228. Despite the *Cronica*, the possibility that Lionel returned to England seems very doubtful.

[23] Actually a large part of the force that Lionel had taken over to Italy with him stayed on after his death under the command of Edward Le Despenser, who, rather ironically, gave his assistance to the Pope and used his force to wage war on the Visconti. See Devlin 1929:270–81.

[24] In his chapter on Chaucer and Boccaccio, Looten summarizes as follows (p. 39): "We are certain today that Chaucer early acquired a practical knowledge of Italian. Bankers and merchants from the Peninsula lived in great numbers in London, in his neighborhood. The Bardi and the Peruzzi were the moneylenders of Edward III, who had farmed out to the former the revenues from the customs, on condition that they turn over a thousand florins a month to the royal coffers. Many other financiers from Genoa, Florence, Lucca, and Pisa operated in England and grew rich there. Chaucer could easily have run into them and so started in on their language." For authority Looten cites "T. Valese, *Rassegna di Studi Francesi*, 1921, Nos. 4–5, p. 170."

that Chaucer was involved in financial dealings for the king during this trip, while it has no documentary support, seems reasonable enough.[25] Although his commission was only "to negotiate with the Genoese about the choice of an English port for their commerce, . . . the records show that he visited Florence as well as Genoa" (Robinson:1957:xxi).[26] Skeat (1912:xi) adds Pisa to the list of towns Chaucer visited, and it should be noted again that, while all three were commercial centers, the largest banking houses in Europe at that time were in Genoa and Pisa. While Chaucer's two companions, according to the commission of 1372 (Kirk 1900, no. 68) were the Italians "Jol[iam]is de Mari Civis Januensis" and "Jacobi Provan,"[27] we should not be misled into assuming that Chaucer, as "the lone Englishman" on the journey, was necessarily the only representative of the crown. It is possible that Provan, as has been mentioned, was a member of the family that served as banker to Edward III, and certainly if the mission had any financial dealings in Italy, such a person would be ideally suited to carry out the negotiations. It is, of course, entirely possible that Chaucer's knowledge of Italian could have been acquired from Provan or Mari during the journey to Genoa,[28] and, with their help, he could probably have carried out the rather complex commercial negotiations that were set forth in his commission. If, however, he was expected to take part in comparatively secret financial operations as the king's representative, or if "on reaching Genoa, Chaucer was detached from his associates and sent on special business to Florence" (Root 1922:257), fluency in the language would have been most advantageous.

To attempt to resolve definitively this extremely complex but highly important question of dating, Hales offers the suggestion that a check could be made by ascertaining "(1) whether the extant translation of the *Roman de la Rose* is by Chaucer, and (2) what is the date of this translation" (Hales 1893:69), for the interpolation on true "gentilesse" and "vilanye" (*Rom*, lines 2185–2202) has definite resemblance to the ideas in *The Wife of Bath's Prologue*, which, in its turn, shows undoubted borrowings from Dante. Unlike *The Wife of Bath's Prologue*, however, which shows clear verbal dependence on Dante, the ideas on "gentilesse" and "vilanye" in *The Romaunt of the Rose* can also be found in Boethius and

---

[25] Actually, of course, the suggestion neither begins nor ends with Cook, though his view has been generally accepted. Young (1913:405–17, esp. sec. 3) was the first to suggest that the trip "toward the region of Florence" was related to the "secret negotiations of the King" (though the phrase itself is common enough) and for the purpose of negotiating a loan for Edward III in return for which certain commercial remunerations were to be given. Lowes (1934:54) is apparently far more definite than the records would warrant when, in speaking of the purpose of the mission, he states that Chaucer "was also to conduct at Florence certain secret business of the King." The objection is not so much to the sense of the statement as to the fact that there is no proof for the finality with which it is made. Root (1922:257), for example, avoids any conjecture on the reason for the Florentine trip and refers, at most, to "diplomatic business."

[26] Unless otherwise noted, all references to Chaucer's works are to Robinson's edition of 1957.

[27] In Kirk (1900, no. 72) he is referred to as "Jakes de Ponan, milite." Manly (1926b:32) identifies these men as Giovanni [*sic*] de Mari and Jacopo de Provano of Carignano. Manly attempts to show that Chaucer, "the lone Englishman [on the mission]," must have been at Lincoln's Inn, since, with 320 of 400 of the personnel of such missions, "the last-named member of the commission is always a person who had some legal training" (p. 33). Manly goes on to suggest that this was the reason for the selection of Chaucer for this mission, but one must ask, first, just what is meant by "some legal training" (i.e., were these all necessarily Inns of Court men?) and, second, whether "some legal training" was not practically a prerequisite for that group from which diplomatic personnel was drawn and (as Tout shows) obtainable elsewhere than the Inns of Court.

[28] Bennett (1948:43) states: "When and how he learnt Italian we do not know. Professor Manly has pointed out that it would not have been impossible for him to have learnt it from one of many Italians resident in London, and it may have been because he already knew Italian that he was sent to Genoa in 1372. Certainly it would seem to explain why he was sent to investigate some affair concerning a Genoese vessel at Dartmouth the next year." On the other hand, there was ample time to develop a working knowledge of the language while on the journey. Root (1922:256–57) and Young (1913:415) generally concur with Mather (1897:1–11) that the trip would have taken about two months during the winter, i.e., from December 1, 1372, to February 1, 1373.

Andreas. If, however, we are willing to accept Dante as the source of these ideas, and if, as Hales concludes, "the translation belongs to the decade 1360–70, as some scholars hold, then we have in it the earliest ascertained reference to Dante in English literature" (Hales, p. 69).

While Hales's view seems open to question, its rather startling conclusion throws into striking relief the amount of precise work that tacitly depends on an approximate date. It is in this final review of the scholarship and criticism that the importance of the time when Chaucer learned Italian and was exposed to the *Commedia* can be seen. As with all other Chaucer scholarship, the disturbance of one atom of information can cause reactions throughout the whole structure built up by the careful and delicate linking of fact to fact, frequently through the attractive power of conjecture. The question of dating Chaucer's knowledge of Italian is hardly an exception, since any resetting of the date necessitates a degree of revaluation that will vary in direct ratio to a scholar's dependence upon a particular year, which is most often 1372.

Tatlock (1950), for example, is adamant in his assertion that Chaucer did not know Italian before his *Italienischereisen* of 1372–73 and 1378. What must be recognized, however, is that Tatlock's critical view of Chaucer is strongly in favor of the clear and distinct divisions of his work into French (courtly and limited), Italian (humanistic and broadening), and English (realistic and mature) periods.[29] Tatlock, therefore, needs to maintain this precise pattern of thesis, antithesis, and synthesis not only for his general approach to Chaucer but also for his early dating of *Troilus and Criseyde*[30] and his consideration of *The Parliament of Fowls* as a mature and relatively late work (Tatlock, chap. 6). From the outset Tatlock speaks of "the influence of the three towering Trecentisti [Dante, Petrarch and Boccaccio] who forced him from the ascendancy of fashionable French poetry, promoted the action on him of classical poetry and freed his own literary personality" (p. 10). Again, in his chapter on *Troilus and Criseyde* (which he considers the first work done under the Italian influence), he must assume that there is a distinct break with the earlier poetry:

> The most important thing that ever happened to Chaucer as a writer was his months in Italy in 1373. Had his years in the customhouse come before this they

---

[29] The divisions were originally proposed by ten Brink (1870) and given support by Furnivall (1871:6 et passim) in his suggested dating of Chaucer's works. For an early rejection of the hypothesis, see T. R. Lounsbury (1877:6–7). In discussing the triple division and the dependence on the date of 1372, Lounsbury states: "There is nothing impossible about any of these statements; but they certainly cannot be disproved, for the very good reason, that, in the present state of our knowledge, they cannot be proved. There are, however, two weak points in the argument upon which the theory is founded. The poet may have been in Italy before 1373, for anything we know to the contrary. He may have become intimately acquainted with the language and literature of that country before he went thither in person. That facilities for studying it, and that from the mouths of native Italians, should not have existed at the splendid court of Edward III, is almost incredible: indeed, in the balance of probabilities, it seems fair to assume that Chaucer was more likely to have been selected for the mission of 1372, in consequence of his knowledge of the tongue of the country to which he was sent, than that he should have made his first acquaintance with its literature in consequence of the mission. There is no evidence that ignorance of the language of a people on the part of an envoy accredited to them was looked upon as a qualification for that particular post in the time of Edward III, at least in the case of a person occupying no higher rank in life than did the poet. The theory of Prof. Ten Brink must, therefore, be looked upon only as a theory, worthy of all respect and consideration, on account of the character and attainments of the man who proposed it and of the men who hold it; but it is only a theory, and ought never to be advanced, as it has already been advanced, as a statement of fact." Lounsbury's remarks have been given at length since they are a succinct statement of this point of view; as well, the closing caveat is worth bearing in mind.

[30] Tatlock (1950), who views *Troilus and Criseyde* as Chaucer's first major poem showing Italian influence, hardly considers 1377 as too late for a poem which he sees as the work of a writer "immensely endowed but inexperienced" (p. 51). Tatlock dismisses Root's astrological dating of 1385 by saying that it would crowd Chaucer's writing too much in the 1380s.

might have given him already some knowledge of the language of Italy, with which England had important commercial relations;[31] but there is no reason to suppose that he had any linguistic qualification for his embassy except his familiarity with French and Latin, of which Italian was merely the local colloquial form. He had already proved his possession of the other traits to fit him for negotiations. This new broadening experience not only contributed greatly to his personal development but led to his use of the three eminent Trecentisti, and above all freed him from the domination of the French poetry of his day, elegant and charming but limited. [P. 33][32]

The concept of the Goethe-esque *Italienischereise* presupposes not only a total conquest of Chaucer's literary personality that Tatlock himself has difficulty in maintaining when positing his date for *The Parliament of Fowls*, but also the somewhat unrealistic view of "the three eminent Trecentisti" who "forced him from the ascendancy of a fashionable French poetry, promoted the action on him of classical poetry and freed his own literary personality." It is difficult, it would seem, to reconcile this view with the astonishing aptitude for literary assimilation and synthesis that Chaucer displays in his writing.

In 1915, Kittredge attacked "this neat triplicity" with characteristic incisiveness and wit:

> This plan has a neat and almost epigrammatic symmetry which commends it to orderly minds, and it is undeniably convenient. The trouble is, that the three adjectives—*French, Italian,* and *English*—do not apply to their several periods with anything like the same degree of descriptive accuracy. [Kittredge 1915:26][33]

Having redefined these adjectives with far more contextual accuracy, Kittredge then added what has since proved one of the most telling blows: "Besides, this neat triplicity obscures the whole process of Chaucer's career, which, of course, was cumulative. Chaucer did not forget French when he studied Italian, and he took with him into the English period all the lessons he had ever learned" (p. 27). Kittredge recognized that the older trichotomic view omitted a "period of transition" and the vitally important reading that Chaucer had done in Latin literature wherein, as Baugh (1948:252) remarked, "Ovid is his Bible."

Shelly (1940:40–41) in his appreciation of Chaucer, expands Kittredge's arguments to what are probably their legitimate limits:

> It was once an accepted commonplace that Chaucer's career might be divided into three periods—the French, in which he imitated the French love-poets; the Italian, in which he was inspired and supposedly "emancipated" by Dante, Petrarch, and Boccaccio; and the English, in which he freed himself from foreign influence and came to the full maturity of his powers in dealing

---

[31] When faced with the probability of Chaucer's knowing Italian before 1372, Bethel (1927:19) simply asserts that "even if Chaucer did know Italian before he went to Italy, it is more than improbable that manuscripts of Dante, Petrarch and Boccaccio should have fallen into his hands before he undertook the journey."

[32] In this Tatlock echoes the view of Kissner (1867), though Kissner considers Boccaccio the dominant figure throughout, Dante's influence being limited principally to *The House of Fame*, the Ugolino passage, and several references to the poet.

[33] Kittredge (1951:26–27) pointed out: "In the French Period, Chaucer was literally under the control of French methods and French conventions. . . . He was, to all intents and purposes, a French love-poet. . . . In the Italian period, on the contrary, Chaucer was nobody's disciple. Dante and Petrarch and Boccaccio were his emancipators. They enlarged his horizon. . . . It was a time of originality. . . . And finally, the third period is called 'English'. . . because his genius turned to English life and English character."

with English life of his own day. The scheme is neat and has some warrant in fact. It is roughly suggestive of certain phases of Chaucer's literary development. But its shortcomings are many, and in some ways it is downright misleading. Professor Kittredge pointed out certain of its weaknesses some years ago. But there are still others. It leaves altogether out of consideration the Latin influence, which was great, especially that of Ovid. It implies that during the French and Italian periods there was little or no orginality in Chaucer's work. It seems to indicate that his escape from the dominance of the French school was due to Italian influence alone, and that Chaucer did not reach his full stature or achieve mastery in his art until the period of the *Canterbury Tales*, although the *Troilus and Criseyde*, done in the so-called Italian period, is as great and perfect a work of art as the *Canterbury Tales*, and in the opinion of some a greater and more perfect work. But its chief defect is that it lays too much stress upon the influences and tends to underrate Chaucer's contribution to his own development. It seems to imply that his growth was chiefly from without, that there was little virtue or genius, other than the power of assimilation, in the man himself. It is part and parcel of the naïve belief that the explanation of all things is to be sought in the indication of influences and the determination of sources.

This citation has been given at length not only because it presents some highly pertinent objections to the view that overemphasizes and depends too heavily upon the date of Chaucer's knowledge of Italian but also because it gives voice to a principle that should be made clear from the start, namely, a belief in Chaucer's poetic genius.

There is no denying, of course, that the date when Chaucer learned Italian is extremely important, since it sets the anterior limits of composition for certain minor poems and limits the possible interpretations of at least one major one, *The Parliament of Fowls*. Tatlock (1950), for example, tries to imply as late a date as possible for the learning of Italian to sustain his view of *Troilus and Criseyde* as the work of an "immensely endowed but inexperienced" (p. 51) author and as the first major poem in which the Italian influence is to be found. In so doing, he remains as indefinite as possible concerning a precise date,[34] since otherwise the disparity in time between the very heavily stressed importance of the Italian trip of 1372 and the first work that resulted from it (1377 at the latest) would be too evident. The date again becomes important when one is considering the anterior limits of those poems showing Italian influence. Pratt, in his excellent "Chaucer and the Visconti Libraries" (1939), gives the following summary (pp. 191–92):

> During the interval between the two journeys (1373–1378) Chaucer is thought to have written several poems showing the influence of Dante's *Commedia*: these are the *Complaint unto Pity*, the *Complaint to His Lady*, the *House of Fame* and perhaps the *Invocation* to the Life of St. Cecilia. After 1378, the date of the second journey, are to be placed the *Canterbury Tales* showing Italian influ-

---

[34] See, for example, Tatlock (1950:10): "For his own career the most important missions were to Italy: in 1372–73 to Genoa and Florence, in 1378 to Milan, involving in all at least four or five months stay in the country. There is little reason to doubt that this was when he learned the Italian language, and above all came under the influence of the three towering Trecentisti." The grouping together of the two missions and the indefinite antecedent of the pronoun "this" make it virtually impossible to ascertain a date.

ence,[35] the framework, *Troilus and Criseyde*, the *Legend of Good Women*, *Anelida*, and perhaps the *Parlement of Foules*. This chronological survey shows that most of Chaucer's poems indebted to Italy came after 1378; and that the earlier poems derive chiefly from one Italian writing, Dante's *Commedia*. It is only after the second journey that Chaucer would seem definitely to have used Dante's *Convivio*, and works of Boccaccio and Petrarch.

It should be noted that of the first four "earlier" poems only one, *The House of Fame*, has any proof of its anterior limit other than the asserted influence of Dante and the assumption that this influence cannot be earlier than 1373. One can see, therefore, just how central to problems of interpretation, criticism, and scholarship have become these questions of when Chaucer learned Italian, when copies of the *Commedia* first came into England, and when Chaucer read Dante.

Above all, however, it is not the intention of these opening pages to court chaos by denying any single date. The purpose has rather been to reconstruct, however cursorily, the social and cultural relations with Italy that were active in Chaucer's immediate society and that must, consequently, be taken into account when we consider the question of dating. The year 1372 (the year *by* which Chaucer must have known Italian) happens to be the year that certain scholars have accepted, but, it must be repeated, it is not so much that particular year that is being subjected to scrutiny as the reasons and probabilities implied in such phrases as "There is little reason to doubt that..." (with reference to the date when Chaucer learned Italian) or "It is more than improbable that..." (with reference to the presence in England of manuscripts of the *Commedia*). If a definite date could be reasonably offered, the task of investigating the Chaucer-Dante relationship would be aided immeasurably, but, lacking such information, one can only present the contemporary situation and hope that it will give, if nothing else, a historical background for the investigation that follows.

Whether we see Chaucer's discovery of Italian literature as a "private Renaissance" that changed the course of English poetry (Lowes 1934:56) or as simply the acquisition of a new stock of material upon which his own "virtue or genius" could work (Shelly 1940:41),[36] we are inevitably faced with the necessity of distinguishing, however grossly, between medieval French and Italian poetry. Any such comparison must perforce be both painfully brief and embarrassingly general, for there is really no middle ground between an approach admittedly limited to establishing certain rough terminology and that which devotes to it a lifetime of careful analysis. Since there is the additional problem here of relating this comparison to Chaucer's writing, it will be immediately apparent that it must indeed be limited and perhaps even platitudinous in part. Nonetheless, a review and realignment of certain aspects might evolve some new relationships and will, in any event, provide the foundation necessary for the further investigation of the Chaucer-Dante relationship.

In attempting a short survey of medieval verse, Speirs (1954:27) remarked:

> Allegory was the way the medieval mind characteristically worked; by its means what was dimly thought or felt was made tangible or visible, the abstract

---

[35] Pratt (1939) lists *The Knight's Tale*, *The Merchant's Tale*, *The Clerk's Tale*, *The Franklin's Tale*, *The Pardoner's Tale*, *The Shipman's Tale*, and *The Monk's Tale*, adding that Griselda's and the Monk's tragedies are often dated in the period 1373–78.

[36] See also the conclusions of Cummings (1916:198–99).

made concrete, the barely intelligible made imaginable and so more clearly intelligible. Allegory is essentially a technique of vision.[37]

Yet there are differences in allegory and in visions so great that the genre itself seems to change. Let us look at what would have been for Chaucer the foremost vision poem of French and of Italian, the *Roman de la Rose* and the *Commedia*, and perhaps in distinguishing here certain techniques, we can hint at one or two of the more general differences between the two literatures.

Lowes, in contrasting the two poems, stresses the representative nature of the *Roman de la Rose* (p. 83):

> I am inclined to think there is, on the whole, no book so thoroughly typical of the Middle Ages as the *Roman de la Rose*—of their strange contradictions, and their conflicting ideals; of their blind reverence for authority, and their rebellious skepticism; of their worship of woman and their contempt of women; of their ethereal idealism and their brute realism; of their deadly monotony and their surging variety. The *Divine Comedy* is typical too, but every detail in it has passed through the alembic of Dante's personality; the Middle Ages are there, but they are moulded by the compelling power of a supreme selective artist. In the *Roman de la Rose* the elements are present in something of their own warring chaos, yet pregnant with the poems of the next two centuries. It is one of the great germinal books of the Middle Ages.[38]

De Wulf's discussion (1953:105) of the two poems tends to compare somewhat more than contrast: "A work like the *Roman de la Rose* is a sort of encyclopaedia of everything that a cultured layman of the middle of the thirteenth century ought to know. The *Divine Comedy*, a work which has not been imitated and which is inimitable, is a symphony of the whole time." We have, then, a general distinction in the encyclopedic nature of the French poem and the more personal, synthesizing nature of the Italian.

On a more specific level, certain distinctive poetic techniques are immediately apparent. Take, for example, the following lines from the *Roman* (2020–27): "Danger then sprang from where he had lain hid; / Hairy and black and great was he; his eyes / Were red as fire; his nose upturned; his face / Most horrible. And maniac-like he cried: / 'Fair Welcome, why have you this gallant brought / So nigh the rose?'" (translation by Robbins, p. 63). We have no difficulty recognizing the allegory of French love poetry, of Daunger, Disdayn, Plesaunce, Bialacoil, or the Rose; but there is, as well, a technique of far greater complexity in the poetry of Dante and his followers. Thus, if we see, in Dante, such tercets[39] as

---

[37] The importance of allegory in the period has, of course, been long recognized. Cf., among others, the view of Saintsbury (1901:71): "The allegorizing and the length which repel readers of today did not disgust generations whose favorite literary style was the allegorical, and who had abundance of leisure." Muscatine (1964:14) is more understanding: "Medieval culture as a whole is much more receptive to the production of non-representational art than ours is. The medieval audience is ready and able to see effortlessly beyond the surface representation of form and image to a higher reality, and to see the concrete itself as a metaphor and symbol." Among other essential discussions see Goodridge (1959, intro.), Tuve (1966), and Wimsatt (1970).

[38] The view of the *Roman* as all-inclusive can again be traced back at least as far as Saintsbury (1901:71): "...the real secret of its vogue, as of all vogues, is that it faithfully held up the mirror to the later middle ages. In no single book can that period of history be so conveniently studied. Its inherited religion and its nascent free-thought; its thirst for knowledge and its lack of criticism; its sharp social divisions and its indistinct aspirations after liberty and equality; its traditional morality and asceticism, and its half-pagan, half-childish relish for pleasures of sense; its romance and its coarseness, all its weaknesses and all its strength, here appear."

[39] A tercet has been chosen in each of the *cantiche* from pages taken at random.

I looked up and saw its shoulders clad in the rays of the planet that leads men aright by every path [*Inf.*, p. 3]

or

Beneath so fair a sky as I describe came four and twenty elders, two by two, crowned with lilies [*Purg.*, p. 321]

or

Here is the Rose wherein the Divine Word became flesh; here are the lilies by whose odor the good way was taken [*Par.*, p. 261],

we are not at all surprised to find, in the first tercet, that the sun is symbolic of God, or, in the second, that the twenty-four elders represent the books of the Old Testament, and the trifoliate fleur-de-lis, the Church; or, in the third, that the Rose symbolizes Mary; the lilies, the apostles; and the way, the way of the Lord. Unlike French allegory, with its frequent one-for-one equivalence of personification and trait, the Italian symbolic representation brings with it multiple levels of meaning and, charged as it always is with biblical connotation, becomes a kind of poetic iconology. The *Roman de la Rose*, in short, works by the more self-contained method of personifying the characteristics of human personality that exist within the closed world of medieval love poetry; Dante, on the other hand, seeks out the single event that will epitomize a whole course of action or that one person who will serve as the symbol of an entire state of mind (be it sinful or philosophical). In other words, the *kind* of image informs and in some respects governs the nature and scope of each of these works. The ramifications of this difference of imagistic structure are pointed out most forcefully and, in a sense, most unfairly, by Gilson (1939:72–73) in a passage well worth quoting at length:

If the sacred poem still lives, it is because its creator has peopled it only with living beings. Himself in the first place, by a unique decision which no poet had ever dared to take or has ever taken since. Then all the others, for not only have all the characters that move in it lived in history or legend, but they live in the poem more intensely than ever, in their individual essence as finally manifested by the inflexible law of divine justice. There is not a single dead man in the whole of the *Divine Comedy*. That is why the text of Dante has nothing in common with any *Pélerinage de Vie Humaine*, *Roman de la Rose*, or other allegorical rubbish with its poverty of human stuff. When people tell us that one should study here "the *Roman de la Rose* as Dante Alighieri is studied in the institutes of Rome and Tuscany," they confuse art with philology purely and simply. When, for example, Jean de Meun tells us about Charlemagne, Abélard and Héloise, we fall too greedily upon these drops of water in his desert of allegories, but Slander, Giving-Too-Much, and Mad Bounty soon reassert their rights, and Jean's few profoundly human lines on Guillaume de Lorris and on himself are quickly buried beneath the chatter of Fear, Shame, Danger and Hypocrisy. The adventures of these PROPER NAMES leave us cold, and we no longer read what they say because it is completely and utterly insipid, but we shall always read Dante because the *Divine Comedy* is the story of a living being in the midst of other living beings. [This and subsequent translations of Gilson are mine.]

With these preliminary distinctions between the *Roman de la Rose* and the *Commedia* constantly in mind, we can now begin to look more closely at a few of the general poetic techniques of Dante in order to compare them to Chaucer's. This can probably best be done by taking up first some of the differences and then some of the similarities of the two poets. The foregoing discussion of imagery and allegory offers a convenient basis on which to develop certain distinctions between the allegory of Dante and that of Chaucer. Recent criticism and explications have tended to see as almost identical in kind the allegory of the two poets, but it would seem upon closer investigation that there are certain distinctive features in Dante that do not appear in Chaucer.

Certain of the more salient distinctions of Dante's allegory can be pointed out with the aid of an article by Caplan (1929:282–90), based principally on a "late Dominican tractate" (Caplan 1925), in which he discusses the fourth of the nine methods which the compiler of the tractate offers for the expanding of a sermon.[40] This method is through a "multiplication of senses":

> Senses are multiplied in four ways: (1) according to the *sensus historicus* or *literalis*, by a simple explanation of the words; (2) according to the *sensus tropologicus*, which looks to instruction or to the correction of morals. It is well to introduce the ways of the world, in order to dissuade the hearers from vice. This sense may be used either mystically or openly...; (3) according to the *sensus allegoricus*. Exposition by this sense is exposition by a "sense other than the liberal.".... The *sensus allegoricus* uses exemplification by simile, as when the life of Christ, or lives of the Saints, are introduced, with an injunction that the hearer follow in their footsteps. With (4) the *sensus anagogicus*, used mystically or openly, "the minds of the listeners are to be stirred and exhorted to the contemplation of heavenly things."....
>
> In a similar fashion Guibert [de Nogent] illustrates how to interpret the word "Jerusalem." Literally, it is the city of that name; allegorically, it represents Holy Church; tropologically, it signifies the faithful soul of whosoever aspires to the vision of eternal peace; anagogically, it denotes the life of the dwellers in Heaven who see God revealed in Zion. [Caplan 1925:283]

After having traced a tripartite method back to Origen, and having mentioned the variant practices in the multiple explications of Augustine, Jerome, and Thomas Aquinas, Caplan then remarks the "the quadruple method of the kind noted in our tractates on preaching was used by Cassian, Aldhelm, Hrabanus Maurus, Bede, John of Salisbury, St. Thomas Aquinas, Dante, and many others" (pp. 285–86). We have here been indulging, perhaps, in expanding the sermon "through concordance of authorities,"[41] but there is both a reason and an excuse for this digression. First, it should be noted that Dante is the only poet in Caplan's list, but an even more important point is that the quadruple explication was not just another form of allegory but a strict and formal device very closely tied to

---

[40] The nine methods offered are through (1) concordance of authorities, (2) discussion of words, (3) explanation of the properties of things, (4) a multiplication of senses, (5) analogies and natural truths, (6) marking of an opposite, (7) comparisons, (8) interpretations of a name, and (9) multiplication of synonyms.

[41] See note 40 above.

religious and homiletic writing.[42] Osgood (1930:xxvii–xxix), in an introduction that has been cited with reference to Chaucer's allegory, observes that

> this allegorical theory of poetry, deriving from the Ancients, and sustained in early medieval times by a naturally strong inclination to symbolism and allegory, supports the allegorical quality of literature and art from Prudentius to Spenser. Nor is it confined only to formal allegory such as the *Divine Comedy*, but suspects and seeks ulterior meaning in all art and poetry worthy of the name.[43]

While this is undeniably true, we must not allow degree to be vizarded; we must not confuse "formal allegory such as the *Divine Comedy*" with writings that partake of the allegorical spirit of the time. To take the example of another genre, we can easily distinguish between Horatian and Juvenalian satire, and we are able, when reading in the eighteenth century, to see at once many of the gradations that exist between the formal satiric epistles of Pope and the scurrility of broadside doggerel. It is this same ability to differentiate within a genre that must be maintained when we are dealing with medieval allegory. The statement that "profane letters were thought of as being allegorical in much the same way as the Bible is allegorical" (Robertson 1951:25)[44] is true, but in a delicate sense that should point out, rather than obliterate, the differences in allegory in the *Roman de la Rose*, the *Commedia*, and Chaucer.

While it would be difficult indeed to maintain that all profane letters were allegorical, the statement would probably be true in a general sense for poetry and art, both of which are highly imagistic. Whether or not these two media were "allegorical in much the same way that the Bible is allegorical" depends upon the degree of distinction we make when speaking of allegory. In a very broad sense, it is true, we can divide poetry into the theurgic and the goetic in much the same way that Augustine could divide his world into *caritas* and *cupiditas*, but the fact that some poetry is written *ad maiorem Dei gloriam* and other poetry is not should not lead us to equate the parts within these divisions. The allegory of Dante,[45] as I have tried to show, is different from that of the *Roman de la Rose*, and both differ from Chaucer. The distinction between Dante and de Lorris relates only to a comparison of their general techniques and is not offered as a means of dividing in two the poetry of the age. There were probably as many degrees of allegory as there were allegorical writers, all of whom can be considered, to one extent or another, as products of the times in which they lived. Undoubtedly the patristic writings of the previous generations—and particularly those of the Augustinian school—offered these writers *a* framework upon which they could construct allegory, but, while we must be constantly aware

[42] This is not meant to imply that the method was at all unusual. Quite the contrary. Caplan has traced it back "at least to Greek theologians of the fourth century," and he cites the famous mnemonic device "Letters teach what has been done, allegory what you should believe; ethics shows what you should do, anagogy where you will go," with an interesting variant of the final phrase in the reference: "Cassian, *ed. cit.*, p. 962. *Speres* sometimes appears for *tendas*; see v. Dobachutz, *op. cit.*, pp. 1ff." He gives also Hugh of St. Cher's thirteenth-century teaching: "History teaches what has been done, tropology what is meet to be done, allegory what ought to be understood, anagogy what ought to be desired." The method, however well known, was precisely formalized and had its roots set firmly in religious grounds.

[43] The passage is used by Robertson (1951:25).

[44] The statement immediately precedes the passage from Osgood (1930) cited above. Robertson's article is a highly sensitive and provocative investigation, and the subsequent discussion has to do not so much with his specific critiques as with the idea of allegory which he offers here.

[45] The lack of a proper term for the tetrachotomic structure of the *Commedia* is at once apparent. Obviously, when Osgood and others refer to the *Commedia* as an allegory, they mean not just the *sensus allegoricus* but the entire work. One is tempted to adopt from art the term "iconological."

in dealing with Chaucer, or any other writer of the era, that such an interpretation is a very real possibility, we must first be sure that we are dealing with allegory and then have very strong proof that the allegory is primarily patristic. Allegory offers a consistent interpretation to the sustained imagery of a work, but on the one hand, we should not assume that the interpretation is necessarily patristic (though it may well be moral), nor, on the other hand, should we let our desire to read sermons in stones convince us that the stone is an altarpiece. In short, we should not uncritically equate medieval poetry with allegory nor automatically assume that all allegorical writing finds a common frame of reference in patristic writing. While many of the foregoing points are undoubtedly self-evident, their restatement here is necessary to underline the range and varieties of allegory in medieval literature. Unless there is additional evidence, it would seem fruitless to attempt to make any specific connections between Dante and Chaucer on so undefined a generalization as the prevalence of allegory in the Middle Ages. The very fact that Dante was able to compose his "inimitable...symphony" with the sustained basis of a quadruple explication in which the *sensus allegoricus* is but one of four highly integrated levels of meaning is reason enough to set the work in a class by itself, completely apart from anything Chaucer ever attempted.

Not only does Dante differ from Chaucer through the unique complexity of his poem, but all his works show him to be a writer who composed with more than just an artistic purpose. The *Commedia* is actively and consciously engaged in the expression of certain moral, political, theological, and social doctrines which in synthesis make up Dante's philosophy. Croce (1922:20), in his appreciation of Dante, has stressed that "Dante himself was strictly bound by the doctrine that poetry must exist primarily in the sense of allegory conveying religious or moral truth." Dante's own bitter experiences in the internecine wars of the city-states molded the political doctrine which he propounded outspokenly and by the eternal judgments that he boldly passed upon his contemporaries. No less vigorous was his stand on theological and philosophical questions, and here his vast reading, assimilated and transformed into a highly personal doctrine, gave him a firm foundation for the views that he set forth: "The text of the *Divine Comedy* much sooner suggests the idea of a moralistic and reformative Dante who had armed himself with all the theses required for his reform and by his morals" (Gilson 1939:273).

Poetry of social protest, poetry of theological disputation, poetry on moral issues had been written before, but one looks in vain for any synthesis such as Dante so fiercely forged. Dante was in almost every sense a poet with a doctrine, and for him the purpose of his poetry was to give voice to that doctrine. Gilson is correct in seeing him as moralistic and reformative, and it is here that one realizes how acutely different in fundamental intention Dante is from Chaucer. Certainly it would be wrong to see Chaucer as no more than a maker of courtly *jeux d'esprit*, and just as certainly Chaucer has a moral and religious viewpoint, but there is nowhere the outspoken political view or the aggressive didacticism that informs Dante's writing.[46] Like any other writer of his age, Chaucer, when he

---

[46] Thus Shelly (1940:29) says: "Chaucer did not write as a vicar of God or as a reformer. Not even in his satire is he a reformer. Nor did he write as one who believed that the business of the poet is to answer the question How to live, or that 'the noble and profound application of ideas to life is the most essential part of poetic greatness.'" Compare this with Gilson (1939:274) on Dante: "The adversary that haunts his thoughts is the clergy that betrays its sacred mission and usurps that of the Emperor: 'Ahi, gente che dovresti esser devota / e lasciar seder Cesare in la sella, / se bene intendi ciò che Dio ti nota!' (*Purg.* 6, 91–93). ['Ah, people that ought to be obedient and let Caesar sit in the saddle, if you rightly understand what God notes to you!' (*Purg.*, p. 61, Singleton's translation)].

"Priests, monks, or Popes—Dante hunted this detested breed with an anger that knew no pity. Just as he enlists saints in aid of his cause, the poet does not hesitate to make God the executor of his exalted purpose."

wished to indulge in *luce* (as opposed to *dulce*), was not one to hide his didacticism under a story. *The Parson's Tale*, *The Treatise on the Astrolabe*, "the translacion of Boece de Consolacione, and othere bookes of legendes of seintes, and omelies, and moralitee, and devocioun" (*ParsT* 1088) show that Chaucer was capable of writing didactic works. The differences between Chaucer and Dante are at once apparent. Chaucer is not the determined reformer of politics, morals, and theology that Dante is; Chaucer's didacticism, with rare exception, seems confined specifically to the separate didactic tracts and treatises, while Dante's didacticism is the very core of the *Commedia*. It is perhaps best to reemphasize that Chaucer has little if any writing that does not have a moral viewpoint, but that does not make the work didactic; nor does he ever attempt that synthesis of didacticism that Dante's astonishing mind transformed to the highest poetry.

Closely allied to the doctrines propounded in the *Commedia* are the consequent judgments that Dante unsparingly passes on his fellow man. This "burning passion for temporal justice" (Gilson 1939:277) is most evident in the *Inferno*, the *cantica* that is probably most concerned with temporal affairs. Gilson has, once again, gone to the heart of the matter (p. 278):

> The *Divine Comedy* accordingly appears as the projection, on the artistic plane, of the vision of that ideal world which Dante dreamed of—a world in which majesty would always be honored according to its rank and every act of treason chastised as it deserved. In short, it is the final judgment passed on the medieval world by a God who will consult Dante before making his adjudications.

Such decisive, explicit, and uncompromising judgment is far from Chaucer's view of his fellow man. Moral reprimand may be given the Summoner or the Friar, Alisoun or Criseyde, but Chaucer's sympathy (though not his approval) seems always to temper the weaknesses that he portrays. The Summoner's description of the infernal resting place of friars can scarcely be said to evoke terror, and it is doubtful that anyone ever lost his soul to the devil with as much *bonne volonté* as does the Summoner in *The Friar's Tale*; Alisoun dares to chop logic with saints, and Criseyde is let go with one of the most sympathetic farewells that an author ever gave an erring heroine. We need only recall Dante's name for an instant to realize how vast a difference there is in the two writers' views of this world and the next.[47]

In structure, in motivation, and in judgment Dante and Chaucer show the most fundamental differences in their poetry, but there are certain areas where, if they do not meet, they at least converge. Gilson's critique of Dante points the way to one of these (p. 267):

> The *Divine Comedy* contains as great a wealth of figurative meanings as the *Roman de la Rose*, but it expresses them differently. Instead of employing a system of frigid allegories and presenting us with personified abstractions, as Greed, Justice, Faith, Theology and Philosophy would have been, Dante employs a system of symbols, i.e., representative characters: Beatrice, Thomas Aquinas, Siger of Brabant, Bernard of Clairvaux. It was a prodigious artistic invention, a sheer stroke of genius, to people the poem in this way with a crowd of living beings, each having a spiritual signification as concrete and

---

[47] Clemen (1963), who perceives the immediacy and the vividness of Dante's poetry as the principal influence on Chaucer (pp. 90–91), nonetheless carefully points out that "the truth is that Chaucer stands a whole world apart from Dante and Boccaccio" (p. 71).

alive as the character that personifies it. The wonderful poetic triumph that is the *Divine Comedy* fully justifies this technique.

In the *Roman de la Rose*, as has been remarked, those abstract qualities that were within the limited scope of love poetry were personified. With certain significant changes Gilson's remarks on Dante could serve as well for Chaucer. Leaving aside his translations,[48] Chaucer too almost completely avoided the "frigid allegories" of the *Roman de la Rose*.[49] If, indeed, we think in terms of *The Canterbury Tales*, the parallel to Dante seems even closer, for where in Dante persons are representative of concepts, in *The Canterbury Tales* they seem representative of social groups. This is not to say that there was a living person behind every one of the pilgrims – though the identification of a number of them has been made or very convincingly argued – but rather that Chaucer scrupulously avoided any use of abstraction and, even where no original is known, seems to have had in his mind a strikingly precise picture of a very human being.[50] Behind the earlier poems stands a whole array of recognized or suspected personages who are the subjects of Chaucer's occasional verse; behind *The Canterbury Tales* there seems to be a gallery of actual or superbly realized figures who are representative of various segments of Chaucer's world. This does not mean that *The Canterbury Tales* is a *poème à clef* or that Chaucer was governed by the historicity of his models. Gilson's rules for this problem in Dante can apply equally well to Chaucer:

> A character in the *Divine Comedy* conserves only as much of its historical reality as the representative function that Dante assigns it requires. . . . The historical reality of Dante's characters may influence their interpretation only insofar as it is essential to the representative function which Dante himself assigns to them and in view of which he has chosen them. [Gilson 1939:267–68][51]

The sense of actuality and the vigor of both the *Commedia* and *The Canterbury Tales* certainly derive a great deal of their force from this seeking out of living or highly realized figures.[52]

One possible reason for this rejection of personification and emphasis on actuality may perhaps be found in a comment that Croce (1922:244) makes on Dante:

> . . . there is in Dante . . . a very wide and complex conception of the world – the conception of a spirit that has observed, tried, and thought all things, that has had full experience of human vice and virtue – an experience gained not in vague, easy, second-hand manner, but in direct contact and imaginative sympathy with life itself. The intellectual and ethical frame of Dante's thought holds and dominates this tumultuous experience, subjugating it entirely.

---

[48] Yet even here Chaucer is inclined to de-allegorize; thus in *PF* 183–294 he has vitalized Boccaccio (*Tes.* 7.51–56) by having the Dreamer rather than Palemone's prayer relate what is seen, and by carefully transforming Boccaccio's Temple of Venus into a temple of *luxuria* or excess (Schless 1974:197–207).

[49] The sole exception would seem to be the God of Love and the Lady in the *Prologue* to *The Legend of Good Women*, though this might well be a disguised compliment. Cf. Burlin (1977:42) and Galway (1938:145–99). It goes without saying that there is a great deal of allegory in Chaucer other than the *Roman's* type which is based on the personification of an abstraction. On Machaut's part in Chaucer's development away from personification and toward realistic portrayal, see below.

[50] The only comparable contemporary view of the social structure is, of course, *Piers Plowman*, but here the author has made use of personification as the basic frame into which his brilliant descriptions of society are set.

[51] Gilson's two rules are given in italics, which I have taken the liberty of translating in normalized roman.

[52] See also Speirs (1951:27): "As in Dante, so in Chaucer frequent similes promote the distinct visualization which is an essential part of allegory and is still an aspect of the 'realism' of the *Canterbury Tales*."

We need only glance at any one of the scholarly first chapters that relate Chaucer to his historical background (or, indeed, that make him a representative of his age)[53] to see that "the world of affairs" was as vital an element in his poetry as "the world of books," that "from this brief sketch of Chaucer's life we may make certain observations which will be helpful in understanding his character as a poet" (Baugh 1948:251). Judging by his works, Chaucer looked on the world with a far different view from that of Dante, but Chaucer too was "in direct contact and imaginative sympathy with life itself." Here the relationship of the two poets has been most sensitively delineated by Donald Howard (1976:41):

> Exactly such an interest in one's surrounding, in one's contemporaries and in one's own city, was an interest Chaucer shared with Dante. But Chacer had a different temperament and a different experience of life. Dante was a disillusioned idealist; he was bitter, and an exile. Chaucer, though not without idealism, adopted an ironic view of the world; and, far from being an exile, he was a dutiful member of the establishment. Dante in exile looked at his contemporaries and saw the meaning of their lives from the viewpoint of eternity; Chaucer looked at his contemporaries close at hand with a certain even-tempered detachment. Dante's *Commedia* and Chaucer's "comedy" are miles apart in this respect.

Or again (p. 45):

> Chaucer, like Dante, was a Christian poet, but he was a poet of the secular world in a narrower sense—possibly a stricter sense—than Dante was; his comedy leaves out the eschatological side of Christianity which makes all life a comedy and which makes all that happens happen for the best. From the larger point of view we might say Chaucer showed things more nearly at their worst, that he was a gloomier poet than Dante. That greater eschatological vision which Dante wrote about must be implied or understood in *The Canterbury Tales*, for it was prominent enough in people's thoughts; but it is not expressed.

Even in his most ambitious work, *The Canterbury Tales*, Chaucer was not trying explicitly to put (in Croce's words) an "intellectual and ethical frame" around the universe but rather was attempting to portray and make comprehensible a representative group of the society he knew best, within the microcosm of the pilgrimage. Whatever their *Weltanschauungen*, the concern of both the Florentine exile and the English civil servant led them to "people [their] poem[s] in this way with a crowd of living beings," to seek not for abstractions but for symbolic representations. This in itself sets their poetry apart from a very great deal of the other writing of the fourteenth century.

While the comparisons made in these pages have had perforce to be couched in generalizations, a few specific differences and similarities in the works have been essayed. Having taken allegory as the most typical method for the structure of imagery, I have tried to emphasize the degree of variation in the genre by comparison of the *Roman de la Rose* and the *Commedia* and have suggested that one of the most notable differences between

---

[53] So, for example, the first chapter of Kittredge (1951) is entitled "The Man and His Times"; of Tatlock (1950), "London, Chaucer and His English Generation"; and of Malone (1951), "Geoffrey Chaucer and the Fourteenth Century," while Bennett's book is *Chaucer and the Fifteenth Century* (1948). Lowes (1934) has emphasized the equal importance by devoting his second chapter to "The World of Affairs" and his third to "The World of Books"; pp. 68–69 are particularly relevant to this interrelationship.

the *Roman* and the *Commedia*—the rejection of personified abstractions—is found likewise in comparing the *Roman* and Chaucer. A further investigation of Dante suggests that certain very fundamental characteristics—the complexity and formality of his poetic structure, his didactic aims, and his ethical judgments—are rarely found as the central tenet around which Chaucer constructs his poetry. Finally, the use of living or highly realized persons for symbolic representations has been posited as a fundamental similarity in the poetic techniques of the two writers with whom we are concerned. How much Chaucer owes this view to Dante it is difficult to say. The extent to which both men were involved in the world of affairs of their times might well have been what convinced them that their poetry should be conceived in terms of human beings rather than personified abstractions or formalized lovers.

There is as well in the early works of both men an analogous admiration and partial transformation of the popular poetry of their day. Dante admired greatly the Provençal poets of his youth, but, taking his cue from the writings of Guinizelli and Cavalcanti, he transformed the courtly and formal love poems of the troubadours into the more personal, more realistic, and more philosophical poetry of the *Vita Nuova*'s famed "*dolce stil nuovo.*" A somewhat analogous case exists for Chaucer. Chaucer's admiration of the *Roman de la Rose* is undoubted, but the earliest dated work that we have, *The Book of the Duchess*, indicates that he must have recognized almost at once the essential weaknesses in the *Roman*'s dependence on personified abstractions: "Under the influence of Machaut 'he substituted human beings for the personified abstractions of the *Roman de la Rose*' but 'went much further than Machaut in the way of realism'" (Shelly 1940:48, citing Legouis 1913:81–82). Despite his heavy dependence upon Machaut, Froissart, and the *Roman*, he "'introduced into the most factitious of all poetic styles a sense of reality and a dramatic force, which brought life and colour to the conventions he dealt with'" (Shelly, p. 48). The humor and colloquialism of the opening section are in marked contrast to the polished formality of Machaut.[54] With regard to the attempt at a realistic basis for the poem as a whole, whether we accept Kittredge's view (1951:53) that "the Dreamer, impelled by simple kindness, conceals his knowledge to tempt the knight to relieve his mind by talking," or Malone's opinion (1951:38) that "Chaucer deliberately sacrificed the virtue of consistency to gain the greater virtue of dramatic irony," we are, in either case, far from the undramatic stylization of Machaut, Froissart, and the *Roman de la Rose*. Finally, in the last section of the poem, Chaucer's virtual transformation of his sources—principally Machaut's *Jugement dou Roy de Behaingne*—is seen at once in his vitalization of the mood, the feeling, and the sensibilities of the principal characters:

> Chaucer took this unpromising material and made it over. His man in black is no debater, though traces of the old debating technic survive. He is a mourner, and his words are an outpouring of his feelings. As we know, he stands for John of Gaunt, and his grief is no fiction, invented by the poet for debating purposes, but a sad reality. Chaucer's sympathy and his wish to comfort the mourner are likewise no literary concoction but come from the heart. The tone and spirit of Chaucer's dialog with the man in black differ correspondingly from what we find in Machaut's debate. [Malone, p. 37]

[54] Malone (1951:28) and Winny (1973:142–48). Muscatine (1964:101) has astutely observed that "the burgeoning vein of realism in Chaucer's early poems, then, is not so much a revolt from the sphere of Machaut as a divergent response to a common endowment of convention and experience—common, too, to Deschamps and Boccaccio and to the whole secular literature of the late Middle Ages."

Like Dante, Chaucer early took his cue from a worthy master whom he was soon to surpass by virtue of his matured inclinations.

There are, then, specific indications that Chaucer's poetic view owed as much to his sensitivity to the world of reality as to a specific literary guide from the world of books. If such were the course of his development, in the *Commedia* he would have found the ultimate confirmation of an artistic technique to which he was naturally inclined.

On the whole, scholarly opinion of this century has regarded Dante's effect on Chaucer as an extremely profound one. Legouis (1913:113), while stressing that Chaucer was never capable of achieving equal heights, feels that "there is no doubt that Chaucer was fully aware of the greatness of Dante, and that he himself felt it."[55] Kittredge (1951:26–27) sees Dante as one of the "emancipators" of Chaucer's style, though he considers Boccaccio the most important Italian influence. Root (1922), like Legouis, stresses that Chaucer must have "felt the power of Dante's divine poem" (p. 17), though he then goes on to enlarge upon the importance of the Italians in general.[56] In his British Academy lecture four years later Manly (1926a:5) hints at a deeper importance of Dante, though in much the same terms:

> The great debt of Chaucer to the Italians — and I suspect that his debt to Dante was as great as that to either Petrarch or Boccaccio — was perhaps not so much because they furnished new models for imitation, as because they stimulated his powers of reflection by forms and ideals of art different from those with which he was familiar.

The depth and quality of Manly's insight may be found again, just half a century later, in Howard's suggestion (1976:139–40) of yet another consonance:

> Memory, central to the experience of reading *The Canterbury Tales*, is embodied in it as its central fiction and becomes the controlling principle of its form. The expressed idea of the work is that the pilgrim Chaucer, like the pilgrim Dante of the *Commedia*, reports an experience of his own which includes stories told by others. Both are returned travellers, both rely on memory. Frances Yates has even suggested that Dante relied for his structuring principles upon the artificial memory systems prevalent in the Middle Ages. This fictional premise, probably Chaucer's greatest debt to Dante, is hardly ever noted.

Yet all these comments, both the impressionistic and the insightful, must eventually respond to specific examples of dependence. And in this regard Bethel's thesis — the only full attack on the problem that has been made — is an attempt to show just how deeply Dante's words and thoughts might have informed Chaucer's poetry. Among the more famous critiques of these decades, the most vigorous claims for Dante's importance are those set out by Lowes (1934), who feels that "Dante did for Chaucer what Greek a century later did for Europe" (p. 29). Lowes then goes on to assert that "it was inevitable that Dante's influence should be profound" (p. 130). Shelly's view (1940:41 et passim) does not

---

[55] Dante's critical impact continues to be asserted in much the same terms; see, e.g., David (1976:21, 42).

[56] Root's passage (p. 17) emphasizes the effect of the Renaissance on Chaucer: "He felt the power of Dante's divine poem; he breathed the atmosphere of humanism which emanated from Petrarch and his circle; he found in Boccaccio a great kindred spirit, an author of keen artistic susceptibility, who in character and temperament had much in common with himself. He found in Italy not only a new set of models, superior in art and in depth of thought to those of France; he received as well a new and powerful intellectual stimulus, which set him to thinking more deeply on the problems of philosophy, and gave him keener interest in the intricacies of human character."

so much deny Dante's influence as elevate Chaucer's personal genius, while Bennett (1953) sees Dante's effect mostly in the change of direction of Chaucer's poetry (p. 46).[57] Tatlock's opinion (1950) of the importance of the "three eminent Trecentisti" has been discussed above, and he is equally definite in asserting that "for Dante, Chaucer had deep reverence, and knew the *Divina Commedia* intimately throughout" (p. 34).

Critical opinion has tended to express impressionistically the feeling that Dante's effect on Chaucer is to be found principally as the profound influence of one great writer on another. Lowes, who has probably offered as many specific examples of the Chaucer-Dante relationship as any other critic, underlined this feeling succinctly when he remarked that "Chaucer's recollections of Dante's words are the least of his debts to him. Those are, for us, little more than hints that keep us aware of something which never found expression in words—the silent workings of the *Divine Comedy*, not unlike those of life, within or beneath Chaucer's consciousness" (Lowes 1934:130). The impressions of so eminent a scholar as Lowes must be kept in mind, but we must recall as well that Chaucer tended to make full use of his reading, as specific studies on Statius, Boethius, the *Roman de la Rose*, and Boccaccio have shown.

What we must also recall when reviewing the scholarship is that the use of Dante, the constant reference to Dante that one finds in Chaucer criticism, seems frequently more a function of the scholars' need than of Chaucer's poetry. Ruggiers (1965) indicates this when he notes, "Yet Dante serves with his highly structured moral system and encyclopaedic range, as a referent, even a touchstone, for much in Chaucer that is merely glancing or oblique" (p. 30, n.11). Often, however, that "referent" is justified in terms more of the reader or the scholar than of the work itself. The reason for this is that Dante supplies the modern reader with the most readily available and masterful depiction of an ordered and didactic universe, and so it is not surprising that time and again his work should be invoked for comparison and contrast with Chaucer and his work. But how often is this a comparison of convenience, used because Dante's encyclopedic lore is more accessible than that of, let us say, Vincent of Beauvais? How justified are we in trying to determine the nature of *The Canterbury Tales* by comparing it with the nature of the *Commedia*, or of posing questions that may not in the end be pertinent? We do not know exactly when Chaucer read the *Commedia*, just as we do not know exactly when most of his own works were written, just as we do not even know for sure how much of Dante Chaucer read or whether Chaucer was as traumatized as some would have us believe by whatever reading he did do. All these uncertainties are possible—the reading of the whole of Dante, the critical impact on Chaucer, the pervasiveness of Dante's moral and poetic presence. All this may well be so, but it tends to rest on conjecture and convenience which, while meriting the most serious kind of consideration, remain opinion that in the final analysis we must recognize has not been proved.

It is the purpose of the remaining chapters of this book to evaluate those lines and passages in Chaucer on which there has been a reasonable claim of Dante's influence and, as well, to suggest corrections and additions where they seem warranted. In the admittedly simplistic category of number of derived lines, Boccaccio, Boethius, the *Roman de la Rose*, Ovid, and many another work and author are far ahead of Dante. And in the scarcely less simplistic category of factual information, further reading in the period has shown that what may once have been thought of as a unique connection is now seen as a matter of multiple authority or common knowledge. That Chaucer's reading was wide

---

[57] "What Chaucer got from Dante was a glimpse of the possibilities open to poets outside the charmed circle of French erotic poetry" (Bennett, p. 46).

and that he himself was well aware of the more important ideas current in his time are perhaps remarks that need no repetition, but they are once more set down here to stress that the following investigation studiously avoids approaching Chaucer's text with only the writings of Dante for comparison. Obviously, it is more than a lifetime's work to recapture Chaucer's reading and the ideas of his age, but insofar as possible this revaluation of the Chaucer-Dante relationship has been attempted in that spirit.

CHAPTER 2

The House of Fame

F ROM THE VAST amount of scholarship on *The House of Fame* relating to Dante, two principal problems seem to emerge: the one, that of interpretation, the other, that of dating. Apart from the various explications of Lydgate's famous "Dante in ynglyssh" phrase, the problem of interpretation is centered upon the extent to which Chaucer made use of the *Commedia*. Of those critiques that interpret the poem as an intensely personal and philosophical work to be read solely and strictly in terms of the *Commedia*, the spiritual and autobiographical view of ten Brink (who was answered by Kittredge), the more moderate view of Chiarini (whose work was reviewed by Robinson), and the more philosophical view of Ruggiers seem fairly to represent the group as a whole. The individual scholar's opinion of the importance of Dante enters, likewise, into the problem of dating, first, in the matter of a single or dual date of composition, second, in the place of the poem in the Chaucer chronology, and, finally, in the matter of an absolute date of composition. Since this work assumes *The House of Fame* to be the first major poem to show the influence of Dante, I need hardly emphasize the importance of establishing the position of the work in the Chaucer canon as closely as possible. *The House of Fame*, in both the biographical problem of dating and the critical problem of interpretation, illustrates more strikingly than any other poem the significance of the Chaucer-Dante relationship.

The highly conjectural and improbable interpretations that have evolved from a solely Dantesque view of this poem have probably done more to confuse the problem of its relationship to Dante than any other single factor. This confusion finds a pattern and part of its source in an early remark of Lydgate, who, in listing Chaucer's works in the Prologue to the *Falls of Princes*, stated:

> He wrot also / ful many a day agone
> Dante in ynglyssh / hym-sylff so doth expresse
> The piteous story / of Ceix and Alcyone
> and the Deth also of blaunche the Duchesse.[1]

Essentially three views have been taken of this assertion. The first can be represented by Bale, who, "in making up his list of Chaucer's works, probably got his 'Dantem Italum

---

[1] Quoted thus in Brusendorff 1925:148–49. Brusendorff's note reads: "From Harl. 1776, f. 8, quoted by Spurgeon I, 28." Hammond (1908:58–60) cites the twelve stanzas in Lydgate relevant to the Chaucer canon from the 1554 Tottel edition of the *Falls of Princes*. In this version the pertinent stanza reads: "He wrote also ful many day agone, / Daunt in English him self so doth expresse / The piteous storye of Ceio and Aclion / and the death also of Blaunche the duches / And notably dyd his businesse / by great aduise his wittes to dispose, / to translate the Romaynt of the Rose."

transtulit' from Lydgate's ambiguous phrase" (Hammond 1908:375).[2] Brusendorff frankly admits (1925:150) that "the natural sense of *He wrot — Dante in ynglyssh* surely is that Chaucer translated Dante, and thus the passage was understood by Bale," but he notes (p. 150) his doubts of Lydgate's opinion[3] and is quick to point out that no trace of such a translation has come down to us. It seems to me that this faint hint that Chaucer translated a work of Dante — presumably the *Commedia* — can be dispelled most rapidly by the comparatively simple process of looking at the explicit statements of Chaucer himself.[4] We may be reasonably certain that if Chaucer had translated as long and complex a work as the *Commedia* it would have been mentioned along with Boethius, Origen, or Pope Innocent's "Wretched Engendryng."

The second view of Lydgate's phrase sees a reference to a specific work, or passage, of Chaucer which Lydgate might have considered as "Dante in ynglyssh." Here many suggestions have been offered, principally those of Skeat, who believed it to be the whole of *The House of Fame*;[5] Hammond (pp. 374–75), who offered the longest direct translation from Dante, the Ugolino episode in *The Monk's Tale*; and Brusendorff, who felt that Lydgate did not "know enough about Dante to recognize Chaucer's actual borrowings" (pp. 149–50, n.7) and therefore, after having misread *WBT* 1125–32, considered the whole of *The Wife of Bath's Tale* as a translation from Dante (p. 151).

The third view of Lydgate's verses is perhaps the wisest, for it frankly accepts the fact that the lines are both "maddening"[6] and syntactically so confused as to be uninterpretable.

While these views have varying degrees of merit, we should not forget that Lydgate's purpose is to praise "my maister Chaucer" as one who had purified "our vulgare." Thus he states at the opening of these verses:

> And semblably, as I ha told toforne,
> my maister Chaucer did his busines,
> And in his dayes hath so well him borne
> out of our tong tauoyden al rudenes,
> And to reforme it with colors of swetenes.
> Wherfore let vs yeue him laude and glory,
> and put his name with Poetes in memory.[7]

Lydgate's purpose not only is explicitly stated here but is implied as well in the emphasis which he gives to the translations,[8] to the moral tone of Chaucer's works, and, finally, to Chaucer's sources. No matter how unscholarly Lydgate's list (and one suspects that it is very much so), the complete exclusion of French poets and the particular emphasis which Lydgate gives to Chaucer's works indicate that one who looked for the moral and

---

[2] Bale's phrase is found in his 1557 *Index Britanniae scriptorum* (reprinted in Hammond, pp. 63–65, from R. L. Poole's ed.), though it is not in his 1548 *Summarium* (*Illustrium Maioris Britanniae scriptorum*, fol. 198, reprinted in Hammond, pp. 8–9).

[3] Brusendorff's note to the preceding statement, after citing Hammond (pp. 62, 375), Spurgeon ("I. 38, 122, & 233 about later statements to this effect"), and Lounsbury (1.425; 2.236), states: "That Chaucer mentions Dante in *Fame* 450 can scarcely have misled Lydgate; it is very doubtful indeed whether he had read Chaucer's poem at all (the passages collected by Skeat I. 24 do not prove anything, cf. Hammond, p. 374)."

[4] See, principally, *LGWP* F 417–41, G 405–31; *MLT* B 53–76; *CT* I (*Retraction*) 1083–87.

[5] Brusendorff's citations (p. 149, n.5): "I. 24 & III. ix; cf. the ed. by C.M. Drennan, p. 15ff., and Wells, pp. 621 & 653." Bennett (1968:51) seems to accept this view.

[6] The apt and oft-quoted description is Kittredge's. See his note in *Nation* 2 (1894):310.

[7] From the Tottel edition of 1554; cited in Hammond, p. 58, stanza 1.

[8] That such work was highly approved is seen in Deschamps's well-known tribute to Chaucer as "Great translateur, noble Geffroy Chaucier."

utilitarian element in literature turned not to the courtly writing of French poets but rather to Latin and also Italian poets, among whom Dante was eminently acceptable.

Of these various explanations it is Skeat's fundamental view of *The House of Fame* as a purely Dantesque work that is closest to our central problem of the poem's interpretation. Skeat's view goes back to that of Sandras (1859), ten Brink (1870:101–10), and, in part, Rambeau (1880:209–68), but it does not seem necessary to exhume all these interpretations, which were, for the most part, thoroughly investigated by scholars many years ago.[9] Sypherd's point-for-point reply to Rambeau's article appears, on the whole, to have put an end to the extreme opinion that saw in *The House of Fame* a *Commedia anglicisée*. More persistent, however, are the variations on ten Brink's interpretation of the poem as an allegorical autobiography and an expression of an inner *Weltschmerz* to which Chaucer, as poet, gave voice by means of the plot and symbolism of the poem. Ten Brink's views, which were the foundation of Rambeau's article, were not encumbered by the forced parallelisms with which the latter tried to support his view, though the final interpretation, in both cases, seems to have lost sight of the poem that Chaucer wrote. Sypherd's reply to Rambeau includes ten Brink by implication, but a more direct answer is made by Kittredge (1894:80–84):

> Great poets, no doubt, address themselves to posterity; and posterity is free to interpret them, for its own comfort and inspiration, in any terms that it finds useful. But they address themselves, in the first instance, to their immediate contemporaries.... What Chaucer meant to his contemporaries is, then, a pertinent question. It stands at the threshold. If there is an inner shrine, we must enter it through the portal of the obvious.
>
> To ten Brink, the temple of glass is a figure for the "charmed circle of poetry in which Chaucer lives under the spell of his study of the great masters." The paintings on the wall are "those pictures of life which he sees in his beloved authors, and which serve as the sole intermediaries between him and the world of men." The sandy desert is "the loneliness that encompasses him whenever he ventures beyond the four walls of his little book-room."
>
> Now these sentimental equations, we must frankly admit, are quite unlike anything that Chaucer's contemporaries would have gathered from the story. The announcement at the outset, that he is to tell them a dream – accompanied as it is by a discussion of dreams which recalls the exordium of the Romance of the Rose, the most popular of all poems with the courtly circle of the time – meant to them, undoubtedly, that they were to hear one more variation on the favorite theme of the love-vision. And this idea was confirmed when they found the poet in a Temple of Venus, admiring a love-tale painted on the walls.... They felt, therefore, – these fortunate knights and ladies of the middle ages, – no such temptation as besets us ingenious moderns to apply the temple, or the lack of worshippers, or the poet's interest in the decorations, to anything in the actual circumstances of Chaucer's life, or to his relations, good or bad, with the world about him.
>
> Moreover, if we scrutinize the supposed allegory a little, we shall perceive its ineptitude. The temple in which Chaucer finds himself is quite unfamiliar to him. He infers that it is dedicated to Venus, because he sees portraits of her and

---

[9] See the reviews of scholarship given in Hammond, pp. 375–76; Brusendorff, pp. 148–51, 160 n.3; and particularly W. O. Sypherd 1907:13 n.1, 14 n.1.

Cupid, but he has no idea in what country it is. Indeed, he leaves the building with the express hope of discovering somebody who can answer this question. . . .

Obviously, this unknown temple cannot stand for Chaucer's habitual literary studies, and the desert for his loneliness outside his book-room. . . .

In short, all attempts to read personal allegory into the First Book of the House of Fame break down completely when tested by comparison with actual narrative. And there is no necessity to have recourse to personal allegory. The temple and the desert are simply devices to transport the poet into the fantastic regions of dreamland, where the eagle can swoop down upon him conveniently: Jove can hardly send his bird to the custom house, or to Chaucer's city lodgings. We are now dispensed, I should hope, from following the allegorical school in its further explorations, and equating the huge eagle that bears Chaucer aloft with "philosophy," or "poetic genius," or "productive Phantasie."[10]

The primary fault of the ten Brink–Rambeau theories, it would appear, is that they failed to take into account that the poem is extraordinarily humorous from the very moment that their symbol of Philosophy, the eagle, begins to speak.

Chiarini's attempt (1902) to take a stand between the position of Rambeau and the reaction of Lounsbury (1892:2.236–48) shows by its untenability the weaknesses of the autobiographical approach. After having cited the views of ten Brink and Sandras, Chiarini states (p. 74):

It will not be difficult to find and follow the thin thread of the allegory, and understand the reason and signification of this poem that is a curious, characteristic document of the playful nature of a poet who, even in a moment of spiritual discomfort, does not know how to speak any language other than that of wit and jest. [This and subsequent translations from Chiarini are mine.]

Following the interpretation of ten Brink generally, Chiarini attempts to add some modification (p. 76):

In the flight with which Chaucer, transported in the talons of the divine messenger, unexpectedly rises from the earth to free himself from his state of spiritual misery, there appears clearly and obviously the concept of the triumph of his talent, which, having broken its chains to pieces, and having overcome every earthly obstacle, soars victorious toward the ideal summits of its glory. But it would be no small error to believe that the eagle in its allegorical signification represented simply the symbol of poetic talent or fancy.

The eagle, Chiarini says, is also "a direct emanation of the Dantesque Virgil" (pp. 76–77), but, to his credit, the ludicrousness of the picture of Chaucer's flight intrudes strikingly (p. 77):

So that the Chaucerian eagle, despite its weighty teachings on the subject of the destined place of every body in the world, on the subject of the law of gravity and the theory of sounds, despite its limited knowledge of Aristotle and Plato, in the end is the symbol of a quite sprightly and humorous philosophy.

---

[10] Cf., also, Brusendorff's succinct remark, p. 160, n.3: "No doubt it is the most personal of all Chaucer's poems, but it is a complete mistake to make it into a sort of autobiographical allegory."

> Dante, in the great figure of Virgil, wished to represent human philosophy in its highest and most noble signification; Chaucer, in the grotesque figure of the eagle, has represented his own particular philosophy, that of a singularly bizarre and witty spirit.

The citation has been given at length to point out the inevitable cul-de-sac into which such an argument leads by the end of the study. When faced with the brilliant comedy of the eagle's remarks in lines 853–63, Chiarini says (p. 108–09):

> This, to me, is pure and simple irony: writing this, Chaucer, I believe, must have had in mind those questions of physics, theology, and philosophy of the Dantesque poem, which are rarely easy or pleasant. And perhaps, as in the preceding case, by the parallelism which I have pointed out between certain points of the two poems that have their exact correspondence, one can guess that the satiric allusion is referred more particularly to the long discussion of Beatrice on lunar spots in canto 2 of the *Paradiso*.

We must assume, therefore, that the symbol of Philosophy, the Dantesque eagle, is used to satirize the very core of Dante's philosophy, theology, and physics; we must assume that Chaucer, at one and the same time, could seriously employ the framework of the *Commedia* to express his inmost feelings on "the difficulty and the hardships of life, and above all the injustice and indifference of men" (p. 71), as well as bewail his fate, "condemned from morning to evening to material and oppressive labor" (p. 70), and yet, at the same time, satirize Dante's poem to the point of ridicule.

Robinson's review (1903:292–97) of Chiarini's study has both specific and general relevance to the present investigation. Even, says Robinson (p. 292), were we to grant every parallel that Chiarini asserts, still "there is no real similarity between the poems in plan and structure; and as for their supposed similarity in spirit and purpose, the 'inner meaning' of the *House of Fame* is entirely a matter of conjecture." Robinson strikes at the very heart of the problem when he writes (p. 293):

> Chiarini, like Rambeau before him, constantly errs, because he sees the *House of Fame* from only one point of view. Both these scholars study it solely in its relation to the *Divine Comedy*, and of course they find numerous points of contact. Dante embodied in his encyclopedic poem nearly all the philosophic doctrine and very much of the current learning of the middle ages, and the same ideas were bound to reappear in any poem of the period that dealt, whether seriously or humorously, with philosophic subjects. Chaucer had read Dante, and his deliberate quotations and unconscious reminiscences add much to the common stock of thought, which would in any case have been inevitable.[11]

Chaucer, adds Robinson, "certainly wrote no other piece which displays such obscure and unskilful use of symbols as is here assumed" (p. 296). Robinson's comments on the fallacy of citing parallel passages and on the nature of the *Divina Commedia* with relation to works of the same era seem eminently just and applicable whenever Chaucer and Dante are juxtaposed *in vacuo*.

---

[11] Cf. Tatlock's statement, "It is no more fair to say that the *House of Fame* is primarily a poem of love than an autobiographical allegory or a parody of the *Divine Comedy*. A striking but unfair case can be made out for any of these theories by picking out seemingly favorable evidence and disregarding all else and all proportion. Chaucer's poems have often been misinterpreted thus."

The observations that Kittredge and Bennett[12] have made on the awareness of Chaucer's audience, combined with the strictures of such scholars as Robinson and Tatlock, should give warning against an overingenious explication of *The House of Fame*, and yet one of the later interpretations of the poem[13] has, in part, depended so heavily upon the *Commedia* that it recalls to a certain degree the interpretations of ten Brink and Rambeau. The article, if it has been read correctly, has four principal assumptions: (1) on the basis of the suggestions of Sypherd (1907:16–17, 114ff.; cited in Ruggiers 1953) and Patch (1927:112, 96; cited in Ruggiers 1953) that there is a possible confusion in some medieval views of Venus, Fortune, and Fame, the writer asserts a total "conflation" of the three; (2) lines 349–60 are taken as the central reason for book 1, with the stress put on Dido's cursing of Fame (instead of Fortune or Venus); (3) the fullest possible philosophical and symbolic interpretation that Dante scholars have evolved must be given to the two eagles—Jove's and God's—in the *Commedia*; and (4) the dominant philosophy in Chaucer's writing is that of Boethius. With the second and fourth points one can agree in part, though it must be remembered that Dido's concern for her reputation is one of several arguments she is presenting to Aeneas in attempting to persuade him to stay; and, while Boethius is vitally important, we can hardly think that he is the "man of gret auctorite" who appears in the closing lines of the poem.

On the "conflation" of Venus, Fame, and Fortune there is perhaps more fundamental doubt that bears directly on the Dantesque interpretation that is given. As Sypherd plainly demonstrates, Chaucer thought of Fame in terminology and images that were ordinarily applied to Fortune. Not only do the suggested sources of these lines bear this out,[14] but Chaucer explicitly states of the suppliants (*HF* 1545–48):

> They hadde good fame ech deserved
> Although they were dyversly served;
> Ryght as her suster, dame Fortune,
> Ys wont to serven in comune.

Now the reason for this seems obvious. Fortune, while still part pagan and part Christian under the Boethian concept, ruled this world,[15] and in this sense Fame would be her lieutenant. Fortune had very precise powers over men and their actions, their love, happiness, wealth, well-being, and so forth. Sypherd, it seems, presses this last point—the relation of Fortune to love (or Venus)—somewhat too strongly since everything in this world—including love and fame—is under Fortune. Being under the same code does not, however, make them equivalents. Fortune, the common goddess, never does appear in *The House of Fame*, and, indeed, not one of the seven groups of petitioners that comes

---

[12] Bennett, p. 48: "Chaucer's contemporaries must have found all this much to their taste. The retelling of the story of the *Aeneid*, with special attention to Dido, revived many memories, while the constant employment of detail suggestive of the old French romances pleased and fascinated his cultivated audience. Then again there was the brilliant reproduction of the Eagle's conversation, the descriptions so full of detail and gusto of the Houses of Fame and Rumour, all expressed in easy-moving octosyllables, which helped to make up a poem unlike anything that had previously appeared in English."

[13] Ruggiers 1953:16–29. Other major studies include Koonce 1966; Bennett 1968; Delany 1972; and Burlin, chap. 2. I tend to endorse Burlin's objection to Koonce's "patristic allegorical illogicalities" (p. 46), though I have great difficulty accepting his assertion that Chaucer "set out to produce a 'big work,' to imitate, either in earnest or in game, the reach of Dante. But once the sizable plan was laid out, he found himself filling in the pieces mechanically" (p. 46). Presently Delany's seems the most thoughtful book on the poem.

[14] Cf. Sypherd 1907:117–28, particularly the citation for *La Panthère d'amour*, p. 118.

[15] See the discussions below under the individual entries *passim*, but especially *Troilus and Criseyde* 1.568–69, 3.617–20, 622–23, 5.1541–45; and the poem *Fortune*. Dante, it should be noted here, elevated Fortune to an angelic power.

before Fame is made up of lovers.[16] The presence of a Temple of Venus in book 1 and a Palace of Fame in book 3, as well as the fact that Chaucer nowhere else confuses these two deities, should, it would seem, be taken as an indication that he had a remarkably distinct picture of the goddesses as separate powers. The "conflation" upon which the article under discussion depends so heavily is, therefore, even more doubtful since it lets pass all distinction between Venus, Fortune, and Fame and asserts almost a total inter-changeability of the goddesses. This, it is felt, loses sight of not only the function but also the rank of these deities.

Finally, the emphasis given to the Dantesque aspect of the eagle seems dangerously overstressed. First, the article assumes that the eagle in Dante was – along with Boethius's mounting Philosophy – the only significant symbol in Chaucer's mind at the time of composition.[17] In addition it assumes that both eagles – that of Jove and that of God – in the *Commedia*, as well as their philosophical implications, were the elements of the poem in which Chaucer was primarily interested. The Chaucerian and Dantean passages are then treated *in vacuo*, though with some confusion, since, in attempting a contextual parallel, the article strongly suggests that Chaucer's (that is, the Dreamer's?) wonder at seeing what happens to the petitioners under Fame's arbitrary dictates comes before, or just as, he leaves the Temple of Venus and is a fundamental crisis for him. On the basis of the confusion, it is asserted that

> just as Dante needed to be presented with his reassuring vision [of the eagle in his dream], so Chaucer now needs his reassuring answer to what he has just recently seen.[18] He prays

> > "O Crist!" thoughte I, "that art in blysse,
> > Fro fantome and illusion
> > Me save!"[19]

The final remarks on Dante's importance (p. 25) seem to echo the explications that ten Brink and Rambeau had long ago offered:

> The relationship to Dante which I have indicated earlier suggests that the mysterious and capricious injustice of the Lady Fortune is to Chaucer's poem what the impenetrable mystery of God's justice is to the *Divine Comedy*; both poets are led to the threshold of an answer by an eagle who is the messenger of the Almighty.

We are, perhaps, once more in danger of losing sight of Chaucer's humor. Actually, the eagle would seem to be a compound of many literary sources and traditions; and while good cause must be shown for the selection of one of these to the exclusion of all others, even better cause must be shown for reading the poem as an allegorical description of a philosophical autobiography. This does not mean that Chaucer was not a serious, or even a profound, poet, but Dante was evidently not that well known, nor (judging by the scholarship of the last hundred years) is the allusion sufficiently clear that confusion would not have beset the audience of Chaucer's time. If we accept the interpretation of philosophical autobiography, we would have to assume a deliberate obscurantism on

---

[16] The sixth and seventh groups are not lovers but those who wish to have the reputations of lovers.

[17] See below, entries under *HF* 496–508, 529–48.

[18] Actually all that the Dreamer has seen so far are the conventional carvings in the conventional Temple of Love.

[19] Ruggiers 1953:21. The lines are *HF* 492–94.

Chaucer's part—an attempt, that is, to hide his meaning behind the complex structure of Dantesque images and the clean contrary tone of the poem itself. In concluding this review of the Dantesque interpretations of *The House of Fame*, I feel justified in citing again Kittredge's opening remark (1894:80–81) on ten Brink's view:

> Great poets, no doubt, address themselves to posterity; and posterity is free to interpret them for its own comfort and inspiration, in any terms it finds useful. But they address themselves, in the first instance, to their immediate contemporaries.... What Chaucer meant to his contemporaries is, then, a pertinent question.

The dating of *The House of Fame* is affected, quite naturally, by the critical view of the poem's unity. Critics such as Jack (1920:39)[20] and Speirs (1951:43)[21] and, by implication, Lowes, believe that there are two dates of composition, one for the "Aeneid" section, and another for the two remaining books.[22] Lowes's is an interesting and balanced summary of this approach to the poem (1934:133):

> Up to the very end of Book I, to repeat, the poem is in the French vein. Then, within forty-four lines, Chaucer draws upon the *Inferno*, the *Purgatorio*, and the *Paradiso*. In a word, when he ended Book I and began Book II, he was familiar with all three parts of the *Divine Comedy*, of which not a trace appears in the poem until Book I is within thirteen lines of its close. And from the moment when Dante's presence makes itself felt the poem is vivid with life. I wish one could know just what had happened. Had Chaucer, all the while knowing Dante, continued with growing boredom a theme which Dante (as he knew) had touched with a pen of fire? Or had he gone through Dante, while a poem in process of composition waited? Or had the manuscript of Book I been lying in his chest since a date near that of the *Book of the Duchess*, with which in the Invocation it is linked, to be thriftily retrieved (for Chaucer was thrifty) as prologue to the swelling act of a new and freshly animating theme?

Lowes considers, first, that there is a total change of direction occurring at about line 495 and, second, that this change is due almost entirely to the influence of Dante. Now if, as has been often stated, Dante's influence went deeply into Chaucer's character, it is curious that he should, just at this point of meeting a freshly animating theme, make use of the *Aeneid* summary—assuming that it is structurally irrelevant—merely because he happened to have done it at some time in the past.[23] Why, in short, did Chaucer not begin by leading directly up to the flight of the eagle and so present a poem exhibiting the unified structure that Dante so eminently exemplifies?[24] That there is a marked difference in tone

---

[20] "Not to speak further, I take this whole Aeneas to be an insertion of quite early work."

[21] "The miniature of the *Aeneid* in the first book (The Prologue) looks like earlier work."

[22] For another division see Heath, von Westenholz, and Pollard (citations in Hammond, p. 376), who consider that book 3 was written later.

[23] For other works that Lowes would consider available at that time, see below, n.33.

[24] Lowes's subsequent suggestion (p. 134) that the invocation to book 2, "O Thought, that wrot all that I mette," comes from *Inf.* 2.7 (correctly, 2.8), "O Memory that wrote down what I saw" (*Inf.*, p. 13), and that this is but a few lines after Virgil's "I was a poet, and I sang of that just son of Anchises who came from Troy after proud Ilium was burned" (*Inf.*, p. 7), is ingenious but too heavily dependent on the association for Lowes's assertion: "And that is precisely what Chaucer too had sung in his own First Book. In a word, in that Invocation, present by no accident, he has now bound together, however baffling their relations otherwise, Books I and II, as if with hoops of steel." Even granting Chaucer this association of ideas, his audience would certainly never have seen in so obscure a reference the "hoops of steel" that were binding the poem together.

between book 1 and book 2 is reasonably evident, but could not this change be due to Chaucer's moving from the comparatively uninspiring work of reshaping a version of the *Aeneid* (like that of Simon Aurea Capra)[25] with Ovidian material to the freer and more creative work of imaginative description in books 2 and 3? While it is true that a certain number of biographical problems may be set aside if we accept the concept of dual dates of composition, we must recognize that such an acceptance is made at the sacrifice of the poem's possible unity. Such an acceptance does not, however, avoid the problem of "a date near that of the *Book of the Duchess,* with which in the Invocation it is linked," since there is just as much reason to connect the Invocation to the whole poem as to the first book alone. In book 1 the mention of Dante would in itself seem to indicate that Chaucer knew the *Commedia* at the time that the first section was composed or rewritten. At least insofar as the question of chronology is concerned, it would seem far sounder to consider *The House of Fame* as a poem with a single date of composition.

As has been previously mentioned, a critic's view of Chaucer's relationship to Dante may determine fundamentally his approach to the chronology of Chaucer's poems. A striking example of overdependence on Dante can be seen in the confusion that previously existed in the chronological relation of *The House of Fame* and *Troilus and Criseyde.* The concomitant difficulties are exemplified in the study on Boccaccio and Chaucer by Trigona (1923), who, after dealing with the Monk's tragedies, says (p. 95):

> That the English poet was not thinking, not even distantly, of imitating the *Commedia* of Dante with this work of his, and much less of having already attempted it, we are easily able to deduce by referring to the noted verses that are read in the leavetaking to his poem *Troilus and Criseyde,* redone, as we shall see, from the *Filostrato* of Boccaccio:
>
> > Go litel book, go litel myn tragedie,
> > Ther god my maker yet, er that I dye,
> > So sende might to make in som comedie!
>
> There clearly is the old dream of the poet: to be able to imitate Dante. And Chaucer makes the attempt afterward in his *House of Fame,* which while left incomplete, even as it now is, shows clearly enough what was the ideal that was spurring his energies and, perhaps, moving his spirit:
>
> > . . . God my maker yet, er that I dye
> > So sende might to make in some comedie![26]

---

[25] Friend 1953:317–23. The text is reprinted by André Boutemy et al. 1946–47:267–88. Boutemy et al. note that there is also a fourteenth-century English transcription of the second edition in Bibliothèque Nationale MS Lat. 4126, as well as other examples in "Mss. de la Reine Christine (Vatican) nᵒ 344" and Bodleian MS Rawlinson G 109. Claes Schaar (1954:33 n.5) had evidently completed his work when Friend's article appeared. Schaar's note, however, is illuminating in the light of his close comparisons of the narrative technique in Chaucer with both Chaucer's sources and other writers of narrative. While Schaar feels that there are few direct verbal parallels, he adds: "What is of real interest is Friend's demonstration of the arrangement of the story and the changes in the narrative made by Chaucer, it seems, under the influence of [Simon's] *Ilias.* As Friend points out (p. 323): 'they are alike in what we may call the management of the story or the scenario made with similar abbreviations, short cuts, and a shift of material to emphasize the role of Venus.'" Pointing out the difference in style between Chaucer and Simon, Schaar concludes: "And when moulding his details, Chaucer keeps closer to Virgil than to the somewhat frigid exhibition of rhetorical skill in the later poet, even if Simon's influence, in other respects, seems probable enough."

[26] See also Trigona, p. 132 ("The poet attempts in fact the imitation of the divine poem in his *House of Fame,* . . . seeking thus to carry into effect his old dream") and p. 150 (". . . this work [*The House of Fame*] which was supposed to be like the realization of his dream: 'There god my maker yet, er that I dye, / So sende might to make some comedie!'"). In all fairness it should be recalled that the original title of Dante's major work was simply *Commedia.*

Trigona's interpretation finds its basis in ten Brink (p. 122)[27] and perhaps the only really surprising fact is that eighteen years after Lowes's searching articles on the chronological relations of Chaucer's works an argument such as this should be used for placing *The House of Fame* after *Troilus and Criseyde*. Lowes (1905:854) had seen at once the central tenet of this view:

> For it is a fair statement of the case to say that the whole argument for the later date of the *Hous of Fame* [ca. 1384] rests on the supposed fact that the "som comedie" in which Chaucer prayed that he might "make" before he died, referred by anticipation to the *Hous of Fame*. In other words, it is upon the sole suggestion of the single word "comedie" that the whole laboriously constructed parallel between the *Hous of Fame* and the *Divina Commedia* depends.[28]

Lowes showed with conviction that "comedie" is used in *Troilus and Criseyde* in opposition to its natural antonym, "tragedie," and he then proceeded, on the basis of a mistranslation, a similarity with the meter of *The Book of the Duchess*, and a maturer humor, to set *The House of Fame* before *Troilus and Criseyde*.[29]

The importance of the order of works in discussion of the Chaucer-Dante relationship is obvious, since we are here assuming that the first major poem to show Dante's influence is, indeed, *The House of Fame*. The objections to such a chronology have been given by Tatlock (1950:63–64), whose argument rests principally on *The House of Fame*, lines 1468–70, where, among the names of those who are authorities on the Trojan cause, we find:

> he Lollius,
> And Guydo eke de Columpnis,
> And Englyssh Gaufride eke, ywis.

Tatlock felt that Lollius, who is mentioned in *Troilus* twice (1.394, 5.1653) as Chaucer's primary source of information, was Chaucer's invention of a fictitious source, but Pratt (1950b:183–87) has demonstrated that the belief in the actuality of Lollius was probably due to a scribal error in Horace *Epistolae* 1.2. In other words, Chaucer might well have inserted the name not for the purpose of "confirming the feigned authenticity of the *Troilus*" (Tatlock, p. 64) but rather through a mistake of his sources.[30]

While it would be quite in keeping with Chaucer's sense of humor to name himself among the authorities on Trojan affairs, the reference to "Englyssh Gaufride" does not seem to bear out such an interpretation. Tatlock's arguments against the usually accepted idea that this is a reference to Geoffrey of Monmouth are: (1) "Geoffrey's *Historia Regum Britanniae* does not tell the story of Troy, but that of some of its refugees, practically

---

[27] "We have made it apparent that at that point Chaucer recalled to mind the Dantean notions of comedy and of tragedy, and thus that he thereby remembered Dante's divine poem."

[28] For a discussion of "make in some comedye" and *The Canterbury Tales*, see Howard 1976, esp. pp. 31–37.

[29] In addition to the mistranslation of *pernicibus alis* which suggests (though only on the assumption that Chaucer would have recognized the error) that *The House of Fame* preceded the *Troilus*, one might note two bits of negative information that would indicate that *The House of Fame* preceded *The Legend of Good Women* and *The Parliament of Fowls*: (1) the "stock list of faithless lovers," to use Lowes's phrase (p. 132; cf., however Lowes's view of another such list in 1917:706–708, discussed below under *PF* 288) contains no hint of material from *The Legend of Good Women*; (2) *The House of Fame* would seem to have preceded the *Parliament of Fowls* since there is no use in the former of what would have been the very convenient description of the Temple of Venus given by Boccaccio in *The Teseida*. This description was, of course, later incorporated in *The Parliament of Fowls*. The foregoing are, admittedly, but additional hints to an order already agreed upon generally.

[30] Kittredge's earlier hypothesis to this effect is set forth in 1909:58–59.

starting with Aeneas' descendants" (Tatlock, p. 64); (2) Geoffrey of Monmouth "is a British-Celtic and strongly anti-English" (Tatlock, p. 64); (3) Chaucer should therefore have named him more exactly "Britoun Gaufride" if he named him at all. On the first point, Chaucer does not say that these authorities tell only of the Trojan war, but rather that "ech. . . / Was besy for to bere up Troye" (Tatlock, p. 64). One of the most fundamental concepts of English medieval historians was, of course, that Britons were the direct descendants of Aeneas and the Trojan race—that, in effect, Trojan culture had moved westward with the fall of Troy and had civilized Europe. In this sense Geoffrey of Monmouth was showing the glory of the Trojan race.[31] Tatlock's second point—that Chaucer would refrain from mentioning Geoffrey's *Historia* because of its anti-English view—seems negated by the tremendous popularity of the work, which would have made it one of the first sources to come to the mind of his audience.[32] Finally, Chaucer's reference to "*Englyssh* Gaufride" is readily accounted for simply on the basis of national pride. Certainly it would have been the very essence of political tactlessness in the bitter years of discontent that closed the reign of Edward III and inaugurated Richard II to have emphasized the existing factional strife by reference to "Britoun Gaufride." Indeed, if Chaucer were referring to himself, it would seem that he would have employed the same version of his name that he had had the eagle use and that he would have written "Englyssh Geoffrey." The use of "Gaufride" seems certainly to reflect the Latin version of the name, which would have been constantly used in connection with the *Historia Regum Britanniae*.

The various arguments for chronological order have been thus carefully reviewed since they are central to our problem of the Chaucer-Dante relationship. *The House of Fame* would certainly appear to precede the other works discussed and can, therefore, be taken as the earliest major poem of Chaucer that shows Dante's influence.

We come, then, to the question of an absolute date, and it is here that we can only test the critical assertions on their own merit. Sypherd's acceptance (1907:11 n.1, 162–63) of Lowes's hypothesized date 1379 (1905:862) has probably lent support to the generally hesitant acceptance of this year of composition. Sypherd has added no evidence to Lowes's suggestion, which itself seems open to discussion. Lowes dates *The House of Fame* in the late seventies, though with no other apparent reason than that it follows the 1378 journey to Italy. This he feels is "a supposition which the presence of passages from Dante (whom Chaucer would certainly read as soon as he became acquainted with Italian) bears out" (p. 862). Whether or not Chaucer would have read Dante first is a matter of individual conjecture, but what is most surprising is Lowes's implicit statement that Chaucer was not acquainted with Italian until after the 1378 journey. Unless this statement has been very badly misread, it not only seems contrary to the generally accepted date 1372 or earlier as the period in which Chaucer learned Italian but also seems to be contradicted by Lowes's later writings (e.g. 1934:128) as well as by the list of works which he, in his early article,

[31] Cf. Robinson, p. 786. An extremely valuable application of this historical concept to *Troilus and Criseyde* was made by Kellogg (1954).

[32] Baugh, p. 170, n.18, in speaking of the popularity of Geoffrey's *Historia*, notes: "This is evident from the more than 200 manuscripts still extant. Alfred of Beverly, writing about 1150, says that it was such a common subject of conversation that any one who did not know its stories was considered a fool. A part of its popularity may have been due to the satisfaction it gave the Anglo-French court to point to something in the past history of Britain comparable to Charlemagne and his peers in France. See G. H. Gerould, 'King Arthur and Politics,' *Speculum*, II (1927), 33–51."

assigns to the 1369–79 period.[33] The date 1379 must, I believe, be rejected until some more definite proof has been offered in support of it.

The *terminus a quo* of *The House of Fame* has been generally set at 1374, since on May 10 of that year Chaucer obtained the house above Aldgate, and on June 2 he was made "Controller of the Customs and Subsidy of Wools, Skins and Hides in the port of London on condition that he should write his rolls with his own hand" (Robinson 1957:xxii), a manual task from which he was not relieved until 1385. It is to this period that the apparently autobiographical passage in *The House of Fame* (lines 644–60) is directed:

> . . . thou has no tydynges
> Of Loves folk yf they be glade,
> Ne of noght elles that God made;
> And noght oonly fro fer contree
> That ther no tydynge cometh to thee,
> But of thy verray neyghebores,
> That duellen almost at thy dores,
> Thou herist neyther that ne this;
> For when thy labour doon al ys,
> And hast mad alle thy rekenynges,
> In stede of reste and newe thynges,
> Thou goost hom to thy hous anoon,
> And, also domb as any stoon,
> Thou sittest at another book
> Tyl fully daswed ys thy look,
> And lyvest thus as an heremyte,
> Although thyn abstynence ys lyte.

Concerning the date of the poem, Robinson states (p. 779):

> In general, the probabilities favor the early years of the Italian period, before the composition of the *Palamon* or *Troilus*. The use of the octosyllabic couplet would have been more natural at that time than later. This date would account for the transitional character of the poem—a French love-vision in type, but clearly under the influence of Dante.[34]

A great deal can be said in favor of an earlier date for *The House of Fame*,[35] though it is admittedly neither more nor less factual than arguments for any other year. There was, of course, no "ten year silence" between 1369 and 1379, since most scholars have agreed in

---

[33] Great caution should be exercised with regard to the hypothesized list of writings which Lowes assigns to fill out the 1369–79 period. He follows Pollard in attributing to this period *The Second Nun's Tale, The Monk's Tale, The Man of Law's Tale, The Clerk's Tale, The Physician's Tale*, and *The Manciple's Tale*, and he adds, with some caution, the translation of the *Roman de la Rose*, a number of minor pieces, balades, roundels, virelayes doubtless lost, Origenes upon the Maudelayne and, with this last, *Melibee* and *The Parson's Tale*. This list in itself, however, rejects a date as late as 1379 for the learning of Italian, for Lowes himself leaned heavily upon a posited Dante allusion in *The Man of Law's Tale* (Lowes 1917a:707–708), as well as citing yet another from *The Complaint unto Pity* (p. 722–24). In addition, there are direct translations from Dante in *The Second Nun's Tale* and *The Monk's Tale*, and Dantesque influence has been seen in *The Clerk's Tale* and *The Parson's Tale*. As well, the influence of the *Roman de la Rose* on *The Book of the Duchess* seems pervasive enough to warrant the translation's being done before rather than after 1369. Finally, although the lost works might very well come from this decade, there is actually no reason to assume that they were all done during 1369–79.

[34] See Robinson, p. 779. See also pp. 330–31, for a fuller treatment.

[35] Patch (1919:321–28, esp. p. 327) supports a view of 1379 or later on the supposition that "perhaps he [Chaucer] consulted the learned and important manual *De Genealogia Deorum*, written by Boccaccio, and available in its first form by 1378. If he heard of it in Italy, I feel confident that Geoffrey Chaucer would have tried

assigning to this period varying amounts of work, usually including several of the Canterbury tales, some translation, and a fair number of the Minor Poems. Although one should not be overcome by the rage for order nor consider that Chaucer was unable to return to a former prosody, Robinson's remarks on the continuity of the octosyllabic line seem justifiable, for a return to the comparative strictness of octosyllables after working in the freer decasyllabic line of any of the poems assigned to this decade seems rather less than more likely. Lowes's impression (1905:862) that *The House of Fame* would naturally follow Chaucer's exposure to Dante is probably valid but far more sound factually if we think in terms of the journey of 1372—if not earlier. It is Lowes, likewise, who has remarked that book 1 is probably of "a date near that of the *Book of the Duchess*, with which in the Invocation it is linked," and this can be most easily explained not by assuming dual dates of composition but by considering *The House of Fame* itself as of an earlier date, closer to that of *The Book of the Duchess*. Finally, while one of the principal works used is undoubtedly the *Commedia*, we should not forget that almost the whole of book 1 is based on the *Aeneid* (or a medieval version thereof) and on Ovid[36] and that echoes of French love visions (among which the more important would certainly seem to be Nicholas de Margival's *Panthère d'amour*[37]) are found throughout the poem. This balance and interweaving of Chaucer's earlier reading in French love poetry with what would have come with his knowledge of Italian literature, while it might very well have continued through the 1369–79 decade, was most certain to have been in the stage of transition represented by *The House of Fame* around the mid-1370s. While it must be pointed out again that one is dealing only in circumstantial evidence, the most plausible explanation of these circumstances points to a period closer to 1374 than to 1379.

If the later date of 1379 is accepted, one can only explain the circumstances as a series of exceptions; that is, we must assume that Chaucer returned to an octosyllabic line; that the poem (probably occasional) has two dates of composition; that Chaucer waited six or seven years before using the *Commedia* (if, as some critics assume, this is the first work that Chaucer wrote under Dante's influence) or, alternatively, that Chaucer did not know Dante until after 1378; and, finally, that Dante's influence dominates the entire poem, though in a manner too deep to be seen in the actual lines.[38] While these exceptions can be granted, of course, the explanation of an earlier date of composition satisfies most simply and most naturally the circumstances surrounding the poem.

From an investigation of the actual lines in *The House of Fame* which have been ascribed to Dante, it would appear that, with the exception of the well-known allusion to *Purg.* 9, Chaucer draws exclusively from the first and last cantos of the *Commedia*'s *cantiche*. There

---

to find a copy" (Patch 1939:40). But if the cost of books was as high as Schramm (1933:139–45) has estimated—that is, about £60 for a book of thirty quires with modest illustrations—we should be cautious what titles we put among Chaucer's "sixty bokys, olde and newe." Not only do the date and the cost of the work militate against Chaucer's acquisition of it at this time but the basis on which Lowes determined the position of *The House of Fame* in the Chaucer chronology—namely, the *pernicibus alis* phrase (n.29 above)—could not possibly have been mistranslated had Chaucer read this passage (bk. 1, chap. 10) in the *Genealogia deorum*. Boccaccio cites the phrase at the opening of his discussion (cf. Boccaccio 1951:1.36, line 27) and goes on to explain (p. 38, lines 9–10): "For he is nimble, that is, swift, since, as he says himself, nothing is swifter."

[36] See, for example, Shannon (1929:48ff.) and Friend (1953) on Chaucer's version of the *Aeneid*. The most perceptive treatment of the Ovidian relationship is Fyler (1979:23–64).

[37] Sypherd, *passim*; Patch 1919, esp. pp. 321–26. Also noteworthy is the use made of Deschamps's *Lay du desert d'amour*.

[38] That is, even though the framework and the largest number of ascribable lines come from French and classical (or medieval classical) sources. Muscatine (1964:108) believes that for "the Dantean material in this poem, the incipient seriousness...is swallowed up in...parody."

are, of course, analogous passages that are more widely scattered, but these usually are the result of a common source or common knowledge. Naturally it is tempting to try to make the bond between the greatest English poet and the greatest Italian poet of the era as strong as possible, but, when faced with a common source or common knowledge, such dependence should not be posited, it seems, unless some unique feature in Dante's treatment can be shown to appear in Chaucer. Considerations of the two poets *in vacuo*— whether by the simple means of extracted parallel passages or by the more subtle psychological method of a posited recreation of the poet's thought process—entail so many questionable assumptions that such a basically exclusive procedure should only be employed with the utmost caution. Robinson's caveat (1903:293) is worth recalling: "Dante embodied in his encyclopedic poem nearly all the philosophic doctrine and very much of the current learning of the middle ages, and the same ideas were bound to appear in any poem of the period that dealt, whether seriously or humorously, with philosophic subjects."

The House of Fame

Book 1

Bethel: "81: God the mover of all things; phrase from *Par.* I, 1—doubtful."

And he that mover ys of al[39]   La gloria di colui che tutto move[40]

The glory of the All-Mover [*Par.*, p. 3][41]

There is no contextual parallel whatever, and one certainly does not need a source for a medieval reference to God as the prime mover of the universe. For some reason Robinson accepts the line from the *Paradiso* as Chaucer's source.

Bethel: "152f.: allusion to Sinon; phrasing due partly to *Inf.* XXX, 98."

[First sawgh I the destruction]   l'altr' è 'l falso Sinon greco di Troia.
Of Troye, thurgh the Grek Synon,
[That] with his false forswerynge....   The other is the false Sinon, Greek from Troy. [*Inf.*, p. 321]

The citation from the *Inferno* is very doubtful as either source or parallel. The omission of line 151 is highly questionable since line 152, given out of context, must consequently receive some such incorrect interpretation as "through Sinon the Greek of Troy." Such a reading is nullified by the context, which shows that "of Troye" is simply part of the preceding line. Sinon, of course, was famed for his treachery,[42] and his act would have

---

[39] Although these works have been cited previously, it would perhaps be convenient to give them again together at this first entry. Unless otherwise noted, citations from Chaucer are from *The Works of Geoffrey Chaucer*, ed. Robinson (2d ed., 1957).

[40] Unless otherwise noted, citations are from *The Divine Comedy*, translated, with a commentary, by Charles S. Singleton, 6 vols. Princeton, 1970–75.

[41] I have used Singleton's translation (1970–75) throughout, unless otherwise noted.

[42] Thus Scartazzini (Dante 1921:274) remarks that Sinon "was noted for his treason."

been particularly infamous to those who considered themselves descendants of the Trojan race. Chaucer need hardly have depended on Dante's single reference to supply him with the information that Sinon was a Greek and indulged in "false forswerynge"; among other works Virgil's *Aeneid* (2.57-194) or a medieval version thereof[43] would supply him with a far more likely source.

In speaking of Sinon in this fashion, Dante is following a tradition that is not in Chaucer. Scartazzini (Dante 1921:274), explaining Dante's reference to "the Greek from Troy," says: "...though Greek, [Sinon] is called by the name of the place where he committed it [the act] cfr. Virg., *Aen.* II, 147 sq., where Priam says to Sinon: 'Whoever thou art, from now on forget the Greeks...; thou shalt be *ours'*" (1.305; Scartazzini's italics). For another instance of the "false forswerynge," and one where Chaucer gives his sources for the Sinon reference, see *SqT* 209-10.

Bethel: "198–201: allusion to Juno's hatred of the Trojans; phraseology influenced by *Inf.* XXX, 1f."

Ther saugh I thee, cruel Juno,	Nel tempo che Iunone era crucciata
That art daun Jupiteres wif,	per Semelè contra 'l sangue tebano
That hast yhated, al thy lyf,	
Al the Troianysshe blood	In the time when Juno was wroth for Semele
	against the Theban blood [*Inf.*, p. 315]

There seems to be neither source nor parallel here.[44] It should be pointed out that Chaucer's reference is to Troy, not Thebes; that the previous 47 lines and a goodly portion of the following 173 lines, as well as 38 lines (427–65) farther on, are based on the *Aeneid*; that Chaucer gives his sources;[45] and that a perfectly good source (if one is needed) can be found in the long passage in which Virgil establishes the motivation for the *Aeneid* in his description of Juno's anger.[46] In short, neither verbal nor contextual parallel is established here.

---

[43] Friend, p. 318, compares *HF* 151–56 with "the rather long treatment by Simon Aurea Capra, who also stresses the false swearing of the traitor" (lines 343–51, 365–66): "And Synon, surrendering him to the Teucrians, that he might surrender the city / Did not fear Priam once captured, nor did he fear the gods. / For calling upon his very own head, and also the godhead, / He swore that the bulk of the horse of Pallas was holy. / He swore that he with his blood would have softened a godhead / Enraged at the Danaans, except that fleeing had saved him. / He swore that the Danaan hope had been broken, that Troy had prevailed, / If a dutiful hand should set up the Palladium in the city. / The Trojans believed in the perjury [MS: Perjuror]. / ... Look, the city is captured, the foe is attacking the townsfolk / And Synon by lying has driven the wooden horse to give birth" (my translation). To these citations Friend notes: "Cf. *Aeneid*, II 195ff. The references to the poem of Simon are from *Scriptorium*, I, 269ff, Boutemy's transcription of Nat. Lat. 8430. In two cases above I have restored the original reading of the manuscript altered by Boutemy." Both citations are found in *Scriptorium* 1.275. For comment on these lines from Simon in comparison with the corresponding passage in Virgil, see Schaar 1954:33 n.5.

[44] See discussion under *TC* 5.599–602.

[45] *HF* 376–79: "And alle the wordes that she [Dido] seyde, / Whoso to knowe hit hath purpos, / Rede Virgile in Eneydos / Or the Epistle of Ovyde...."

[46] Cf. *Aen.* 1.19–20: "Yet in truth she had heard that a race was springing from Trojan blood." Chaucer seems closer to Virgil than to Simon, who, though he stresses Juno's anger, "But in violent hatreds, but unfair, but envious Juno / Is not enough satisfied, even as yet, with evils" (Boutemy et al., lines 511–12, pp. 277–78, my translation), and its cause in Jupiter's choice of Ganymede and Paris's choice of Helen, concludes with "For this double reason she hated the Trojans, and them / She hurt with whatever art she could use to hurt" (Boutemy et al., lines 519–20, p. 278, my translation).

Bethel: "445–50: Dante named (450) and the *Inferno* alluded to."

And every turment eke in helle
Saugh he [Aeneas], which is longe to
    telle;
Which whoso willeth for to knowe,
He moste rede many a rowe
On Virgile or on Claudian,
Or Daunte, that hit telle kan.

The group of names itself and the fact that Chaucer could name Dante this casually seem to indicate that the Italian poet may have been fairly well known and held in reasonably high esteem[47]. It shows, at least, that Dante was to be taken into account and was considered in better company than that of the *visio* writers of the time, whom Chaucer does not bother to mention.

Bethel: "458: spelling Lavyna due possibly to *Purg.* XVII, 37; doubtful."

And wan Lavina to his wif
                                   Ancisa t'hai per non perder Lavina

                                   You have killed yourself in order not to lose Lavinia [*Purg.*, p. 181]

No relationship at all is established here. Bethel might have also listed *Inf.* 4.126 and *Par.* 6.3 as other examples of Dante's use of this spelling, but the line above (458) can also be found spelled Lavyna[48] and the four other uses of the name (even with the references to the town) are spelled Lavyne.[49] Oddly enough, in his text Bethel (p. 201) states that "there are, finally, one or two instances in which Dantesque influence has been mistakenly urged. The allusion to 'Lavina,' where the argument is based merely on grounds of spelling, I have already discussed."[50] It seems strange that, having once rejected the possibility of a source in Dante, Bethel should go on to include it in his summary in the appendix, even with the "doubtful" evaluation. Sypherd (1907:52), taking this as an example of the danger of basing any part of an argument on "shadowy parallelisms," shows the fallacy of incomplete comparison. According to the texts given by both Scartazzini and Grandgent, the argument is even weaker than Sypherd supposed, since the example of a Lavinia reading in *Inf.* 4.126 given in his text is apparently not valid, both of the aforementioned editors having Lavina.

Although it is questionable whether any authority is necessary at all, another source for most of the spellings (i.e., Lavyne or Lavine) might be added. In the *Roman d'Eneas*, which Chaucer used and which was "classical with a difference," as Patch (1939:37) aptly puts it, one finds constantly the expected French version of Lavinia's name, i.e., Lavine.[51] Undoubtedly many other precedents for the spelling can be found, but all point up the danger of attempting to establish parallelisms with a limited historical approach.

---

[47] See Chap. 1; see also Tatlock 1950:34.

[48] Cf. Tatlock and Kennedy 1927.

[49] *BD* 331; *HF* 148; *LGW* 257, 1331.

[50] Bethel's discussion is in chap. 2, where he cites the above spelling and that in *BD* 331.

[51] Cf., e.g., *Eneas: Roman du XII* Siècle*, line 3315 (Salverda de Grave 1925:1.101). See also the Middle English noncycle romance *Floris and Blauncheflour*, written about 1250. In speaking of the marvelous cup received in part payment for Blauncheflour, it says that Eneas won it at Troy "And gaf it to Lauine, his amy" (line 180).

Bethel: "480–95: Details in the description of the desert have been suggested as parallels to *Inf.*, I, 64–6, XIV, 8f., 13–5. All seem doubtful."

When I out at the dores cam,
I faste aboute me beheld.
Then sawgh I but a large feld,
As fer as that I myghte see,
Withouten toun, or hous, or tree,
Or bush, or grass, or eryd lond;
For al the feld nas but of sond
As smal as man may se yet lye
In the desert of Lybye;
Ne no maner creature
That ys yformed be Nature
Ne sawgh I, me to rede or wisse.
"O Crist!" thought I, "that art in blysse,
Fro fantome and illusion
Me save!" and with devocion
Myn eyen to the hevene I caste.

Quando vidi costui nel gran diserto,
  "*Miserere* di me," gridai a lui,
  "qual che tu sii, od ombra od omo certo!"

dico che arrivammo ad una landa
che dal suo letto ogne pianta rimove.

Lo spazzo era una rena arida e spessa,
  non d'altra foggia fatta che colei
  che fu da' piè di Caton già soppressa.

When I saw him in that vast desert, I cried
to him, "Have pity on me whatever you are,
shade or living man!" [*Inf.*, p. 7]

I say we reached a plain which rejects all
plants from its bed. [*Inf.*, p. 141]

The ground was a deep dry sand, not
different in its fashion from that which once
was trodden by the feet of Cato. [*Inf.*, p. 141]

The intervening lines in the last two examples from Dante tend to rule them out as sources,[52] and the first example has no other parallel than the word *diserto*, which in this instance refers to a wild, barren, or deserted place rather than to a sandy plain. It is rather strange that Sypherd (1907:52–53) accepted this as a parallel, particularly since in his notes he cites two other parallels, both of which indicate generic traditions which later scholarship tends to uphold. Sypherd cites the *Espurgatoire Saint Patriz of Marie de France*, lines 301–304, the original of which, as Spencer shows (1927:177–200), was extremely popular and probably used elsewhere by Chaucer. Sypherd's other citation is *La Prison amoreuse*, lines 1521–22. In addition, this symbol of the desert in the genre of love poetry is seen again, as Robinson notes (p. 781) in Deschamps's *Lay du desert d'amour*, and he adds that "in the imagery of the love-vision, as Professor Patch has shown, it may well represent the state of the despairing lover. See *MLN* XXXIV, 321ff."[53] Finally, as Robinson again points out (p. 781), Chaucer may have used the same source as Dante, i.e. Lucan's *Pharsalia*[54] or the *Hystore de Julius Ceasar* of Jehan de Tuim. Of all the possible sources Dante certainly seems among the least likely, as Bethel's "doubtful" justly implies.

[52] *Inf.* 14.10–12: "The woeful wood is a garland round about it, as round the wood the dismal ditch. Here we stayed our steps at the very edge" (*Inf.*, p. 141).

[53] This remark, of course, agrees with Sypherd's suggestion of the importance of the genre in medieval literature in general and *The House of Fame* in particular. Patch (1919) gives a perfectly adequate source from the *Lay du desert d'amour* (lines 236–40): "Ne venez pas en ce desert / Ou il n'a fueille, ne boys vert, / Herbe, fleur, fruit, n'autre verdure; / Tout chant d'oisel y ert desert" ("Come not into this wasteland where there is neither leaf, nor green tree, grass, flower, fruit, nor other verdure; every birdsong has gone"). It seems unnecessary to strain for a connection with Dante either through noting that there is a *fosse* in the *Panthère d'amour* and the use of the word *fosso* in *Inf.* 14.11 (see n.52), or through remarking on the fact that *Inf.* 14 is within the vicinity of *Inf.* 17, where Geryon appears, and that Geryon is somewhat like Boccaccio's comment on the monster Fama in the *De genealogia deorum* (*habeant hominis effigiem*) which Chaucer might perhaps have read at this time (however, for the commonness of figures similar to Geryon from the time of Rev. 9.7–11 through Brunetto Latini, see Grandgent (Dante 1933:151–52) and the partial bibliography cited there).

[54] See specifically *Pharsalia* 9.378, 394–96, for the source of the passage in Dante. Bennett (1957:47–48) perceptively adds to the discussion Ovid (*Met.* 11.600–01, and cf. *BD* 157–59) and Virgil (*Aen.* 1.338; 4.257, 466–68). The fullest investigation is the excellent article by Steadman 1961:196–201.

Bethel: "496–508, 529–548: Description of the golden-feathered eagle due chiefly to *Purg.* IX, 19–24, 28–30. But the wording of ll. 505f. is closely modelled on *Par.* I, 62 f.; while ll. 534–9 take a hint from *Purg.* XXXII, 109f., 112."

Thoo was I war, lo! at the laste,
That faste be the sonne, as hye
As kenne myghte I with myn yë,
Me thoughte I sawgh an egle sore,
But that hit semed moche more
Then I had any egle seyn.
But this as sooth as deth, certeyn,
Hyt was of gold, and shon so bryghte
That never sawe men such a syghte,
But yf the heven had ywonne
Al newe of gold another sonne;
So shone the egles fethers bryghte,
And somwhat dounward gan hyt
    lyghte.

This egle, of which I have yow told,
That shon with fethres as of gold,
Which that so hye gan to sore,
I gan beholde more and more,
To se the beaute and the wonder;
But never was ther dynt of thonder,
Ne that thyng that men calle fouder,
That smot somtyme a tour to powder,
And in his swifte comynge brende,
That so swithe gan descende
As this foul, when hyt beheld
That I a-roume was in the feld;
And with hys grymme pawes stronge,
Withyn hys sharpe nayles longe,
Me, fleynge, in a swap he hente,
And with hys sours ayen up wente,
Me caryinge in his clawes starke
As lyghtly as I were a larke,
How high, I can not telle yow,
For I cam up, y nyste how.

In sogno mi parea veder sospesa
    un'aguglia nel ciel con penne d'oro,
    con l'ali aperte e a calare intesa;
ed esser mi parea là dove fuoro
    abbandonati i suoi da Ganimede,
    quando fu ratto al sommo consistoro.

Poi mi parea che, poi rotata un poco,
    terribil come folgor discendesse,
    e me rapisse suso infino al foco.

[. . . e fissi li occhi al sole oltre nostr'uso. . . .]
e di sùbito parve giorno a giorno
    essere aggiunto, come quei che puote
    avesse il ciel d'un altro sole addorno.

Non scese mai con sì veloce moto
    foco di spessa nube, quando piove
    [da quel confine che più va remoto,]
com' io vidi calar l'uccel di Giove
    [per l'alber giù, rompendo de la scorza,
    non che d'i fiori e de le foglie nove;
e ferì 'l carro di tutta sua forza;
    ond' el piegò]. . . .

I seemed to see, in a dream, an eagle poised in the sky, with feathers of gold, its wings outspread, and prepared to swoop. And I seemed to be in the place where Ganymede abandoned his own company, when he was caught up to the supreme consistory.[*Purg.*, p. 89]

Then it seemed to me that, having wheeled a while, it descended terrible as a thunderbolt and snatched me upwards as far as the fire. [*Purg.*, p. 89]

[. . . and I fixed my eyes on the sun beyond our wont. . . . And suddenly day seemed added to day,] as if He who has the power had adorned heaven with another sun. [*Par.*, p. 7]

Never with so swift a motion did fire descend from dense cloud, when it falls from the confine [that stretches most remote,] as I saw the bird of Jove [swoop downward through the tree, rending the bark as well as the flowers and the

new leaves, and it struck the chariot with all its force, so that it reeled]. . . .
[*Purg.*, p. 359]

It would be almost impossible to review here all the scholarship that has gone into this passage on the eagle, varying as it does between the extremes of Rambeau and the folklorists.[55] Robinson's remarks (pp. 781–82) on possible specific sources summarize this condition: "How far the suggestion for the eagle came from Dante and how far from the description of Ganymede in both Virgil and Ovid is a matter of dispute."[56] The best approach and review of the problem is still Sypherd's (p. 54), and his division of it seems a precise and totally valid one: "I agree [he says] with Rambeau that Chaucer no doubt got some of the physical characteristics of his eagle from Dante. . . . But for the *idea* of the eagle, of his journey through the air, we must look elsewhere than to the *Divine Comedy*."[57]

While Bethel's ascription of lines in *The House of Fame* is somewhat generous, his basis for the eagle's description in Dante is valid, and his reference to *Par.* 1.62–63 as the source of lines 505–506 seems justified.[58] The "hint from *Purg.* XXXII" should be treated with much more caution, however. The source in Ovid (*Met.* 155–61) makes a strong connection between Jove and the eagle, which can be only indirectly arrived at through Dante — that is, by connecting the eagle of *Purg.* 9 with that of *Purg.* 32(where it is representative of the Roman Empire) and finally with the eagle of the angelic formation in the sphere of Jupiter in *Par.* 20. Ovid's description is (*Met.* 10.157–60 [4.75]): "Still he did not deign to take the form of any bird save only that which could bear his thunderbolts. Without delay he cleft the air on his lying wings and stole away the Trojan boy." Extracted from *Purg.* 32, the lines that Bethel cites are striking, but in context one can see that *l'uccel di Giove* is a fairly common euphemism[59] for the word "eagle" which Dante had found in his source in the biblical parable.[60] Likewise, one can see that there is actually very little here that would have led Chaucer to make a selection of particular lines which have no contextual parallel to his picture of the eagle in *The House of Fame*.

One of the most interesting studies of Dante's influence in this passage is that made by Schaar (1954) on the basis of comparative stylistic techniques. While verbal similarities are, perhaps, passed by too lightly, the discussion seems worth citing at some length (p. 195):

> The most important of the passages which are said to have exerted an influence on this episode, is no doubt the eagle episode in *Purgatorio* IX, 19ff, a paragraph which seems to have been in Chaucer's mind when he related his

[55] See, for example, the following: ten Brink 1870:92; Rambeau 1880:232; Sypherd 1907:54; Lounsbury 1892:2.246; Lowes 1934:135; Kittredge 1909:86; Patch 1939:40; Tatlock 1950:59; Bennett 1957:49–51. Naturally, almost any critique of *The House of Fame* will have some reference to this problem.

[56] Delany (1972:69) rightly assumes multiple influence: "As a figure with an illustrious traditional background the garrulous bird is well qualified to convey important information: his literary antecedents are found in the Greek myth of Ganymede, in the Bible, in patristic biblical commentary and in Dante's *Divine Comedy*."

[57] Sypherd's italics. See also part 3, chap. 4, esp. pp. 86–95, for the many possible sources for the eagle, as well as a discussion of its functions within *HF* itself. Robinson notes, for example, that the descent of the eagle "is partly imitated from Dante. . . and partly from Machaut's Jugement du Roy de Navarre. . . and Confort d'Ami" (p. 782).

[58] Certainly it is more justified than Robinson's citation of *Purg.* 2.17–24, where Dante describes the approaching angel as a light growing greater in size and intensity.

[59] Cf. *Aen.* 1.394, *Jovis ales* ("bird of Jove").

[60] Ezekiel 17.3–4. Delany (p. 69, n.1) also cites Exod. 19.24; Job 39.27; Jer. 48.40, 49.22.

adventure with the eagle.[61] Other suggested originals are the Ganymede episode in Ovid's *Metamorphoses* X, 155ff,[62] and some passages in Machaut's *Jugement dou Roy de Navarre*, 301ff, and *Confort d'Ami* 1899f.[63] The latter two passages, however, afford parallels only to certain limited details in Chaucer's episode, and have less interest for an examination of his technique in describing the descent of the eagle. One might also refer to another analogous passage in Machaut, which is somewhat more relevant from our point of view, i.e., the episode of the descent of the eagle in the *Dit de l'Alerion* 4569ff. Let us examine the parallels in Dante, Ovid, and Machaut from the point of view of narrative technique.

After citing Clemen on the differences of content and similarities of form,[64] Schaar points out certain distinctions of technique between Dante's episode and that in Chaucer:

> In Dante, then, there is no even recording of events in a chronological order, interlaced with digressions, but rather a division of the episode into two equal halves, one static and descriptive, the other abrupt and sudden. While the lightning simile in Dante becomes part of and lends precision to the act of descending, it is more expanded in Chaucer and rather assumes a digressive character, being elaborated into a piece of independent description (*Ne that thyng that men calle fouder,* / *That smot somtyme a tour to powder*[65] etc.).

Passing by the parallel in the *Metamorphoses* with perhaps undue haste,[66] Schaar concludes (p. 196):

> The episode in the *Dit de l'Alerion*, finally, is a little more suggestive of the eagle episode in the *Hous of Fame*, but even more so of that in *Purgatorio*. There is the same contrast as in Dante between the description of the eagle soaring in the sky (4569–4574) and the sudden descent (. . . *Qu'eins qu'on peüst fourmer* *.VI. mos.* / *Il fu sus mon poing descendus*) etc., and the continuation deals with the poet's reactions. In short, the episode in Dante has many similarities to that in Chaucer, but there are also striking differences of technique, similar to those between Chaucer and Machaut.—Chaucer's paragraph, along with the close continuation, leads up to the main episode in Book II, the conversation with the eagle. It is also, of course, dramatic in itself.

---

[61] Schaar (1954) cites the first four scholars given in n.55 above, adding Clemen (1938:114ff.) and continuing: "The parallels traced by Dilts between Chaucer's eagle passage and certain details in Paradiso (*Observations on Dante and the Hous of Fame*, MLN LVII, 1942, p. 26ff) seem to me to be of less interest. It is quite possible that the latter passages were present to Chaucer's mind, but they are hardly of interest in an examination of his technique, and seem in any case far less important than the *Purgatorio* passage referred to by ten Brink and others."

[62] "Suggested by Lounsbury, *ibid.*" (Schaar's note).

[63] "Cf. Robinson, p. 891" (Schaar's note).

[64] Schaar (p. 196) cites Clemen 1963:91: "What influenced Chaucer in the *Divine Comedy* was not the basic conception, the thoughts, the 'content'; it was Dante's method of presentation, the intensity and perception with which he reproduced sensuous detail, visual impressions of movement and light for the most part, but also of sounds."

[65] "The parallel in *Navarre*, referred to by Robinson, reads: 'Chei li tempes et la foudre / Qui mainte ville mist en poudre' (301f)" (Schaar's note).

[66] Schaar (p. 196) says merely: "The eagle episode in the *Metamorphoses* has very little in common, from the technical point of view, with Chaucer's. The whole act of descending and carrying away the boy is compressed to one line and a half (*nec, mora, percusso mendacibus aere pennis* / *abripit Iliaden*); and no further stages of the process are given." One should not forget, however, the preceding lines in Ovid, nor the connection made there between Jove and the eagle. Cf. the previous discussion in this entry.

Schaar's investigation here, as elsewhere in his study, helps considerably to illuminate the way in which Chaucer transformed his sources. In this particular passage it would appear to explain at least one major aspect of the still tantalizing problem of Chaucer's degree of dependence on Dante.

Dilts (1942:26): Compares *HF* 497–99 with *Par.* 1.47–48:

As Chaucer wrote that in his dream he turned his eyes to heaven and

> faste by the sonne, as hye
> As kenne myghte I with myn ye,
> Me thoughte I sawgh an egle sore . . .

his mind seems to have been dwelling upon Beatrice in the *Paradiso,* who is described as looking into the sun:

> riguardar nel sole

There, too, as in Chaucer we find the eagle:

> aguglia sì non gli s'affisse unquanco

Again, the consideration *in vacuo* of Chaucer's lines with the *Paradiso* (translated below) must be carried out with great caution. What makes Dilts's suggestion feasible is the presence of other lines in *The House of Fame* based on this canto.[67] As far as the narrative situation is concerned, Chaucer, after all, wants to have his dreamer look up in order to see the eagle, and there seems no more natural way than for him to look up to God in prayer. The lines from the *Paradiso,* when put in their context, are perhaps less striking. It is noon in the Earthly Paradise for Dante (*Par.* 1.46–48):

> quando Beatrice in sul sinistro fianco
> vidi rivolta e riguardar nel sole:
> aguglia sì non li s'affisse unquanco.

when I saw Beatrice turned to her left side and looking at the sun: never did eagle so fix his gaze thereon. [*Par.*, p. 5]

The words *aguglia* and *sole* are indeed in suggestive juxtaposition, but the context and use of them are radically different. Beatrice is gazing directly into the sun (an act of adoration that Dante unsuccessfully tries to emulate): Chaucer's dreamer merely locates the eagle's position by relating it to the most readily available celestial point, the sun. Second, the reference in Dante is not to *the* eagle (i.e., the golden eagle) but to the fact that eagles (according to general belief) are capable of gazing into the sun, as Dante's sources had stated.[68] There is, then, little if any contextual parallel here, and, while the combination of *aguglia* and *sole* might possibly have stayed in Chaucer's mind, there would seem to be little basis for saying that he was "dwelling upon Beatrice" or that he saw here a reference to "the eagle."

When considered *in vacuo,* the passages may be given more weight than they rightly should be asked to bear. Thus Bennett, whose "'hooking' power of Chaucer's poetic

---

[67] *HF* 504–06 and *Par.* 1.63. Dilts notes (p. 27) that this parallel was pointed out to her by Patch, but it had already been cited by Bethel (see preceding entry) and Lowes 1934:136.

[68] Lucan, *Pharsalia* 9.902ff; and Latini, *Tesoro* 3.8. Cf. Dante 1921:649.

memory" (p. 154) recalls Lowes's theory of "linked atoms,"[69] is led to suggest a creative process which, while possible, seems finally to beget the same doubts as did Lowes's (Bennett, p. 51):

> In the *Paradiso* the image of the eagle-sighted Beatrice serves to show that she can gaze unflinchingly on the supernal glory. Chaucer's esemplastic imagination has seized on the bestiary association suggested by this faculty, and, having envisaged his glittering eagle as likewise hovering near the sun, he substitutes it for the sunlike Beatrice. The transmutation of diverse Dantean images, the adapting of them to novel purposes, the swift dramatic effect of the eagle's appearance—all these foreshadow the developments, and the density, that make the next part of the poem so rewarding, and indicate that the poet is by now wholly absorbed in his creation.

In an artistic universe inhabited only by Chaucer and Dante, such esemplastic power would be quite understandable, but the multiplicity of Chaucer's reading and interests must make us, in the final analysis, extremely cautious about accepting such tempting, and certainly not impossible, assertions.

Book 2

Bethel: "523–8: Chaucer invokes his Thought −: l. 523 is closely modelled on *Inf.* II, 8/ ll. 524 f. derive from *Par.* I, 11/l. 528 adapts *Inf.* II, 9."

O Thought, that wrot al that I mette,
And in the tresorye hyt shette
Of my brayn, now shal men se
Yf any vertu in the be,
To tellen al my drem aryght.
Now kythe thyn engyn and myght!

[O Muse, o alto ingegno, or m'aiutate;]
  o mente che scrivesti ciò ch' io vidi,
  qui si parrà la tua nobilitate.

[Veramente quant' io del regno santo]
  ne la mia mente potei far tesoro,
  [sarà ora materia del mio canto.]

  [O Muses, O high genius, help me now!] O memory that wrote down what I saw, here shall your worthiness appear! [*Inf.*, p. 13]
  [Nevertheless, so much of the holy kingdom] as I could treasure up in my mind [shall now be the matter of my song.] [*Par.*, p. 3]

Since the tercet from *Inf.* 2 is undoubtedly the basis for this passage from the Invocation, we can perhaps see here the way in which Chaucer molds his sources to fit his poetic intention. In the first place, Chaucer varies in having "thought" for *mente*, and "mette" (dream) for *vidi*. As well, in Dante's phrase ("Qui si parrà la tua nobilitate"), the reference is to the nobleness of his *mente*, not to its capabilities. This is borne out by the phrase just preceding this tercet: "la mente che non erra" ("memory which does not err"). Dante, unlike Chaucer, worries not about the powers of his memory but rather about the nobility, the stature, and the heights, that it can attain. His invocation, after all, is to the Muses and the *alto ingegno*. On the other hand, Chaucer, despite the commas that break up the text, is

---

[69] See Lowes 1927. For a critique of this method when applied to Chaucer and Dante, see Schless 1960:136–37, 1974:184–86, and chap. 3, below.

clearly asking his thought to show whether or not it has the ability or power ("vertu") to recount his dream correctly; that is (if I interpret this passage correctly), Thought has noted down all his dream and shut it up in the treasury or storehouse of his brain; now he wants to see whether Thought has the ability to recount that dream. Such an interpretation seems to be supported by the last line: now display your workings and your strength. If Chaucer was faced with the problem of translating *mente*, he thought of it not in terms of *memory* but rather in terms of the considerative power of the mind. Where Dante is asking for an even more heightened nobility, Chaucer seems to be asking for a display of simpler narrative powers. Chaucer, in other words, has not translated literally but, by a shift of emphasis, has brought Dante's tercet into line with his own poetic intention. This apparently minor change is really quite significant since it seems to indicate that Chaucer was making practical use of his source and not attempting to link it to the whole structure and ethos of the *Commedia*.

Considering the amount of interest that this passage has evoked, and considering that even so careful a critic as Burlin (1977:52) can remark that "the rendering of 'mente' by 'thought' may have been due to an imperfect grasp of Italian," it may not be entirely out of place to point to the nature of Dante's work. Dante's title for it was *La Commedia*; it was only later referred to as *Il Visione*, and still later as *La Divina Commedia*. These new titles detract from what I suggest is the essential boldness of the work from a theological point of view, for Dante did not claim that he saw Hell, Purgatory and Paradise in a dream; in a manner of speaking, he wrote the whole of the *Commedia* without evasion, that is to say, as a matter of direct and immediate experience – an awesome assumption of divine election. I would further suggest that, contrary to indicating "an imperfect grasp of Italian," Chaucer's change from *mente* to "thought" may well demonstrate his awareness that Dante's primary experience was to be dealt with by *mente* while his secondary experience of dream was more properly to be ordered by "thought."

Whether or not Chaucer was forced to take to *Par.* 1.11 (sixty-six cantos later) for the image of the mind as a treasury or storehouse is not quite so clear, though it is highly probable that he did so. In context, however, Dante's phrase is not outstanding, certainly not so outstanding as the phrase "ne la mia mente potei far tesoro" would be by itself, particularly in the light of Dante's previous discussion of the powers of the intellect and memory before so awesome a subject as *la gloria di colui che tutto move*. In all fairness one must not omit the possibility that this image can be thought of as a commonplace which both poets used, as is pointed out below.

In summation, then, although there may be some doubt of Chaucer's use of *Par.* 1, he most certainly had *Inf.* 2 in mind when he was composing these lines of the Invocation; however, the most important fact seems to me to be that this latter borrowing clearly shows that Chaucer was primarily making use of Dante's words and not attempting either to parody the *Commedia* or to make Dante's philosophic context his own. Sypherd (1907:78) has offered a possible composite source of two lines from Dante plus the lines that might have come from the *Teseida*.[70] He has noted also the following interesting parallel from Boccaccio's *Amorosa visione* (1944, text A, 2.1-12), which is given here more extensively:

---

[70] The error, common to the two works, concerning Helicon (*Teseida* 11.63.3-4; Boccaccio 1938), "sopra Parnaso, presso a l'Elicone fonte," was not, however, an unusual one. For the general confusion about the habitation and location of Apollo and the Muses, see below, entry under *Anel.* 15-19; see also Lowes 1917a:150-51; and Vincent of Beauvais 1473, vol. 1, bk. 2, chap. 72, fol. 42v.

"O high and gracious intelligence that moves the third heaven, O holy goddess, place your power in my breast; / *Not suffering, O Citherea, that the talent for this present work flee from me,* but rather grow more subtle and more in me. / *Let your excellence come into my mind,* so that my speaking of Orpheus recall the sound that brought him to regain his spouse. / *Inflame me so much more than I am,* that your ardor, which I wish wholly to enfold me, may make pleasing that of which I speak." [My translation][71]

Chaucer, like Boccaccio, is invoking the aid of Venus, and line 3 ("metti nel petto mio la tua potenzia") bears a striking resemblance to the close of the Invocation to book 3 ("Now entre in my brest anoon!"). Chaucer's use of the *Amorosa visione* has been generally denied,[72] and, on the whole, justifiably. It is probably best, therefore, to consider this parallel with Boccaccio as due rather to the common genre of the two passages. Invocations, broadly speaking, follow a pattern, and there are, consequently, certain stylized phrases that are almost inevitable.

Dilts: Compares *HF* 534–39 with *Par.* 1.74–75, 92–93; also Bennett (1968:56–57).

But never was ther dynt of thonder,	[Trasumanar significar *per verba*
Ne that thyng that men calle fouder,	non si poria; però l'essemplo basti
That smot somtyme a tour to powder,	a cui esperïenza grazia serba.
And in his swifte comynge brende,	S'i' era sol di me quel che creasti]
That so swithe gan descende	novellamente, amor che 'l ciel governi,
As this foul	tu 'l sai, che col tuo lume mi levasti.
	[e cominciò: "Tu stesso ti fai grosso
	col falso imaginar, sì che non vedi
	ciò che vedresti se l'avessi scosso.
	Tu non se' in terra, sì come tu credi;]
	ma folgore, fuggendo il proprio sito,
	non corse come tu ch'ad esso riedi."

[The passing beyond humanity may not be set forth in words: therefore let the example suffice any for whom grace reserves that experience.
   Whether I was but that part of me which Thou didst create last,] O Love that rulest the heavens, Thou knowest, who with Thy light didst lift me. [*Par.*, p. 7]

[and (she) began: "You make yourself dull with false imagining, so that you do not see what you would see had you cast it off. You are not on earth, as you believe;] but lightning, fleeing its proper site, never darted so fast as you are returning to yours." [*Par.*, p. 9]

There is, apparently, the similarity of the comparison of an action being as swift as lightning, but several other sources, much closer verbally, have been suggested.[73] Chau-

---

[71] The most important changes in text B's version of this passage are in line 2 ("che muovi il terzo cielo e ogni sua idea") and lines 8–9 ("tal che 'l mio dir d'Orfeo risembri il suone, / che placò il duca della morta gente"). The verses cited by Sypherd are in italics.

[72] Cummings 1916, chap. 2, denies all the suggestions of Koeppel (1891–92:227–67) and Child, though he does not cite these particular lines from *The House of Fame*.

[73] See discussions above under entry from Bethel for lines 496–508 and 529–48.

cer's Dreamer, well aware of having been "hente . . . in a swap," has nothing to do with the ecstatic love of God that elevates the soul of Dante, and, unless we are willing to follow the questionable interpretation that Chiarini (1902) has given, we should be extremely wary of casting aside our regard for the context of a work. The whole genre of love visions, as well as *visio* literature, was common knowledge of Chaucer's time, and it would be a mistake to force connections with the *Commedia* that could only show Chaucer's complete misunderstanding of the work. Even considered *in vacuo*, Dilts's parallels are radically different and in the light of other poems seem, for all practical purposes, not very strong.

Bethel: "586–604: Chaucer's doubts and the eagle's reassurance. The whole passage seems to have been suggested by Dante's musings and Virgil's remarks in *Inf.* II. Specific references follow—: 586–9; cf. *Inf.* II, 31f. [589: mention of Ganymede due to *Purg.* 9.23f.], 598, 601–4: cf. *Inf.* II, 49–51."

["O God!" thoughte I, "that madest
　　kynde,
Shal I noon other weyes dye?
Wher Joves wol me stellyfye,
Or what thing may this sygnifye?
I neyther am Ennok, ne Elye,
Ne Romulus, ne Ganymede,
That was ybore up, as men rede,
To hevene with daun Jupiter,
And mad the goddys botiller."
Loo, this was thoo my fantasye!
But he that bar me gan espye
That I so thoughte, and seyde this:
"Thow demest of thyself amys;
For Joves ys not theraboute—
I dar wel putte the out of doute—
To make of the as yet a sterre.
But er I bere the moche ferre,
I wol the telle what I am,
And whider thou shalt, and why I cam
To do thys, so that thou take
Good herte, and not for fere quake."

"Ma io, perché venirvi? o chi 'l concede?
　　Io non Enëa, io non Paulo sono;
　　me degno a ciò né io né altri 'l crede.
Per che, se del venire io m'abbandono,
　　temo che la venuta non sia folle.
　　Se' savio; intendi me' ch'i' non ragiono."
E qual è quei che disvuol ciò che volle
　　e per novi pensier cangia proposta,
　　sì che dal cominciar tutto si tolle,
tal mi fec' ïo 'n quella oscura costa,
　　perché, pensando, consumai la 'mpresa
　　che fu nel cominciar cotanto tosta.
"S'i' ho ben la parola tua intesa,"
　　rispuose del magnanimo quell' ombra,
　　"l'anima tua è da viltade offesa;
la qual molte fïate l'omo ingombra
　　sì che d'onrata impresa lo rivolve,
　　come falso veder bestia quand' ombra.
Da questa tema a ciò che tu ti solve,
　　dirotti perch' io venni e quel ch'io 'ntesi
　　nel primo punto che di te mi dolve . . . ."

[For the reference to *Purg.* 9.23–24, see entry
　　under *HF* 496–508.]

"But I, why do I come there? And who allows it? I am not Aeneas, I am not Paul; of this neither I nor others think me worthy. Wherefore, if I yield and come, I fear that the coming may be folly. You are wise; you understand better than I explain it." And like one who unwills what he has willed and with new thoughts changes his resolve, so that he quite gives up the thing he had begun, such did I become on that dark slope, for by thinking on it I rendered null the undertaking that had been so suddenly embarked upon.

　　"If I have well understood what you say," the shade of that magnanimous one replied, "your spirit is beset by cowardice, which oftentimes encumbers a man, turning him from honorable endeavor, as false seeing turns a beast that shies. To free you from this fear I will tell you why I came and what it was I heard when I first felt pity for you . . . ." [*Inf.*, pp. 15, 17]

Insofar as the reference to *Purg.* 9 is concerned, there is no verbal parallel save in the mention of the name of Ganymede, for which—if Chaucer needed a source—Ovid[74] would certainly prove closer with the phrase "Invitaque Jovi nectar Junone ministrat." Chaucer's reference to Ganymede as "botiller" parallels, with reasonable closeness, the *Ovide moralisé* 10.3362–67: "Now I will tell you of the youth who was made bottler of heaven, for whom Jupiter, to take and watch and seek him out, came from heaven to earth and took the shape of an eagle and flew and embraced the youth." It would hardly seem necessary, however, to have a source for such generally known information. Likewise, if one is thinking up a list of those who have previously been carried up into the heavens, Ganymede would certainly come to mind without the necessity of any one particular source. Both Sypherd and Robinson point to the differences between Chaucer and Dante, and Sypherd continues (p. 55): "Ovid also tells of the carrying off of Romulus (*Met.* xiv, 824). The story of Enoch is told in Gen. v. 24; of Elijah in 2 Kings ii, 11."[75] Both men also cite Holthausen, who points to passages in the *Ecloga theoduli* that mention Enoch, Helia (Elijah), and Ganymede together. Of course, as Robinson says (p. 782), "Enoch and Elijah were constantly associated,"[76] and one is tempted to think that the limited number of those who traveled by air, just like the limited number of those who had made the infernal journey, were constantly associated, if by nothing other than glosses. Certainly, in the present case, there is little in common—save for Ganymede—in those chosen from the list of eligible referents.

Bethel's suggestion of a contextual parallel must be treated with equal caution. To parallel "Chaucer's doubts and the eagle's reassurances" with the situation of Dante and Virgil is a highly questionable procedure. One need hardly mention the poetic convention of humility or the natural reaction that the reader might expect of a traveler in the face of an "other-world" journey. But Sypherd, however, as I have already mentioned, shows that "this element of fear in the presence of a guide or other allegorical visitant is very common" (p. 57), and he cites instances in Saint John (Rev. 1.17), the *Pélerinage de la vie humaine*, Cicero's *Somnium Scipionis*, Boethius's *De consolatione*, and Froissart's *Paradys d'amours*. Sypherd concludes with the following remark and accompanying note (p. 57, n.3):

[74] *Met.* 10.155–61. See above. A full commentary on *Jovis ales* (*Aen.* 1.394) with the various legends of Ganymede etc. is found in Servianus (1946:2.191–93). Bennett (1968:56–57) suggests a rather complex relationship to Dante.

[75] Ganymede is also mentioned, of course, in *Aen.* 1.28. For other heavenly flights and their tendency toward similarity, see also Sypherd, p. 103, n.1, where the *Apocalypsis Goliae episcopi* and Lucian's dialogue between Menippus and a friend are mentioned. In the latter, mention is made of Ganymede, who was "rapt up into heaven by an eagle to fill out wine to Jupiter," and of Daedalus. Menippus soars very high, becoming full of anguish. "Then he sees a great light below" and goes on to the court of Jupiter. The connections with Chaucer, as Sypherd points out, are unlikely or impossible, but the inevitable similarities should certainly give one pause before making hasty ascriptions.

[76] The examples of this association are innumerable. The two prophets were constantly pictured in the iconology of the age. Twining (1885:54), in explaining various symbols of Christ's life, states: "Besides this [aforementioned] means of illustrating the fact of the Ascension by a symbol, there were other *typical* illustrations of it in the scenes from the Old Testament, which were believed to bear a prophetic allusion to it. The two principal of these were the Translations of Enoch and Elijah." And again (p. 89): "Amongst the events of the Old Testament which were selected to typify the Resurrection of the Body, the Ascent of Elijah could not be omitted." In his *Liber gratiae* (printed in the *Opuscula*), Vincent of Beauvais explicates the life of Christ. Book 4, chap. 42, is given over to a discussion "on the excellence of His ascension in comparison to that of other holy persons." Enoch and Elijah are the two examples used, though, unlike Christ, they needed to be carried up to heaven. Enoch was a husband and a father, wherefor the fine distinction: "For indeed, Enoch was removed into heaven, who was begotten in coition and who begot in coition. Elias was caught up into heaven, who was begotten in coition but who did not beget in coition. But indeed the Lord was *assumed* into heaven—who neither begot nor was begotten in coition" (my translation; my emphasis). There is a further discussion in bk. 4, chap. 101.

It is the most natural thing for the hero to feel fear and for his guide to comfort him.... See instances in folk-tales collected by Mr. Garrett. Also Schofield, *The Pearl, Mod. Lang. Pub.* xix. p. 179, 1904. Also J. L. Lowes, *Two Versions of Prologue to Legend of G. W., Mod. Lang. Pub.* xix, pp. 653–4.

There would seem to be, then, no real basis for *verbal* ascription since the two examples which Dante gives are not mentioned by Chaucer, who, rather, starts off with the more common liaison of Enoch and Elijah and then adds Romulus and Ganymede. The closest verbal similarity is in the construction "I neyther am..., ne..., ne..." and Dante's "Io non..., io non...sono."[77] Yet, while taking into account Sypherd's impressive list of thematic parallels, we must not forget that there is reasonably certain evidence that Chaucer was thinking of this canto of the *Commedia* at other parts of *The House of Fame*. The passage in the *Commedia*, though not a verbal source or even the sole narrative source, would have fitted in with Chaucer's poetic intention and, as such, might very well have been in his mind at the time of composition. Certainly the section in Dante is analogous to "Chaucer's doubts and the eagle's reassurances," and the general tone of Chaucerian whimsicality would have fused this with the other sources, but it would be too rash to claim that Dante is the sole source for these nineteen lines in Chaucer.

Bethel: "729–36, 753–5; 826–37; 840–2: scientific discourse of the eagle; chief source Boethius, *Cons. Phil.*, III, pr. xi, but also verbal indebtedness to *Conv.* III, iii, 2–5."

"Geffrey, thou wost ryght wel this,
That every kyndely thyng that is
Hath a kyndely stede ther he
May best in hyt conserved be;
Unto which place every thyng,
Thorgh his kyndely enclynyng,
Moveth for to come to,
Whan that hyt is awey therfro

Thus every thing, by thys reson,
Hath his propre mansyon,
To which hit seketh to repaire,
[Ther-as hit shulde not apaire.]

This, mayst thou fele, wel I preve.
And that same place, ywys,
That every thyng enclyned to ys,
Hath his kyndelyche stede:
That sheweth hyt, withouten drede,
That kyndely the mansioun
Of every speche, of every soun,
Be hyt eyther foul or fair,
Hath hys kynde place in ayr.
And syn that every thyng that is
Out of hys kynde place, ywys,
Moveth thidder for to goo,
[Yif hyt aweye be therfroo,

[Non sanza cagione dico che questo amore ne la mente mia fa la sua operazione; ma ragionevolemente ciò si dice, a dare a intendere quale amore è questo, per lo loco nel quale adopera.] Onde è sapere che ciascuna cosa, come detto è di sopra, per la ragione di sopra mostrata ha 'l suo speziale amore. Come le corpora simplici hanno amore naturato in sè a lo luogo proprio, e però la terra sempre discende al centro; lo fuoco ha amore a la circumferenza di sopra lungo lo cielo de la luna, e però sempre sale a quello. Le corpora composte prima, sì come sono le minere, hanno amore a lo luogo dove la loro generazione è ordinata, e in quello crescono e acquistano vigore e potenza; onde vedemo la calamita sempre da la parte de la sua generazione recevere vertù. Le piante, che sono prima animate, hanno amore a certo luogo più manifestamente, secondo che la complessione richiede; e però vedemo certe piante lungo l'acque quasi cansarsi, e certe sopra li gioghi de le montagne, e certe ne le piagge e dappiè monti: le quali se si transmutano, o muoiono del tutto o vivono quasi triste, sì come cose disgiunte dal loro

---

[77] In this regard we should recall the "rhythmic echoes" that Everett refers to when discussing *PF* 127ff. in her fine essay (1965:143).

As I have before preved the,]
Hyt seweth, every soun, parde,
Moveth kyndely to pace
Al up into his kyndely place.

amico. [Li animali bruti hanno più manifesto amore non solamente a li luoghi, ma l'uno l'altro vedemo amare. Li uomini hanno loro proprio amore a le perfette e oneste cose. E però che l'uomo, avvegna che una sola sustanza sia tutta sua forma, per la sua nobilitade ha in sè natura di tutte queste cose, tutti questi amori puote avere a tutti li ha.]

[Not without good cause do I say that this love carries on his work 'in my mind'; but this is affirmed with reason in order that we may apprehend what is this love by means of the place in which it performs its task.] Wherefore we must know, as has been said above, for the reason there shown, that everything has its own special love; as, for instance, simple bodies have in themselves a love inspired by nature for their own proper place, and therefore earth always tends downwards to the centre: fire has a natural love for the circumference above, adjoining the heaven of the moon, and therefore always leaps up towards that.

The primary composite bodies, such as minerals, have a love for the place which is adapted for their generation, and grow in that and derive strength and potency from that. Hence we see that the loadstone always receives its virtue from the quarter where it was generated.

Plants, which are the primary objects endowed with soul, still more evidently have a love for a certain place in accordance with the requirements of their constitution; and therefore we see that certain plants almost always do well by the water, certain others on the ridges of the mountains, certain others on the shores or at the foot of the mountains, which if they are transplanted either die altogether or live as it were sadly, like things detached from the place they love.

[Dumb animals not only more plainly have a love for their place, but we see that they also have a love for one another.

Mankind have their own proper love for all perfect and noble things. And since man, although his whole form consists of one substance alone, has on account of nobility a portion of the nature of every one of these things in himself, he can feel all these loves and does feel them all.]

Chaucer is here writing in the full tradition of the medieval, semitheological approach to the physical sciences. For this reason the list of possible parallels is extraordinarily large, and, being of general knowledge, any ascription must show fairly definite verbal parallels. After all, that everything in the universe had its order and its natural place was the basis of the Christian philosophy.[78] Dante, in *Convivio* 3.3, attempts to show how Love works in the universe. He speaks of five kinds of Love: first, the love of the simple body to remain or to return to its natural location; second, the love of the mixed body for its place of generation; third, the love for certain foods and nutrition; fourth, sensual love; and fifth, the Rational or Angelic love of Truth and Virtue. It is in the discussion of the first of these — though it has nothing to do with Chaucer's topic — that Lowes (1915:28–29) found, of

---

[78] Cf. Aquinas, *Summa Theologica* 1.21.1: "This world is called one by the oneness of its order, since some things are set in order for others. But whatever things are from God, have order for each other, and for God Himself" (my translation).

course, an emphasis on place. Dante was not totally original here but seems to have been following mainly Saint Thomas's explanation of inclination, as given in the *Summa* 1.59.1, 2 (Aquinas 1947:1.294–95):

> Since all things flow from the Divine will, all things in their own way are inclined by appetite towards good, but in different ways. Some are inclined to good by their natural inclination, without knowledge, as plants and inanimate bodies. Such inclination towards good is called *a natural appetite*. Others, again, are inclined towards good, but with some knowledge; not that they know the aspect of goodness, but that they apprehend some particular good; as the sense, which knows the sweet, the white, and so on. The inclination which follows this apprehension is called *a sensitive appetite*. . . . But the inclination towards something extrinsic comes from something superadded to the essence; as tendency to a place comes from gravity or lightness.

As Robinson (p. 783) so aptly phrases it: "The doctrine. . . that every natural object has a natural place which it tries to reach, and in which it tries to remain, was the predecessor of the law of gravitation. . . . It is not easy to assign Chaucer's statement to a definite source."[79] Since one would naturally expect to meet in Boethius an idea as universally accepted as this, it is not surprising to find that Fansler (1914:216) considers that Boethius was probably the source for both Chaucer and Dante, and, in fact, *De cons.* 3, pr. 11, might certainly be used as a parallel idea that shows up also in *The Romaunt of the Rose*, lines 1693–99. One can see the idea again, as Sypherd has pointed out, in the last line of *De cons.* 3, m. 2, which in Chaucer's translation (and with the gloss) reads:

> Alle thynges seken ayen to hir propre cours, and alle thynges rejoysen hem of hir retornynge ayen to hir nature. Ne noon ordenaunce is bytaken to thynges, but that that hath joyned the endynge to the bygynnynge, and hath maked the cours of itself stable (*that it chaunge nat from his propre kynde*).

The "verbal indebtedness" to which Bethel refers revolves mainly around the phrase *loco proprio* or the word *loco* in Dante. Now none of the instances given by Dante is used by Chaucer's eagle in his long and comically pedantic discourse. The reference that both Lowes and Bethel point to is the constant appearance of the word "kindely" (natural) and the term "kyndely stede." So fundamental to the thinking of the Middle Ages is this view of an assigned place for everything in the universe that only the demonstration of some unique feature common to two writers can serve as internal evidence of the dependence of one on the other.[80] Not only is there a difference of context between the discussions of

---

[79] See also, among others, Delany 1972, esp. pp. 72–74, and Bennett, n.80 below.

[80] This concept of the physical workings of the universe is at the very core of official doctrine as expounded by Saint Thomas. See the citation from *Summa theologica* 1.69.1,2 in the text; also "For the appetite of a thing is moved and tends towards its connatural end naturally" (Aquinas 1.853). Dilts (pp. 27–28) feels that "Beatrice's explanation of Dante's cosmic flight. . . is in substance identical with the learned discourse of Chaucer's eagle upon the scientific reason for the ascent of sound to the House of Fame." She seems, however, to have lost sight of the medieval world picture when comparing *HF* 753–55 (cited in this entry) with *Par.* 1.103–11 (the context of which has been added in brackets): "[And she began,] 'All things have order among themselves, [and this is the form that makes the universe like God. Herein the high creatures behold the imprint of the Eternal Worth, which is the end wherefor the aforesaid ordinance is made]. In the order whereof I speak all natures are inclined by different lots, nearer and less near their principles; [wherefore they move to different ports over the great sea of being, each with an instinct given it to bear it on; this bears fire upward toward the moon; this is the motive force in mortal creatures; this binds together and unites the earth']" (*Par.* pp. 9, 11). See Bennett's discussion (1957, esp. pp. 71ff). While Bennett constantly invokes the name and work of Dante, the breadth of his sources for these ideas shows that they were, as he puts it, "commonplaces, to be sure" (p. 77 and n.1).

Dante and Chaucer, which has already been mentioned, but it must be recognized that "kyndely stede" does not seem to be a strict enough translation of *loco proprio* to warrant an ascription of these lines to Dante. The difference in the terms is seen, in part, in the gloss to the passage from Boethius given above, where Chaucer has "that it chaunge nat from his propre kynde." "Propre mansioun" (line 754) is perhaps a much closer interpretation, but the term *proprio* has specific relevance to Dante's argument, which is explaining universal order, while "kyndely" has specific relevance to Chaucer's discussions of natural science or philosophy and how it controls sound. Under the medieval philosophical system, both Dante's discussion of the order of the universe and Chaucer's discussion of the nature of sound would be based on the unified view of the macrocosm and God's pervading plan, but this relation to a Whole does not make the parts equivalent. In summation, then, there would appear to be differences both in context and in intent that are reasonably significant, and, as well, it would seem evident that *Convivio* 3.3.3–5 is in no way a necessary source for Chaucer, who would have been as familiar with the basic idea as we are, let us say, with the laws of Newtonian physics.[81]

Nor must we forget that the whole idea for a House of Fame is based primarily on Ovid's description in *Met.* 12.39–63, which begins: "There is a place in the middle of the world, 'twixt land and sea and sky, the meeting-point of the threefold universe. From this place, whatever is, however far away, is seen, and every word penetrates to these hollow ears" (Ovid 1916:4.183). The *Ovide moralisé* emphasizes that this is the "mancions" of all human sound: "There was a spot set equally between heaven and earth and sea, equidistant from the world. From there one sees around whatever is done all over the world; there one knows all the news, all the speakings, all the tales that are said in every region. It is the spot, it is the mansion where Fame is dwelling" (12.1588–97). Obviously, neither the Ovid nor the *Ovide moralisé* is being suggested as a source for the eagle's view of the nature of sound, but these should be given to counterbalance any idea that one of the many medieval scientific treatises may have evoked the concept of the House of Fame. Chaucer, in typically medieval manner, is revaluating a classical source in the light of the then current *Weltanschauung*.

Bethel: "887–918: the eagle's command to Chaucer to look down at the earth has been compared to a similar command of Beatrice's to Dante, *Par.* XXII, 124–53; but any indebtedness here seems doubtful."

As Sypherd (p. 58) says, "There is not the slightest reason for presenting this likeness as evidence of influence of the earlier on the later work." That one is away from and above the earth should not make unusual the correlative that one must look down to see it. Robinson, after noting the suggestion of *Par.* 22.128,[82] adds that "the similarities of language may be due only to the similarity of situation" (p. 783). Sypherd negates any

---

[81] Robinson, p. 783, mentions other possible sources, such as Alanus de Insulis's *De planctu naturae* and Saint Augustine's *Confessions* 13.9. For the discussion of sound, see Sypherd (pp 96–100), who parallels *HF* 765–81 with Vincent of Beauvais's *Speculum naturale* 5, chap. 14 (given by Skeat and Robinson as 4.14) and Macrobius's *Commentarius ex Cicerone in somnium Scipionis* 2, chap. 4; and *HF* 781ff. with Boethius's *De musica* and the *Speculum naturale* 5.18 (Skeat and Robinson give 4.18). As well, Sypherd mentions Skeat's references to *De musica* 1.3 and *Speculum naturale* 25.58, adding *Speculum naturale* 5.12 and the comment that "the entire treatment of voice and sound in the *Speculum naturale* has so many points of contact with Chaucer's descriptions that I am inclined to doubt the wisdom of ascribing much influence to Boethius" (p. 97).

[82] Beatrice's words are: "...look back downward and behold how great a world I have already set beneath your feet" (*Par.* p. 253).

connection between Dante's *aiuola* (line 151) and Chaucer's "no more semed than a prikke" (line 907), by citing, among several other possibilities, *De cons.* 2, pr. 7, and *Somnium Scipionis* 6.16, both of which use the closer term *punctum*. Actually, no sources whatever are needed, and certainly the passage in Chaucer is distant enough from that of Dante to make even a parallelism questionable. I agree completely with Bethel's opinion.

Bethel: "919–24: reference to Daedalus and Icarus possibly suggested by *Inf.* XVII, 109f."

Ne eke the wrechche Dedalus,
Ne his child, nyce Ykarus,
That fleigh so highe that the hete
Hys wynges malt, and he fel wete
In myd the see, and ther he dreynte,
For whom was maked moch
    compleynte.

nè quando Icaro misero le reni
    sentì spennar per la scaldata cera,
    gridando il padre a lui "Mala via tieni!"

nor when the wretched Icarus felt his loins unfeathered by the melting wax, and his father cried to him, "You go an ill way!"
[*Inf.*, p. 181]

Once again, it is very doubtful that a source was necessary for so familiar a story. Nonetheless, both Robinson and Sypherd note parallels. Robinson summarizes briefly (p. 783):

> Daedalus and Icarus are likewise mentioned in RR, 5226–27. But Chaucer certainly knew Ovid's version of the familiar story (Met., viii, 183ff.) and the brief reference here points to no special source. Comparisons have been made with Inf., xvii, 109–14, the Ecloga Theoduli, ii. 101–03, and Boccaccio's Amoroso Visione, xxxv.

The one piece of positive information that we can get is that the passage in the *Commedia* could not have been the source for Chaucer, since he has details very few of which appear in Dante and all of which are in Ovid.

Bethel: "926–31: reference to Plato's doctrine that souls proceed from stars and return to them may have been suggested by *Conv.* II, iv, 5."

["Now turn upward," quod he, "thy
    face,]
And behold this large space,
This eyr; but loke thou ne be
Adrad of hem that thou shalt se;
For in this region, certeyn,
Duelleth many a citezeyn,
Of which that speketh Daun Plato.
[These ben the eyryssh bestes, lo!"]

[Altri furono, sì come Plato, uomo eccellentissimo, che puosero non solamente tante Intelligenze quanti sono li movimento del cielo, ma eziandio quante sono le spezie de le cose (cioè le maniere de le cose): sì come è una spezie tutti li uomini, e un' altra tutto l'oro, e un' altra tutte le larghezze, e così di tutte.] E volsero che sì come le Intelligenze de li cieli sono generatrici di quelli, ciascuna del suo, così queste fossero generatrici de l'altre cose ed essempli, ciascuna de la sua spezie; e chiamale Plato "idee," che tanto è a dire quanto forme e nature universali.

[There were others, like Plato, a most eminent man, who assumed not only that there are as many Intelligences as there are movements of the heaven, but also as many as there are species of things, just as there is one species for all men, and another for all gold, and another for all riches, and so on:] and they would have it that as the Intelligences of the heavens are producers of these movements, each one of its own, so these other Intelligences are producers of everything else, and exemplars each one of its own species; and Plato called them "ideas" which is equivalent to calling them universal forms and natures. [P. 82]

As can be seen by setting these two passages in context, Chaucer and Dante are speaking of entirely different aspects of Plato. Dante is discussing the Platonic (or perhaps Neo-platonic) concept of ideas and essences; Chaucer, as all the commentators have pointed out, is speaking of "many a citezeyn" in apposition with "eyryssh bestes" (a line which Bethel omits), without any reference to the philosophical problems involved in Dante's argument. Robinson's summary notes (p. 783):

> Skeat took the "beasts" to be the signs of the zodiac. But with the term of "citizen" he compared several passages in the Anticlaudianus of Alanus de Insulis, where the reference is to the aerial powers. See iv, 5 (Migne, Pat. Lat., CCX, 525), "aerios cives"; v, 7 (Migne, 537), "cives superi"; v, 9 (Migne, 538), "superos cives."[83]

Chaucer's reference to Plato seems, indeed, so superficial that it might be suspected to come rather from some brief glossarial or textual appeal for authority than from a detailed discussion of the philosophy itself. This suspicion gains support from the remarks of Ker, who cites (again using Robinson's summary [p. 783]) "the term 'animalia...corpore aeria' in St. Augustine's De Civ. Dei, viii, 16; in viii, 15, Plato is acknowledged as an authority on the powers in question."[84] The only point, then, that these passages from Chaucer and Dante have in common is the word Plato, but his name was so widely used in medieval writing that it is almost impossible to ascribe any single source without having very close verbal similarity as supporting proof for the ascription. Chaucer's appeals to "auctoritee" must always be handled with the utmost caution.

Bethel: "936–59: the discussion of the Galaxy and its origins depends partly on *Conv.* II, xiv, 1ff."

"...Se yonder, loo, the Galaxie,
Which men clepeth the Milky Wey,
For hit ys whit (and somme, parfey,
Kallen hyt Watlynge Strete)
That ones was ybrent with hete,
Whan the sonnes sone, the rede,
That highte Pheton, wolde lede
Algate hys fader carte, and gye.
The carte-hors gonne wel espye

...e sì come la Galassia, cioè quello bianco cerchio che lo vulgo chiama la Via di Sa'Iacopo.... [2.14.1]

[E per la Galassia ha questo cielo similitudine grande con la Metafisica. Per che è da sapere che di quella Galassia li filosofi hanno avute diverse oppinioni. Chè li Pittagorici dissero che 'l Sole alcuna fiata

---

[83] Francis (1949:339–41) supports Skeat's view of the "beasts" as referring to the zodiacal signs, as opposed to Ker's view (1899:38–39), which took them to be demons of the air, on the basis of the *Anticlaudianus*. Francis points to the Phaëthon story (*HF* 940-56) from Ovid's *Metamorphoses*, where, he notes, there is not only Phoebus's warning to beware the various zodiacal signs (*Met.* 2.78-83) but also a reference to *vastorum simulacra ferorum* (*Met.* 2.193-94). He concludes that there is probably a combination of Ovid's "beasts" and Alanus's "citizens."

[84] Robinson's reference here reads: "(See Migne, Pat. Lat., XLI, 240f. The reference to Plato in Dante's *Par.*, iv, 22-24, seems to be irrelevant here)."

That he koude no governaunce,
And gonne for to lepe and launce,
And beren hym now up, now doun,
Til that he sey the Scorpioun,
Which that in heven a sygne is yit.
And he, for ferde, loste hys wyt
Of that, and let the reynes gon
Of his hors; and they anoon
Gonne up to mounte and doun
    descende,
Til bothe the eyr and erthe brende;
Til Jupiter, loo, atte laste,
Hym slow, and fro the carte caste.
Loo, ys it not a gret myschaunce
To lete a fool han governaunce
Of thing that he can not demeyne?"

errò ne la sua via e, passando per altre parti
non convenienti al suo fervore, arse lo luogo
per lo quale passò, e rimasevi quella
apparenza de l'arsura: e credo che si
mossero da la favola di Fetonte, la quale
narra Ovidio nel principio del secondo di
Metamorfoseos. [2.14.5][85]

[Altri dissero, sì come fu Anassagora e
Democrito, che ciò era lume di sole
ripercusso in quella parte, e queste
oppinioni con ragioni dimostrative
riprovaro. Quello che Aristotile si dicesse
non si può bene sapere di ciò, però che la
sua sentenza non si truova cotale ne l'una
translazione come ne l'altra. E credo che
fosse lo errore de li translatori; chè ne la
Nuova pare dicere che ciò sia uno
ragunamento di vapori sotto le stelle di
quella parte, che sempre traggono quelli: e
questo non pare avere ragione vera. Ne la
Vecchia dice che la Galassia non è altro che
moltitudine di stelle fisse in quella parte,
tanto picciole che distinguere di qua giù non
le potemo, ma di loro apparisce quello
albore, lo quale noi chiamiamo Galassia; e
puote essere, chè lo cielo in quella parte è
più spesso, e però ritiene e ripresenta quello
lume. E questa oppinione pare avere, con
Aristotile, Avicenna e Tolomeo. Onde, con
ciò sia cosa che la Galassia sia uno effetto di
quelle stelle le quali non potemo vedere, se
non per lo effetto loro intendiamo quelle
cose, e la Metafisica tratti de le prime
sustanzie, le quali noi non potemo
simigliantemente intendere se non per li loro
effetti, manifesto è che 'l Cielo stellato ha
grande similitudine con la Metafisica.]
[2.14.6–8]

...and the Galaxy, that is, the white circle, which is commonly called St.
James's Way.... [2.14.1]

[And in the Galaxy this heaven has a close resemblance to Metaphysics.]
Wherefore it must be known that the Philosophers have had different opinions
about this Galaxy. For the Pythagoreans affirmed that the sun at one time
wandered in his course, and in passing through other regions not suited to
sustain its heat set on fire the place through which it passed, and so these traces
of the conflagration remain there. And I believe that they were influenced by
the fable of Phaeton, which Ovid tells at the beginning of the second book of

---

[85] These are the passages cited by Lowes (1915:29–30).

the *Metamorphoses*. [2.14.5] [Others, as, for instance, Anaxagoras and Democritus, said that the Galaxy was the light of the sun reflected in that region. And these opinions they confirmed by demonstrative reasons. What Aristotle may have said about it cannot be accurately known, because the two translations give different accounts of his opinion. And I think that any mistake may have been due to the translators, for in the New Translation he is made to say that the Galaxy is a congregation, under the stars of this part of the heaven, of the vapours which are always being attracted by them, and this opinion does not appear to be right. In the Old Translation he says that the Galaxy is nothing but a multitude of fixed stars in that region, stars so small that they are not separately visible from our earth, but the appearance of whiteness which we call the Galaxy is due to them. And it may be that the heaven in that part is more dense, and therefore retains and reproduces that light; and this opinion Avicenna and Ptolemy appear to share with Aristotle. Therefore, since the Galaxy is an effect of those stars which cannot be perceived except so far as we apprehend these things by their effect, and since Metaphysics treat of primal substances which in the same way we cannot apprehend except by their effects, it is plain that there is a close resemblance between the starry heaven and Metaphysics.] [2.14.6–8]

Chaucer's source here in all probability is not the *Convivio* but rather a combination of common knowledge, folk etymology, and (at least in the case of the *Metamorphoses*) the same source that Dante had used. In the comparison of *HF* 936–39 and *Convivio* 2.14.1 it is at once evident that Chaucer has the additional information that the "Galaxie" is also called the "Milky Wey," and he then gives the reason: "For hit ys whit." When the origin of a word was given (very frequently the first step in any medieval discussion), details such as these were commonly included. Thus Vincent of Beauvais, speaking of the zodiacal signs, writes in the *Speculum naturale* (bk. 4, chap. 16): "Another of the visible phenomena was called *galaxias* by the Greeks, that is, 'milky circle.' For 'milk' is called *galac* in Greek, and 'circle' *xios*"; or "The track which appears on the sphere is the 'milky circle,' called 'milky' from its purity, because it is white. Some have said this is a track or way because the sun went around and in transit, from its own splendor [caused the Milky Way] thus to shine."

Slightly more complex is the question of the Galaxy and its origin, but this too is based on common sources and knowledge, mainly on that evolving from the commentaries on Aristotle's *De meteoris*. Basically two traditional views were held on the beginning of the Galaxy, and each can be subdivided: (1) the "classical," composed of (a) the mythological tale of Phaëthon which can be found in Ovid's *Metamorphoses* and (b) the Pythagorean view that the sun wandered from its course,[86] and (2) the physical explanation of Anaxagoras and Democritus[87] divided into (a) the concept that the galaxy is composed of

[86] This is essentially the Phaëthon story with the sun in place of "the sonnes sone." Cf. the *Philosophumena* of Aetius, 2.17 (Aetius 1879:346).

[87] Cf. Dreyer (1953:29): "Demokritus appears to have had a remarkably correct conception of one celestial phenomenon, the Milky Way, the light of which is said to have explained as caused by a multitude of faint stars." Dreyer cites other philosophers (Aetius, Macrobius, Manilius, etc.) who "quote the opinion but do not mention Demokritus. On the other hand Aristotle, *Meteor.* I. 8, p. 345a, says that Demokritus shared the peculiar opinion of Anaxagoras, so perhaps Demokritus did not think that there are more stars crowded together in the Milky Way, but only that we see them better there."

innumerable stars, too small to be distinguished, and (b) the concept that the Galaxy is white and shining through a reflection of the sun's rays. Aristotle's *De meteoris* was, of course, the basis of all later speculation, and those whose primary intent was to give commentary on the text—for example, Saint Thomas or Averroës—recorded the mythological argument with the others. Among the patristic writers on natural philosophy more "modern" views were advanced, but these men were inclined to make their *impugnationes* only against the last three arguments, evidently ignoring the first because it was pagan, mythological, and unscientific.[88] Dante's position is unique in that he tries to achieve a resolution by finding the common ground of all the major hypotheses.[89]

An approach such as Dante's was entirely different from that of Chaucer, who, as can be seen, was following the oldest and most literary of the arguments. The connection between the Galaxy's formation and the Phaëthon story can be considered, for all practical purposes, common knowledge. Saint Thomas had explicated Aristotle (*Meteor.* 1.8.12) as follows: "Certain people have said that this was the track of some star, which traversed this part of the heavens after it had lost its proper course at the time of the wreck of heaven, which is said in fable to have been caused by Phaethon" (my translation).[90] Averroës's famous commentary on Aristotle gives the following on the "Opinio pythagoricorum" (1530, chap. 9 ["De lactea"], fol. x, sign. BB2r):

> Moreover, as touching both what the cause may be and what the milky color is, let us say now (having also, moreover, learned about this before) what others have earlier said, others indeed of those called Pythagoreans. Some say that this is a track, these indeed say, of the fallings of certain stars, after the disturbance said to have happened under Phaëthon. On the other hand, others say that the sun at some time wandered into this zone, as if the place were scorched, or had suffered some other such torment, by exhalation of the heavenly bodies themselves.

Chaucer, then, does not mention any of the other opinions on the origin of the Galaxy, let alone the review and resolution which Dante attempted. Instead, Chaucer uses only

---

[88] Albertus Magnus, in *Meteor.* 1.2.2: "Therefore we now begin to take into consideration the *galaxy*, which is the same as the Milky or White Way, or in Arabic *majaraterii*, which translates '*alcha* that is moved.' This should be said first of the galaxy, indeed: because it is itself practically and materially not among the parts of the celestial orb, as will be shown below. Indeed, we shall after this take under consideration other celestial phenomena, and we shall speak of these things by means of an elegant argument, as is our custom, and that of every philosopher great in philosophy. Indeed there were some who [*Marginal notation*: early opinions] have said, that at some time the sun was moved into that place (where the galaxy now is), and by its light and heat scorched the celestial orb in that place: chiefly, indeed, having been burnt—if it be earthly—it was made white, just as appears in chalk: and therefore the sun by its combustion impressed on the orb this track which is called the galaxy." Albertus goes on to refute this and the arguments of Democritus and Anaxagoras, but it will be noted that his basic assumptions eliminate the mythological concept from the very start.

[89] For further discussion of the symbolic implications of Dante's view, see Gilson, pp. 105–106. To attempt a resolution of the conflicting views was no mean feat. The Pythagoreans were basically a mystical cult whose fundamental belief was that the universe is based on, or rather, could be resolved to, real numbers, that the concept of real number was the only valid measure. That this view opposes itself to supernatural schema need hardly be stressed. On the other hand, inherent in the Christian belief of a universe of crystalline spheres with their mechanically attached stars and their motion coming from intelligences of varying order, there is a rigidity that forbids any variation from the formalized view. On this basis astronomical aberrations (such as comets and meteors) must have divine purpose, since they are able to traverse the solid crystalline spheres; likewise, those who have their visions of God do so only by way of the spirit, which, by divine permission, is capable of passing through the material boundaries of the universe.

[90] Cited in *Il Convivio* (1934:217, note to line 3). Saint Thomas continues: "But others say that through that zone the sun ever passes; and thus, through the motion of the sun or of a star, this part of heaven is as if burned, or has suffered some such torment, so that a certain whiteness appears there."

the well-known fable of Phaëthon, which he probably found in Ovid or a medieval version thereof. That Chaucer was using the *Metamorphoses* seems clear enough; thus (*Met.* 2.198–200): "When the boy sees this creature reeking with black poisonous sweat, and threatening to sting him with his curving tail, bereft of wits from chilling fear, down he dropped the reins" (Ovid 1916:3.75)[91] can be compared with *HF* 948–52, it being remembered that "there is one place where the Scorpion bends out his arms into two bows" (Ovid 1916:3.73–75). The pedantic eagle, with his usual loquaciousness and industry, gives a rapid history and survey of the heavens. Coming first to the zodiac, he warns Chaucer not to be "adrad of. . .eyrish bestes," and it is possible that this, plus their arrival at the galaxy, is what reminds him of the Phaëthon story.

This reasonably close investigation of the suggested Dantean source for *HF* 936–59 has, it is hoped, illustrated once more the importance of an acquaintance with the common knowledge of the period. Robinson's early remarks on the inclusiveness of Dante's writings and the danger of comparison *in vacuo* cannot be recalled too often.

Bethel: "981f.: the Biblical quotation was probably suggested by *Par.* I, 73–75."

"...But wher in body or in gost I not, ywys; but God, thou wost!"	Si' i' era sol di me quel che creasti novellamente, amor che 'l ciel governi, tu 'l sai, che col tuo lume mi levasti.

Whether I was but that part of me which Thou didst create last, O Love that rulest the heavens, Thou knowest, who with Thy light didst lift me. [*Par.*, p. 7]

Bethel's evaluation here seems valid. Since Chaucer can be shown to have used *Par.* 1 at other points in the poem, the lines cited here might well have reminded him of one of the most famous heavenly flights, that of Saint Paul. On the basis of the indirect allusion in the *Commedia*, Chaucer's recognition of Dante's source shows, not surprisingly, a very close knowledge of the Bible, for the lines in *The House of Fame* are undoubtedly from 2 Cor. 12.1–4 (Douay-Rheims):

If I must glory (it is not expedient indeed): But I will come to visions and revelations of the Lord.

I know a man in Christ above fourteen years ago (whether in the body, I know not, or out the body, I know not; God knoweth), such a one caught up to the third heaven.

And I know such a man (whether in the body, or out of the body, I know not: God knoweth):

That he was caught up to paradise, and heard secret words, which it is not granted to man to utter..

Saint Paul's doubts about whether or not he took his body with him or left it behind on his journey or vision of Heaven are not, of course, settled by the biblical text, and they

---

[91] Francis (1949) has noted the following parallels: *HF* 941–42 and *Met.* 1.751; *HF* 950ff. and *Met.* 2.200 (similar to that given in the text here); *HF* 955–56 and *Met.* 2.312–13. Nor should one forget the more general (2.201–207): "When the horses feel these [reins] lying on their backs, they break loose from their course, and, with none to check them, they roam through unknown regions of the air. Wherever their impulse leads them, there they rush aimlessly, knocking against the stars set deep in the sky and snatching the chariot along through uncharted ways. Now they climb up to the top of heaven, and now, plunging headlong down, they course along nearer the earth" (Ovid 1916:3.75).

soon become a point of theological discussion, which Grandgent summarizes as follows (Dante 1933, note to *Par.* 1.74):

> St. Augustine (in De Genesi ad Litteram, XII, iii–iv) and St. Thomas discuss the question, but leave it undecided. . . . Whether St. Paul actually beheld God or not is a matter on which theologians have disagreed, St. Augustine and St. Thomas holding the affirmative opinion. Cf. Exod. xxxiii, 20; "Thou canst not see my face: for no man shall see me, and live."

Dante, continues Grandgent, "considers his rapture as similar in kind to St. Paul's"[92] and therefore paraphrases the apostle's words in such a way as to continue the progressive elevation of his vision and his theme. Chaucer, however, cites almost directly from 2 Corinthians, converting Saint Paul's words to his narrative purpose. The dreamer is suddenly and not unnaturally frightened at his peculiar situation, first remarking (lines 979–80):

> Thoo gan y wexen in a were,
> And seyde, "Y wot wel y am here; . . ."

After the biblical quotation he explains the reason for his sudden concern (lines 983–84):

> For more clere entendement
> Nas me never yit ysent.

The problem is not a major issue in the mind of the Dreamer, for immediately thereafter he is busy checking what he is actually observing against the accounts that he had read in Martianus Capella and Alanus de Insulis—and the primary and secondary material happily agree.[93] The mind-reading eagle suddenly breaks into his train of thought with comic insistence (lines 991–93):

> With that this egle gan to crye,
> "Lat be," quod he, "thy fantasye!
> Wilt thou lere of sterres aught?"

In his use of 2 Corinthians, Chaucer has brought in a reference to yet another famous flight, but he has very neatly avoided any theological argument by maintaining a light, almost whimsical touch. Dante's reference to Saint Paul's words would have shown Chaucer (if he had not known otherwise) that there were elements of doctrinal dispute here; but where Dante's paraphrase points up the theological implications, Chaucer's more direct quotation is used primarily to advance narrative intention. Recognition of Chaucer's source would have given an added fillip to his audience, but while Chaucer's poem does not suffer in the least if one does not know the source, Dante's lines depend not only on a recognition of the source but on an awareness of its theological implications as well. Chaucer, it would seem, recognized the reference in Dante but intentionally avoided the emphasis that Dante had given. This, indeed, may be one of the places where Delany's view (p. 118) particularly pertains: "Chaucer is no ideological poet like Jean de Meun or Dante. Religion is not his first idea but his last, so that it enters the structure of his work, not as a credible solution to dialectic, but in fact as another term in dialectic."

---

[92] Grandgent continues further: "In the following narrative Dante seems to think of himself as still in the flesh, although he ultimately sees God."

[93] On the comic and ironic uses that Chaucer made of "the mediaeval device of reference to authorities," see Levy (1942:25–39). On *The House of Fame* see pp. 30–35, and on this passage, pp. 34–35.

Ruggiers (1954:34–36): A comparison of *HF* 1068–82 with *Par.* 4.37–48:

But o thing y will warne the	Qui si mostraro, non perché sortita
Of the whiche thou wolt have wonder.	sia questa spera lor, ma per far segno
Loo, to the Hous of Fame yonder,	de la celestïal c'ha men salita.
Thou wost now how, cometh every	Così parlar conviensi al vostro ingegno,
speche;	però che solo da sensato apprende
Hyt nedeth noght eft the to teche.	ciò che fa poscia d'intelletto degno.
But understond now ryght wel this,	Per questo la Scrittura condescende
Whan any speche ycomen ys	a vostra facultate, e piedi e mano
Up to the paleys, anon-ryght	attribuisce a Dio e altro intende;
Hyt wexeth lyk the same wight	e Santa Chiesa con aspetto umano
Which that the word in erthe spak,	Gabrïel e Michel vi rappresenta,
Be hyt clothed red or blak;	e l'altro che Tobia rifece sano.
And hath so verray hys lyknesse	
That spak the word, that thou wilt	
gesse	
That it the same body be,	
Man or woman, he or she.	

These showed themselves here, not because this sphere is allotted to them, but to afford sign of the celestial grade that is least exalted. It is needful to speak thus to your faculty, since only through sense perception does it apprehend that which it afterwards makes fit for the intellect. For this reason Scripture condescends to your capacity, and attributes hands and feet to God, having other meaning; and Holy Church represents to you with human aspect Gabriel and Michael and the other who made Tobit whole again. [*Par.*, p. 39]

Ruggiers, after citing two previously suggested sources in the thirteenth-century Hebrew *Zohar*[94] and in Boethius,[95] proposes that there is a "more probable source for the accommodation of words into images in the *Divina Commedia*" (p. 35). He continues (p. 36):

In canto iii of *Paradiso*, Dante mistakes the faint outlines of the blessed spirits for reflections. He is assured by Beatrice that they are *vere sustanze*, real beings,[96] and he then proceeds to speak with the spirit of Piccarda. There is, however, a question remaining in his mind about the appearance of spirits on the various planets, a question which is answered by Beatrice to the effect that the blessed actually have their permanent dwelling in the Empyrean, and that their appearing to him on the various planets constitutes both an accommodation to his sight and a vehicle for their words.[97]

Justifiably, Ruggiers does not press verbal parallels but rather bases his case on the fact that in Dante the spirits are made visible and that in Chaucer the rumors are visualized. Ruggiers, with fine insight, concedes (pp. 36–37):

No other poem illustrates so much as this one the difference between the two poets: Dante determined to explain away a poisonous heresy, the enslavement

---

[94] Cf. J. T. Williams 1947:488–90.
[95] Ziegler 1949:73–76. The suggestion is *De cons.* 4, pr. 1, m. 1.
[96] Ruggiers's note here cites *Par.* 3.29 in the Grandgent edition.
[97] Following this citation Ruggiers quotes the lines from *Par.* 4 given at the beginning of this entry.

of souls to a material universe; and Chaucer stripping the philosophy away from the bare bones of a device, the accommodation of words into images, and writing with the unadorned directness of his genius.

There is undoubtedly some analogy here, but the question seems to be whether or not Chaucer had need of the concept as presented in the *Commedia*. The device of giving human form to words is not, one feels, that unusual. We should not forget, first of all, that the foundation of the Christian faith is based on this very image, namely, the Word made flesh. Second, to controvert the heresy inherent in the Platonic doctrine which Dante is considering in this canto, Saint Thomas (and many other patristic writers) dealt with this very subject:

> It is befitting Holy Writ to put forward divine and spiritual truths by means of comparisons with material things. For God provides for everything according to the capacity of its nature. Now it is natural to man to attain to intellectual truths through sensible objects, because all our knowledge originates from sense. Hence in Holy Writ spiritual things are fittingly taught under the likeness of material things.[98]

In poetry the same device is used in Boccaccio's *Teseida* 7.50–69, a passage which Chaucer later used as the basis for *The Parliament of Fowls* (lines 183–294). Here, while Palamone remains below, his prayer assumes human shape, goes up to the temple of Venus, observes the outer Garden of Love, enters the temple, notes the painted stories and the statues therein, is spoken to and led into the goddess's chamber, sees Venus, and makes its request successfully.

Yet with all these parallels of the visualizing of words, one tends to neglect the most obvious source, Ovid's description of the abode of Fama (Rumor) in *Met.* 12.39–63.[99] Since the *Metamorphoses* (or a medieval version thereof)[100] had given Chaucer the basic framework for the setting of his last two books, one should regard Ovid's lines with particular care. It would certainly appear, especially on the basis of lines 53–58, that Ovid has pictured his rumors as essentially human beings and has done so with skill and intention. The whole passage, moreover, shows Ovid's careful development of the image, first as noises, then as persons, and finally as personifications. The device is, therefore, in Chaucer's primary source, and, until a more exact parallel is found, there seems no reason to reject the Ovidian original.

---

[98] Aquinas, *Summa Theologia* 1.1.9, cited in Dante 1921:678–79.

[99] The passage is given here for the convenience of immediate comparison (it will be referred to again at *HF* 2060): "There is a place in the middle of the world, 'twixt land and sea and sky, the meeting-point of the threefold universe. From this place, whatever is, however far away, is seen, and every word penetrates to these hollow ears. Rumour dwells here, having chosen her house upon a high mountain-top; and she gave the house countless entrances, a thousand apertures, but with no doors to close them. Night and day the house stands open. It is built all of echoing brass. The whole place resounds with confused noises, repeats all words and doubles what it hears. There is no quiet, no silence anywhere within. And yet there is no loud clamour, but only the subdued murmur of voices, like the murmur of the waves of the sea if you listen afar off, or like the last rumblings of thunder when Jove has made the dark clouds crash together. Crowds fill the hall, shifting throngs come and go, and everywhere wander thousands of rumours, falsehoods mingled with the truth, and confused reports flit about. Some of these fill their idle ears with talk, and others go and tell elsewhere what they have heard; while the story grows in size, and each new teller makes contribution to what he has heard. Here is Credulity, here is heedless Error, unfounded Joy and panic Fear; here sudden Sedition and unauthentic Whisperings. Rumour herself beholds all that is done in heaven, on sea and land, and searches throughout the world for news" (Ovid 1916:3.18–85).

[100] See below, entry under *HF* 2060–75.

Chaucer's contribution seems to lie chiefly in having the rumors take on the configuration of their individual speakers. This is unlike Dante's far more orthodox approach where a spirit becomes visible in order that it can be seen or heard by the cruder senses of human beings. It would seem that we must credit this invention to what Ruggiers refers to as "the unadorned directness of Chaucer's genius," though the device as a whole seems most plausibly to come from Ovid.

Book 3

Bethel: "1091–3; 1101–9: Invocation; some of the material is borrowed from *Par.* I, 13–15, 22–27, 19."

O God of science and of lyght,
Appollo, thurgh thy grete myght,
This lytel laste bok thou gye!
[Nat that I wilne, for maistrye,
Here art poetical be shewed;
But for the rym ys lyght and lewed,
Yit make hyt sumwhat agreable,
Though som vers fayle in a sillable;
And that I do no diligence
To shew craft, but o sentence.]
And yif, devyne vertu, thow
Wilt helpe me to shewe now
That in myn hed ymarked ys—
Loo, that is for to menen this,
The Hous of Fame for to descryve—
Thou shalt se me go as blyve
Unto the nexte laure y see,
And kysse yt, for hyt is thy tree.
Now entre in my brest anoon!

O buono Appollo, a l'ultimo lavoro
   fammi del tuo valor sì fatto vaso,
   come dimandi a dar l'amato alloro.

O divina virtù, se mi ti presti
   tanto che l'ombra del beato regno
   segnata nel mio capo io manifesti,
vedra'mi al piè del tuo diletto legno
   venire, e coronarmi de le foglie
   che la materia e tu mi farai degno.

Entra nel petto mio, e spira tue....[101]

O good Apollo, for this last labor make me such a vessel of your worth as you require for granting your beloved laurel.

O divine Power, if you do so lend yourself to me that I may show forth the image of the blessed realm which is imprinted in my mind, you shall see me

---

[101] Bethel's italics and line arrangement are given here. In context and in order the lines read (*Par.*, pp. 3, 5): "The glory of the All-Mover penetrates through the universe and reglows in one part more, and in another less. I have been in the heaven that most receives of His light, and have seen things which whoso descends from up there has neither the knowledge nor the power to relate, because, as it draws near to its desire, our intellect enters so deep that memory cannot go back upon the track. Nevertheless, so much of the holy kingdom as I could treasure up in my mind shall now be the matter of my song.
"O good Apollo, for this last labor make me such a vessel of your worth as you require for granting your beloved laurel. Thus far the one peak of Parnassus has sufficed me, but now I have need of both, as I enter the arena that remains. Enter into my breast and breathe there as when you drew Marsyas from the sheath of his limbs. O divine Power, if you so lend yourself to me that I may show forth the image of the blessed realm which is imprinted in my mind, you shall see me come to your beloved tree and crown me with those leaves of which the matter and you shall make me worthy."

come to your beloved tree and crown me with those leaves of which the matter and you shall make me worthy.

Enter into my breast, and breathe there.... [*Par.*, pp. 3, 5]

Once again we can observe Chaucer's method of molding Dante's lines to suit the tone of his poem. While Dante's influence is observable throughout the lines from *The House of Fame* cited above, it is strongest in lines 1101–1103 and 1106–1109. Still one must not forget that certain conventions of invocations are also active here. Apollo is, of course, the conventional god to whom invocations for poetic inspiration would be addressed, and the appeal "Entra nel petto mio" is found as well in Boccaccio.[102] Nor, it would seem, should the verbal parallelism be too strongly pressed between "this lytel laste bok" (line 1093) and Dante's *ultimo lavoro*, which, when placed in context – where Dante has spent the previous ten lines in awe of his subject – seems rather to refer to the crowning task of describing Paradise and God himself than to the "last work" (that is, the final *cantica*). The more literal interpretation is, however, most certainly plausible.

The intervening lines (1094–1100), with their dry humor of self-abnegation, seem to indicate clearly that Chaucer has been playing upon the formality of invocations from the very start. While few people would take Chaucer's disclaimer of "art poetical"[103] at face value, an incorrect impression can be given by omission of these intervening lines, which make of the entire invocation a fine piece of high comedy.[104] Having gone through all the stylized reverences and formal phrasings of the invocation, Chaucer suddenly changes pace and, with a businesslike efficiency, ends up with the last, conventional line:

Now entre in my brest anoon!

Scholars have tended to seize on these lines (frequently omitting the contratone of lines 1094–1100) as examples, one suspects, of the long-sought-for "high seriousness" that Arnold found wanting in Chaucer. J. A. W. Bennett (1968:101) declares that "behind Chaucer's appropriation of this prayer lies the fact that he is the first Englishman to share Dante's sense of the worth of poetry and of the act of poetic creation."[105] As given, this evaluation takes too little account of Chaucer's contemporaries – of Langland or Gower or the Pearl Poet, among others – and even were we to add a modifying "explicitly" after "first Englishman," we would still not have dealt properly with the Chaucerian balance that is established by lines 1094–1100. Disregarding some such perspective, Bennett (p. 101) almost seems ready to find his high seriousness in an *o altitudo*: "It is in the light of the long-standing suspicion or disregard of poetry as such...that we must view the reverence with which Dante regards Virgil, and the devotion with which Chaucer follows

---

[102] Cf. *Amorosa visione* 2.3: "place your power into my breast." As well, the following two lines ("not suffering, O Citherea, that the talent for this present work flee from me") could be compared with *HF* 1092–93 ("thurgh thy grete myght, / This lytel laste bok thou gye!"), and line 7 ("Let your excellence come into my mind") with *HF* 1101–1103 ("thow / Wilt helpe me to shewe now / That in myn hed ymarked ys"). The *Amorosa visione* is certainly not being offered here as a source, only as a demonstration of some of the conventions of invocations.

[103] For other such disclaimers see *MLT* B 47–48; *Th* B² 1899 and *Th* B² 2118. For a more precise discussion see Everett 1955.

[104] For distinctions within this relatively neglected genre, see Ruggiers 1977; for my present understanding see "Dante: Comedy and Conversion," in Ruggiers. *The House of Fame* is, I feel, a deeply serious *investigation* of "the worth of poetry and...the act of poetic creation," but that does not mean that it is not comedic or that it does not sustain the balance, distance, and unflinching honesty that constitute the hallmark of Chaucer's high comedy.

[105] See also Burlin, p. 56.

in Dante's steps." Even Bethel, concerning these lines, remarks that "the change in the nature of the promise made to the God should the poem be successfully completed is characteristically Chaucerian. Dante promises to crown himself with a laurel wreath...; Chaucer, more humbly, merely promises to kiss Apollo's tree." One might suggest substituting "effectively" for "humbly" if only because the former seems more easily provable than the latter. Nor must we forget that the prayer is for the poem to "be successfully completed" — but it is not, at least not in the conventional sense, and in this respect the prayer may very well be seen as "characteristically Chaucerian."

We should not, however, consider that Chaucer is parodying the *Commedia in se*, but rather that his essential balance has worked upon the genre of the formal invocation and brought it into line with the general tone of his poem. As Patch (1939:45) has remarked, Chaucer's audience would not have recognized the reference to Dante. That does not mean that this was purely a private joke of Chaucer's; his audience would have recognized at once that the classical invocation was being made the object of some gently comic gibing.

Bethel: "1229: mistake as to the sex of Marsyas due to *Par.* I, 19–21."

And Marcia that loste her skyn,
[Bothe in face, body, and chyn,
For that she wolde envien, loo!
To pipen bet than Appolloo.]

Entra nel petto mio, e spira tue
    sì come quando Marsìa traesti
    de la vagina de le membra sue.

Enter into my breast and breathe there as when you drew Marsyas from the sheath of his limbs. [*Par.*, p. 5]

The recollection of Marsyas's name is due in all probability to this passage in Dante, which, as discussed above, can be seen in the opening of the invocation. The mistake about Marsyas's sex would be due not to any parallel mistake on Dante's part but only to the fact that the Italian does not show in this passage what the sex of the subject is, one way or the other. Another source is indicated by Chaucer's subsequent lines, which give many details not in Dante but all of which can be found in Ovid's account of the legend.[106] It is difficult, however, to reconcile those actions that Chaucer ascribes to a woman with the fact that Marsyas was a satyr, thus making it rather unlikely — unless Chaucer's knowledge of mythology was particularly weak on this point — that there would be any ambiguity in Ovid insofar as Marsyas's sex is concerned. If Ovid were the source, to account for the mistake in sex, one would have to grant not only this weakness on Chaucer's part but also a faulty reading of the opening lines of the legend in the *Metamorphoses* (6.383–85): "Another recalled the satyr whom the son of Latona had conquered in a contest on Pallas's reed, and punished" (Ovid 1916:3.315). It must be noted, however, that, beyond the words *satyri*, *quem*, and *victum*, there is no further indication of the sex given by either word or grammatical construction. An obvious misreading can be made of *Satyri fratres* (line 393) which would tend to confuse the issue, and lines 392–95 might more plausibly be expected to be the tribute to a female than a male: "The country people, the sylvan deities, fauns and his brother satyrs, and Olympus, whom even then he still loved, the nymphs, all wept for him, and every shepherd who fed his woolly sheep or horned kine on those mountains" (Ovid 1916:3.315). Finally, Ovid gives the name only at the end of his account: "Marsya nomen habet," where, as a first declension Greek noun, its

---

[106] *Met.* 6.382–400. Cf. Koch 1923.

spelling is the same as that used by Dante. Chaucer might have mistaken the noun ending for the far more common feminine declension, but his spelling of the name with a *c* is different from that of both Ovid and Dante and—though not as important as forgetting Marsyas's mythological genealogy—suggests that there might be some other source than the two that have been mentioned.

A far more plausible answer to the problem is that of Alfred David (1974:19–29), who shows that the sexual confusion can easily be derived from a subbranch of the manuscripts of the *Roman de la Rose* "in which Apollo flays a female satyr called 'Marse'" (p. 26). David's subsequent caveats may be worth considering (p. 26):

> More significant than the establishment of the source in this case is the elimination of some other hitherto possible sources. These include Ovid and the numerous Christian moralizations of the *Metamorphoses* and other pagan myths such as the *Ovide moralisé*. . . . As with so much else in Chaucer, before searching the Roman poets, Boccaccio, or Dante, not to mention arcane medieval Latin sources, one should ask, "Does it occur in the *Roman de la Rose*?"[107]

What I might suggest occurred in the present instance is that Marsyas's name may well have come from Chaucer's reading of the *Paradiso* (as seen in the Invocation); Chaucer would then seem to have gone to his copy of the *Roman de la Rose* for further information— or in this case, misinformation.

Bethel: "1460–63: mistake as to the birthplace of Statius due to *Purg.* XXI, 88–92."

The Tholosan that highte Stace,	Tanto fu dolce mio vocale spirto,
That bar of Thebes up the fame	che, tolosano, a sé mi trasse Roma,
Upon his shuldres, and the name	dove mertai le tempie ornar di mirto.
Also of cruel Achilles.	Stazio la gente ancor di là mi noma:
	cantai di Tebe, e poi del grande Achille

> So sweet was my vocal spirit that me, a Toulousan, Rome drew to itself, where I was deemed worthy to have my brows adorned with myrtle. Men yonder still speak my name, which is Statius. I sang of Thebes, and then of the great Achilles [*Purg.*, p. 231]

Unlike the previous entry, this was not a "mistake" in Chaucer's time. Statius's two great epics, the *Thebaid* and the unfinished *Achilleid*, "highly artificial and ornate in style, were looked upon as models of rhetorical elegance."[108] They were the only works of Statius known at the time, though a third work, a miscellany known as the *Silvae*, was recovered after the fourteenth century. It is from the *Silvae* alone that we learn of Naples as Statius's birthplace. Dante, Chaucer, and their contemporaries, however, did not know this work and therefore confused the epic poet with Lucius Statius Ursolus, a rhetorician of Toulouse who lived in the time of Nero.[109] The appearance of Statius and the naming of his two known works is natural, since this is a listing of all the principal writers of the matter of antiquity. To Chaucer's age, naming Toulouse as Statius's birthplace was not a

---

[107] The question, though fair enough, immediately invites other names, such as the encyclopedist Vincent of Beauvais.

[108] Grandgent (Dante 1933:509).

[109] Dante 1933, note to *Purg.* 21.76–102.

mistake but a commonplace;[110] nonetheless, one must not overlook that Dante's tercet contains facts paralleling those in Chaucer, namely, that Statius was born in Toulouse and "cantai di Tebe, e poi del grande Achille." While this does not, of course, make the *Purgatorio* passage the only possible source for Chaucer's lines, it does make it worth consideration.

Bethel: "1511f: wording of this reference to Proserpine due to Dante's description of her, *Inf.* IX, 44."

Of Pluto, and of Proserpyne,	[le meschine]
That quene ys of the derke pyne.	de la regina de l'etterno pianto
	[the handmaids] of the queen of eternal lamentation [*Inf.*, p. 91]

There is obviously a case of analogous subject matter here, though the question of direct source might be considered somewhat more debatable. Verbally there are two points of comparison: the word "quene" with *regina* and the phrase "of the derke pyne" with *de l'etterno pianto*. In the case of the latter, "derke pyne" translates the spirit if not the words of *de l'etterno pianto*, though Chaucer's description of Proserpine can be paralleled also in Ovid (*Met.* 5.507–508): "But yet she was a queen, the great queen of that world of darkness, the mighty consort of the tyrant of the underworld" (Ovid 1916:3.273). Proserpine was, by the tradition of centuries, the queen of the infernal regions, and neither Chaucer nor Dante varies in this view. Indeed, Chaucer, making his brief allusion, could very well have had Dante as much in mind as Ovid or any of the other classical authors.

Bethel: "1802f: reference to the wind in Hell; wording seems due to *Inf.* V, 28–33."

He gan to blasen out a soun	Io venni in loco d'ogne luce muto,
As lowde as beloweth wynd in helle	che mugghia come fa mar per tempesta,
	se da contrari venti è combattuto.
	La bufera infernal, che mai non resta,
	mena li spirti con la sua rapina;
	voltando e percotendo li molesta.

>   I came into a place mute of all light, which bellows like the sea in tempest when it is assailed by warring winds. The hellish hurricane, never resting, sweeps along the spirits with its rapine; whirling and smiting, it torments them. [*Inf.*, p. 49]

Bethel is generous in the number of lines that he cites as source of the single line 1803, or, rather, the single word "beloweth," since Chaucer is emphasizing not the tempestuous quality of the wind but the noise that is made.

As for the wind itself, Spencer (1927:192–93) shows that it was as common an attribute of hell as was the stench. He gives as examples the *Poema morale* ("Hwilc hete is þer woule wuneð, hu biter winde þer blaweð"), *St. Patrick's Purgatory* ("a smart wind blewz wel faste"), and the warning given to Owayn that the fiends will send "such a wynde" that he will be blown down to hell.

---

[110] Cf., for example, Boccaccio, *Amoroso visione* 5.34, which refers to "Stazio di Tolosa."

The noise of the winds of hell is mentioned, as well, in the *Ayenbite of Inwit*, where in hell there is "ver bernynde, brenstone stinkinde, tempeste brayinde," and the noise of hell can be heard from some distance by Saint Brendan and his companions (Spencer, p. 193).[111] The howls of the tortured and damned souls and the shouts and cries of their tormentors are consistently mentioned in the descriptions of the infernal regions. The precise description of the bellowing, the winds, and the tempestuous seething is found in one of the best-known works of this genre, the *Visio Tundali*, which Vincent of Beauvais gave *in extenso* in the *Speculum historiale* (38.88–104). From the start Tundale's *Vision* is striking. Describing the "pena insidiatorum et perfidorum" ("punishment of traitors and lurkers in ambush"), he states: "From one part of this mountain was fire, filthy, sulfurous, and full of darkness; from the other part, icy snow and a frightful wind" (chap. 90). In lines that could have been a common source to both Dante and Chaucer, the English visionary recounts the horrors he has seen: "Whence going further, they saw an immensely broad swamp whose waves, flung up by tempests, did not permit them to see heaven. There was full many a multitude of terrifying beasts, bellowing to devour souls" (chap. 92). The bellowing and howling is continued to an even greater pitch:

> Indeed, those beasts, wishing to get out, when they could not drag their tails with them, never gave over turning their fiery and iron-hard fangs back against the very bodies from which they sprang, until they consumed those right to the tendons and right to the dry bones. And thus as if yelling together the roar of the overflowing icepacks and the howls of the souls sustaining such torment and the bellow of the beasts getting out from among them reached heaven. [Chap. 94]

Dante, who is emphasizing the unending restless torment of the souls, might possibly have reminded Chaucer of the volume of sound carried by the infernal winds, but he is certainly not the sole source. *Visio* literature was extensive at this time, and while it is generally acknowledged that Dante wrote the supreme example of the genre, the traditional descriptions of so vast a body of writing are more likely to be the source from which Chaucer almost unconsciously drew his image.

Bethel: "2034–40: description of the throng in the House of Rumor seems to be modelled on *Inf.* III, 55–7."

But which a congregacioun	e dietro le venìa sì lunga tratta
Of folk, as I saugh rome aboute,	di gente, ch'i' non averei creduto
Some wythin and some wythoute,	che morte tanta n'avesse disfatta.
Nas never seen, ne shal ben eft;	
That, certys, in the world nys left	
So many formed be Nature,	
Ne ded so many a creature	

> ...and behind it [the whirling ensign] came so long a train of people that I should never have believed death had undone so many. [*Inf.*, p. 29]

There is not, of course, any contextual parallel whatsoever. Dante is describing the mass of neutrals, of Laodiceans, who are rejected by both heaven and hell and are condemned

---

[111] As Spencer puts it, "In *St. Patrick's Purgatory*, the fiends do little else but yell."

for eternity to clash against each other in blind mass movements from one side of their circle to the other. Chaucer is describing the crowds in the House of Rumor and saying that there are not as many creatures alive, or, for that matter, as many creatures dead, as there are (personified) rumors in that hall. The two writers would seem to converge on the point of the vast number of the dead.

Much closer contextually to this and the following passages in Chaucer are the lines from Ovid (*Met.* 12.55–57) describing the house of Fama: "Crowds fill the hall, shifting throngs come and go, and everywhere wander thousands of rumors, falsehoods mingled with the truth" (Ovid 1916:4.185). Verbally Chaucer often makes use of the sweep of all generations (lines 2037–40), most often to imply (excellence among) great numbers,[112] but the similarity of line 2040 with the image in Dante's tercet should be borne in mind.

Bethel: "2060–75: the expansive quality of rumour; discussion very similar to *Conv.* I, iii, 7ff; I, iv, 1."

Whan oon had herd a thing, ywis,	La fama buona principalmente è generata de
He com forth ryght to another wight,	la buona operazione ne la mente de l'amico,
And gan him tellen anon-ryght	e da quella è prima partorita; chè la mente
The same that to him was told,	del nemico, avvegna che riceva lo seme, non
Or hyt a forlong way was old,	concepe. Quella mente che prima la
But gan somwhat for to eche	partorisce, sì per far più ornato lo suo
To this tydynge in this speche	presente, sì per la caritade de l'amico che lo
More than hit ever was.	riceve, non si tiene a li termini del vero, ma
And nat so sone departed nas	passa quelli. E quando per ornare ciò che
Tho fro him, that he ne mette	dice li passa, contra conscienza parla;
With the thridde; and or he lette	quando inganno di caritade li fa passare,
Any stounde, he told him als;	non parla contra essa. La seconda mente che
Were the tydynge soth or fals,	ciò riceve, non solamente a la dilatazione de
Yit wolde he telle hyt natheles,	la prima sta contenta, ma 'l suo
And evermo with more encres	riportamento, sì come quasi suo effetto,
Than yt was erst.	procura d'adornare; e sì, che per questo fare
	e per lo 'nganno che riceve de la caritade in
	lei generata, quella più ampia fa che a lei
	non viene, e con concordia e con discordia di
	conscienza come la prima. E questo fa la
	terza ricevitrice e la quarta, e così in infinito
	si dilata. E così, volgendo le cagioni sopra
	dette ne le contrarie, si può vedere la
	ragione de la infamia, che simigliantemente
	si fa grande. Per che Virgilio dice nel quarto
	de lo Eneida che la Fama vive per essere
	mobile, e acquista grandezza per andare.
	Apertamente adunque veder può chi vuole
	che la imagine per sola fama generata
	sempre è più ampia, quale che essa sia, che
	non è la cosa imaginata nel vero stato.

[112] See, for example, *MLT* B 1077–79: "save the joye that lasteth everemo, / There is noon lyk that any creature / Hath seyn or shal, whil that the world may dure"; *FranT* F 929–30: "He syngeth, daunceth, passynge any man / That is, or was, sith that the world bigan"; *TC* 5.832–33: "Oon of the beste entecched creature / That is, or shal, whil that the world may dure"; *LGW* F 285–89: "And after hem coome of wymen swich a traas / That, syn that God Adam hadde mad of erthe, / The thridde part, of mankynde, or the ferthe, / Ne wende I not by possibilitee / Had ever in this wide world ybee."

The good report of a man is generated in the first place by the favourable process in a friend's mind, and by this it is first brought to the birth: for the mind of an enemy, although it receives the germ, does not quicken it. The mind which first brings it forth, both in order to embellish its own gift, and through affection for the friend who receives it, does not keep within the bounds of truth but oversteps them. And when the mind in order to embellish what it affirms oversteps the bounds of truth, it speaks against conscience; when affection misleads it to overstep them, it does not speak against conscience. The second mind which receives what is said is not content merely with the exaggeration due to the first, but is careful to embellish its own repetition of it, as being in this case the effect proper to itself; and so, by this action and by the deception which the affection generated in it practises on it, makes the report greater than it was when received, whether in agreement or in disagreement with conscience, as with the first mind. The third mind that receives it does the like, and so the fourth, and thus the report is enlarged to infinity. So when the action of the causes above mentioned is reversed, the reason for ill fame which is magnified in like manner may also be perceived. Wherefore Virgil says in the fourth book of the *Aeneid* that 'Fame thrives on motion and acquires greatness by going onward'. Anyone who wishes can therefore see clearly that the image which is generated by fame alone, is always greater, of whatever kind it be, than the thing itself of which it is the image in its true condition. [Pp. 38–39]

The question of source in this citation is both complex in itself and important to the general view of the Chaucer-Dante relationship. Broadly speaking, it would seem that Chaucer's treatment of the subject is of the same general nature as that which Dante gives in *Convivio* 1.3.7ff.,[113] while the subject matter itself is almost certainly indebted ultimately to Ovid's description of Fama in *Met.* 12 (which Chaucer undoubtedly knew). Let us look first at the subject matter. The relevant lines of the *Metamorphoses* (12.55–58) read: "Thousands of rumors and confused reports flit about. Some of these fill their idle ears with talk, and others go and tell elsewhere what they have heard; while the story grows in size, and each new teller makes contribution to what he has heard" (Ovid 1916:4.185)[114] The *Ovide moralisé* (13.1601–20) seems even closer to the subject matter in Chaucer's description:

One can enter through more than a thousand apertures without portals and without doors. Day and night the house is open, without fastening or partition wall. And without rest and without silence, voices repair and recommence, without clamor, in a soft murmur, of truth and countertruth. They come there no matter what the day. There, those who go about finding news go and come without stay, so they only batter the wind and the ears of their hearers, and so they give many unfounded joy. Others recall and repeat the word that has been told them. Some bear witness to the truth; others speak the emptiness of falsehood and, in recounting, make the tale grow and go about lying.

---

[113] The reference to *Convivio* 1.4.1 does not seem worth giving since it is only the briefest possible transitional summary of the material in the preceding chapter.

[114] For these lines in context, see above, n.99.

While Dante is dealing not directly with rumor but, as his source shows,[115] with the more moral question of the way good report increases and the psychological motivation of the person who adds to the report, the manner in which his subject is developed is closer to Chaucer than to any other source. The numerical order with which Dante follows the growth of good report ("Quella mente che prima...La seconda mente...la terza...la quarta, e così in infinito") is similar to Chaucer's "...oon...another wight...the thridde," and, although a common stylistic device, it is found only indirectly in the *Metamorphoses* ("Hi...hi...") and the *Ovide moralisé* ("Li autres...Li un...Li autre").[116] Most striking of all, however, is that Dante develops the more vital image of one person telling another, just as Chaucer does in *The House of Fame* description. On the other hand, it must be admitted that Dante's interest is primarily in the question of praise and the psychological reason that causes *la mente* to exaggerate the good report while the Ovidian passage, it must be recognized, is in the proper context and supplies the source for a large number of lines (particularly in the previous 120 verses) in other parts of *The House of Fame*.[117] What we may have, then, is a blending, in which Chaucer, following more closely the matter of the Ovidian passage, made use of the more vital Dantesque image, thus presenting an almost ludicrously dynamic picture of the physical workings of rumor.

Although the passage in the *Convivio* cannot be definitively offered as a source, since the construction of the Ovidian original could have suggested Chaucer's treatment, we should recognize that Dante's handling of an analogous subject in a similar manner is striking. In any event, if Chaucer had read the *Convivio* by the time he was engaged in *The House of Fame*, he would undoubtedly have recognized the similarity of Dante and Ovid at once, and this might have served as an addition to, or reminder of, the Ovidian description. The question of date, however, presents one of the fundamental problems in ascribing *The House of Fame* passage to Dante, for there would appear to be no other valid instances at this time of Chaucer's use of the *Convivio*, and Chaucer was not one to leave so rich a source untapped. If we accept the posited source, therefore, we must reconsider, concomitantly, the question how early Chaucer had read the four tractates of Dante that make up the *Convivio*.

[115] In this discussion Dante is principally dependent on Saint Thomas's commentary on Aristotle's *Nicho-machean Ethics*. Thus, for example, 2.2.q.115, a.1: "To praise anyone touches upon both good and evil, according naturally to whether due circumstances are observed or neglected. Again, if anyone wishes to please anyone else by praising him,...other due circumstances being observed, this will pertain to the virtue of friendship having been made public." Dante is following Saint Thomas in the investigation of "laus," or *buona fama*, as opposed to rumor. Rather interestingly, a discussion paralleling the moral element in Dante and Saint Thomas can be found in Layamon's *Brut* (1847:2.541–42, lines 22954–80), where Arthur's reputation is being spoken of.

[116] This is one of the principal devices that Schaar traces through the various types of narrative in Chaucer's poetry. See particularly chaps. 3 and 4 and, for two examples among many, pp. 183, 198.

[117] Sypherd gives the following: 2.714–15; 3.1945–47, 1951–58, 2034–36, 2043–48.

CHAPTER 3

Anelida and Arcite

HE EXTENT to which Dante's influence is present in *Anelida and Arcite* depends almost wholly on the individual scholar's acceptance or rejection of that particular kind of association of ideas best known in Chaucerian studies as "linked atoms." With one exception the lines in this poem that are ascribed to Dante have been suggested not on the basis of a direct indebtedness but through the medium of another poem or poems, that is, a primary source (generally Boccaccio) contains a word or phrase that is said to remind Chaucer of a more or less similar word or phrase (usually in Dante), and this, in turn, is offered as a probable source for some proximate word or phrase in a given Chaucerian passage. The assumptions of such a procedure appear to be twofold: first, it must be assumed that Chaucer composed these posited Dantesque lines from memory (i.e., without consulting the text) and that he was capable of total recall of Dante (though not necessarily of other authors or common knowledge); second, it must be assumed that, on the basis of a limited number of works (usually, for *Anelida*, by Chaucer, Boccaccio, and Dante), treated *in vacuo*, one can reconstruct the creative process of the poet. On the basis of these two assumptions one can then proceed to connect similar words and phrases in Chaucer's known source with others in Dante and thus attempt to show the use of the *Commedia*.

It is not my purpose to discuss here the methodology as such, except in those cases where it directly affects the Chaucer-Dante relationship. In these cases, however, it is necessary to inspect closely the individual atoms of suggestion that are the links in the proposed chain of causal relationships. Since the majority of the posited ascriptions to Dante are based on an extremely complex process of scholarly conjecture, it has been necessary to take up each point, step by step, to check the ultimate validity of the connection between Chaucer and Dante. We must recognize from the very start that all these connections have been proposed in those lines which make up Chaucer's Invocation. That in itself makes the procedure somewhat questionable, since the very nature of the Invocation's stylized form and stock imagery would appear to militate against the results of a process that makes its connective links solely on the basis of three authors—in this case, Chaucer, Boccaccio and Dante—treated *in vacuo*. In any such minute inspection one is naturally aware of the danger of anatomizing the subject to death, and there has been a definite effort to avoid deadening categorization, but at the same time it would certainly seem legitimate—considering the importance to our subject—to revaluate carefully those ascriptions to Dante based on the theory of "linked atoms."

Anelida and Arcite

Bethel: "8–10: phraseology possibly influenced by *Par*. I, 7–12."

Bethel, who gets this parallel from Lowes, has been careful to use the words "phraseology possibly influenced by," while Lowes takes this as a positive parallel in support of another passage, *Anel*. 15–19. In other words, Lowes must assume this parallel to be definite to uphold what would appear to be an even weaker one. Lowes sets out his evidence thus (1917a:729):

> There is, however, still further evidence that the first canto of the *Paradiso* enters into Chaucer's fabric. The lines (7–9) just preceding those already quoted are as follows:

> > Perchè appressando sè al suo disire,
> > *Nostro intelletto si profonda tanto,*
> > *Che dietro la memoria non può ire.*

> The second stanza of *Anelida* begins:

> > For hit *ful depe is sonken in my minde.*

And it ends:

> > Hath nigh *devoured out of memorie.*

Now with both passages taken out of context, there does seem to be at least a vague similarity of words (*si profonda*, "sonken"; *memoria*, "memorie"), but the two passages, in context, read:

For hit ful depe is sonken in my mynde,	[La gloria di colui che tutto move
With pitous hert in Englysshe to endyte	per l'universo penetra, e risplende
This olde storie, in Latyn which I fynde,	in una parte più e meno altrove.
[Of quene Anelida and fals Arcite,	Nel ciel che più de la sua luce prende
That elde, which that al can frete and	fu' io, e vidi cose che ridire
bite,	né sa né può chi di là sù discende;]
As hit hath freten mony a noble storie,	perché appressando sé al suo disire,
Hath nygh devoured out of oure	nostro intelletto si profonda tanto,
memorie.]	che dietro la memoria non può ire.
	[Veramente quant'io del regno santo
	ne la mia mente potei far tesoro,
	sarà ora materia del mio canto.]

> [The glory of the All-Mover penetrates through the universe and reglows in the one part more, and in another less. I have been in the heaven that most receives of His light, and have seen things which whoso descends from up there has neither the knowledge nor the power to relate,] because, as it draws near to its desire, our intellect enters so deep that memory cannot go back upon the track. [Nevertheless, so much of the holy kingdom as I could treasure up in my mind shall now be the matter of my song.] [*Par*., p. 3]

What Chaucer is saying—and out of context, the indefinite "hit" hides the difference—is that he is determined to tell sympathetically in English the Latin story of Anelida and Arcite which time has almost taken from our memory. On the other hand, Dante, in the context of the opening of this *cantica*, states that he has attained the Empyrean, that those who return neither know how to nor have the power to retell their experience, because the closer they come to expressing what they have seen, the more intellect becomes awed at the majesty of God, thus totally destroying all the power of memory to tell what has been experienced. Except for the coincidence of the words *memorie*—"memoria," there would seem, therefore, to be no basis of parallelism in these passages. As Scartazzini (Dante 1921:646) notes, the *suo disire* is "Dio, sommo bene e fine ultimo dei desiderii dell'uomo," and the intellect "penetra sì a fondo mirando in Dio, che la memoria non lo può sequire." Since the parallel is so weak, Lowes tries to establish it by the same concept of Coleridgean total recall[1] that he uses with *PF* 288–94, though the "interesting association of ideas" is here reversed, working from Dante back through Boccaccio. The most striking weakness in this particular chain—even granting that there is some sort of parallel in the passages given above—lies in connecting the Dante to the Boccaccio. Lowes (1917a:729) states:

> And what is between (line 8 and line 14 of Chaucer) exemplifies once more how Chaucer's imagination hovered creatively over his remembered reading. Dante's eighth line ("nostro intelletto," etc.) has taken the place of the opening words of the *second* stanza ("E'm'è venuta voglia") of the *Teseide*, the rest of which Chaucer now begins freely to translate:

> > E'm'è venuta voglia con pietosa
> > Rima di scriver una storia antica,
> > Tanto negli anni riposta e nascosa.[2]

Actually, however, if the Boccaccio is a source for a portion of this stanza (and one wonders whether it is necessary to have a source for such a general statement as "I'm going to tell an old story about . . ."), then the first line of Boccaccio ("E'm'è venuta voglia con pietosa") is a much closer parallel to Chaucer than that offered by Lowes from Dante. Why and in what manner Dante's eighth line "has taken the place of the opening words of the *second* stanza" is not explained.

Continuing his proof by association, Lowes (1917a:729) concludes:

> But at once he is off on another track! For the words that I have italicized (i.e., from Boccaccio) have recalled to him a passage from Boethius, which he proceeds to paraphrase.

> But how many a man, that was ful *noble* in his tyme, hath the wrecched and nedy *foryeting of wryteres* put out of minde and don away! Al be it so that, certes, thilke wrytinges profiten litel; the which wrytinges *long and derk elde doth awey*, both hem and eek hir autours.

> > That *elde*, which that al can frete and byte,
> > As hit hath freten mony a *noble* storie,
> > Hath nigh *devoured out of our memorie*.

> And in these last three lines Boethius (in "elde," "noble," and the general idea), Boccaccio (in the retention of "storia"), and Dante (in the emphasis upon "memoria") are all present. [Lowes's italics]

---

[1] Cf. Lowes 1934:136: "Chaucer and Coleridge, in so many respects antipodal, were endowed with the same insatiable appetite for books, and the same prehensile, amalgamating memory."

[2] Lowes's italics. The following line is "Che latino autor non par ne dica."

The citation of Dante in connection with this passage in *Anelida and Arcite* would seem to be totally gratuitous. Even if we were to assume that it was possible to reconstruct Chaucer's mind at the moment of his writing these lines in *Anelida*, the silent assumption is that we have in Boccaccio, Boethius, and Dante all the possible material that might have influenced Chaucer at this time. However improbable, let us grant this assumption. On such a basis there might be some argument for accepting the passage from Boethius; indeed, one might even accept the Boccaccio, though only on the basis of the line which Lowes rejects ("E'm'è venuta voglia con pietosa"). But there is not, even granting all this, any apparent reason for looking to Dante for the suggestion of anything in this passage. The contexts of the Chaucer and Dante lines are completely different; the link that is meant to connect a questionable citation in Boccaccio with the passage in Dante would appear to be nonexistent, and the procedure of quoting now a single word, now a line out of context seems the most tenuous kind of proof.

Bethel: "15–19: the inclusion of Polyhymnia, and some of the phrasing are due to *Par.* I, 7–15; XXIII, 55–7. 17: Cirrea; allusion probably due to *Par.* I, 36."

Once more Bethel has evidently taken his parallel from Lowes, though this time with far more positiveness. He is, however, selective in that he rejects Lowes's more inclusive parallelism, which sets lines 15–20 against *Par.* 1.13–21, 25–27, 31–36. Bethel modifies this inclusiveness in the light of Boccaccio's *Teseida* 1.1.1–14, 11.62.6–8, and 11.63.1–5. Since my previous remarks have been on the basis of Lowes's article, and since Bethel's parallels are included in Lowes's citations, I shall continue on the basis of the former, asking the reader to apply the remarks to Bethel where necessary. In the following citations, from Dante and Boccaccio, I have added Lowes's italicizations and supplied those verses which he has omitted:

Be favorable eke, thou Polymya,
On Parnaso that *with thy sustres* glade,
By Elycon, not fer from Cirrea,
Singest with vois memorial *in the shade,*
Under the laurer which that may not
    fade,
And do that I my ship to haven wynne.

O buono Appollo, a l'ultimo lavoro
    fammi del tuo valor sì fatto vaso,
    come dimandi a dar *l'amato alloro.*
Infino a qui *l'un giogo di Parnaso*
    assai mi fu; ma or con amendue
    m'è uopo intrar ne l'aringo rimaso.
Entra nel petto mio, e spira tue
    sì come quando *Marsïa* traesti
    de la vagina de le membra sue.
[O divina virtù, se mi ti presti
    tanto che l'ombra del beato regno
    segnata nel mio capo io manifesti,]
vedra'mi al piè *del tuo diletto legno*
    venire, e coronarmi de le foglie
    che la materia e tu mi farai degno.
[Sì rade volte, padre, se ne coglie
    per trïunfare o cesare o poeta,
    colpa e vergogna de l'umane voglie,]
che parturir *letizia* in su la *lieta*
    delfica deïtà dovria *la fronda*
    peneia, quando alcun di sé asseta.
Poca favilla gran fiamma seconda:
    forse di retro a me con miglior voci
    si pregherà perché *Cirra* risponda.

O good Apollo, for this last labor make me such a vessel of your worth as you require for granting your beloved laurel. Thus far the one peak of Parnassus has sufficed me, but now I have need of both, as I enter the arena that remains. Enter into my breast and breathe there as when you drew Marsyas from the sheathe of his limbs. [O divine Power, if you do so lend yourself to me that I may show forth the image of the blessed realm which is imprinted in my mind,] you shall see me come to your beloved tree and crown me with those leaves of which the matter and you shall make me worthy. [So rarely, father, are they gathered, for triumph of caesar or of poet—fault and shame of human wills] that the Peneian frond ought to beget gladness in the glad Delphic deity whenever it causes anyone to long for it. A great flame follows a little spark: perhaps, after me, prayer shall be offered with better voices, that Cyrrha may respond. [*Par.*, pp. 3, 5]

> *O Sorelle* Castalie, che *nel monte*
> *Elicona* contente dimorate
> D'intorno al sacro gorgoneo fonte,
> *Sottesso l'ombra delle frondi amate*
> *Da Febo* [delle quali ancor la fronte
> Spero d'ornarmi, sol che 'l concediate]
>
> Un bello scudo e di molto valore,
> Nel qual si vedea *Marsia* sonando,
> Sè con Apollo nel sonar provando.
> Vedeasi appresso superar Pitone,[3]
> E quindi *sotto l'ombre graziose*
> *Sopra Parnaso presso all'Elicone*
> *Fonte* seder *con le nove amorose*
> *Muse, e cantar maestrevol canzone*. . . .[4]

O Castalian sisters, who dwell in bliss on Mount Helicon around the sacred Gorgonean fount beneath the shade of those boughs which Phoebus loves, and with which I still aspire to adorn my brow, if you would only grant it: incline your holy ears to my entreaties, and heed them, as it behooves you.

[Aegeus made him accept] a beautiful shield for his greater glory, and it was very valuable, for on it was depicted Marsyas playing in his music contest with Apollo.

Next Apollo was portrayed overcoming the Python, and then seated near the Helicon fount with the nine loving Muses and singing an ingenious song. . . .

Lowes, whose citation of *Teseida* 12.62–63 is certainly valid, attempts to connect the Boccaccio with the passage in Dante to account for the reference to Cirrhea and, by a strained association, the reference to Polyhymnia as well. As will be seen, however, the location of Parnassus in Cirrhea was part of the common knowledge (however confused) of the time, and the ascription to Dante of the suggestion for Polyhymnia seems untenable in itself and based on the assumption that Chaucer was unable to evoke on his own as stock a subject as one of the Muses. Lowes's argument is as follows (1917a:725):

---

[3] My text reads Fitone here.

[4] Boccaccio *Teseida* 1.1.1–6; 11.62, 6–8, 11.63.1–5. See also the discussion under the entry for *PF* 1091–93; 1101–09 (McCoy's translation).

A peculiarly interesting convergence of reminiscences, involving once more a fusion of Boccaccio and Dante, occurs in the Proem to *Anelida and Arcite*. It has long been recognized that Chaucer's three stanzas are based on the first three stanzas (in reverse order) of the *Teseide*. But that is only part of the story. For it has not been observed that Chaucer has, for one thing, combined with the first stanza of the first book of the *Teseide* the sixty-third stanza of the eleventh book.

The passages from Boccaccio and Chaucer are then cited with the italicization as given above. In order to show a direct and "inevitable"[5] relationship between Boccaccio and Dante, Lowes has ignored the distinct possibility that a great deal of this information on the Muses could come from common knowledge of the classics. There is no doubt that Boccaccio is the primary source, but that does not mean that all other material save certain selected sources is to be ruled out. Nonetheless, Lowes's discussion continues (1917a:725–26):

> That the one passage in the *Teseide* should recall the other was inevitable, considering their references in common to Apollo, Helicon and the Muses, and the recurrence of the phrase "sottesso [sotto] l'ombra [l'ombre]."[6] The conjunction of Parnassus and Helicon is therefore Boccaccio's, not Chaucer's.
>
> But in all probability it was not Boccaccio's alone. For in neither stanza does Boccaccio refer to "Cirrea."

Lowes then goes on to show the total confusion concerning the geography of the Parnassus regions that existed among all the commentators of Chaucer's time. He cites Servius, Lactantius, *I Fatti di Cesare*, Junius Philargyrius, and Macrobius, all of whom mention Parnassus, Cirrhea, Helicon, Apollo, and the Muses; and, though it is admitted that "like most of his contemporaries, [Chaucer] was largely indebted to the mass of misinformation provided in the accepted commentaries" (Lowes 1917a:726), not once is it suggested that Chaucer's knowledge of the region could have come from one of these sources nor, indeed, that the confusion of Helicon as both mountain and fountain exists even in the passages that are cited from Boccaccio. Instead, Dante is pressed into service with the statement: "But the immediate suggestion for 'Cirrea' in *Anelida* came probably from another source. Few pages of the *Divine Comedy* seem to have made a deeper impression upon Chaucer than the first part of the first canto of the *Paradiso*" (Lowes 1917a:727). The implications of the conclusions which Lowes reaches are at once far-reaching and fundamental to our view of the Chaucer-Dante relationship. Because of the complexity of the argument I have added numbers occasionally so as to be able to refer to specific points more easily:

> Now to anyone familiar with Canto I, Boccaccio's "*frondi amate Da Febo*" must almost inevitably have recalled Dante's "*l'amato* alloro" and his "la *fronda* Peneia" (not to speak of "tuo *diletto* legno"), while the reference to "Marsia" is common to both [1]. The passage once remembered, the insertion of "Cirrea" (however troubled by the contagion of the commentators) is in the right Chaucerian vein [2]. And the suggestion that the mention of "Cirrea" is immediately due to Chaucer's recollection of Dante [3] is borne out by the fact that "glade" (which scarcely translates "contente") [4] seems to be transferred

---

[5] The word is Lowes's. See Lowes 1917a:728, 729 n.2.
[6] The brackets are Lowes's.

to the Muses from the "lieta" of *Par.*, I, 31, and that Boccaccio's "*frondi* amate" has become specifically "l'amato *alloro*" of *Par.*, I, 15. [Lowes 1917a:728; Lowes's italics]

1. If one could assume that the only two books that Chaucer had ever read were Boccaccio and Dante or that the presence of the adjective *amato* and *amate* ("beloved") were sufficiently striking, one would still have difficulty believing that canto 1 of the *Paradiso* "must almost inevitably" recall the words in Dante. As a matter of fact, the adjective is used by both Boccaccio and Dante, since they are referring to the traditional story of Apollo and Daphne, which is (like references to the Muses, to the protector Apollo, to his domain, and to the fountain of knowledge and inspiration) among the commonplaces in the invocations of classical and medieval poetry. The term *amato alloro* (in one form or another) is used by both men, but Chaucer makes no use whatever of this common reference to the Daphne story, and, if we are to assume that he was using the two Italian works as sources, we are forced likewise to assume that he intentionally avoided any allusion to the well-known tale that they had in common. If we were to follow the process of association of ideas on this basis, the reference in Boccaccio might equally well have evoked the French version of the story in the *Ovide moralisé* (1.3035-51):

> If she [Daphne] was beautiful in body before, she is a tree just as beautiful still. Phebus loves her as before. He feels the breast warm and moving, which trembles under the thin bark. He thinks to kiss her, it seems to me, but the tree flees his kiss. Phebus says: "Since Fortune so torments me that I have you not as wife, you will be my tree and I will make a chaplet and crown of you. You shall be a laurel, and thus I give you a gift of great nobility. For honor and for dignity, in sign of love and of glory, those who will have gained victory will make crowns of you for their heads.

By an association of ideas one could, if he wished, connect the accompanying descriptions of Parnassus, Helicon, Apollo, Muses, fountains, and so on, with any of the other scores of references that can be found throughout Ovid or the moralized Ovid. Boccaccio and Dante are giving traditional descriptions of Apollo and of Parnassus, which, along with the reference to Marsyas, can be linked with equal ease to Ovid, the *Ovide moralisé* or any one of a large number of other places in classical or medieval literature.[7] Certain unique aspects make it highly likely that Boccaccio is the source which Chaucer is using, but unless correspondingly positive evidence is presented, one should not posit an additional source simply on the basis of common knowledge exhibited by two writers. Indeed, the use by both Boccaccio and Dante of Marsyas's name and its absence from Chaucer[8] lead Lowes to add a rather surprising footnote: "I am not imagining all this. It is what happens constantly to everyone who reads at all, and in the case of a tenacious memory like Chaucer's it is inevitable. See Section 1 above" (Lowes 1917a:728 n.2).[9] No one can doubt Chaucer's tenacious memory or the increased concentration involved in the reading process at this time, but that does not mean that, with the limited information that we have at our disposal, we should arbitrarily impose certain mental patterns on a poet's

---

[7] Cf. *Met.* 1.452-575 and 6.382-400, respectively; also *Ovide moralisé* 1.2737-3260, 3408-37; and 6.1921-2057, respectively.

[8] Except, that is, as some kind of mental point of contact.

[9] Section 1 is the Semiramis passage and the list of lovers, which itself is open to debate. See below under the entry for *PF* 288-94.

mind and then call them "inevitable"—above all, not when he is using information that was part of the culture of western civilization generally.

2. It would seem here that Lowes is attempting to prove an extremely important point by the very hypothesis that he tries to establish; i.e., "the right Chaucerian vein" is assumed to be a mind capable of total recall of selected sources. By (3) the validity of this hypothesis is assumed in order to "prove" the next point, though there is no apparent reason why the name "Cirrea" must come from Dante, and Lowes has himself cited at least one source (1917a:726) that not only mentions the name but gives the more suggestive spelling Cirrhaea.[10] As well, the aspect of poetic convention or tradition—the fact that all these were time-honored place-names of the Muses' territories—seems not to have been given sufficient consideration. Finally, there is the assertion at (4) that "glade" "scarcely translates 'contente,'" though I find it a perfectly legitimate translation, far superior to some such word as "content." Yet for the sake of the whole argument some sort of a "convergence of reminiscences" must be established, and it is apparently for this reason that there is the attempt to make *lieta* and *letizia* the basis for Chaucer's reference to the "sustres glade," when actually *lieta* is no closer to "glade" than *contente*.

On looking directly at the passage in *Anelida*, then, we find that the names Parnassus, Helicon, and Cirrhea are used in a number of works in classical and medieval literature, that the adjective "glade" has ample justification in the Italian *contente*, and that Chaucer certainly needed no reference to understand that Boccaccio's word *frondi* referred to the Muses' traditional sign, the laurel. As well, those very elements which are common to both Boccaccio and Dante—the references to the Daphne story and the mention of Marsyas—are nowhere in the Chaucerian passage under discussion. It is at this point in his argument that Lowes offers in support of his ascription the posited parallels in the preceding stanza,[11] though this method of leaning one apparently weak argument against another in the hope that they will be mutually supportable does not seem to constitute the kind of strong independent proof that one would like to have here.

The assumption that Chaucer had total recall of Dante and the correlative assumption that one can reconstruct the poet's creative process form a hypothesis that can lead one ever further astray. Thus, taking up first the *frondi amate* of Boccaccio—which somehow is connected with the passage in Dante, though the phrases of neither of the Italian poets appear in Chaucer—and taking the *memoria* from a previous passage in Dante,[12] Lowes offers these two most dubious sections of a highly tenuous parallel as proof of a third—and equally dubious—parallel by connecting the passage in Boccaccio with one in Dante and then one in Dante with another in Dante. The interweaving of these is ingenious, and I again take the liberty of inserting translations and numbers at points I wish to discuss. Lowes's argument goes as follows (1917a:730; Lowes's italics):

> But why should Chaucer invoke Polyhymnia among the Muses? For one thing, of course, because of Dante's "memoria" in the preceding line [1]. But

[10] This kind of source hunting can, of course, lead one to make all sorts of strange relationships. I note, for example, that Toynbee (1909:lii) has the following thematic citation at the opening of *Dante in English Literature*: "Thou know'st perchance how Phoebus self did guide / Our Tuscan *DANTE* up the lofty side / of snow-clad *Cyrrha*; how our poet won / *Parnassus'* peak and founts of *Helicon*: / How with *Apollo*, ranging wide he sped / Through Nature's whole domain and visited / Imperial Rome, and Paris, and so passed / O'erseas to BRITAIN'S distant shores at last / (Boccaccio to Petrarch)." The capitalization is Toynbee's; the suggestive italicization is mine. The possible conclusions I leave to the reader's imagination.

[11] See above under discussion of lines 8–14.

[12] See, again, under lines 8–14 above.

there is probably an additional association of ideas. Toynbee compares *Anelida*, 15–16 ("Polymnia...with thy sustres") with *Par.*, XXIII, 56 ("Polinnia con le suore") [2]. This tentative suggestion attains practical conclusiveness when we examine the contexts of the two passages [3]. Chaucer has in mind, as he writes with Boccaccio and Boethius before him [4], the ideas of stories *forgotten in old books*, and also the association with the "*Sorelle* Castalie" and the "*frondi amate*." The twenty third canto of the *Paradiso* opens with the line:

> Come l'augello intra l'amate fronde [5]
> [As the bird among the beloved leaves] [*Par.*, p. 257]

And the lines immediately preceding the mention of Polyhymnia are as follows:

> Io era come quei che si risente
>   *Di vision obblita, e che s'ingegna*
>   *Indarno di ridurlasi alla mente,*
> Quando io udi'questa profferta, degna
>   *Di tanto grado, che mai non si estingue*
>   *Del libro che il preterito rassegna.*
> Se mo sonasser tutte quelle lingue
>   Che *Polinnia con le suore fero*, etc. [6]

[I was as one that wakes from a forgotten dream, and who strives in vain to bring it back to mind, when I heard this proffer, worthy of such gratitude that it can never be effaced from the book that records the past.] [*Par.*, p. 259]

[Though all those tongues which Polyhymnia and her sisters made....] [*Par.*, p. 261]

The argument concludes with surprising positiveness on a rather weak note:

> Had he tried, Chaucer could scarcely have helped recalling the passage, and it is difficult to resist the conclusion that the appeal to "Polymnia...with [her] sustres" represents the interweaving of another reminiscence of the *Paradiso*.

As Lowes correctly notes, however, "The figure of the ship in *Anelida*, 20, is as Skeat rightly designates it, 'a common simile.'" Indeed, this is one of the stock similes of the time and can be found, among other places, in the *Teseida*, the *Thebaid*, and the *Filostrato* and throughout Petrarch's sonnets.

With reference to the main statement on Polyhymnia, the following points should be noted:

1. As has been suggested previously, the relevance to the passage of the word *memoria* is highly questionable. Yet, even granting this for the moment, the argument is difficult to accept. Lowes notes that Polyhymnia, in certain works, is connected with memory and cites three points in Bode's *Scriptores rerum mythicarum*, as well as quoting from the *De genealogis deorum gentilium*,[13] which is ascribed to Boccaccio. But the connection here is

---

[13] "Quinta Polymnia, quasi polim [?], id est *multam memoriam faciens* dicimus: quia post capacitatem est *memoria* necessaria." [We call the fifth Muse Polymnia, as it were *polim* (?), that is, *causing much to be remembered*: because after talent, *memory* is needed.] Lowes's italics.

weak, and there is no mention that the usual interpretation of Polyhymnia—which is the way Dante uses her name in the *Paradiso*—is as the muse of sublime hymn, as her name would suggest. Scartazzini notes (Dante 1921:874, note to line 56): "*Polyhymnia*, the Muse *of many hymns*, who presides over lyric poetry. He names the Muse in order that the song that the Poet would wish would be of the highest lyric flight" (Scartazzini's italics). If Chaucer were summoning up the muse of memory or recall, he might just as well have invoked Clio. Any connection with "vois memorial" (line 18), as is suggested by the citations, is highly questionable, since the phrase would have to mean that Polyhymnia with her "sustres glade" sings with a voice that evokes memory or the power of recollection. Actually, the meaning is far more straightforward, if we accept the traditional interpretation of the muse: the muse of sublime poetry sings in a voice that is memorable (a word not in use before 1483), or a voice that is preserved in the hearer's memory because of its sublimity. To make a connection with something Dantesque, one would be forced to evolve a far more difficult and far less satisfactory reading than that which the traditional interpretation affords.

2. Toynbee's note is far more cautious than is apparent here. In speaking of the date at which Chaucer might have become familiar with the *Commedia*, he says (1909:xvi, n.1): "Cf. also the invocation (11. 15–20) with *Par.* xxiii. 56, and *Par.* i. 16, 36; but it is quite possible, of course, that these are mere coincidences." Toynbee evidently recognizes that the representation of a muse with her sisters is not unusual and that the coincidence in two separate works of the same muse is scarcely grounds for a parallel. We might note that Dante also used Clio, Urania, and Calliope. Indeed, it would have been odd if Chaucer had not hit on one of these at some time or another.

3. With still only the name of the muse in common, the two highly questionable passages previously discussed are assumed to give "practical conclusiveness."

4. There is not, of course, any indication what books Chaucer had open before him. The suggestion that Boethius and Boccaccio were actually consulted while Dante was only recalled allows one a tremendous leeway in making associations. In other words, it is felt that there should be a definitive visual text as a starting point for Chaucer's "association of ideas" but that there is to be no visual text of the *Commedia*, since this would not permit Chaucer's mind to range as freely as the argument demands. Without a visual text of some other author one would be unable to search the surrounding lines for a suggestive word, and with a visual *Commedia* one would have to account for the lack of contextual relevance. It is apparently for this reason that there is an insistence on total recall for Dante alone, all other writers or common knowledge of the time being largely excluded.

5. There is no contextual parallel here and sources for the image and the phraseology can be found, according to Scartazzini, in Virgil (*Aen.* 12.473ff.; *Georg.* 1.413) and also in Statius (*Achill.* 1.212ff.). The *amate fronde* here refers to the tree in which a bird has its nest and has nothing to do with the laurel beloved by Apollo or with Chaucer's one word, "laurer," but some common term or link is necessary to transfer the discussion over to the twenty-third canto of the *Paradiso*. With reference to Scartazzini's citation of Statius's *Achilleid*, Chaucer had stated in line 21 that "Stace" was his primary source, "and after him Corynne,"[14] though Chaucer's reference is, as Robinson has noted, to Statius's more famous work, the *Thebaid*.

6. The "etc." unfortunately covers the fact that Dante is asking the muse of sublime hymn to raise him to the grandeur of his subject, as the rest of the text would show.

---

[14] Shannon (1929:17–28), identifies "Corynne" as Ovid, but see Robinson, p. 789, for other suggestions.

To sum up Lowes's pattern: Boccaccio's *frondi amate* is like Dante's *amato alloro* in *Par.* 1, which is like Dante's *amate fronde* in *Par.* 23, in which there is reference to Polyhymnia, who, in turn, is connected in some instances with "memory," which is the word that Chaucer uses in a nearby line in the *Anelida*. The objections to this procedure are not only that every step of the pattern is open to the most fundamental doubts but that the very basis of absolute recall on which it must necessarily be founded is not itself established. With this kind of word association one can connect almost any text with any other and claim a *tertium quid*. That such complexity should lie behind the stylized invocation of a muse is, of course, possible, but the very fact that we are dealing with a conventional form should warn us from considering it only on the basis of certain selected sources examined *in vacuo*. The long tradition of poetic invocation in itself makes the claim of "inevitability" open to grave doubt. If one looks again at the original lines in Chaucer, it becomes apparent how far the association *in vacuo* may be carried.

Bethel: "211, 350: the phrase *the poynt of remembraunce* is a translation of *Purg.* XII, 20; *la puntura de la rimembranza*. See Klaeber, *Das Bild bei Ch.*, 122, 344; Lounsbury, *Studies*, II, 240: Chiarini, *Casa della Fama*, 15 n. Cf. *Kt. T.* A 1501."

So thirleth with the poynt of
    remembraunce
The swerd of sorowe.... [*Anel.* 211–12]

[But as the swan, I have herd seyd ful
    yore,
Ayeins his deth shal singen his
    penaunce,
So singe I here my destinee or chaunce,
How that Arcite Anelida so sore]
Hath thirled with the poynt of
    remembraunce. [*Anel.* 346–50]

Remembrynge on the poynt of his desir,
He on a courser, startlynge as the fir,
Is riden into the feeldes hym to pleye
    [*KnT* A 1501–1503]

[Speaking of those being purged of pride and made humble, Dante says:]

onde lì molte volte si ripiagne
    per la puntura de la rimembranza,
    che solo a' pii dà de le calcagne

Wherefore many a time men weep for them there, at the prick of memory that spurs only the faithful. [*Purg.*, p. 123]

In at least the first two instances—those from *Anelida and Arcite*—the striking phrase from *Purg.* 12 would appear to be a source of Chaucer's lines. While it is true that Dante uses the word *puntura* ("prick") as opposed to *punta*, the terms are almost interchangeable, and what slight difference there is in wording is easily accounted for by the change in the final image. Dante's metaphor is that of a spur and the goading of remembrance; Chaucer's even more forceful image is that of the sword of sorrow with its point of remembrance. Chaucer has enlarged Dante's image almost to the degree of a conceit, and this seems in keeping with the general "tendency to poetic diction" which Robinson (p. 304) sees as the conspicuous feature of the *Anelida*. Both Chaucer and Dante, I strongly suspect, are being influenced by the striking verses of Simeon to Mary at the Circumcision: "And thy own soul a sword shall pierce, that, out of many hearts, thoughts may be revealed" (Luke 2.35). The scene can be found literally interpreted in art and embroidery, with a sword suspended in air, its point aimed at the heart of the seated Mary, thus linking Simeon's statement with the sorrows of the Crucifixion. Withal, however, Chaucer's adaptation of the phrase seems accomplished, and the added complexity of the metaphor makes it as arresting an image as it had originally been in the *Commedia*.

The citation from *The Knight's Tale* does not seem to come from Dante's phrase. "Poynt," in the sense of "aim," "object," "purpose," or "end," is frequently so used by Chaucer. "Remembrynge on the poynt of his desir" has a coincidence of words but lacks completely the distinctive metaphor which, in the *Anelida*, very strongly suggests a source in the *Commedia*.

CHAPTER 4

The Parliament of Fowls

ITH ONE EXCEPTION, all the borrowings from Dante in the *Parliament of Fowls* are from the opening of the *Divina Commedia* and in all probability restricted to *Inf.* 2 and 3. The most outstanding adaptation that Chaucer makes is undoubtedly the one that occurs at the gate to the park, where he joins the solemn rhythms of the lines that Dante inscribes above the entrance to the Inferno and the poetic diction that typifies the love poetry of the French school of courtly writing. Recognizing these two elements as we do, we find the resulting verses almost macabre in their overtones. In Chaucer's audience, however, probably few could have seen the interwoven thread of Dante, though the park would have been at once familiar, as would such terms as "hertes hele," "well of grace," "Disdayn," and "Daunger." Whatever caused Chaucer to use the formidable lines from Dante at this point in his poem we shall probably never know, but the very interesting suggestion of Everett seems to merit consideration and has been cited in the course of the discussion of lines 123–40.

Dante's contribution is not sufficiently extensive to have any fundamental effect on the poem as a whole. Like *The House of Fame*, the *Parliament of Fowls* is basically in three parts, the first section being mainly the paraphrase of a classical work; the second, the centering of the dream vision on a particular scene or sequence; and the third, the application of this sequence to the occasion for which the poem was primarily written. While the Dantesque lines in the *Parliament of Fowls* occur at an important juncture of the poem (i.e., between the first and second sections), they do not vitally affect the understanding of the poem. At most one perhaps can draw a vague relationship between certain narrative facts: that, for example, in the one case the Dreamer is entering the park while in the other Dante is entering the Inferno; that in the *Parliament of Fowls* the Dreamer is in the process of losing his guide while in the *Commedia*, Dante is in the process of gaining one. Such parallels, however, are so general that they can hardly be pressed beyond this point, receiving, as they do, so little actual support in the text. Rather one must recognize that the principal Italian work in the *Parliament of Fowls* is the *Teseida* and that the influence of Boccaccio (beginning in the *Anelida* and culminating in the *Troilus*) is evident in the careful translation and reemphasis that Chaucer makes in *PF* 183–294. Dante's influence was never as extensive as Boccaccio's, but, as I hope to show in the course of this book, it served an entirely different function in the poetry of Chaucer.

The Parliament of Fowls

Bethel: "85f.: description of nightfall; closely modelled on *Inf.* II, 1–3."

The day gan faylen, and the derke nyght, That reveth bestes from here besynesse	Lo giorno se n'andava, e l'aere bruno togliea li animai che sono in terra da le fatiche loro

> Day was departing, and the dark air was taking the creatures on earth from their labors. [*Inf.*, p. 13]

The lines from Dante are very probably the original for the Chaucerian passage, though there is the additional source in Virgil, *Aen.* 9.224–25, as Robinson (p. 793) notes. Moore (1896:359), in connection with Dante, suggests: "Add perhaps viii, 26–7; iv, 522–532"—a reference which could apply to Chaucer as well.

Bethel: "109f., 112: words of Africanus; closely modelled on *Inf.* I, 83f."

But thus seyde he, "Thow hast the so wel born In lokynge of myn olde bok totorn, . . . That sumdel of thy labour wolde I quyte."	vagliami 'l lungo studio e 'l grande amore che m'ha fatto cercar lo tuo volume.

> May the long study and the great love that have made me search your volume avail me! [*Inf.*, p. 9]

This citation is somewhat less certain than the first. The suggested parallel is based on the idea that ardent study of a work is being rewarded by its author's serving as guide on a supernatural journey, but Dante is paying tribute to Virgil as poet, and his long-term zeal now makes him somewhat worthy of speaking to the Mantuan. Dante is not, as might be inferred, offering his past studies as reason for having Virgil guide him—which, of course, is a fact that has not yet been revealed. In addition, the parallel is even less close when it is recalled that Chaucer's dream visions often grow out of his reading in a book just before sleeping and that the subject of his reading not only serves as motivation for the whole vision but often injects itself directly into the first scene.

J. A. W. Bennett (1957:56–57): Lines 112–15 compared to *Purg.* 27.91–99, especially with reference to Cytherea.

Cytherea! thow blysful lady swete, That with thy fyrbrond dauntest whom the lest, And madest me this sweven for to mete, [Be thow myn helpe in this, for thow mayst best!]	Sì ruminando e sì mirando in quelle, mi prese il sonno; il sonno che sovente, anzi che 'l fatto sia, sa le novelle. Ne l'ora, credo, che de l'orïente prima raggiò nel monte Citerea che di foco d'amor par sempre ardente, giovane e bella in sogno mi parea donna vedere andar per una landa [cogliendo fiori; e cantando]

As I was thus ruminating, and thus gazing at them, sleep fell on me, sleep which often knows the news before the event.

In the hour, I think, when Cytherea, who seems always burning with the fire of love, first shone on the mountain from the east, I seemed to see in a dream a lady young and beautiful going through a meadow [gathering flowers and singing]. [*Purg.* p. 297]

On those occasions when he uses the name Cytherea, Chaucer usually refers to the heavenly Venus, though here the firebrand is the standard evocation of the lustful Venus, and one might conclude that the name Cytherea is used to separate her from the Venus that will appear as one of the deities of the temple. While Bennett states that "here Cytherea can hardly be anything but the benevolent planet of a christianized cosmology," we must recall that, as in *TC* 3.1255–57, we seem to balance delicately between the goddess figure (line 1255) and the "wel-willy planete" (line 1257). Bennett continues to associate too generally when he refers to "the cosmology that Chaucer, like Dante, accepts without question"; this is an *in vacuo* comparison that also brings together Scipio's "brekers of the lawe" (*PF* 79) and *Purg.* 26.83–84, which from Bennett's text would seem to relate to Guido Guinicelli but which, in context, actually refers to the hermaphrodites:

> [Nostro peccato fu ermafrodito;
>   ma perché] non servammo umana legge,
>   seguendo come bestie l'appetito.

[Our sin was hermaphrodite: but because] we observed not human law, following appetite like beasts. [*Purg.* p. 285]

Bennett then moves to *Purg.* 27.91–99, comparing it with Chaucer in even broader and more generalized terms (p. 27):

> Thus in Dante as in Chaucer we pass from an account of sleep after toil, to the credibility of dreams, then to the sight of the planet of love burning in the sky, and finally to the vision of an earthly paradise, whither Dante has been led by Virgil and Statius, even as Chaucer is now led into such a paradise by the great African.

Even *in vacuo* it is difficult to accept such an alignment of the two texts or to refrain from noting that Venus, as the morning star, is common knowledge and is too widespread in poetry to be so precisely located. Indeed, Pratt (1946:262–64) has shown conclusively that this is an instance of Chaucer's borrowing from himself, from *HF* 518–28, which itself goes back to *Inf.* 2, *Par.* 1, and *Teseida* 1 and 11.

Bethel: "123–140: The inscription above the park gates; suggestion from *Inf.* III, 1–9."

And over the gate, with lettres large iwroughte,	PER ME SI VA NE LA CITTÀ DOLENTE, PER ME SI VA NE L'ETTERNO DOLORE,
There were vers iwriten, as me thoughte,	PER ME SI VA TRA LA PERDUTA GENTE.
On eyther half, of ful gret difference,	GIUSTIZIA MOSSE IL MIO ALTO FATTORE;
Of which I shal now seyn the pleyn sentence:	FECEMI LA DIVINA PODESTATE, LA SOMMA SAPÏENZA E 'L PRIMO AMORE.
"Thorgh me men gon into that blysful place	

Of hertes hele and dedly woundes cure;
Thorgh me men gon unto the welle of
grace,
There grene and lusty May shal evere
endure.
This is the wey to al good aventure.
Be glad, thow redere, and thy sorwe
of-caste;
Al open am I – passe in, and sped thee
faste!"

"Thorgh me men gon," than spak that
other side,
"Unto the mortal strokes of the spere
Of which Disdayn and Daunger is the
gyde,
Ther nevere tre shal fruyt ne leves bere.
This strem yow ledeth to the sorweful
were
There as the fish in prysoun is al drye;
Th' eschewing is only the remedye!"

DINANZI A ME NON FUOR COSE CREATE
SE NON ETTERNE, E IO ETTERNO
DURO.
LASCIATE OGNE SPERANZA, VOI
CH'INTRATE.

[Queste parole di colore oscuro
vid' ïo scritte al sommo d'una porta]

THROUGH ME YOU ENTER THE WOEFUL CITY, / THROUGH ME YOU
ENTER ETERNAL GRIEF, / THROUGH ME YOU ENTER AMONG THE
LOST. / JUSTICE MOVED MY HIGH MAKER: / THE DIVINE POWER
MADE ME, / THE SUPREME WISDOM, AND THE PRIMAL LOVE. / BE-
FORE ME NOTHING WAS CREATED / IF NOT ETERNAL, AND ETERNAL I
ENDURE. / ABANDON EVERY HOPE, YOU WHO ENTER.

[These words of obscure color I saw inscribed over a portal.] [*Inf.*, p. 25]

To give an even firmer basis to the parallel, Bethel's ascription should have included lines
141–42, comparing them with *Inf.* 3.10–11. It would seem that line 141, "These vers of gold
and blak iwriten were," refers to the lines over the first (gold) side and the second (black)
respectively,[1] in which case there might be a parallel to the *paroli di colore oscuro* of *Inf.* 3.10.
As well there is the parallel of line 123 ("...over the gate, with lettres large iwroughte")
and *Inf.* 3.11 ("Vid' ïo scritte al sommo d'una porta").

Oddly enough, the verbal parallel is far stronger in the words inscribed in gold than it is
in those in black, though Dante's lines are certainly more in the spirit of the latter. There is
nothing, of course, in the black half that strictly parallels *Inf.* 2.1–9. The courtly "Disdayn
and Daunger" are a long way from the *etterno dolore* and *perduta gente* of Dante. Nor must
we consider that the idea for the entrance necessarily comes from the *Commedia*. As
Sypherd (1907:52) notes in connection with *The House of Fame*, inscriptions on gates are
found elsewhere: in the *Amorosa Visione* (cap. 2), in the *Roman de la Rose* (lines 21449–55),
and in Froissart's *La Cour de May* (lines 1140–43), where, on a tablet of gold is written,
"Flee, flee from here slanderers; traitors; envious, brazen liars; false proud ones; per-
jurors; deceivers of women." For the concept, then, it is likely that we are faced with a
convention of the paradisiacal garden of courtly love rather than with a unique source in

---

[1] Robinson (p. 793) also gives this interpretation.

Dante's *Inferno*. This in no way denies Dante's influence (which seems clearly demonstrable), but it does explain the presence of the gates at just this point in the *Parliament of Fowls*, as well as the presence of the terminology of polite, courtly love.

As with *The House of Fame*, we can quickly dismiss any idea of parody of the *Commedia*, since there were few Englishmen who would have been able to recognize lines even so outstanding as these. Nor is it at all likely that Chaucer was either unmoved or giving vent to any personal cynicism by merging Dante's arresting lines with the more stylized ideas of love poetry.[2] An interesting and not at all improbable explanation of this admittedly strange combination is offered by Everett (1955:43) in her "Chaucer's 'Good Ear'":

> Annotators usually refer to Dante's *Inferno* (iii. 1ff.). Yet, though there is an obvious similarity in that both passages record inscriptions over gates leading to non-earthly regions, the two passages are poles apart in true significance, and even more in feeling. The only other link between them is the similarity of their rhythm. I believe what haunted Chaucer's mind was the repeated "Per me si va..." of Dante's lines, and that it is this, perhaps more than anything else, that constitutes his "debt" to the Italian poet.

It is, indeed, noteworthy that the element that Chaucer has seized upon most persistently in his repetition of "Thorgh me men gon into" is just that phrase that, by virtue of its pounding cadence, stands out so sharply in the *Commedia*. Everett has perhaps passed too lightly over the other parallels that have been mentioned earlier in this entry, but the primary appeal to Chaucer might well have been in some such aspect as she has pointed out.

Bethel: "141–7: hesitancy in entering the park; cf. Dante's hesitancy before entering the Infernal portals, *Inf.* III, 12 ff."

These vers of gold and blak iwriten
    were,
Of whiche I gan astoned to beholde,
For with that oon encresede ay my fere,
And with that other gan myn herte
    bolde:
That oon me hette, that other dide me
    colde;
No wit hadde I, for errour, for to chese,
To entre or flen, or me to save or lese.

per ch'io: "Maestro, il senso lor m'è duro."
Ed elli a me, come persona accorta:
  "Qui si convien lasciare ogne sospetto;
  ogne viltà convien che qui sia morta...."

> whereupon I said, "Master, their meaning is hard for me." And he to me, as one who understands, "Here must all fear be left behind; here let all cowardice be dead...." [*Inf.*, p. 25]

The *Commedia* offers no verbal parallel and only a very limited contextual parallel to the Chaucerian passage. Actually there is no equivalent to Chaucer's hesitancy. Dante is expressing the fear that he, as a mortal, is subject to the strictures given by the words above the gate, for *duro* has the dual meaning of (slang) "rough" as well as "difficult." Chaucer, on the other hand, is genuinely hesitant because of the choice presented by the

---

[2] See Patch (1939:46–47), where such possibilities are taken up and disposed of effectively.

two paths which lie open to him. The development of this state of mind is found in the following eight lines, which show clearly that, while there may be hesitancy on the Dreamer's part, there is nothing comparable to the fear that has laid hold of Dante.

It would seem that any dependence here would have to be the result of the position of these lines; that is, the preceding passage echoes *Inf.* 3.1–11, and there are two verses twenty lines ahead (*PF* 169–70) that have strong verbal similarity to *Inf.* 3.19–21. If, therefore, these present lines were to be ascribed to Dante, it would have to be mainly on the basis of their relative position in the poem.

Bethel: "148–56: idea and part of phrasing from *Par.*, IV, 1–12."

Right as, betwixen adamauntes two	Intra due cibi, distanti e moventi
Of evene myght, a pece of yren set	d'un modo, prima si morria di fame,
Ne hath no myght to meve to ne fro—	che liber' omo l'un recasse ai denti;
For what that oon may hale, that other let—	sì si starebbe un agno intra due brame
	di fieri lupi, igualmente temendo;
Ferde I, that nyste whether me was bet	sì si starebbe un cane intra due dame:
To entre or leve, . . . [lines 148–53]	per che, s'i' mi tacea, me non riprendo,
	da li miei dubbi d'un modo sospinto,
	poi ch' era necessario, né commendo.

Between two foods, distant and appetizing in equal measure, a free man would die of hunger before he would bring one of them to his teeth. So would a lamb stand between two cravings of fierce wolves, in equal fear of both; so would a hound stand still between two hinds. Wherefore, if I was silent, urged in equal measure by my doubts, I neither blame nor commend myself, since it was of necessity. [*Par.*, p. 37]

There is no source here whatever, but rather an analogy based on common knowledge. This image is the classical *pons asinorum*, one of the most familiar and famous of the debating points of medieval and classical philosophy. Grandgent's note (p. 684) reads:

The familiar paradox later known as the Ass of Buridan, or the donkey and the two bales of hay, is here applied to Dante, who is eager to ask two questions and cannot decide which to put first. See Aristotle, *De Caelo*, II, xiii; St. Thomas, *Summa Theologiae*, Prime Secundae, Qu. xiii, Art. 6. Cf. *Met.*, V., 164–6.

The scientific image appears in *The Romaunt of the Rose*, lines 1182–86:

> Right as an adamaunt, iwys,
> Can drawen to hym sotylly
> The iren that is leid therby,
> So drawith folkes hertis, ywis,
> Silver and gold that yeven is.[3]

It seems hardly necessary to add that, beside the absence of verbal parallel, there is no contextual similarity either. Bethel's ascription continues:

---

[3] I am only pointing out here Chaucer's awareness of the scientific image. Fansler (1914:95) rightly rejects the *Roman* as the source of the lines in *The Parliament of Fowls*.

til Affrycan, my gide,
Me hente, and shof in at the gates wide,

And seyde, "It stondeth writen in thy
   face,
Thyn errour, though thow telle it not to
   me...."

Io mi tacea, ma 'l mio disir dipinto
   m'era nel viso, e 'l dimandar con ello,
   più caldo assai che per parlar distinto.

I was silent, but my desire was depicted on my face, and my questioning
with it, in warmer colors far than by distinct speech. [*Par.*, p. 37]

The parallel seems definitely questionable. Verbally, one's inner feelings being depicted
in his facial expression is common. There remains the coincidence of juxtaposition, but the
point of the *pons asinorum*—which, it must be remembered, does not originate with
Dante—is that the subject is reduced to complete neutrality, and the only way this can be
shown is by the facial expression. The resulting speechlessness, therefore, follows naturally from the paradox, and the two passages would have to show much more direct
verbal relationship to have that of Dante taken as the source.

Bethel: "157: idea probably from *Inf.* III, 14."
Robinson: "With ll. 157–58 cf. *Inf.*, III, 127–29."

But dred the not to come into this place,
For this writyng nys nothyng ment bi
   the

"Qui si convien lasciare ogne sospetto..."

"Quinci non passa mai anima buona;
   e però, se Caron di te si lagna,
   ben puoi sapere omai che 'l suo dir suona."

"Here must all fear be left behind...." [*Inf.*, p. 25]

"No good soul ever passes this way; therefore, if Charon complains of you,
you can now well understand the meaning of his words." [*Inf.*, p. 33]

Insofar as the first suggestion is concerned, there is certainly no verbal parallel here. The
only connection that one can suppose is that in both cases a kind of reassurance is being
given, but there are many points in world literature that could be so described. I am at a
loss to see either verbal or contextual similarity in Robinson's ascription. Sypherd, with
reference to *The House of Fame*, gives numerous instances of the element of fear in the
presence of a supernatural guide. He cites (p. 57), among others, the *Pélerinage de la vie
humaine*, Saint John (Rev. 1.17), the *Somnium Scipionis*,[4] Boethius, and Froissart. The
reaction is, of course, so natural that its absence would be more noteworthy than its
presence.

Bethel: "169f.: closely modelled on *Inf.* III, 19–21."

With that myn hand in his he tok anon,
Of which I confort caughte, and wente
   in faste.

E poi che la sua mano a la mia puose
   con lieto volto, ond' io mi confortai,
   mi mise dentro a le segrete cose.

---

[4] "No sooner did I know him [Africanus] than I shuddered. 'Draw near,' said he, 'with confidence, lay aside
your dread.'" Quoted in Sypherd, p. 57.

And when he had placed his hand on mine, with a cheerful look from which I took comfort, he led me among the secret things. [*Inf.*, p. 25]

This tercet is almost certainly the source of Chaucer's lines, since the verbal parallel is supported by the contextual parallel, as established in *PF* 123-25. Undoubtedly this is in the same tradition as *HF* 586-604, for which Sypherd, as we have seen, has found many parallels, remarking that "it is the most natural thing for the hero to feel fear and for his guide to comfort him." We might notice also that this same, very natural reaction is outlined in Virgil, *Aen.* 6.261-63, where the Sybil is speaking:

"...now, Aeneas, thou needest thy courage, now thy stout heart." So much she said, and plunged madly into the open cave; he, with fearless steps, keeps pace with his advancing guide.

Despite these many parallels, however, the strong verbal similarity to Dante, plus the contextual parallelism, makes the source of the lines almost certainly the tercet in *Inf.* 3.

Bethel: "*197f.: descriptive detail from *Par.* XIV, 118f., 121-3."

Of instruments of strenges in acord	E come giga e arpa, in tempra tesa
Herde I so pleye a ravyshyng swetnesse	di molte corde, fa dolce tintinno
	[a tal da cui la nota non è intesa,]
	così da' lumi che lì m'apparinno
	s'accogliea per la croce una melode
	che mi rapiva, sanza intender l'inno.

And as viol and harp, strung with many cords in harmony, chime sweetly for one who does not catch the tune, so from the lights that appeared to me there a melody gathered through the cross which held me rapt, though I followed not the hymn. [*Par.*, p. 161]

The ascription is very doubtful. The only thing in common is that both images are taken from music, but this hardly justifies the ascription of a source, even with the omission of the material that cannot be brought into any kind of relevance. The danger of comparison *in vacuo* can be seen here, for these lines are in the section (*PF* 183-294), which, as Robinson notes (p. 794), is "a close imitation of *Tes.*, vii, st. 51-60, 63-66, 61-62." It is not surprising, therefore, to find that stanza 53 of *Teseida* begins: "She seemed to hear, besides, delightful singing and every musical instrument" (McCoy, p. 177).

Bethel: "201-3: descriptive details summarizing *Purg.* XXVIII, 7-18."

Therwith a wynd, unnethe it myghte be lesse,	Un'aura dolce, sanza mutamento
Made in the leves grene a noyse softe	avere in sè, mi feria per la fronte
Acordaunt to the foules song alofte.	non di più colpo che soave vento;
	per cui le fronde, tremolando, pronte
	tutte quante piegavano a la parte
	u' la prim' ombra gitta il santo monte;
	non però dal loro esser dritto sparte
	tanto, che li augelletti per le cime
	lasciasser d'operare ogne lor arte;
	ma con piena letizia l'ore prime,
	cantando, ricevieno intra le foglie,
	che tenevan bordone a le sue rime

A sweet breeze that had no variation in itself was striking on my brow with the force only of a gentle wind, by which the fluttering boughs all bent freely toward the quarter where the holy mountain casts its first shadow; yet were they not so deflected from their upright state that the little birds among the tops ceased practicing all their arts, but singing they greeted the morning hours with full joy among the leaves, which kept such burden to their rhymes. [*Purg.*, p. 303]

While Chaucer is describing the traditional love garden on the basis of Boccaccio's lines in the *Teseida*, this particular passage is close to Dante's description of the earthly paradise. Birds singing in the trees and soft winds moving through the branches are, of course, part of the stock description of the *hortus conclusus*,[5] but the emphasis in both poems on the harmony attained by the singing birds and the sound of the gentle wind in the branches certainly seems to bring the two very close together.[6]

Bethel: "288–94: list of lovers partly from *Inf.* V, 58–69 (see also *Tes.* VII, 62)."

Semyramis, Candace, and Hercules, Biblis, Dido, Thisbe, and Piramus, Tristram, Isaude, Paris, and Achilles, Eleyne, Cleopatre, and Troylus, Silla, and ek the moder of Romulus: Alle these were peynted on that other syde, And al here love, and in what plyt they dyde.

". . . Ell' è Semiramìs, di cui si legge che succedette a Nino e fu sua sposa: tenne la terra che 'l Soldan corregge. L'altra è colei che s'ancise amorosa, e ruppe fede al cener di Sicheo; poi è Cleopatràs lussurïosa. Elena vedi, per cui tanto reo tempo si volse, e vedi 'l grande Achille, che con amore al fine combatteo. Vedi Parìs, Tristano"; e più di mille ombre mostrommi e nominommi a dito, ch'amor di nostra vita dipartille.

[5] Robinson (p. 794), after citing the *Teseida* as the basis of lines 183–294, says: "The Italian passage in turn goes back here and there to the Roman de la Rose; and it is hard to judge whether Chaucer recalled the French poem directly or only followed it at one remove. With 190–96 cf. RR, 1375–82, 661–70; with 204–10, RR, 20395ff., 20559ff., 20655f. . . . 201–3, which depart from Boccaccio, perhaps contain a reminiscence of Dante's Earthly Paradise (Purg., xxviii, 9–15)." Bethel's longer citation from the *Purgatorio* seems preferable, particularly in respect to *PF* 201 and *Purg.* 28.7–9, and *PF* 202–203 and *Purg.* 28.17–18. To Robinson's list one might add that *PF* 197–200 is similar to *RR* 670–85 and *BD* 301–20, in both of which there are long passages on the heavenly music of the singing birds. See also Bennett (1957:75–111).

[6] Boccaccio also describes the traditional singing of birds but does not lay primary stress on their harmony with the sound of the wind. For Chaucer to have gotten anything like this idea from *Teseida* 7.52, we would have to assume that he read the first *three* lines of Boccaccio's stanza together: "She heard birds of almost every kind singing through the branches. She watched them with delight, too" (McCoy, p. 127), and even then did not thoroughly understand them. It seems far more likely that he recognized in the *Teseida* the obvious use of the traditional paradisiac garden. For some examples and discussion of the *hortus conclusus*, see Robertson (1951:24–43), discussed in chap. 1. For other examples of the paradisiac garden, cf. Vincent of Beauvais, *Speculum historiale* (14.73), bk. 24, chap. 120, the vision of Saint Preiectus, and also bk. 30, chaps. 6–10, "De novicio cisterciensi temptato a Sathana. Euit in Anglia eo tempore" (i.e., ca. 1160), particularly chap. 7. The traditional fusion of the garden of love and the earthly paradise can probably be traced back to folk etymology and the ambiguity of *deliciae* which encompasses the various stages between delight and voluptuousness as well as meaning, by metonymy, one's sweetheart or beloved. See Vincent of Beauvais, *Speculum historiale*, bk. 2, chap. 63, for the location, description, and etymology of paradise. For the vast range of graphic representations of the *hortus conclusus*, see particularly van Marle (1931–32, passim, esp. vol. 1, chap. 9, pp. 457–76, figs. 452–75, and vol. 2, chap. 6, pp. 415–51, figs. 444–83. For background see Curtius 1953 and Giamatti 1966, esp. pp. 11–119.

"She is Semiramis, of whom we read that she succeeded Ninus and had been his wife: she held the land the Sultan rules. The next is she who slew herself for love and broke faith to the ashes of Sichaeus; next is wanton Cleopatra. See Helen, for whom so many years of ill revolved; and see the great Achilles, who fought at the last with love. See Paris, Tristan," and more than a thousand shades whom love had parted from our life he showed me, pointing them out and naming them. [*Inf.*, p. 51]

This list has been used as a case in point to show how Chaucer "incessantly fuses two or more bits of his reading into a *tertium quid*" (Lowes 1917a:706). On the basis of Boccaccio and Dante alone, says Lowes (p. 707), "What has happened is clear at a glance"—Chaucer read the stanza in the *Teseida*, the third line of which "is echoing Dante," and this recalls the canto of Dante to his memory: "The result is that he combines Boccaccio's and Dante's lists into one. Not only is every lover in the *Teseide* included (through one at least of each pair), *but every name in Dante's list as well*" (Lowes's italics). The assumption that is the foundation of this view is that Chaucer is capable of total recall; that is, given the suggested echoing of Dante's passage, Chaucer would be able to call to mind the precise list of names in *Inf.* 5 and a specific line therein. It is not that one doubts that Chaucer read this passage—there is later evidence to prove that he did—but rather one wonders whether the assumption of total recall does not avoid the implications of direct consultation of the text and make the creative process more limited and mechanical than it would actually seem to be.

A comparison of Chaucer's text with his primary source—Boccaccio's *Teseida*—will perhaps prove illuminating in the present situation. On closer examination of the passage in the *Parliament of Fowls* we find that there are not sixteen but eighteen names, since Chaucer begins listing the depicted martyrs of love three lines before the point usually cited (lines 285–87):

> of which [maydenes] I touche shal
> A fewe, as of Calyxte and Athalante,
> And many a mayde of which the name I wante.

Boccaccio's stanza preceding the one mentioned is worth giving as well, since it offers not only the source for these lovers (which are *not* "in Dante's list") but the context for Chaucer's passage as well (*Teseida* 7.61–62, McCoy, p. 178):

> She saw there the bows of many of Diana's devotees hung up and broken. Among these was that of Callisto who was transformed into the northern Bear. And there were the apples of the disdainful Atalanta who excelled in running, and the weapons, also, of that other haughty one who gave birth to comely Parthenopaeus, grandson of the Calydonian Oeneus.
> She saw stories painted everywhere, and among these, traced with consummate skill, she saw all the works of the bride of Ninus made clear. She saw Pyramus and Thisbe and the mulberries already stained, at the foot of the wall. She saw the great Hercules on the lap of Iole, and sorrowful Byblis piteously on her way to entreat Caunus.

These stanzas, describing the paintings that Palemone's prayer sees in the temple of Venus, supply seven of the eighteen lovers mentioned by Chaucer. Now, of those remaining, six are unique to Dante's list—Dido, Tristram, Paris, Helen, Achilles, and Cleopatra—but these are the most famous lovers of medieval literature, and Chaucer would scarcely have needed any source other than common knowledge to "recall" them. There is, then, not one unusual name (e.g., Candace, Rhea, Silva, Silla, or Troilus) outside Boccaccio's list that is used by Dante and that would serve as a positive indication of source. Most outstanding of all, however, is the absence—supposing that Chaucer were using the *Commedia*—of Dante's greatest example of lovers, Paolo and Francesca da Rimini, the main subjects of this canto. Eminently suited as they are to the context, these two memorable lovers are conspicuous by their absence from Chaucer's verses.

Boccaccio may have started Chaucer thinking, but his thought would seem to have ranged wider than a simple *primus* and *secundus* leading to a *tertium quid*. Chaucer, who had already given a fair array of lovers in *The Book of the Duchess* (Paris and Helen, Dido and Aeneas, Echo and Narcissus, Sampson and Delilah, Phylis and Demophon, among others) and in *The House of Fame* (Dido and Aeneas, Breseyda and Achilles, Paris and Oenone, Jason and Isiphile, Jason and Medea, Hercules and Dyanira, Theseus and "Adriane," and others) was no novice dependent on sources for such famous names as the half dozen that are found to be (upon comparison with Boccaccio's list) in *Inf.* 5. If a source is necessary, the medieval versions of Ovid could have supplied at least seventeen of the eighteen names, and at least fourteen are found—many with their complete "fable"—in the *Ovide moralisé*. Lowes's later remarks (1934:132) on the catalogue of names in *The House of Fame* seem perfectly appropriate in the present case. Speaking of the first book of *The House of Fame*, he says, "The account of Dido's suicide is followed by a stock list of faithless lovers, drawn in part, either directly or by way of Machaut, from the *Ovide Moralisé*." The *Parliament of Fowls* passage can, I believe, be viewed in much the same way, for, although we might not be able to point to one specific source, it is more likely that Chaucer's stock list of lovers developed from Boccaccio's stanzas on the basis of common knowledge and reading in the standard classical authors.[7]

Bethel: "*442: simile possibly from *Par.* XXII, 55-7; doubtful."

Ryght as the freshe, rede rose newe	così m'ha dilatata mia fidanza, come 'l sol fa la rosa quando aperta tanto divien quant' ell' ha di possanza.

    [Your affection and good seeming] have expanded my confidence as the sun does the rose when it opens to its fullest bloom. [*Par.*, p. 249]

Even if an image as common as Chaucer's needed a source, there does certainly not appear to be any parallel here.

---

[7] There is a further attempt to establish this list by relating it to the mention of Semiramis in *MkT* B[2] 2477 (Nero) and *MLT* B[1] 358-59. In the former, at least, it is certainly *Inf.* 5.56 which supplies the phrase applied to Nero. No connection is made, however, between the mention of only the name in *The Parliament of Fowls* (which undoubtedly can be derived from *Teseida* 7.62) and the other, slightly more extended, remarks in *The Canterbury Tales*. Moreover, these later references to Semiramis (even granting the source of both of them in Dante) have nothing to do with *The Parliament of Fowls* unless we are to assume that (1) Chaucer could only have known of Semiramis from Dante and would not have recognized Boccaccio's allusion to her, and (2) there is no time lapse between the writing of *The Parliament of Fowls*, *The Monk's Tale*, and *The Man of Law's Tale*, so that a single instance of recall binds the allusions in a sort of mutual support. As will be pointed out below (*MLT* B[1] 358-59), Semiramis was a traditional symbol in the Middle Ages; and Chaucer demonstrates (by his most extended reference to her in *LGW* 707-09) that he knew at least the remarks in the *Metamorphoses* on Semiramis.

Bethel: "*518: line closely modelled on *Purg.* X, 57."

For office uncommytted ofte anoyeth   per che si teme officio non commesso.

   because of which men fear an office not given in charge. [*Purg.*, p. 103]

There is undoubtedly a close verbal parallel, though there is no contextual relationship whatever. Robinson (p. 796) offers an explanation by noting that this line is "a proverb equivalent to 'Proffered service stinketh'; cf. *CYT*, VIII, 1066n," and this, in turn, states that "Skeat notes several parallels, . . . EE Prov., p. 121, no. 285; cf. Haeckel, p. 47, no. 161" (p. 761). The proverb is also listed in Whiting (1934:40). Although there is a close verbal parallelism, it is undoubtedly true that in both cases the remarks are sufficiently sententious and divorced from their context to have the distinct air of the proverb.

CHAPTER 5

Troilus and Criseyde

ROILUS AND CRISEYDE in two ways marks a new development in Chaucer's use of Dante. First, the scope of his borrowings seems to have widened considerably. Unlike the earlier occasional poems in which Chaucer tended to confine himself mainly to the opening or closing cantos of the *Commedia*'s three sections (and particularly the first three cantos of the *Inferno*), and unlike those instances where he had taken a single scene and converted it totally to his narrative purpose, he now began to range somewhat more freely through Dante's poem, though the actual amount that he borrowed (in number of lines) does not increase to any noticeable degree.

Even more important than this wider range of the borrowings is the appearance of what may best be described as short units of religious lyrics translated from Dante. Chaucer, it seems, had now begun to use his sources for concepts as well as for phrases,[1] and apparently he turned to Dante for support in verses expressing the mystical quality of religion in much the same way that he turned to Boethius for higher philosophy and to Boccaccio for narrative stimulus. Borrowings at the level of the word or the image continued, but, to quote Lowes's perceptive analysis of this situation (1934:190; see also p. 236):

> Chaucer, when he ended the *Troilus*, was profoundly moved, and he turns, as so often at moments of heightened feeling, to the great passage in Dante, and to the Offices and hymns of the Church. And his sublime invocation is compact of both. For its opening is a word by word rendering of three lines in one of the loftiest cantos of the Paradiso:

> > Quell' uno e due e tre che sempre vive,
> > E regna sempre in tre e due ed uno,
> > Non circonscritto, e tutto circonscrive.

> And its close breathes the very spirit of the beautiful Office of the Virgin.

Troilus is, indeed, an example of what has been aptly termed "the mastered art" (Lowes's title for his chapter on *Troilus*) and the deeper understanding with which Chaucer uses Dante is an additional manifestation of this mastery. In these instances Chaucer does not

---

[1] This does not mean that Chaucer had not understood the works he had previously read, but rather that he was now consciously borrowing from them their concepts as well as their words. Indeed, there is reason to believe that the Marian prayer of Saint Bernard (*Par.* 33), which is echoed in *TC* 3.1261–67 and used more directly in *PrP* B² 1664–70 and *SNP* G 36–56, might have early been committed to memory. See the discussion in the introductory remarks to *CT* and under *PrT* 1664–70.

merely take over a few words, or a felicitous phrase; instead, he seems to add to his poem a further stratum of understanding. This he accomplishes by two means: first, by giving a passage of sufficient length that the original writer's expressed thought can be seen, and, second, by using a passage with sufficiently familiar terminology that its implications are readily apparent. Whether Chaucer had for some time thought of Dante as the great Christian lyricist of his era is probably one more question to which we shall never be able to give a definitive answer, but the fact remains that when he wished to express the intensity of the emotional adoration of religion—particularly Marian adoration—he blended Dante's lyricism with the offices of the church.

It is tempting to think that this more sensitive use of Dante became *the* vital factor in Chaucer's poetry as a whole, but there would appear to be no support for this in the poetry itself. The concepts of Fortune and courtly love in *Troilus* seem to be far closer, respectively, to Boethius (in the first instance) and the generally held view (in the second) than to Dante, and, indeed, in each instance they lack the unique resolution that so clearly marks Dante's interpretation. What must be recognized is that the maturer view that Chaucer took toward Dante in *Troilus* seems to apply to his other sources also, and might well have been evoked by the greater scope and complexity of the poem itself.

Whether there was a rereading, a revaluation, or simply a fuller employment of the *Commedia*, the result seems to indicate that Chaucer thought of Dante, along with the offices of the church, when writing the short, independent lyrics of a devotional nature that appear in *Troilus* 3.1262 and 5.1863 and at certain points in *The Canterbury Tales*. The occasional use of a phrase or an image continues, but the consistent nature of these more extended borrowings seems to show that Chaucer had begun to develop a more definite viewpoint toward Dante's thought and writing.

Troilus and Criseyde

Book 1

Bethel: "*1: phrase possibly from *Purg.* XXII, 56."

The double sorwe of Troilus to tellen   ["Or quando tu cantasti le crude armi]
                                                                 de la doppia trestizia di Giocasta, . . ."

          ["Now, when you sang of the cruel strife] of Jocasta's twofold sorrow . . ."
[*Purg.*, p. 239]

Taking into account the contextual differences, Robinson (1957:814) notes the line from Dante, adding that it is "a phrase which Chaucer may have recalled, though the passages are otherwise quite dissimilar." Grandgent (Dante 1933:523) gives the accepted meaning of the lines from Dante as follows: "By the twofold affliction of Jocasta" is meant her two sons Eteocles and Polynices, whose strife and death are related in the 11th book of the *Thebaid*." The temperate approach of both Robinson and Bethel seems healthy. The uniqueness of the verbal parallel makes it tempting to assign Dante as the source, but the complete lack of contextual parallel or reference makes the caution of the two scholars justified. "Possibly" seems an apt judgment.

Bethel: "6–14: invocation to Tisiphone; phraseology influenced by Dante's description of the Furies, *Inf.* IX, 34–51."

Thesiphone, thow help me for t'endite
Thise woful vers, that wepen as I write.

To the clepe I, thow goddesse of
    torment,
Thow cruwel Furie, sorwynge evere yn
    peyne,
Help me, that am the sorwful
    instrument,
That helpeth loveres, as I kan, to
    pleyne.
For wel sit it, the sothe for to seyne,
A woful wight to han a drery feere,
And to a sorwful tale, a sory chere.

E altro disse, ma non l'ho a mente;
    però che l'occhio m'avea tutto tratto
    ver' l'alta torre a la cima rovente,
dove in un punto furon dritte ratto
    tre furïe infernal di sangue tinte,
    che membra feminine avieno e atto,
e con idre verdissime eran cinte;
    serpentelli e ceraste avien per crine,
    onde le fiere tempie erano avvinte.
E quei, che ben conobbe le meschine
    de la regina de l'etterno pianto,
    "Guarda," mi disse, "le feroci Erine.
Quest' è Megera dal sinistro canto;
    quella che piange dal destro è Aletto;
    Tesifón è nel mezzo"; e tacque a tanto.
Con l'unghie si fendea ciascuna il petto;
    battiensi a palme e gridavan sì alto,
    ch'i' mi strinsi al poeta per sospetto.
["Vegna Medusa: sì 'l farem di smalto,"
    dicevan tutte riguardando in giuso;
    "mal non vengiammo in Tesëo l'assalto."]

And more he said, but I have it not in memory, for my eye had wholly drawn me to the high tower with the glowing summit, where all at once three hellish blood-stained Furies had instantly risen up. They had the limbs and bearing of women, and they were girt with greenest hydras. For hair they had little serpents and cerastes bound about their savage temples. And he, who well recognized the handmaids of the queen of eternal lamentation, said to me, "See the fierce Erinyes! That is Megaera on the left; she that wails on the right is Alecto; Tisiphone is in the middle"; and with that he was silent. Each was tearing her breast with her nails; and they were beating themselves with their hands, and crying out so loudly that in fear I pressed close to the poet.

["Let Medusa come and we'll turn him to stone," they all cried, looking downward. "Poorly did we avenge the assault of Theseus."] [*Inf.*, pp. 91, 93]

First of all, the comparison is a little too generous in the number of lines assigned. It would appear, according to the notation, that there are seven lines of Chaucer that can be given a parallel in Dante. Closer inspection, however, would seem to show that there are fewer than two lines here, namely "Thesiphone, . . . / thow goddesse of torment / Thow cruel Furie, sorwynge evere yn peyne." The same is true of the Dante passage, in which the first tercet is certainly not a part of any possible parallel. We come down, therefore, to possible verbal or referential parallels in the name of the Fury and the line and a half pointed out just above.

As for verbal dependence, even the briefest comparison of the two passages shows that there are no parallels save in the name Thesiphone, and Shannon (1929:121) shows that "Chaucer very properly invokes the aid of one of the Furies, Tisiphone (Thesiphone), for this tale is to be one of Love's tragedies. As this scrap of classical mythology was so well known, it is perhaps useless to try to identify its source, though Virgil in Aeneid, vi, 555, and 571, and x, 76,[2] refers to Thesiphone by name."

Are there any other points on which a similarity could be based? The phrase "goddesse of torment" is certainly not in the Dante passage but is a part of a classical tradition, as is the adjective "cruwel." We are left, therefore, with the phrase "sorwynge evere yn peyne"; Dante's Furies, however, though they might be "yn peyne," are most certainly not "sorwynge." Indeed, one must recall the context of the passage in the *Commedia* to appreciate what it is that the Furies are doing. Dante is still in the fifth circle, where the sin of anger, *rancor*, or *furor*, is being punished, and, as always in the *Commedia*, the occupants of a zone exemplify the vice or virtue of their location. The tercet that follows the lines given by Bethel shows that the Furies that inhabit the City of Dis not only are not "sorwynge" but can be thought of as being "yn peyne" only in the broadest sense that all the other tormentors of the Inferno are "yn peyne," namely, that they have fallen from grace. If Dante's Furies were "sorwynge," there would be no reason for the poet to say "i' mi strinsi al poeta per sospetto." The following tercet shows clearly that the Furies are not being tortured or tormented; they are tearing at themselves in an ecstasy of anger:

> "Vegna Medusa: sì 'l farem di smalto,"
> dicevan tutte riguardando in giuso;
> "mal non vengiammo in Teseo l'assalto."

"Let Medusa come and we'll turn him [the intruder, Dante] to stone," they all cried, looking downward. "Poorly did we avenge the assault of Theseus."

The reference here is, of course, to the rescue of Theseus from the underworld (i.e., out of the control of *medieval* Furies) by Hercules in the *Aeneid* (6.392ff). If Alecto is weeping (line 48), then, it is not from grief but from the frustrated anger of not being able to tear apart the intruders. It becomes evident, therefore, that the phrase "sorwynge evere yn peyne" has little relevance to the condition of Dante's Furies, once it is looked at in context.

The reason that I emphasize this to such a degree is that it is the basis for Lowes's ascription of this and other passages to Dante. He must establish a unique quality common to both Chaucer and Dante, and this he takes to be the "torture undergone by the Furies" (Lowes 1917a:718–19). Lowes puts in this point in an attempt to counterbalance the very strong classical, or traditional, source of the lines. In full he states:

> It is very true that Chaucer must have been familiar, also, with the phrases "*tristis* Erinys,"[3] "*tristes* Dirae,"[4] "*tristes* Furiae,"[5] but the epithet *tristis* is scarcely sufficient to account for his significant emphasis upon the torture undergone by the Furies themselves and upon their lamentations under it. The explanation lies in the fact that Chaucer's conception of the Furies is colored throughout by Dante's.

The validity of this statement can be questioned. First, as has been shown above, the Furies are not being tortured in the passage which has been cited from Dante and which, in the final analysis, is the only link that is offered between Chaucer and Dante. That the Furies were a standard part of infernal description Lowes himself points out by citing Jean

---

[2] This seems to be a misprint. Should it not be "761," the line reading: "Pallida Tisiphone media inter millia saevit"?

[3] "*Aen.*, II, 337; *Her.*, VI, 45: *De Raptu*, I, 225" (Lowes's note and italics).

[4] "*Aen.*, VIII, 701" (Lowes's note and italics).

[5] "*De Raptu*, II, 219" (Lowes's note and italics).

de Meun,[6] but he fails to note the rather significant passage that Spencer (1927:185) was to bring in when discussing this particular passage:

> Chaucer, in translating Boethius, had himself written as follows (Boethius is describing the effect of Orpheus' music upon the inhabitants of hell):[7] "and the three goddesses, Furies, and vengeresses of felonyes, that tormenten and agasten the sowles by anoy, woxen sorwful and sory, and wepen teres for pity."

As I shall attempt to point out in dealing with the "Herenus queen" passage in *The Complaint unto Pity*, the process of assimilating the classical into the Christian world often led to some odd confusions and compromises. The merging of Tartarus into hell should not be surprising. What is surprising is that scholars in general have failed to take into account the directly contradictory evidence of the *Commedia*'s context.

Bethel: "*15: Papal title possibly derived from *Inf.* XV, 112; doubtful."

For I, that God of Loves servantz serve   colui potei che dal servo de' servi
                                                    [fu trasmutato d'Arno in Bacchiglione]

him who [was transferred] by the Servant of Servants [from Arno to Bacchiglione] [*Inf.*, p. 161]

Since the position of the pope as *servus servorum Dei* was such common knowledge, it is surprising to see this put down as a parallel, and even more so in the light of Bethel's statement in his text (p. 115):

> It may seem absurd to remark that Chaucer may have seen the papal title "servus servorum Dei," which he adapts in *Troil.* I, 15, and uses with its proper application in the *Parson's Tale*, I. 773, in *Inf.* XV, 112. The title was, of course, generally known; cf. Boccaccio, *Il Comento sopra la Commedia di Dante* (Mantier), note on *Inf.* XV, 112. Cf. F. N. Robinson, *Speculum* I, 465 (Oct. 1926).

I agree with Bethel's first evaluation, but not his second; the validity of such an ascription seems not "doubtful" but "absurd."

Bethel: "*568f.: from Dante (cf. *e.g.*, Inf. XV, 46f.; XXI,, 82; XXXII, 76f.) appear to have come such deliberate forms of expression as the balancing of alternatives here and in the following lines; *Troil.* IV, 388; *Cant. T.*, Gen. Prol., A 844; *Kt. T.*, A 1074, 1465; *Nun's P.'s T.*, B 4189; *Clerk's T.*, E 812; *Merch. T.*, E 1967–9; *Frank. T.*, F 1508; *Pars. T.*, I 574."

"What cas," quod Troilus, "or what   El cominciò: "Qual fortuna o destino
    aventure   anzi l'ultimo dì qua giù ti mena?..." [*Inf.*
Hath gided the to sen me   15.46–47]
    langwisshinge...?" [*TC* 1.568–69]

---

[6] "...the Furies are 'en enfer justicières Gardes félonesses et fières' ['in hell the female judges, cruel and fierce keepers']; they are 'les trois ribaudes félonesses, Des félonies vengeresses' ['the three cruel ruffians, avengers of felonies'], and their functions are clear: 'Ces trois en enfer vous atendent; Ceus lient, batent, fustent, pendent, Hurtent, hercent, escorchent, foulent, Noient, ardent, greillent et boulent'" ['"These three await you in hell; these bind, beat, cudgel, hang, strike, tear, flay, trample, drown, burn, roast, and boil'"] (Lowes, p. 718).

[7] "*De Cons. Phil.*, iii, met 12. 37ff." (Spencer's note).

Straunger than this, thorugh cas or
   aventure [*TC* 4.388]

Were it by aventure, or sort, or cas
[The sothe is this, the cut fil to the
   Knyght] [*GP* A 844–45]

And so bifel, by aventure or cas [*KnT* A
   1074]

Were it by aventure or destynee [*KnT* A
   1465]

[That oother man was logged wel
   ynough,]
As was his aventure or his fortune [*NPT*
   B² 4188–89]

The strook of Fortune or of aventure
   [*ClT* E 812]

Were it by destynee or aventure,
Were it by influence or by nature,
Or constellacion, that in swich estaat
[The hevene stood, that tyme fortunaat
Was for to putte a bille of Venus werkes]
   [*MerT* E 1967–71]

But thus they mette, of aventure or
   grace [*FranT* F 1508]

Eek if a man, by caas or aventure, shete
an arwe, or caste a stoon, with which he
sleeth a man, he is homycide. [*ParsT* I
574]

sanza voler divino e fato destro [*Inf.* 21.82]

se voler fu o destino o fortuna
non so [*Inf.* 32.76–77]

   He began: "What chance or destiny brings
you down here before your last day . . . ?"
[*Inf.*, p. 155]

without divine will and propitious fate [*Inf.*,
p. 219]

whether it was will or fate or chance I do not
know [*Inf.*, p. 343]

Bethel's list is composed principally of his own and Tatlock's suggestions (1905:371–72) of Dantesque influence, and the claims of the latter have been shown by Jefferson (1917:60–65) to have a more likely source in Boethius. Indeed, Jefferson even has one section devoted to "Cas or Aventure or Destinee, Etc." (pp. 62–65), but he is much closer to the truth, it seems, when he gives a broader view, stating (p. 65) that "the Stoics and Neoplatonists, as well as Boethius, had disputed over the question of the relationship of Providence, destiny, and chance; but of these discussions it is not likely that Chaucer had first hand knowledge." As a matter of fact, this problem, this opposition of terms (to which Bethel has made reference), was, and had been, a standard theme from classical times. Virgil, in *Aen.* 6.531–33, sets the two in the usual relationship: ". . . qui . . . casus, . . . quae . . . fortuna. . . ." The ramifications of the problem run throughout the discussion of Fortune,[8] as Patch has pointed out; they are taken up frequently in Saint Thomas's *Summa Theologica* and, throughout the medieval period, pass like a patterning thread through the main fabric of theological inquiry. H. S. Bennett (1948:27–28) sums up the major issue of which this was a part:

[8] See remarks on that poem below.

On one religious matter there was certainly "endless agitation." From the earliest times the problem of determinism and of man's free will had occupied theologians, and the question was very much alive in Chaucer's time, for, while he was a youth, Bishop Bradwardine in his *De Causa Dei* had stirred the troubled waters afresh. In the *Nun's Priest's Tale*, and in the revised version of *Troilus and Criseyde*, Chaucer shows his interest in the matter....

These subtle arguments were not easily apprehended, but had a similar attraction for thoughtful men to those raised in our day by relativity or dialectical materialism.... Chaucer and his contemporaries exercised their minds on this baffling problem as part of their attempt to understand the ways of God and the place of man in the scheme of things.... The doctrine of *gentilesse*, the nature of chance, the problem of free will are all dealt with by Boethius and helped to form Chaucer's thought on these matters, and to guide him in some of the deepest passages of the *Knight's Tale* and *Troilus and Criseyde*.[9]

Bennett's parallel to discussions of relativity or dialectical materialism is a pertinent one and is borne out by his subsequent remark (p. 27): "Few are fitted to understand these things, but that does not preclude many from trying."

The important point here, finally, is that this question of "hap" or "grace," or "cas" or "aventure," or "sort" or "destynee," or "Fortune" or "influence" was a problem of the era, one in which there was general discussion by almost every trained mind, one which stretches back through the Middle Ages to classical times. Indeed, the alternatives might well have been alluded to by one totally indifferent to theological discussion. Chaucer uses one such pair in *The Book of the Duchess*, a poem written, it will be recalled, before he read Dante. The man in black, describing the moment when he first "sawgh oon / That was lyk noon of the route," says (lines 810–11):

> Shal I clepe hyt hap other grace
> That broght me there?

While Chaucer's concepts of the problem seem to have a number of affinities to those of Boethius, there is nothing in the mere handling of the topic nor in the "balancing of alternatives" (to use Bethel's phrase) that connects it with Dante save—as has been mentioned above—by way of *zeitgeist*.

Bethel: "*871f.: idea of reluctance to enter Hell possibly suggested by *Inf.* III, 12ff.; doubtful."

But tho gan sely Troilus for to quake	per ch'io: "Maestro, il senso lor m'è duro."
As though men sholde han led hym into helle	Ed elli a me, come persona accorta: "Qui si convien lasciare ogne sospetto...."

   ...whereupon I said, "Master, their meaning is hard for me." And he to me, as one who understands, "Here must all fear be left behind..." [*Inf.*, p. 25]

There is neither verbal nor contextual parallel. Whether the Chaucerian simile implies a living person or a dead soul making this infernal entry, the reaction is too natural to allow anything but the closest of parallels to be accepted as a source.

---

[9] For the influence of Augustine and Boethius on historical and fictional narrative, see Pickering 1980.

Bethel: "*894–96: these lines show assimilation of Dante's discussion of the nature of 'love' *Purg.* XVII (esp. 94–105) and XVIII (esp. 34ff.)."

So oughtest thou, for nought but good
    it is
To loven wel, and in a worthy place;
The oughte nat to clepe it hap, but
    grace.

["Né creator né creatura mai,"
  cominciò el, "figliuol, fu sanza amore,
  o naturale o d'animo; e tu 'l sai.]
Lo naturale è sempre sanza errore,
  ma l'altro puote errar per malo obietto
  o per troppo o per poco di vigore.
Mentre ch'elli è nel primo ben diretto,
  e ne' secondi sé stesso misura,
  esser non può cagion di mal diletto;
ma quando al mal si torce, o con più cura
  o con men che non dee corre nel bene,
  contra 'l fattore adovra sua fattura.
Quinci comprender puoi ch'esser convene
  amor sementa in voi d'ogne virtute
  e d'ogne operazion che merta pene...."
    [*Purg.* 17.91–105]

Or ti puote apparer quant' è nascosa
  la veritate a la gente ch'avvera
  ciascun amore in sé laudabil cosa [*Purg.*
  18.34–36]

He began: "Neither Creator nor creature, my son, was ever without love, either natural or of the mind, and this you know. The natural is always without error; but the other may err either through an evil object, or through too much or too little vigor. While it is directed on the Primal Good, and on secondary goods observes right measure, it cannot be the cause of sinful pleasure. But when it is turned awry to evil, or speeds to good with more zeal, or with less, than it ought, against the Creator works His creature. Hence you can comprehend that love must needs be the seed in you of every virtue and of every action deserving punishment...." [*Purg.*, p. 185]

Now it may be apparent to you how far the truth is hidden from the people who aver that every love is praiseworthy in itself. [*Purg.*, p. 191]

First, we must recognize that there are no verbal parallels here. Next, we must see whether there is any parallel in thought or doctrine. In the text of his thesis Bethel, citing the whole of Chaucer's next stanza (*TC* 1.897–903) in an attempt to make connection with Dante, seems to push the otherwise natural association of pity and virtue too far:

"And also thynk, and therwith glade the,
That sith thy lady *vertuous* is al,
So folweth it that there is some *pitee*
Amonges alle thise other in general;
And forthi se that thow in special
Requere nat that is ayeyns hyre name,
For vertu streccheth nat hym self to shame."[10]

[10] Bethel's italics. See, however, Kittredge 1915:69, where the following lines from the *Remède de Fortune* (1671–83) are compared with *TC* 1.897–900: "*Encore dois tu penser aussi / Pour toy mettre hors de soussi, / Non mie*

The connection of pity and virtue is a constant element of courtly-love lyric, as even the most cursory inspection shows.[11] Bethel's plan demands, however, that he equate first pity and virtue and then love and pity. Having "established" these equivalences (and it is this that I wish to investigate further), he then uses the terms interchangeably as bases for ascriptions to Dante.

The attempt to establish the total equivalence of love and pity is the principal basis for Bethel's claim for Dantesque parallels on this topic, "the nature of love." To do this, Bethel attempts to connect the two terms by the conjunction "or." For example, in looking at one specific line in Boccaccio (*Filostrato* 2.23) but at Dante in general, Bethel—on the assumption that the thought in Chaucer must come from one of these two sources only—arrives at the conclusion (p. 144) that

> the causal relationship, then, which Chaucer asserts between pity and virtue is not only not derived from Boccaccio but is thoroughly opposed to the sentiments which the Italian poet's Pandaro utters. On the other hand, in Dante virtue is the *sine qua non* of "gentilesse," and "gentilesse" is associated with love *or* pity as in the line of which Chaucer was so fond; the thought of the second stanza here quoted derives, it seems to me from Dante, and very probably from no one passage in Dante, but from a general assimilation by the English poet of the Italian's doctrine.[12]

Since Bethel is positing proof by association, it is necessary to follow his line of reasoning fairly closely. On the one hand, he seems to imply the following syllogistic pattern:

Virtue and pity are linked in Chaucer.
Virtue is the *sine qua non* of gentilesse in Dante.
Therefore, Chaucer, who stresses virtue, is using Dante for his source.

---

penser, mais savoir, / *Se tu vues joie* et pais *savoir,* / *Que puis qu'elle a parfaitement* / *Tous les biens,* qu'on puet bonnement / Ymaginer, dire, ou penser / Qui croissent en li sans cesser, / *Et qu'elle est des vertus parée.* / Et de tous vices separée, / *Qu'il couvient de nécessité* / *Qu'en li soit Franchise et Pité,* / Humblesse et Charité, s'amie." ["*Again you must also think in order to put yourself beyond care,* not just thinking but knowing if you *want to know joy* and peace, *that since she has perfectly all the attributes* that one can rightly imagine, speak or think of, which grow in her without cease, *and since she is adorned with virtues* and separated from all vices, *then it is necessarily befitting that in her be Candor and Compassion,* Humbleness and Kindness her friend."] The italics are Kittredge's, and he notes here also Machaut's *Jugement du Roy de Behaingne* 458–62: "Son Dous Regret riant m'asseüroit, / Et Dous Espoirs doucement me disoit / En louiauté / Et m'affermoit qu'onques si grant biauté / Ne pot estre qu'il n'i eüst pité." ["Laughing, his Sweet Regret assured me and Sweet Hopes quietly spoke to me in all honesty and confirmed that never could such great beauty exist that did not have compassion."] *TC* 1.895–96 is compared with *Remède* 1790–96: "Car elle t'a fait plus de grace / Que ne porroies desservir / En li cinc cens mille ans servir. / Et si te vueil dire comment: / Amours t'a fait loial amant / A la milleur et la plus bele / Qui vive." ["For she has shown you more grace than you could deserve in serving her five hundred thousand years. And so I want to tell you how: Love has made you an honest lover to the best and most beautiful one alive."]

[11] Cf., for example, Robbins (1952): no. 131, *The All Vertuous She* (John Lydgate, pp. 129–30); no. 139, *A Pitiless Mistress* (MS Sloane 1212, pp. 141–42); no. 140, *A Sovereign Mistress* (MS Sloane 1212, pp. 142–43); no. 177, *The Ten Commandments of Love* (MS Fairfax 16, pp. 165–68); no. 198, *To His Mistress, Root of Gentleness* (MS Cotton Vespasian D-ix, pp. 200–02); no. 201, *An Envoy to his Mistress* (MS Royal 19.A.iii, pp. 206–07); no. 212, *Abuse of Women* (in negative terms) (MS Advocates 1.1.6, pp. 225–26). See also Root's explanation of these lines in his edition of *Troilus* (1945:427).

[12] The italics for *or* are mine. The line "of which Chaucer is so fond" is *Inf.* 5.100, which I shall discuss below. Many scholars have the unfortunate habit of using *gentilezze* and *gentilesse* interchangeably. I am not at all certain that this is valid, since it entails a change not only of cultures but frequently of a century or more. In modern terms it is somewhat like trying to equate nineteenth-century French *explication de texte* with the more recent, though not new, critical use of the phrase.

Now, as I have tried to show, the link between virtue and pity is common. In fact, Chaucer is not stressing this element at all. If we look at the argument that Pandarus is setting forth, we find that he learns who Troilus's love is at line 874, though he has been speaking of love with Troilus since line 603. Pandarus's speech of encouragement runs from line 874 to line 1008, piling reasons and authorities on top of one another. Of these 134 lines, the two and a half verses cited at the beginning of this entry are but one more reason rapidly brought in by Pandarus; these lines do not form a central argument, nor should they, I think, be taken as having any philosophical or contextual parallel to Dante's writing where, to repeat a statement already made, it is not courtly love but "l' amor che muove il sole e l'altre stelle" with which we are dealing. If the Dantean concept of love were as important as Bethel suggests, it would certainly appear clearly and as something more than an aside in one of Pandarus's magnificently garrulous speeches.

Correlatively, Bethel attempts to connect *pity* as closely as possible with Dante in roughly the following manner:

> Dante was one of the exponents of the *dolce stil nuovo*.
> The main element of the *dolce stil nuovo* is *gentilesse*.
> *Gentilesse* is associated with love.
> Love is the same as pity.
> Chaucer emphasizes pity and gentilesse.
> *Therefore*, Chaucer is following Dante (which is verified by his frequent use of
>   *Inf.* 5.100, which shows also that Love and Pity are the same).

This summary is based on the citation from Bethel given above and also on two statements made previously in the body of his thesis (p. 140):

> Now it is this very emphasis upon "gentilesse"—if I may borrow Chaucer's word—and the association with it of Love, or Pity (for the transition from Love to Pity is, as I have remarked, an easy one)[13] which is one of the chief characteristics of the *dolce stil nuovo*; and to illustrate Chaucer's debt to Dante in this respect one need only furnish a list of his references to gentilesse—in the Dantesque sense.[14] . . . For the present I shall content myself with pointing out the frequency with which Chaucer introduces what is virtually a translation—allowing for his substitution of *pity* for *love*—of a particular line of Dante's, which at this time, sufficiently illustrates my point.[15]

It is obvious, then, that the translation from *amor* to *pietà* must be made in order to show that the five citations of *Inf.* 5.100 have their source in Dante. But Dante was neither the first nor the last poet of the *dolce stil nuovo*, which began with Guido Guinizelli and continued on through Chaucer's time, almost a century later. Chaucer, in other words, could have learned the doctrine from any one of the innumerable members of the school. Guinizelli's famous "Al cor gentil ripara sempre amore" probably is the source for *TC* 3.5,[16]

---

[13] Again it should be noted that the unwarranted substitution has been made. No proof or semblance of proof for the "easy transition" has been offered. Bethel is strictly literal in saying "as I have remarked."

[14] The weakness of reasoning in this last remark seems to depend on (1) the exclusion of all material that is non "Dantesque"; (2) weakness of definition, i.e., what is Dantesque and does that mean that Dante wrote it; and (3) begging the question, i.e., assuming that certain material and concepts are from Dante in order to show that Chaucer used Dante.

[15] The line is *Inf.* 5.100.

[16] "[Love] In gentil hertes ay redy to repaire." Cf., for example, Tatlock 1920:443: "'Gentil herte,' 'cuer gentil,' 'gentil core' are a part of the regular fashionable vocabulary of love from the thirteenth century on."

and Boccaccio, Chaucer's principal source for *Troilus*, constantly has lines such as "Benigna donna d'ogni gentil core" (*Filostrato* 3.74). Dante's one great work in the *dolce stil nuovo* is the *Vita nuova*, which, however, Bethel feels certain Chaucer never read (indeed, Bethel [pp. 149–50] is careful to show how many apparent references from the *Vita nuova* come to Chaucer by way of Boccaccio's *Filostrato*). Yet, with reference to the present passage in *Troilus and Criseyde* and those which he claims are based on *Inf*. 5.100, Bethel makes the whole *dolce stil nuovo* school equivalent to Dante and takes the further step of equating *amor* and *pietà*.

Now, although love and pity could function side by side, they are not interchangeable, as many a complaint witnesses. In fact, in most instances pity is invoked where the love has not yet been achieved and serves as a means to an end. True, if a woman accepts a lover, it is assumed—though more rarely stated—that she is being pitiful, or more often *merciful*, but then, to cite only one poem, she also becomes "faire," "fre," "of grete pris," "bright," "fresh," "dere," "amyable," "ground of grace," "most of worthyness," "comfort of this caas," "helper of hevynesse," "rote of stedfastnesse," "honour," "norice of gentilnesse," "comely," "lussom," "soverain," "semely," "strengthe of stablenesse," "counsell of clennesse," "turtill trewe triable," "amorouse," "worthy," "witty," "wys," "derworth," "delitable," "ertly ioy and blisse," "faucon," "Rose," "Carboncle," "prymerose," and "plesaunce," among other things (Robbins 1952:212–13, "A Lover's Farewell to His Mistress"). In brief, pity is very often needed to bring about love; it is even an attribute of the "gentil core" but it is certainly not the same thing as love.

Let us look now, as objectively as possible, at the lines which are "virtually a translation" of *Inf*. 5.100. They are:

> *LGW* G 491 (F 503)   "But pite renneth sone in gentil herte"
> *KnT* A 1761   "For pitee renneth soone in gentil herte"
> *MerT* E 1986   "Lo, pitee renneth soone in gentil herte!"
> *SqT* F 479   "That pitee renneth soone in gentil herte"

and an "adaptation":

> *MLT* B 659–61   "This Alla kyng hath swich compassioun,
>   As gentil herte is fulfild of pitee,
>   That from his eyen ran the water doun."

The line in the *Commedia* is

> Amor, ch' al cor gentil ratto s' apprende

Love, which is quickly kindled in a gentle heart [P. 331]

The only "virtual translation" here is the phrase *al cor gentil* and perhaps the word *ratto*, though this in English is quite definitely the word "swift," as opposed to *tosto* or even *presto*, which would mean "soon." Now the commonest term of the whole *dolce stil nuovo*, and the basis on which Guinizelli started his opposition to the Sicilian school, is found in the phrase *al cor gentil*. Chaucer would have seen it throughout Boccaccio; it permeates Petrarch's *Rime*; and it would have been common coinage with almost any poet in Italy from the middle of the century on. Chaucer's line is most probably a part of the thought of this school of writers (as the "adaptation" seems to indicate), but this by no means makes Dante its author. Robinson, referring to the line and its recurrence, notes (pp. 675–76):

> It expresses a favorite sentiment of Chaucer's, which recalls the familiar doctrine of the poets of the "dolce stil nuovo" that Love repairs to the gentle heart.

See especially, Dante, Inf., v, 100; Vita Nuova, xx (Sonetto x); Guido Guinicelli's famous canzone: "Al core gentile ripara sempre Amore"...and cf. Tr, iii, 5. It should be observed, however, that the association of pity with nobility is also Ovidian. See Tristia, iii, 5, 31–32.[17]

We must, therefore, most seriously doubt the direct ascription of this line to Dante, and, since it serves as the basis of other, more hypothetical ascriptions, we must review those purely on their own merit.

Finally, Bethel (p. 144), in claiming that lines 894–96 in *Troilus* are based primarily on "the discussion of the nature of love in the seventeenth and eighteenth Cantos of *Purgatorio*," tries to overcome the natural objection to the insignificance of their treatment there by finding other references in which the passage from Dante might be taken as being present. He chooses the following (p. 145):

Bethel: "*977–79: no person is without love; Pandarus' words are closely modelled on *Purg.* XVII, 91–93."

There is the distinct possibility of a basic mistranslation here. The lines from Chaucer are cited with the following italicization:

> "For this have I herd seyd of wyse lered:
> *'Was nevere man nor woman yit bigete*
> *That was unapt to suffren loves hete,*
> *Celestial, or elles love of kynde.'*
> Forthy some grace I hope in her to fynde."

with the comment that this is

> a passage the source of which has not hitherto been identified. The Dantesque lines which Chaucer is following here:

> "Nè creator nè creatura mai,"
>   cominciò el, "figliuol, fu sanza amore,
>   o naturale o d'animo; e tu 'l sai."[18]

Since *TC* 977 is underlined, and all of *Purg.* 17.91 is given, one is forced to conclude that these two lines are meant to be taken as parallels. If this is so, then *creator* and *creatura* may have been mistranslated as the masculine and feminine (i.e., "man" and "woman") of the same word, when they refer, of course, to the Creator and every living thing he has created.

Let us assume, however, that the citation should have begun with *creatura*; is there anything here to indicate a source in Dante? First, there are no verbal parallels. We come, then, to the question of whether the thought is Dante's. The concept of the pervasiveness of love is, of course, as traditional as the Bible's "God is Love." Likewise, the direction of man's love toward either a celestial or a natural object is not the discussion in the passage from the *Commedia*. Pandarus, in this instance, is saying that the ardor of love that is in all

---

[17] See discussion of Shannon, pp. 178–79. Whiting (1934:44) lists the line as a sententious remark. An interesting point is made by Preston (1951:617), who, in speaking of Machaut's use and reuse of a certain theme, says: "An analogy in Chaucer is his use of the beautiful sentence derived from Guido Guinicelli, that 'pitee renneth soone in gentil herte': we may think we know what it means, until it has been applied to Theseus, to Alceste, to the wife of January, and to Canacee." See also Tatlock's remark (1920:443) cited above, n.16.

[18] See translation at beginning of previous citation.

human beings must be channeled toward either the celestial or the natural. To imply that these two categories of human love are paralleled by Dante's *o naturale o d'animo* shows that one either has badly misread the passage oneself or else is attributing to Chaucer a very bad misreading. In the *Commedia*, Virgil is stating that love itself is either natural (i.e., instinctive) or rational (i.e., elective.)[19] Dante's concept of natural love is, as a matter of fact, almost diametrically opposed to "love of kynde" in humans. For Dante, "natural love, as that of heavy bodies for the centre, of fire for the circumference, or of plants for their natural habitat, is unerring."[20] As well as the fact that there is neither verbal nor contextual parallel between Dante's *amore...naturale* and Chaucer's "love of kynde," there is the additional basic difference in the subjects under discussion: Virgil is speaking of the two kinds of love that rule the created universe, while Pandarus is speaking only of human passion. Nor is there any parallel in *Troilus* to *amore...d'animo*, which is elective by virtue of man's free will. According to Dante, this rational love, if directed toward primal good (like *amore naturale*) or if directed temperately toward secondary goods (i.e., worldly blessings), is unerring and becomes sinful only when it is misdirected or when it is excessive in its desire for worldly things. There is no parallel to this in Chaucer, either in words or in sense. Pandarus is stating the commonplace that the passion that is in all human beings can be directed either to God or to a fellow human being.[21]

Purg. 17.94–105 is cited (Bethel, p. 146) not in its entirety but rather as a collage of quotations which unfortunately tend to give a false impression by virtue of their juxtaposition:

> Lo naturale è sempre sanza errore,
>   ma l'altro puote errar per malo obietto...
> Mentre ch'elli è nel primo ben diretto,
>   e ne' secondi sè stesso misura,
>   esser non può cagion di mal diletto;
> ma quando al mal si torce....

[19] Cf. Grandgent, p. 468, Argument to *Purg.* 17; Singleton, *Purg.* Commentary, pp. 390–95.

[20] *Divine Comedy*, Carlyle-Wicksteed translation, p. 288, Introduction to *Purg.* 17. It is important here to establish the differences clearly, since the prevalence and ambiguity of the theme of *amor* can lead to a great deal of confusion. The differences here are fundamental enough to be reasonably evident. Being elective, Dante's "amore...d'animo" in itself includes both "celestial or elles love of kynde." Chaucer, it will be noticed, does not mention any equivalent to "amore...naturale." Now Chaucer's alternatives were commonplaces of the time and the very basis of Augustinian theology. This is admirably pointed out by Makarewicz (1953:94): "[Love] is good if it tends directly to God and subordinates all other loves to that; it is evil, if it tends to disrupt this order or this hierarchization and to make an inferior object the recipient of what is rightly due to the Superior Being. In virtue of this definition love may be considered under two categories: divine and profane love or as Chaucer calls it 'celestial, or elles love of kynde.' Such a distinction between divine and profane love is given by St. Augustine in his definition of *charitas*: 'Charitatem voco motum animi ad fruendum Deo propter ipsum et se atque proximo propter Deum; cupiditatem autem, motum animi ad fruendum se et proximo et quoliber corpore non propter Deum.' ['I call Charity the soul's motion toward delighting in God for His own sake, and in itself and its neighbor for God's sake; but I call Cupidity the soul's motion towards delighting in itself and its neighbor and anything corporeal *not* on God's account.' The passage is *De doctrina Christiana* 3.16.10, following D. W. Robertson. My italics.] This doctrine of charity regulates the relation between man and his Creator as well as between man and man, and man and any created object. By this doctrine, St. Augustine brought about an integration between the temporal and the spiritual." Makarewicz cites the *De doctrina Christiana* in Migne, *Patrologia Latina* 34.72 and *Sermo* 21 in Migne, 38.143.) I have taken the liberty of quoting *in extenso* not only to differentiate the various meanings of *amor* in relation to the immediate problem but also to establish a basis for future references to the Augustinian concept of *caritas* and *cupiditas*.

[21] Bethel mentions the possibility of other sources later and in connection with a passage in *The Knight's Tale*: "...just after he has drawn the distinction between 'natural' and 'celestial' love, Arcite quotes the 'olde clerkes' Boethius and Boccaccio." The sources, as Bethel has noted, are "*De Cons.* III, met xii, 59–62; IV, met. iv, 37ff. (Root); *Troil.* IV, 618; *Filos.*, IV, 75. Cf. Root, *Troilus*, 511."

contra 'l fattore adovra sua fattura.
Quinci comprender puoi ch'esser convene
amor sementa in voi d'ogne virtute
e d'ogne operazion che merta pene.[22]

In context these lines would seem to have little relevance to the subject that is being discussed in *Troilus and Criseyde*.

As has already been mentioned, Pandarus's "wyse lered" is not expounding anything by way of original thought; he is merely repeating a biblical division—to which the Wife of Bath gives a gloss in the supreme comedy of her Prologue, a division based on the even more general categorization of *vita activa* and *vita meditiva*. Even if we were to grant, for the sake of argument, Bethel's fairly fundamental proviso that "due allowance [be made] for the dissimilarity of setting," it does not seem to follow that it is therefore (to use Bethel's words, p. 146)

> fairly safe to say that Chaucer is adapting in a greatly condensed form this exposition [i.e., the lines taken from *Purg*. XVII, 94-105] when he makes Pandarus argue:

> "...for noght but good it is
> To loven wele, and in a worthy place."

As noted earlier, this period in religion is marked by the prevalence, indeed, one might say the cult, of *amor*; it is this concept which was, of course, the basis of the Augustinians' basically positive creed of *caritas* and *cupiditas*, as well as the "speculative mysticism of the thirteenth and fourteenth centuries."[23] "To loven wele and in a worthy place" was a kind of virtuous expediency, a venial sin,[24] according to a very large segment of the religious thinking of the era. Pandarus has converted the phrase to his own uses, but the result is that his original is too generally known to have any specific source, and his particular interpretation bears little resemblance to Dante's more conventional discussion.

Book 2

Bethel: "1-4: metaphor derived from Dante; lines closely modelled on *Purg*. I, 1-3."

Owt of thise blake wawes for to saylle,	Per correr miglior acque alza le vele
O wynd, o wynd, the weder gynneth clere;	omai la navicella del mio ingegno,
	che lascia dietro a sé mar sì crudele

---

[22] Bethel, p. 146. Bethel cites other passages: *Purg*. XVIII, 34ff.; *Par*. XXXIII and *Par*. X, 83f. In this last he tries to establish a parallel between Chaucer's "The oghte not to clepe it hap but grace" (*TC* 1.896) with "lo raggio de la grazia, onde s'accende / verace amore e che poi cresce amando" ("the ray of grace, by which true love is kindled and which then grows by loving"). Bethel, who has been trying to show the connection of the two passages in *Troilus* (lines 894-96 and 976-80), has already suggested (p. 145, n.1) that the word "grace" in line 896 connects with the same word in line 980 ("Forthy som grace I hope in hire to fynde") and—although the use of the two words seems different—he is here evidently attempting to further the connection by giving the word the authority of his suggested source.

[23] See the monumental work of Gilson (1955), in particular pp. 70-80 (on Saint Augustine), pp. 164-71 ("Speculative Mysticism"), pp. 340-46 (on the Bonaventurian School), and pp. 447-71 (for the thirteenth- and fourteenth-century metaphysical group known as the Second Augustinian School).

[24] Cf. the Parson's definitions, *ParsT* I 358-68.

For in this see the boot hath swych
 travaylle,
Of my connyng, that unneth I it steere.

  To course over better waters the little bark of my genius now hoists her sails,
  leaving behind her a sea so cruel. [*Purg.*, p. 3]

The lines from the *Purgatorio* are, in all probability, the source for Chaucer's passage, though Cummings (1916:53) remarks: "Dante...is often assigned as the origin of these lines; but the comparison of a poem or a poet to a bark at sea is a common one in Italian poetry. Cf. Petrarch, Canzone VII (*Vergine bella.*), 66–71; Boccaccio, *Ninfale Fisolano*, VII, 65; *Sonnetto* 95; *La Teseide*, XI, 12; *Fil.* IX, 3."[25] Robinson believes (p. 929) that this is "almost surely a reminiscence of Dante" but adds, as other possible sources, Ovid *Ars Amat.* 1.772, 3.26, 748; *Rem. Am.* 811–12; and, one might add, Ovid *Elegy* 10.

 The scholars differ on the lines to which the sources should apply; Robinson cites, in *TC*, lines 1–3; Cummings cites line 1–7; and Root, for whom "these lines somewhat resemble Dante" (1943:435), refers to lines 1–6. That the image is a common one there can be little doubt, but it seems to me vital to include Chaucer's line 4 to establish the one point which most indicates a source in Dante, namely, the phrase *la navicella del mio ingegno*. This is not, of course, conclusive evidence, since the idea is at least implied in most of the boat images, but the phrasing in this instance is certainly close and serves to bear out, in part, the reading *konnyng* (of H³ H⁴ H⁵ S¹ CX TH) as opposed to *commyng* (of γ J H² Ph), which, as Root says (p. 435), "does not seem to make much sense in the context."[26]

Bethel: "22f.: discussion of changes of language brought about by passage of time; *Conv.* I, v, 9."

Ye knowe ek that in forme of speche is chaunge Withinne a thousand yeer	Onde vedemo ne le cittadi d'Italia, se bene volemo agguardare, da cinquanta anni in qua molti vocabuli essere spenti e nati e variati; onde se 'l picciol tempo così transmuta, molto più transmuta lo maggiore. Sì ch' io dico, che se coloro che partiron d'esta vita già sono mille anni tornassero a le loro cittadi, crederebbero la loro cittade essere occupata da gente strana, per la lingua da loro discordante. Di questo si parlerà altrove più compiutamente in uno libello ch' io intendo di fare, Dio concedente, di Volgare Eloquenza.

  Hence in the cities of Italy, if we will look attentively back over some fifty years, we see that many words have become extinct and have come into existence and have been altered; wherefore, if a short time so changes the language, a longer time changes it much more. Thus I say that if those who

---

[25] Singleton's note (*Purg.* Commentary, p. 3) discusses the figure of the poet as navigator, quotes Virgil *Georgics* 4.116–19, cites *Georgics* 2.39–41, and refers "for many other examples before Dante" to Curtius 1953:28–30.

[26] Cf., among others, Aristotle's *Rhetoric* 3.3.

have departed from this life a thousand years ago were to return to their cities, they would believe that these had been occupied by some foreign people, because the language current there would be at variance with their own. This will be much more fully discussed elsewhere in a book which I intend to compose, God permitting, on the *Eloquence of the Vulgar Tongue*. [Pp. 43–44]

For the following three and a half lines of *Troilus* (see next entry), Bethel has given another source, which is, as he indicates, doubtful. The argument would have been stronger if the citations had been based on the single passage from the *Convivio* given above—if one is unwilling, that is, to accept the scholarship already offered. The entire passage in Chaucer (*TC* 2.22–26) reads:

> Ye knowe ek that in forme of speche is chaunge
> Withinne a thousand yeer, and wordes tho
> That hadden pris, now wonder nyce and straunge
> Us thinketh hem, and yet thei spake hem so,
> And spedde as wel in love as men now do.

As Seibert noted (p. 306), in all probability the ultimate source for the lines is Horace's *Ars poetica*, lines 69–72: "[M]uch less shall the glory and glamor of speech endure and live. Many terms that have fallen out of use shall be born again, and those shall fall that are now in repute, if Usage so will it, in whose hands lies the judgment, the right and the rule of speech" (Horace 1936:457). Seibert states that the passage might have been found at two points in John of Salisbury's *Metalogicon*: 1.16 and 3.3. Root (1943:436) compares Wace's *Roman de Rou* 77–80, and both he and Robinson note the possibility of a parallel in Seneca's *Epistles* (19.5, 13), as well as the parallel in Dante which Bethel considers doubtful, i.e., *Convivio* 2.13.10. In this last-mentioned passage Dante, comparing the discipline of Grammar to the Moon, says (Dante 1924b:107):

> And Grammar has these two properties, because on account of its infinitude the rays of the reason are not brought to a stand in any direction, especially in the case of words; and it shines now from this side, now from that, in so far as certain words, certain declensions, certain constructions are in use which formerly were not, and many formerly were in use which shall hereafter be in use again, as Horace says in the beginning of the *Poetry*, when he affirms that "many words shall revive which formerly have lapsed, &c."

Of these two passages from the *Convivio*, I would choose the former, mainly on the basis of negative information. First, the passage from 2.13.10 develops the concept of a cyclic pattern to vocabulary and declensions and constructions. Chaucer, on the other hand, is emphasizing only that words drop out of use. Second, Chaucer does not make reference to the "auctoritee" which Dante has given in 2.13.10, while he does use the same generally anecdotal approach that Dante employs in 1.5.9. By citing only lines 22–23, Bethel appears to have chosen this last passage from the *Convivio* only on the basis of the phrase *mille anni*, which he underlines in his text; however, this phrase, as Dante indicates, is hardly more than a vague, general term used to signify a large number or amount, and it does not serve as conclusive identification. There is no reason, however, why the entire passage, i.e., lines 22–26, could not be based, for its idea, on *Convivio* 1.5.9, in which case the phrase *mille anni* along with the general similarity of the topic would become far more positive evidence.

In any event, if it is necessary to have a source other than the Horatian original for these lines in Chaucer, the *Convivio* seems the most likely possibility.

Bethel: "24ff.: continuation of the discussion; possibly influenced by *Conv*. II, xiii, 10; doubtful."

See discussion in preceding entry.

Bethel: "64–66: the swallow's sorrowful mourning song; lines closely modelled on *Purg*. IX, 13–15."

The swalowe Proigne, with a sorowful
    lay,
Whan morwen com, gan make hire
    waymentynge,
Whi she forshapen was

Ne l'ora che comincia i tristi lai
    la rondinella presso a la mattina,
    forse a memoria de'suo'primi guai

    At the hour near morning when the swallow begins her sad lays, perhaps in memory of her former woes [*Purg.*, p. 87]

In order to ascribe these lines to the *Commedia*, one is forced to approach the tercet from the *Purgatorio* as "an interesting illustration of the way in which Chaucer uses Dante in combination with classical material"—rather, that is, than as an exclusively Dantean source. The reason is, of course, that Dante here and in *Purg*. 17.19–20 is following the Greek version of the story—which Virgil also adopted—which makes Progne the nightingale and Philomela the swallow. Grandgent (Dante 1933:470 n.19) summarizes as follows: "...the Latins, followed by modern poets, usually made Philomela the nightingale. But Ovid (*Met*. VI, 424ff.), the Latin poet from whom Dante got the story, does not tell, and Virgil (*Eclogue* VI, 79) seems to follow the Greek version, which Dante also adopted." If Chaucer also followed Ovid here or in the legend of Philomela, he too would have been faced with the confusion of "One flies to the woods,, the other rises to the roof" (*Met*. 6.668–69; Ovid 1916:3.335). The reference in Boccassio's *Teseida* 4.73 ("Then hearing Philomena singing") continues the Greek version, but Chaucer did not carry the story in *The Legend of Good Women* to the point of the transformation, and so was not faced directly with the problem there.

    The possibilities in the present situation, then, would seem to be that (1) Chaucer was using this *description* from Dante with a non-Dantesque version of the story, (2) Chaucer had another source which definitely made Progne the swallow, or (3) Chaucer used this or some other description (perhaps even that of Ovid) but nevertheless did not succeed in figuring out which of the two women became the swallow and which the nightingale.

    Now this passage in *Troilus* is possibly from the description in the *Purgatorio*, as Bethel and others have noted, but it must also be admitted that "Chaucer seems to have been unaware of Dante's usage" (Bethel, p. 194) of Progne as the nightingale. By using the word "unaware," Bethel avoids having to take into account the possibility (which would cast some doubt on the "linked atoms" basis of total recall) that Chaucer had simply forgotten the closely allied *empiezza* reference in *Purg*. 17.19–20. It would seem far sounder to consider that Chaucer did indeed use the descriptive tercet in *Purg*. 9 and simply did not remember Dante's later remarks.

Bethel: "967–70: flowers closing at night and re-opening in the morning; from *Filos*. II, 80, 1 f. Possibly Chaucer remembered *Inf*. II, 127 f. as well; the parallel with Dante is, however, doubtful."

But right as floures, thorugh the cold of nyght	Quali fioretti dal notturno gelo
Iclosed, stoupen on hire stalke lowe,	chinati e chiusi, poi che 'l sol li 'mbianca,
Redressen hem ayein the sonne bright,	[si drizzan tutti aperti in loro stelo]
And spreden on hire kynde cours by rowe	

> As little flowers, bent down and closed by chill of night, straighten and all unfold upon their stems when the sun brightens them. [*Inf.*, p. 21]

Root's note to lines 967–73 summarizes the predominant view that this stanza follows closely *Filostrato* 2.80. Boccaccio's lines, as Rossetti pointed out, are taken almost verbatim from Dante, *Inf.* 2.127–32 (Root 1945:450).

Book 3

Bethel: "5: close adaptation of Guinizelli's line, "Al cor gentil ripara sempre amore", which Chaucer found quoted in *Conv*. IV, xx, 7."

In gentil hertes ay redy to repaire	...sì come disse quel nobile Guido Guinizzelli in una sua canzone, che comincia: *Al cor gentil ripara sempre Amore.*

> ...as that noble Guido Guinicelli remarks in a Canzone of his which begins, "To the gentle heart Love ever repaireth." [P. 262]

The line in Chaucer is almost certainly based upon the opening of Guinizelli's famous canzone. Where Chaucer might have found the Guinizelli line is excellently summarized by Robinson (p. 823):

> Closer to this [line in Chaucer] than in Fil. iii, 74 ("Benigna donna d'ogni gentil core") or Inf. v, 100 ("Amor, che al cor gentil ratto s'apprende") is Guido Guinizelli's line, "Al cor gentil ripara sempre Amore.". . . If Chaucer had not read Guido's poem, he might have known this single line from Dante's citation of it in the Convivio, iv, 20.[27]

Both parts of Robinson's last sentence seem admirable; the first half admits the strong possibility that Chaucer would have very likely read Guinizelli's poem if he had had anything at all to do with Italian poetry, and the latter half gives the most likely source second to this possibility.

Bethel: "*39:a phrase possibly from *Par*. XXXIII, 16; doubtful."

---

[27] See also Tatlock 1920:443, cited above, n.16.

Now, lady bryght, for thi benignite   La tua benignità non pur soccorre

    Thy loving-kindness not only succors [*Par.*, p. 371]

Unlike *TC* 3.1262–67 below, there is not enough of a reference here to determine Chaucer's source. The terminology of *amor* was used for many purposes (see Robertson 1951:28), and, while there is no evidence to deny Dante's influence here, the rest of the passage seems to be predominantly in the terms of the invocations of love poetry.

Bethel: "45–48: idea of invoking Calliope probably from *Purg.* I, 7–9."

Caliope, thi vois be now present,   Ma qui la morta poesì resurga,
For now is nede; sestow nought my   o sante Muse, poi che vostro sono;
  destresse,   e qui Calïopè alquanto surga
How I mot telle anonright the gladnesse
Of Troilus, to Venus heryinge?

    But here let dead poetry rise again, O holy Muses, since I am yours; and here let Calliope rise up somewhat. [*Purg.*, p. 3]

Whatever parallel there is here should obviously apply only to lines 45–46. Verbally, there is only the use in both invocations of Calliope's name, but for the factual information about so generally known a convention as the Muses, one can hardly cite Dante as the specific source. Calliope, properly, is the muse of epic poetry and, as the mother of Orpheus (cf. Virgil *Eclogue* 4.57), in invocations to the Muses is often named as their chief. Thus Virgil has the verbally closer, though equally conventional, invocation (*Aen.* 9.525): "Vos, O Calliope, precor, adspirate." If both Root and Robinson had not noted Dante's reference to Calliope in connection with these lines from *Troilus*, it would hardly seem worthwhile taking the matter further.

    It must be remembered that Chaucer has followed the invocation convention in each book so far: in the first with the Fury Tisiphone and in the second with Clio, the muse of history. In both instances we must recall that it is possible that Chaucer, if he does not have his tongue in his cheek, is at least perfectly aware that he is not writing in the full tradition of Suetonius or Virgil. The stanzas that open book 3 indicate that the mood is not what one could refer to as the heaviest imaginable, and if the muse of epic poetry is being here invoked, then the material of the book indicates that it is a *poème épique d'amour*. Chaucer's preceding forty-four lines of ever-increasing "heryinge" of Venus are magnificently undercut by his comic desperation in "sestow nought my destresse?" This is a far cry from Dante's invocation of all the *sante Muse* and of their chief, Calliope. Dante is passing from *la morta poesì*, poetry of despair, to poetry (*Purg.* 1.4–6)

        di quel secondo regno
      dove l'umano spirito si purga
      e di salire al ciel diventa degno.

    [of that second realm where the human spirit is purged and becomes fit to ascend to Heaven. (*Purg.*, p. 3)]

There is then only the vaguest possible contextual parallel in that both poems are coming to a more hopeful section, or perhaps to the next step of two different *scalae amoris*, but there seems to be scarcely more than this.

Bethel: "617–20: influence of Dante's conception of Fortune, *Inf.* VII, 67–96."

But O Fortune, executrice of wyrdes,   [See citation under the poem *Fortune*.]
O influences of thise hevenes hye!
Soth is, that under God ye ben oure
        hierdes,
Though to us bestes ben the causes
        wrie.

While the principal treatment of this question is in the discussion of the poem *Fortune*, a primary investigation here may point out the fundamental error in the assignment of Chaucer's passages on Fortune to Dante. In his text Bethel cites Root's note to the above passage, which states that "Chaucer here accepts the orthodox opinion that astrological influences are subject to the will of God and are, like Fortune, a means through which the divine providence is executed" (Root 1945:475). It would be a mistake, however, to try to establish here an either-or based on the false assumption that whatever is not "pagan" is Dantesque. With this oversimplified dichotomy in mind, Bethel unfortunately goes on to find instances where Chaucer uses the pagan idea of planets and Fortune, citing *KnT* A 1086–91 and asserting that there we see "the stoical resignation to whimsical or malignant fate rather than that of Christian submission to an unfathomable divine scheme, which we should expect when the influence of Fortune and of the heavens is directly subordinated to the control of God" (Bethel, p. 268). Such an oversimplification would appear to beg the question completely, as the subsequent attempted elimination of a *tertium quid* shows (p. 268):

> If we associate the thought of [the citation from *Troilus* given above], which places Fortune under God's control, with that of the other passages in which she is similarly treated,[28] the goddess becomes, by implication, the minister of God; and, if we carry this implication a step farther, the "influences of thise hevenes hye" are raised to the same exalted position.
>   Now this is exactly what Dante has Virgil do with Fortune...she is associated in rank with the other gods[29] "l' altre prime creature" who conduct the heavens.[30]

The expansion and explication of the text seem completely unwarranted. Patch (1922:201) has very carefully explained the difference in approach:

> [Dante's] Fortuna is pagan and Boethian in that she embodies the pagan whimsicality in outward manner and is yet subordinate to a greater Deity; she does not award necessarily according to merit, and yet her madness has method because she is obeying the decrees of a superior will. To give her official recognition as an angelic power with her own peculiar duties, was a step Boethius and Albertus Magnus did not take.

With the additional corroboration of Patch's explanation and Root's note, it can be seen that the "compromise"[31] position which Boethius took is precisely that of Chaucer. In

---

[28] "E.g., *Tr.* v, 1541–5; *Fortune* 65ff. See Tatlock, *Mod. Phil.*, III, 371" (Bethel's note).

[29] "*Inf.*, VII, 87" (Bethel's note).

[30] "*Ibid.*, 95, 74" (Bethel's note).

[31] The term is Patch's. See p. 190 and his statement four pages later that with Boethius "you have almost the Christian conception."

Boethius too the implication that Fortune was a specific aspect of the Divine Plan was strong but never made.[32] Dante's contribution was to take this step: to create Fortune as "an angelic power" in charge of a sphere. As a matter of fact, Bethel's argument serves only to prove how very close Chaucer is to Boethius on this particular point.

Bethel: "*622 f.: shows assimilation of the doctrine of *Conv.* II, iv, *passim*."

| But execut was al bisyde hire leve The goddes wil; for which she moste bleve. | [Dante's description of the ten Heavens of the Christian universe which emanate from God, and of their movements, which are directly proportional in physical influence to their proximity to God.] |

Although Root's note includes these two lines with the three given in the entry immediately above, Bethel treats them separately to point out that they "seem to mean that Chaucer regards these several powers [i.e., the spheres of the universe] as gods." Bethel is faced with the problem of accounting for the very embarrassing and un-Christian plural, "goddes." These lines must be Christianized to maintain the interpretation that he has given for the previous three lines. To this explanation of line 623 he adds (p. 270 n.3):

> Unless one prefers to think that *goddes* refers to the pagan-gods. This, however, involves an inconsistency in Chaucer's lines, owing to the fact that the poet has already, only a line or two before this, placed these guiding forces under the governance of the Christian God. Cf. Jefferson, *Ch. & Cons. Phil.*, 59, no. 30.

There is, of course, total inconsistency here, but it is that inconsistency, that confusion of classical character and Christian tradition, that (as has been pointed out many times) is so typical of the Middle Ages. If we are dealing with a serious theological subject (as is proposed above), then Chaucer would not speak in polytheistic terms. If we do not think of the lines in terms of a credal sermon, however, Chaucer's reference is seen to be as casual as our modern references to "the gods."

Indeed, if we look at this entire stanza in context, we can see that it is not deeply religious but superbly ambivalent, that it is not formal philosophy but is touched by mock seriousness, accentuated by Chaucer's "this mene I now." Looking at the stanza in context, we can see at once that, if these are Christian powers at work, their wonders are being performed in a highly immoral way. In brief, the fates are helping bring about the seduction of Criseyde. There is no reason to make of this an ontological argument for the Church Triumphant, nor is there any need for anagogical or eclectic consistency.

Bethel: "*1147f.: shows general influence of Dante's attitude to *gentillesse*."

>   for every wyght, I gesse,
> That loveth wel, meneth but gentilesse.

There is neither verbal nor contextual parallel for these lines in Dante. To assign any line that mentions "gentilesse" to Dante, in spite of the tradition not only of courtly love but

---

[32] Patch, p. 194, says: "An inference of such a figure [as the goddess Fortuna] in subordination to Divine Providence is easily drawn, but Boethius did not draw it."

also of the whole century of *dolce stil nuovo* that followed Dante, is an extremely tenuous position.[33]

Bethel: "1262-7: Troilus's hymn to Love—:1262f. very close adaptation of *Par.* XXXIII, 14 f./1264-7: modelled on *Par.* XXXIII, 16-8."

[Benigne Love, thow holy bond of thynges,]
Whoso wol grace, and list the nought honouren,
Lo, his desir wol fle withouten wynges.
For noldestow of bownte hem socouren
That serven best and most alwey labouren,
Yet were al lost, that dar I wel seyn certes,
But if thi grace passed oure desertes.

[Donna, se' tanto grande e tanto vali,]
che qual vuol grazia e a te non ricorre,
sua disïanza vuol volar sanz' ali.
La tua benignità non pur soccorre
a chi domanda, ma molte fiate
liberamente al dimandar precorre.

[Lady, thou art not so great and so availest,] that whoso would have grace and has not recourse to thee, his desire seeks to fly without wings. Thy loving-kindness not only succors him who asks, but oftentimes freely foreruns the asking. [*Par.*, p. 371]

Chaucer's lines are undoubtedly from Dante. There is an even closer connection when one considers that this prayer to the Virgin which opens *Par.* 33 emphasizes (1) the elements of both *l' amore* (Nel ventre tuo si raccese l' amore," line 7 [In thy womb was rekindled the love (*Par.*, p. 371)]) and *caritate* ("Qui sei a noi merïdiana face / Di caritate," lines 10–11 [Here thou art for us the noonday torch of charity (*Par.*, p. 371)]), while Troilus begins, "O Love, O Charite" (line 1254); and (2) the Boethian doctrine of love as the "holy bond of thynges" in the following tercet: ". . . in te s' aduna / Quantunque in crëatura è di bontate" (lines 20–21 [. . . in thee is found whatever of goodness is in any creature (*Par.*, p. 373)]).

What makes the connection with Dante particularly strong in these lines is not only the verbal but also the thematic parallel. Paradoxically, it is the latter that makes the stanza (181) seem somewhat out of place when spoken by Troilus—though this statement needs some explanation. In the preceding stanza (180), Troilus's hymn begins with an address to Cupid (and secondarily to Venus and Hymen), but the very terms with which it opens— *amor* and *caritas*—are the most fundamental concepts of the Augustinian belief.[34] The stanza with which we are most concerned, however, does not develop the sense of *amor* that one connects with Cupid, but rather proceeds in terms of the Christian *amor*, the "Benigne love" that became the basis of Marian worship.[35] In its turn the final stanza (182) does not develop this religious lyric but rather tends to convert it to the reverential terms of love poetry. In short, Chaucer has attempted to weave together three elements:

---

[33] For extended discussions of the relationship of Chaucer's *gentilesse* and Dante's *gentilezza*, see under *TC* 1.894-96, *The Franklin's Tale, The Squire's Tale*, and *Gentilesse*.

[34] See above, n.20.

[35] Cf. "La tua benignità," also 5.1869, and the last line of *Troilus* ("For love of mayde and moder thyn benigne"), and finally note Root's remark (1945:485) that verses 1266-67 have echoes of Chaucer's Marian poem, *An ABC*, line 180, "That, nere thy tender herte, we weren spilt." See the introductory remarks to *The Canterbury Tales* and *PrP* B² 1664-70 for further suggestions on the *Paradiso* passage. On the subtle interweaving of *amor, amicitia*, spiritual and carnal, see the fine study of Patterson 1979:297-330.

Troilus's classical god of love, Cupid; the Christian concept (on the basis of the reference to Cupid as amor and caritas) in the Marian tradition; the courtly poetry of love (on the basis of "serven" and "labouren" in line 1265), which is somewhat closer to the character of Troilus that has been presented and a great deal closer to the situation in which he finds himself.

While it is interesting to observe the way in which Chaucer has attempted to interlock these elements, the central stanza (with the exception of line 1265) departs radically from the values and situation of the context in which it is found. This does not constitute a question of applicability or nonapplicability but is rather an instance of Chaucer's more mature use of Dante. He is not, I believe, trying (as he did in the earlier poems) to adapt Dante's words to his immediate task; rather he seems to be attempting to add to the scope of his poem by using a lyric unit from the *Commedia*. Troilus has just reached the zenith of his love, and Chaucer, probably wishing to show his lover's exultation, heightens his verse with Dante's lines. Lowes has said of Chaucer that "when he is deeply moved he is apt to remember Dante" (1934:236), and perhaps we are not too far astray if we add that Chaucer also is likely to remember Dante when he wishes to move his audience deeply. In any event, these lines would appear to be an early example of Chaucer's view of Dante as a religious lyricist worthy of emulation.

Bethel: "1373–9 (Root), 1387–95 (Skeat): Midas and Crassus as examples of covetousness; cf. *Purg.* XX, 103–17."

As wolde God tho wrecches that dispise
Servise of love hadde erys also longe
As hadde Mida, ful of coveytise,
And therto dronken hadde as hoot and
    stronge
As Crassus dide for his affectis wronge,
To techen hem that they ben in the vice,
And loveres nought, although they
        holde hem nyce.

"...Noi repetiam Pigmalïon allotta,
    cui traditore e ladro e paricida
    fece la voglia sua de l'oro ghiotta;
e la miseria de l'avaro Mida,
    che seguì a la sua dimanda gorda,
    per la qual sempre convien che si rida.
Del folle Acàn ciascun poi si ricorda,
    come furò le spoglie, sì che l'ira
    di Iosuè qui par ch'ancor lo morda.
Indi accusiam col marito Saffira;
    lodiamo i calci ch'ebbe Elïodoro;
    e in infamia tutto 'l monte gira
Polinestòr ch'ancise Polidoro;
    ultimamente ci si grida: 'Crasso,
    dilci, che 'l sai: di che sapore è l'oro?'"

"...Then we recall Pygmalion, whom insatiate lust of gold made traitor, thief, and parricide; and the misery of the avaricious Midas which followed on his greedy demand, whereat men must always laugh. Each then remembers the foolish Acan, how he stole the spoils, so that the wrath of Joshua seems to sting him here again. Then we accuse Sapphira with her husband; we celebrate the kicks which Heliodorus had; and in infamy the name of Polymestor who slew Polydorus circles all the mountains. Last, the cry here is, 'Tell us, Crassus, for you know, what is the savor of gold?'" [*Purg.*, p. 219, 221]

In the text of his thesis Bethel arranges the citation, giving only lines 103, 106–107, and 116–17, which, though perhaps unduly selective, does attempt to extract from the list a more plausible source than that given by Dante contextually.

If a source were necessary for Midas or Crassus, it need not have come from the *Commedia*. Shannon comments (1929:133):

> The tale of the covetousness of Midas and of his ass's ears is found in *Met.* xi, 100–193. Chaucer himself tells the story in the *Wife of Bath's Tale*, II. D. 951–982. For the incident of the dead Crassus forced by Orodes to drink molten gold, Chaucer was no doubt indebted to Boccaccio's *De Casibus Virorum*, vi, vii.

Shannon goes on to note (pp. 133–34, n.2):

> Professor Lowes thinks the dominant influence upon Chaucer here was Dante (*Mod. Phil.*, XIV, 135–137). As the ass's ears are not mentioned in Dante, that information certainly came from Ovid. Dante's reference to Crassus (*Purg.* xx, 116–117) would be unintelligible without a further knowledge of the story. For this Mr. Lowes suggests Florus. But I show (p. 181) that in the only place where Chaucer has been thought to borrow from Florus, viz., in the Legend of Cleopatra, he was using *De Mulieribus Claris* and *De Casibus Virorum*. As all that Chaucer has about Crassus may be found in *De Casibus Virorum*, Mr. Lowes' reference to Jehan de Tuim's *Hystore de Julius Cesar* is also unnecessary. Ovid, Boccaccio, and possibly Dante, contributed to Chaucer in this passage.

Bethel himself is admirably cautious in his text: "I should not wish to lay too much stress upon what may be mere coincidence [i.e., the names Midas and Crassus], in view of the fact that a similar occurrence of the two names in juxtaposition and under the head of (implied) avarice is to be found in Petrarch's *Trionfo della Fama*."[36] One might also cite, as does Lowes (1917a:137), the same combination of names and the same spellings that appear in Boccaccio's *Amorosa Visione* 12.5–12.

The most likely answer, however, is that given by Root (1945:487): "Both Midas and Crassus are stock examples to prove that "coveytise is vice." They are also used by Dante, *Purg.* 20.106–8, and by Gower, *Conf. Am.* 5.141–332, 2068–224." This use of names is, in other words, one more example of Chaucer and Dante drawing on the same source, in this instance, common knowledge. Despite this, however, Bethel continues (p. 189):

> ...but Mr. Lowes' next observation bears out this possibility [of Dante as the source]. He shows that the phrase "for his affectis wronge" is derived from Chaucer's reading of the three cantos of the *Purgatorio* immediately preceding the one we are discussing, which deal with the nature of love, and that its occurrence here shows how complete was his assimilation of Dante's doctrine.[37]

As a matter of fact, Lowes cites only two points in the preceding three cantos where Dante uses the word *affeto* (17.111 and 18.57), and in the first of these occurrences there is a definite textual problem, both Singleton and Grandgent giving the reading *effeto*. Lowes states (1917a:137):

> Not only is "affect" (which Chaucer seems to use only here) a characteristically Dantean word, but it occurs twice...in the fundamental discussion in Cantos

---

[36] "I, 56–57: '...Mida o Crasso con l'oro a *virtu* furon rebelli....' I merely wish to show here how easily the matter of juxtaposition and spelling may be accounted for here as mere coincidence, unless of course it is suggested that Petrarch is drawing upon Dante, which is perfectly possible, but absurd to urge without further evidence" (Bethel's note).

[37] Bethel, p. 189. Bethel's note here reads: "Cf., e.g., *Purg.* XVII, 100."

XVII and XVIII of the *Purgatorio* concerning the nature of love. Crassus' "affectis wronge" represent love "quando al mal si torce" (XVII, 100), and Chaucer's use of the phrase shows his complete assimilation of Dante's doctrine.

First, there is nothing "characteristically Dantean" about the word *affeto*, which is the usual Italian word for "emotion," "love," "affection of mind or heart," and so on. There is no reason, in other words, for supposing that Dante, more than any other Italian, would be the source of Chaucer's word "affectis." From seeing together these bits of Chaucer and Dante, taken out of context, one might gain the impression that Crassus and "affectis wronge" are somehow connected with *quando al mal si torce*, which in turn is somehow connected with *affeto*, but there is, as far as can be seen, no basis for this suggestive juxtaposition.

Finally, we are asked to assume that Boccaccio's use of the term *gli dolorosi avari* (*Filostrato* 3.38), which Chaucer is said to be translating at line 1373, recalled the fifth circle of Purgatory (Lowes 1917a:135–36),[38] which in turn served to recall Crassus and Midas from Dante's list of names and at the same time not only recalled the general discussion of Divine Love two and three cantos before but even went so far as to recall a single word that appears perhaps a single time in those cantos. This would seem to represent an incredible feat of memory.

Bethel: "1415–20: reference to *Fortuna Major* taken from *Purg.* XIX, 1–6."

But whan the cok, comune astrologer,	Ne l'ora che non può 'l calor dïurno
Gan on his brest to bete and after crowe,	intepidar più 'l freddo de la luna, vinto da terra, e talor da Saturno
And Lucyfer, the dayes messager,	–quando i geomanti lor Maggior Fortuna
Gan for to rise, and out hire bemes throwe,	veggiono in orïente, innanzi a l'alba, surger per via che poco le sta bruna–
And estward roos, to hym that koude it knowe,	
Fortuna Major	

At the hour when the day's heat, overcome by Earth and at times by Saturn, can no more warm the cold of the moon–when the geomancers see their *Fortuna Major* rise in the East before dawn by a path which does not long stay dark for it– [*Purg.*, p. 201]

The suggested parallel should probably be limited to include only lines 1419–20 in *Troilus* and lines 4–6 in *Purgatorio*.

Fortuna Major is a particular conformation of stars[39] which had prophetic significance in the fairly popular medieval art of geomancy. The geomanticist first sets down at random a series of dots within a given framework. According to Root (1945:488), the figure thus arbitrarily arrived at by the geomanticist "will refer him to one of the signs of the zodiac, and to one of the seven planets. Thus, *Fortuna Major* refers to the sun, and to the sign of Aquarius." Root continues (p. 489):

---

[38] With such total recall, one is tempted to look for a hint of the fourth circle of the Inferno as well.

[39] These are θ Pegasi and α, π, γ, ζ, η Aquarii. I wish here to express my thanks to Miss Lockwood, of the Swarthmore College observatory, for her assistance in the astronomical aspects of this problem.

> ...the name, Fortuna Major, seems to have been applied to a group of six stars in the constellations of Aquarius and Pegasus, which conform roughly in disposition to the geomantic figure. . . . When the first light of dawn appeared in Troy, the group of stars called Fortuna Major, by "hym that koude it knowe," was about half-way between the eastern horizon and the zenith, and was still rising "estward," with the four stars properly placed above the other two.

The problem of ascription here is extremely complex. The art of geomancy was probably fairly familiar to Chaucer, who mentioned it by name in *ParsT* 1600–1605 and who liked to display his astronomical and astrological knowledge.[40] Dante obviously is not Chaucer's sole source of information on geomancy and geomantic figures, since, as Root points out, he mentions two other figures, Puella and Rubeus, in *KnT* 2045.

The one strong point in favor of Dantean source is that both poets, in speaking of Fortuna Major, refer to the hour before dawn. Dante is correct in this connection: "As these constellations immediately precede Aries, in which the sun is from March 21 to April 21, the figure in question can be seen in the east shortly before sunrise at that season" (Dante 1933:489–90). If Chaucer is following Dante's image, however, he has allied the geomantic figure (incorrectly, according to Root's calculations) more closely to the sunrise than the facts would warrant.

Of course, Chaucer may not have been thinking in such strict astronomical terms. If such were the case, we could not entirely dispense with Curry's remark that the emphasis here is not so much on the geomantic figure as on the term as synonymous with the sun, so that the passage simply means, "The sun rose" (cf. Robinson, p. 826). Favoring this interpretation are the following: (1) the image pattern set up by the crowing cock and Lucifer (i.e., Venus) as heralds of the day (i.e., the name Fortuna Major as the astronomical configuration already halfway to the zenith has no poetic function, either metaphorically or informatively, in the stanza, whereas the term has a definite function if Chaucer is using it as synonymous with, or closely allied to, the sun); (2) five manuscripts which read "afterward" or "after that" for "estward"; and (3) the definite possibility that "roos" means not "was rising" but "appeared on the horizon" (as it does in the previous line), in which case, if Chaucer's calculations were correct, the term as used for the geomantic configuration could not apply (since the group of stars was already "between the eastern horizon and the zenith"), but as a synonym for the sun the term would, of course, be applicable.

Three more general facts argue against the Dantean source. First, if this passage is from Dante, it is the only instance of Chaucer's borrowing astrological or astronomical information from him. Second, nothing in the rest of the description of the dawn in *Troilus* is dependent on Dante. Third, Chaucer shows in *The Knight's Tale* that he had other sources for his knowledge of geomancy, and these may very well have supplied him with his reference to Fortuna Major.

Despite all this evidence to the contrary, however, the coincidence of the hour that is being described and the fact that Chaucer's evident miscalculation can be accounted for by the line in Dante seem strong arguments in favor of the *Commedia* as source.

Bethel: "*1600: spelling Flegiton probably due to Dante; cf. *Inf.* XIV, 131."

Fro Flegetoun, the fery flood of helle   Flegetonta e Letè? ché de l'un taci

---

[40] *MLP* B¹ 1–14.

...Phlegethon and Lethe...? for about the one you are silent [*Inf.*, p. 149]

Despite Bethel's previous objections to ascriptions made on mere grounds of spelling,[41] this is his only basis for ascribing the Flegitoun[42] line to Dante. He says (pp. 204–205) that it "might have been taken from any one of a number of sources;[43] but the spelling with an initial 'F' may possibly show that he had Dante in mind."

To base this ascription on the initial *F*[44] is extremely dangerous in a period when orthographic regulation depended upon the individual writer. In Chaucer, for example, initial *f* replaces (if such a word can be used) *ph* in the following instances: *fenix* ("phoenix") *BD* 981; *frenetik* ("phrenetic") *TC* 5.206; *Frigius* (Phrygius) *BD* 1069; *Fysic* ("physic") *RR* 5739; *fisycien* ("physician") *Bo* 1, pr. 3, 65–70; *Fermacies* ("pharmacies") *KnT* 2713; *fantom* ("phantom") *MLT* 1037, *HF* 11, *HF* 493.

Bethel's ascription, therefore, seems highly unlikely.

Bethel: "1625–28: both idea and phrasing may be due solely to *Inf.* V, 121–23; but are probably due in part to Boethius, *Cons. Phil.* II, p. iv, 3–6."

"For of fortunes sharpe adversitee
The worste kynde of infortune is this,
A man to han ben in prosperitee,
And it remembren, whan it passed
   is...."
	E quella a me: "Nessun maggior dolore
	   che ricordarsi del tempo felice
	   ne la miseria;..."

   And she to me, "There is no greater sorrow than to recall, in wretchedness,
the happy time" [*Inf.*, p. 55]

Dante was most likely translating from Boethius here. Root evidently considers that Chaucer's primary source was also the *De consolatione*, for he notes at this point (1945:492):

> A free rendering of Boethius, 2pr. 4.4–7: "Sed hoc est quod recolentem vehementius coquit. Nam in omni adversitate fortunae infelicissimum est genus infortunii fuisse felicem." Chaucer here follows the Latin more closely than in his translation of Boethius; "But this is a thing that greatly smarteth me whan it remembreth me. For in alle adversitee of fortune, the most unsely kinde of contrarious fortune is to han ben weleful."[45]

Bethel's use of "solely" and "in part" at the opening of this citation are misleading. Certainly Chaucer was closer to the Latin than to the Italian in the phrasing, for example, of "The worste kynde of infortune" (*infelicissimum est genus infortunii*), "to han ben in prosperitee" (*fuisse felicem*), "for of fortunes sharpe adversitee" (*Nam in omni adversitate fortunae*), while the idea of the vexing recollection can be seen in *Sed hoc est quod recolentem*

---

[41] Cf. his discussion of "Lavyna," *HF* 458 above.

[42] Or Flegiton (Root) or *flegtoun* (Cp), or *flagitoun* (HlJ); not to mention the MS corruptions of Cocytus in H3 H4 R Cx.

[43] "Cf. Wise, *Influence of Statius*, 12, and *Thebiad*, IV, 523; VIII, 29. Root, *Troilus*, 491 compares *Aeneid* VI, 550f.; cf. Spencer's article" (Bethel's note).

[44] It will be noted that here, as in the other line (116) where he uses the name, Dante gives the spelling Flegetonta, never Flegeton.

[45] Both Root and Robinson (p. 827) also cite Saint Thomas *Summa*, part 2, Secunda Secundae, q. 36, art. 1, as well as, of course, the lines from the *Inferno*. Singleton (*Inf.*, Commentary, p. 93) adds Saint Augustine *Confessions* 10.14.

vehementius coquit. Though Dante's version is far more dramatic, Chaucer's seems a great deal nearer the common source.

Bethel: "1688f., 1693f.: the impossibility of describing the joy of the lovers; modelled closely on *Par*. XIX, 7–9."

This is no litel thyng of for to seye;	E quel che mi convien ritrar testeso,
This passeth every wit for to devyse; . . .	non portò voce mai, né scrisse incostro,
This joie may nought writen be with inke;	né fu per fantasia già mai compreso
This passeth al that herte may bythynke.	

And that which I must now tell, never did voice report nor ink record, nor was it ever comprised by phantasy [*Par*., p. 209]

There is no contextual parallel here, of course. Dante is describing his wonder and awe of the eagle, which, though made up of innumerable individual souls, speaks with a single voice and acts as an entity. Chaucer is describing the "joie" of Troilus and Criseyde, after "Pandarus hem two / Abedde brought" for the second time. Robinson is probably correct in remarking that "no source need be sought for so familiar a formula" (p. 827), and we can probably dispense with lines 1688–89 as an example of the common rhetorical device of inexpressibility.[46] However, the image which Chaucer has employed in lines 1693–94 is so strikingly similar to that of Dante that there would appear to be no reason to doubt the possibility of its source in *Par*. 19.

Bethel: "1807f.: allusions to Venus and Cupid; modelled on *Par*. VIII, 7ff."

Thow lady bryght, the doughter to Dyone,	ma Dïone onoravano e Cupido,
Thy blynde and wynged sone ek, daun Cupide	quella per madre sua, questo per figlio,
	e dicean ch'el sedette in grembo a Dido

. . . but they honored Dione and Cupid, the one as her mother, the other as her son, and they told that he had sat in Dido's lap. [*Par*., p. 83]

Any relationship here is highly doubtful. As Lowes, Robinson, and Root mention, the kinship of Dione, Venus, and Cupid could also have been learned from Virgil (*Aen*. 3.19), Claudian (*De Rapt. Pros*. 3.433, 4.102), Ovid (*Ars Am*. 2.593, 3.769; *Amores* 1.14, 33), Boccaccio (*Teseida* 1.3.3–5; *Gen. Deor*. 11.4), or Servius (1.339), among others, so that it is not at all unreasonable to consider this common literary knowledge. The weakness of parallels based on the concept of total recall is that they must often be constructed on an overly complex suggestive pattern to maintain their linkages, and thus the simpler and more probable explanations are ignored. Bethel, for example, in his text explains his reason for this ascription as follows (pp. 193–94):

---

[46] See Sypherd (1907), where he discusses Chaucer's inability to describe the beauty of the House of Fame. Sypherd adds (p. 61) that "this is one of the most conventional commonplaces in mediaeval poetry." See Curtius 1953:159–62.

A similar collocation [to that which Lowes points to in the invocation to Polymnia in the *Anelida*] of Dante and Boccaccio occurs in *Troilus* III, 1807–10.... The first two lines Chaucer draws chiefly from Dante...on a hint from Boccaccio, while in the reference to the Muses he returned to Boccaccio and translated, in "listen for tabide," a phrase he had neglected to include in the *Anelida* passage already discussed.

The more direct suggestion of common literary knowledge seems far more likely.[47]

Book 4

Bethel: "22–24: invocation to the Furies; phrasing influenced by Dante's description of the Furies, *Inf.* IX, 34–51."

O ye Herynes, Nyghtes doughtren thre,   [See under *TC* 1.6–14.]
That endeles compleignen evere in
        pyne,
Megera, Alete, and ek Thesiphone

Lowes (1917*a*:720 n.1) gives a wide range of possible sources (of which Dante is not one) for line 22 above. For line 23 see the discussion under *TC* 1.6–14. The argument that the spelling of Alete is indication of a borrowing from Dante is extremely weak. First, Dante uses the spelling Aletto; second, Chaucer does not follow Dante's spelling Tesifone for the third Fury, which – if he were following the Italian text as closely as has been suggested – would certainly have made itself felt.[48] All that is left, then, is the coincidence of the order of the first two names, since the third must come last by the demands of meter and rhyme. This seems hardly sufficient grounds for an ascription to Dante.

Bethel: "225–27: comparison of Troilus, bereft of hope, to trees stripped by winter; closely modelled on *Inf.* III, 112–14."

And as in wynter leves ben biraft,   Come d'autunno si levan le foglie
Ech after other, til the tree be bare,   l'una appresso de l'altra, fin che 'l ramo
So that ther nys but bark and braunche   vede a la terra tutte le sue spoglie,
        ilaft,   [similemente il mal seme d'Adamo
[Lith Troilus, byraft of ech welfare,   gittansi di quel lito ad una ad una,
Ibounden in the blake bark of care,   per cenni come augel per suo richiamo.]
Disposed wood out of his wit to breyde,
So sore hym sat the chaungynge of
        Criseyde.]

As the leaves fall away in autumn, one after another, till the bough sees all its spoils upon the ground, [so there the evil seed of Adam: one by one they cast themselves from that shore at signals, like a bird at its call.] [*Inf.*, p. 33]

The additional lines in Chaucer's stanza have been given since Bethel makes use of them

---

[47] Pratt (1947:263 n.17) considers lines 1807–13 as a reworking of *HF* 518–22.
[48] The other use of the name in Chaucer (*TC* 1.6) has the same spelling as that given in line 24 above.

in his text. I have added the following tercet from Dante so that a fuller comparison of these two images may be carried out. Bethel, like most of the other scholars, finds (pp. 223–24):

> In a comparison of Troilus, stripped of everything save the "blake bark of care," to trees whose foliage winter has stripped away, Chaucer is obviously following Dante, is "clearly writing with the pages of Dante open before him."[49] . . . The first three lines are imitated from the third canto of the Inferno:[50] . . . where Dante applies the simile to the embarkation of the souls of the damned from the spheres of Acheron.[51]

In checking this entry, we should recognize that there is no parallel, as Bethel's appendix (though not his text) indicates, after line 227 in Chaucer.

Now just what are the similarities and differences in these two similes? First we should note that there is no contextual parallel: in Chaucer we have Troilus's mounting grief at the coming loss of Criseyde; in Dante, a visual picture of the souls leaving Acheron. Verbally, Dante's simile is set in autumn, Chaucer's in winter. Chaucer's phrase "leves ben biraft, / Ech after other" is paralleled by Dante's "si levan le foglie / l'una appresso de l'altra." Finally, the rest of the two images again diverge: "fin che 'l ramo / vede a la terra tutte le sue spoglie" is far different from "til the tree be bare / So that ther nys but bark and braunche ilaft." What we have here, it would seem, is certainly not a direct translation but rather a common image of the gradual falling away of leaves from a tree. Virgil's lines read: "...thick as the leaves of the forest that at autumn's first frost dropping fall" (Virgil 1918:1.527), and Horace uses the image in lines 58–63 of the Ars poetica shortly before those which are the basis of TC 2.22–26:

> It has ever been, and will ever be, permitted to issue words stamped with the mint-mark of the day. As forests change their leaves with each year's decline, and the earliest drop off: so with words, the old race dies, and like the young of human kind, the new-born bloom and thrive. We are doomed to death—we and all things ours. [Horace 1936:455]

Axon (1900:93) early remarked that "the simile, however, is an obvious one, and at the most the words of Dante can only have reminded Chaucer of what he must himself have often seen." While, therefore, there is an analogy in the Commedia, it would seem that there is nothing unique in this comparison.[52]

As well, if we look at the image itself, we see that Dante is emphasizing the fate of the leaves and that the simile, poetically, is weak in that there are no equivalents to the tree and the branch in the vehicle; it is, in short, used only for its visual effect in describing the movement of the souls from the shore of Acheron. On the other hand, Chaucer's image is not merely visual but circumstantial, for the emphasis is on the barrenness of the tree (i.e.,

---

[49] Root (1945:xliv). At this point Bethel cites TC 4.225–31.

[50] Inf. 3.112–14 are given, and Bethel notes that they are "modelled in turn upon Aen., VI, 309–12, cf. Kuhns, Tr. Nature., 29."

[51] Singleton (Inf., Commentary, p. 55), after quoting Virgil, points out Dante's "strikingly new elements—the bough 'sees' (vede) its leaves (il mal / seme d'Adamo) fall away; there is a shift to falcon imagery (line 1217)—but these distinctive features are not in Chaucer.

[52] One finds the image throughout literature: thus, for example, Boethius, De consolatione (1, m. 5.180–85), "Wynter wakeneth al my care" (ca. 1300), Shakespeare's sonnets (e.g., no. 73), Shelley's odes ("To the West Wind"), Verlaine's "Les Sanglots Longs," and the sentimentality of popular song lyrics ("Autumn," "September Song") to name but a few that come first to mind.

Troilus) which is the central figure of the image and the part from which the dependent images (i.e., leaves and branches) derive their meaning and their relevance.

Bethel, in rejecting Rambeau's theory on *The House of Fame* in general and lines 1521–24 in particular (p. 216) cited Lounsbury's well-known comment that "it was not necessary for Chaucer to go to Italy to be reminded of the particular kind of noise occasioned by the humming of a bee."[53] One wonders whether such a trip was necessary to discover that "leves ben biraft, / Ech after other," be it in autumn or in winter.

Bethel: "*388: See under *Troil.* I, 568f."

...thorough cas or aventure.   [See citations under *TC* 1.568f.]

Very little need be added to the previous discussion, but it is interesting to note that Dante is urged as a source for this conventional division. Bethel after noting how important Boethius was in western Europe in general and in Chaucer's philosophy in particular, with specific reference to "free-will and predestination, fate and fortune, true and false felicity" (pp. 239–40) suggests (p. 243):

> No question, for instance seemed to interest him [Chaucer] so much as the age-old speculation about free-will and determinism, or rather predestination.... No one can read very widely in Chaucer's poetry without realizing how thoroughly and deeply interested he was in the most important philosophical question of his day—and for that matter of our own.

The important point to be noted here is that it was indeed an "age-old speculation" and that it is not at all necessary to look solely to Dante for the source of this opposition.

Bethel: "473f.: reference to Proserpine; phrasing probably due to *Inf.* IX, 34–51."

but down with Proserpyne,   [See citation under *TC* 1.6–14.]
Whan I am ded, I wol go wone in pyne

The reference here is merely to the lower regions. Troilus, bewailing the loss of Criseyde, says, in context:

> "The deth may wel out of my brest departe
> The lif, so longe may this sorwe myne;
> But fro my soule shal Criseydes darte
> Out nevere mo; but down with Proserpyne,
> Whan I am ded, I wol go wone in pyne,
> And ther I wol eternaly compleyne
> My wo, and how that twynned be we tweyne."

If this is meant to be the Christian hell, Troilus's concept of it is far different from Dante's. Rather, this seems to be the standard, classical conception of the lower world, which was, of course, the region of Proserpine. See further discussion under *TC* 1.6–14.

---

[53] "*Studies*, II, 244" (Bethel's note).

Bethel: "776: the figure of *unsheathing* one's soul is taken from *Par.* I, 21."

Til I my soule out of my breste unshethe   de la vagina de le membra sue

from the sheath of his limbs. [*Par.*, p. 5]

There is no contextual parallel here. Troilus is telling how he will kill himself by starvation "till I my soule out of my breste unshethe," while Dante is invoking the help of Apollo

Entra nel petto mio, e spira tue
sì come quando Marsïa traesti
de la vagina de le membra sue.

The entire parallel is thus made to rest on the word "vagina," which in Chaucer is "the figure of *unsheathing* one's soul." This is not, however, the use that Dante has for the word, as Root (1945:514) points out succinctly: "Boccaccio says, *Fil.* 4.89: 'sen va la smarrita Anima fuor del corpo.' Chaucer's curious metaphor suggests Dante, *Par.* 1.20–1. . . . But Dante is referring to the *flaying* of Marsyas."[54] If this word did make such an impression on Chaucer, it is surprising that he did not use it in his longest reference to Marcia in *The House of Fame* (lines 1229–32)—if that passage is indeed based on Dante.

Bethel: "925–27: speech compared to the *flat* and *edge* of a sword; cf. *Inf.* XXXI, 1–6; *Purg.* XXXI, 2–3."

And shapeth yow his sorwe for
    t'abregge,
And nought encresse, leeve nece swete!
Beth rather to hym cause of flat than
    egge,
[And with som wisdom ye his sorwe
    bete.
What helpeth it to wepen ful a strete,
Or though ye bothe in salte teeris
    dreynte?
Bet is a tyme of cure ay than of pleynte.]

Una medesma lingua pria mi morse,
    sì che mi tinse l'una e l'altra guancia,
    e poi la medicina mi riporse;
così od'io che solea far la lancia
    d'Achille e del suo padre esser cagione
    prima di trista e poi di buona mancia.

volgendo suo parlare a me per punta,
che pur per taglio m'era paruto acro

One and the same tongue first stung me, so that it tinged both my cheeks, and then it supplied the medicine to me; thus I have heard that the lance of Achilles and of his father was wont to be the cause, first of a sad and then of a good gift. [*Inf.*, p. 327]

. . .turning against me the point of her speech, which even with the edge had seemed sharp to me [*Purg.*, p. 339]

Actually line 927 (the only line concerned in this projected parallelism) has nothing to do with speech, but is concerned with Criseyde's attitude. Evidently the "speech" element has been introduced not because it is in Chaucer but because it is the subject on which Dante bases his images. Nor is the *Commedia*'s comparison of speech as a weapon so unusual; both the Pardoner (line 712) and Pandarus (*TC* 2.1681) can "wel afilen" their

---

[54] Root's italics. Griffin and Myrick's translation reads: ". . .the bewildered soul parteth. . .from the body" (Boccaccio 1967:329).

tongues when the occasion demands. The second citation from Dante, then, has nothing to do with the line from Chaucer that is under consideration.

Root, quite properly, only suggests a similar notion in Dante to that found in line 927, adding Scartazzini's remark (p. 227): "Our ancient poets love to compare to the spear of Peleus the glance and the kiss of the lady."

The reference to Achilles could, of course, have been easily found in Ovid,[55] and there is every indication that Chaucer had the classical source in mind in his other mention of Achilles and of the magic spear in *The Squire's Tale* (lines 238–40), since Achilles' victim, "Thelophus the kyng," is mentioned at the same time in both places. On the other hand, what makes any source in Dante even less likely in the present instance is that "flat" and "egge" refer, in all probability, to a sword and not to a lance or a spear.

The magic sword in *The Squire's Tale* (lines 156–67) fits more closely the brief description given in line 927 above. Whether or not the mythical lance of Achilles suggested the sword that "the kyng of Arabe and of Inde" sent to Cambyuskan or whether Chaucer had another tale in mind is difficult to say. Certainly, if there is a source, the detail of *The Squire's Tale* would indicate one more precise than that which the classical — to say nothing of the *Dantesque* — descriptions could have afforded him.

Examples of similar conceptions in Oriental literature, as Robinson notes (pp. 717, 718), have been collected by Clouston (1889) and strengthen the theory that the tale was to be composed by piecing together "episodes of different origin" (Robinson, p. 717). In any event, there is no clear indication that line 927 has its source in Dante, while there is much that points to a totally different, and probably folkloric, source.

Bethel: "1187f.: Minos as judge of the souls of suicides; cf. *Inf.* XIII, 94–96; cf. V, 1–15; cf. XX, 35f."

So that his soule hire soule folwen myghte
Ther as the doom of Mynos wolde it dighte

Quando si parte l'anima feroce
  dal corpo ond' ella stessa s'è disvelta,
  Minòs la manda a la settima foce.

Così discesi del cerchio primaio
  giù nel secondo, che men loco cinghia
  e tanto più dolor, che punge a guaio.
Stavvi Minòs orribilmente, e ringhia;
  essamina le colpe ne l'intrata,
  giudica e manda secondo ch' avvinghia.
Dico che quando l'anima mal nata
  li vien dinanzi, tutta si confessa;
  e quel conoscitor de le peccata
vede qual loco d'inferno è da essa;
  cignesi con la coda tante volte
  quantunque gradi vuol che giù sia messa.
Sempre dinanzi a lui ne stanno molte:
  vanno a vicenda ciascuna al giudizio,
  dicono e odono e poi son giù volte.

E non restò di ruinare a valle
  fino a Minòs che ciascheduno afferra.

---

[55] *Met.* 12.112, 23.171–72; *Rem. am.* 44–48; *Trist.* 5.2.15–18. Cf. Grandgent (Dante 1933:276): "In Provençal and early Italian poetry there are many references to this spear; it was believed in the Middle Ages that a hurt inflicted by it could be healed only by another wound from the same weapon."

When the fierce soul quits the body from which it has uprooted itself, Minos sends it to the seventh gullet. [*Inf.*, p. 135]

Thus I descended from the first circle into the second, which girds less space, and so much greater woe that it goads to wailing. There stands Minos, horrible and snarling: upon the entrance he examines their offenses, and judges and dispatches them according as he entwines. I mean that when the ill-begotten soul comes before him, it confesses all; and that discerner of sins sees which shall be its place in Hell, then girds himself with his tail as many times as the grades he wills that it be sent down. Always before him stands a crowd of them; they go, each in his turn, to the judgment; they tell, and hear, and then are hurled below. [*Inf.*, p. 47]

And he stopped not from falling headlong down to Minos, who seizes every one. [*Inf.*, p. 205]

Tatlock (1904:97) suggests that this is an allusion that makes a parallel between Troilus and Criseyde and Paolo and Francesca. Briefly his line of argument is that the description of Minos at the beginning of canto 5 of the *Inferno* should, per se, be evoked in the reader's (or audience's) mind by Chaucer's mention of Minos in *Troilus* and that this in turn should connect with the story of Paolo and Francesca—which occupies the last half of Dante's canto. But surely this is an oversubtle technique if Chaucer is in fact trying to make the allusion; surely, if Chaucer wished to make reference to the Paolo and Francesca story he would not have been so circuitous about it. There are no verbal parallels here, and, aside from the fact that the Paolo and Francesca story deals with two lovers, there is no contextual parallel either.

Bethel follows Root, who notes (p. 522):

Fil. 4.120 reads

> Acciochè il suo spirto seguitasse
> Quel della donna con si trista sorte,
> E nell' inferno con lei abitasse.

Rossetti explains that *inferno* means only Hades; but Chaucer has preferred to soften the idea. Minos is the judge who passes judgment on the souls of suicides.[56]

In other words, Root, thinking in Christian terms, sees Chaucer giving the reason why Troilus and Criseyde should be united after death, since, as Bethel (pp. 190–91) puts it, "Minos assigns the souls of suicides to the same place." But if Chaucer were trying to get a point as delicate as this across to his audience, he would not base himself on an obscure cross reference to a work they had probably not read; on the contrary, he would have to base his allusion on a fairly generally accepted tradition if it was to get across at all. In the final analysis, of course, there is no positive evidence that Chaucer was trying to establish so subtle a point.

It would, naturally, be more consistent if Troilus were to descend rather to the pagan underworld than "to the (Christian) regions of eternal punishment (Spencer 1927:186),

---

[56] Griffin and Myrick's translation reads: ". . . in order that his spirit might follow that of his lady in so sad a fate and dwell with her in hell" (Boccaccio 1967:345).

but, as Grandgent says (Dante 1933:47), "it is not strange to find in a Christian Hell many classic personages, especially such as were already associated with the lower world." What is important is that there is nothing in this reference to Minos that is outside traditional view as established from the time of the eleventh book of the *Odyssey* on. Chaucer could have run across the idea in Virgil[57] or Claudian,[58] among other sources. What principally serves to deny Dante as a source is what Chaucer does not say. In classical literature, as Grandgent points out (Dante, p. 47): "Minos...holds...the noble office of judge of the dead.... In Dante he has become a hideous demon, arbiter of the damned—the symbol, it would seem, of the guilty conscience." The lurid portrait that Dante paints at the beginning of canto 5 is nowhere found in Chaucer, either here in *Troilus* or in any one of the fourteen references to him in the Legend of Ariadne in *The Legend of Good Women*. On the contrary, all of them fall within the scope of the classical and traditional concept of Minos as king of Crete or as the holder of "the noble office of judge of the dead."

Bethel: "1538–40: allusion to Athamas; phrasing possibly indebted to *Inf.* XXX, 1–4."

Saturnes doughter, Juno, thorugh hire myght,	Nel tempo che Iunone era crucciata per Semelè contra 'l sangue tebano,
As wood as Athamante do me dwelle	come mostrò una e altra fiata,
Eternalich in Stix, the put of helle!	Atamante divenne tanto insano

In the time when Juno was wroth for Semele against the Theban blood, as she showed more than once, Athamas became so insane.... [*Inf.*, p. 315]

There is here a possible use of Dante,, but this is based not so much on a verbal as a contextual similarity. As Root (1945:525) notes: Atamante "is a type of the 'falsitori' who dwell in the tenth 'bolgia' of the eighth circle. Criseyde prays that Juno may condemn her to hell, mad as Athamas, if she is ever *false* to Troilus."

Bethel's reticence ("possibly indebted") is well advised, considering the vigorous argument that Spencer offers against Lowes's original ascription of the lines to Dante. Spencer's conclusion (p. 186) is that,

> as Mr. Lowes himself remarks, the form "Athamante" could have come from Ovid, Met. iv, 470: "Athamanta," and Ovid is probably the source for Chaucer's knowledge of that character's woodness. Further, we have already seen[59] that the phrase, *Stix, the put of helle*, derives by no means from Dante alone; hence we cannot use its employment here as additional evidence to show that Chaucer had Dante in mind when writing Athamante. The passage can be accounted for by Ovid and the convention of mediaeval hell; if Dante was in Chaucer's mind here at all, the portion of it he occupied was, I think, very small.

Nearly all the elements in Chaucer's passage are to be found in Ovid (*Met.* 4.416–562): an extended description of Styx ("nebulas exhalat iners: umbraeque recentes / Descendunt

---

[57] *Aen.* 6.531–33: "Yet not without a lot, not without a judge, are these places given; Minos, presiding, shakes the urn; 'tis he calls a court of the silent, and learns men's lives and misdeeds" (Virgil 1918:1.537).

[58] *De Raptu* 2.332: "Minos' urn of judgment throws no ambiguous lots" (Claudian 1918:2.343).

[59] See following entry.

illac.... / Pallor hiemsque tenent late loca senta", lines 434–46), constant references to madness (lines 429, 485, 499, 512), the use of noun forms identical to Athamante (lines 467, 471, 497), and references to Juno as the daughter of Saturn (lines 448, 464), though the last (as Lowes says) is a commonplace. Finally, it must be recalled that the reason for Dante's use of Athamas as an example of the "falsitori" is not completely clear. Evidently Athamas is mentioned in the lowest part of the eighth circle either because he was falsifying in the sense that he was *fuor di se*[60] in his madness or because he had falsely accused his first wife, Nephele, of madness; but the first reason is obscure in Dante and not hinted at in Ovid, while the second reason is in neither work.

While no source clearly explains the reason for Chaucer's selection of Athamante, certain elements seem to suggest strongly that he may have had the *Commedia* in mind. First, Ovid does not speak of Athamas in the infernal regions, while Dante does; second, however obscure its motivation, the fact remains that the canto from which this reference comes is a particularly appropriate one insofar as Criseyde and her oath are concerned. If the reference was made by chance, it was a particularly felicitous stroke.

Bethel: "1540: reference to "Stix, the put of helle" possibly from *Inf.* VII, 106, etc.; doubtful."

Eternalich in Stix, the put of helle!   In la palude va, c'ha nome Stige
                                                        questo tristo ruscel

> This dismal little stream...flows into the marsh that is named Styx. [*Inf.*, p. 75]

There is no basis for dependence here. Spencer's argument is conclusive. If one were to consider only Virgil, Claudian, and Dante as possible sources, then Dante's conception is closest; but, adds Spencer (p. 181), "there were other descriptions of hell." He begins by listing the Book of Job and *Piers Plowman*, which refer to "the put of helle." The most convincing argument, however, comes from his long list of medieval visions which use the same description (p. 181): "Drihthelm in the seventh century,[61] Tundale,[62]

> and the phrase "put of helle" is a favourite one with the English author of *St. Patrick's Purgatory*, where in the twenty lines (vv. 357–377), hell is spoken of eight times as a "put." Examples from the visions could be multiplied almost indefinitely. Indeed the Middle Ages rarely thought of hell as anything else, and we cannot say that Chaucer's description of it as such or as a "swolow"[63] comes from Dante alone. And it is equally doubtful if he was thinking of Dante's description of Styx as *una palude...che ha nome stige* (as has been suggested[64]) when he called Styx the "put of helle"; for a marsh and a pit are not, after all, quite the same thing.

---

[60] Rossetti 1881:58.

[61] "Bede, *Eccles. Hist.*, v. 12" (Spencer's note).

[62] "There are fifty-four Latin MSS alone of Tundale's vision (cf. A. Wagner, *Visio Tungdali*, Erlangen, 1882) extending from the twelfth to the fifteenth centuries—and his account was translated into French, German, English, Italian, Irish, and Icelandic. Owayn's adventures in *St. Patrick's Purgatory* had an almost equal popularity. In this case, too, we are confronted with a large number of MSS in Latin, French and English. Cf. E. J. Becker [*Mediaeval Visions of Heaven and Hell*, Baltimore, 1899] pp. 81ff." (Spencer's note).

[63] Cf.. *TC* 4.1540 (Root 1945), *BD* 171, *HF* 1654.

[64] "J. L. Lowes, "Chaucer and Dante," *Mod. Phil.*, XIV (1917), 705–35" (Spencer's note).

I have cited this passage at some length for two reasons: first, because Lowes depends on the line from *Troilus* for many other posited sources, and, second, because Spencer's review of the *visio* literature points up the danger of paralleling passages *in vacuo*.

Bethel: *1674–76: Shows the general influence of Dante's ideas of *gentillesse*."

"Eke gentil herte and manhod that ye
    hadde,
And that ye hadde, as me thoughte, in
    despit
Every thyng that souned into
    badde. . . ."

[See discussions under *TC* 1.894–96, *FranT*, *SqT*, *Gent*.]

There is neither verbal nor contextual similarity in Dante. The ascription is evidently based on the word *gentil*, but it ignores the vast body of love and courtly-love poetry of medieval literature.

Book 5

Bethel: "6f.: reference to Lachesis; phrasing possibly due to *Purg*. XXV, 79; doubtful."

And Troilus shal dwellen forth in pyne
Til Lachesis his thred no lenger twyne.

Quando Làchesis non ha più del lino

And when Lachesis has no more thread
[*Purg*., p. 273]

As far as I can determine, there is no connection whatever between these two passages. Bethel cannot possibly mean to imply that Chaucer was dependent on Dante for either the idea or the name of one of the Parcae. The only basis on which this suggestion can be made is that in both cases there is the idea of the fates being under God (at least to the extent that they are both mentioned by Christian writers), but this idea was so general and the suggestion of it here is so vague that there would seem to be no valid relationship at all.

Bethel: "*267–73: several phrases in a similar appeal to the reader suggest *Inf*. XXXIV, 22–27."

Who koude telle aright or ful discryve
His wo, his pleynt, his langour, and his
    pyne?
Naught alle the men that han or ben on
    lyve.
Thow, redere, maist thiself ful wel
    devyne
That swich a wo my wit kan nat diffyne.
On ydel for to write it sholde I swynke,
Whan that my wit is wery it to thynke.

Com' io divenni allor gelato e fioco,
    nol dimandar, lettor, ch'i' non lo scrivo,
    però ch'ogne parlar sarebbe poco.
Io non mori' e non rimasi vivo;
    pensa oggimai per te, s'hai fior d'ingegno,
    qual io divenni, d'uno e d'altro privo.

How frozen and faint I then became, ask it not, reader, for I do not write it, because all words would fail. I did not die and I did not remain alive: now think for yourself, if you have any wit, what I became, deprived alike of death and life! [*Inf*., p. 363]

Robinson (p. 832), noting that "the address to the reader has been ascribed to the influence of Dante," cites this and other passages in the *Commedia* but adds, justly, that "it is hardly necessary to assume that Chaucer had any literary model for so natural a device."

The direct appeal to the reader is one of Chaucer's most engaging devices and one that he uses most frequently. Throughout his writing, for example, there is the direct command to his audience to follow up his remarks with recommended reading.[65]

As well, the inability of the poet to describe something, as has been mentioned frequently, was almost a convention of poetry of the time. Certainly one finds it throughout those poems in which the writer tries to describe in courtly terms the beauty of his mistress,[66] and Chaucer uses the device more than once. In the Proem to *The House of Fame*, for example, he says (lines 12–18):

> but whoso of these miracles
> The causes knoweth bet then I,
> Devyne he; for I certeinly
> Ne kan hem noght, ne never thinke
> To besily my wyt to swinke,
> To knowe of hir signifiaunce
> The gendres. . . .

And later, in book 3 (lines 1174–80), Chaucer would have us again believe that poetic ability is failing him:

> hit astonyeth yit my thought,
> And maketh al my wyt to swynke,
> On this castel to bethynke,
> So that the grete craft, beaute,
> The cast, the curiosite
> Ne kan I not to yow devyse;
> My wit ne may me not suffise.

What we have here, as Robinson implies, is a poetic convention rather than a literary source.

Bethel: "549: 'O ryng, fro which the ruby is out falle'—: Cary compares *Purg.* XXIII, 31; (cf. Root, *Troilus*, 539). But the application of the figure is totally dissimilar in the two cases, and any borrowing here seems doubtful."

The fact that the figure of the ruby, as Robinson notes (p. 833), is not in the *Filostrato* has sent scholars off to look for it elsewhere. Bethel, looking at the context, is right in saying that the application is totally dissimilar; the line in Dante refers to the dark- and hollow-eyed spirits, with pallid faces and bodies so wasted away that the skin took the form from the bones and "parean l'occhiaie anella sanza gemme," their eye-sockets seemed gemless rings (cf. lines 22–24, 31).

The image of the gem, more specifically the ruby, and still more precisely the ruby in the ring, is found at 2.344, 585, 1087; 3.1371, and 5.549, and is often, as here, a Chaucerian

---

[65] Cf. e.g., *MkT* B² 3769–70, 4453; *PardT* C 742; *ClT* E 183; *MerT* E 2232; *ManT* H 344–45; *TC* 1.147, 5.1771; *LGW* 1367, 1457, 1557, also *MkT* B² 3650, 4519; *PardT* C 586; *WBT* D 982, 1168, which are directed to the reader, though through the primary audience of the other pilgrims.

[66] Cf. "The Ten Commandments of Love," MS Fairfax 16, printed in *Secular Lyrics of the XIVth and XVth Centuries*, p. 165, stanza 1; or "The Beauty of His Mistress, III," MS Rawlinson C 813, *ibid.*, p. 126, stanza 1. See also Sypherd 1907:61; Curtius 1953:159–62.

addition to the *Filostrato* (thus, at 2.585, *la gemma* becomes "the ruby"). In these instances Chaucer can be seen establishing a specific image and then developing it through its use as a token of consummated love (3.1371) and finally, in pathos, as the symbol of the lost love (5.549: "O ryng, fro which the ruby is out falle").

Specific interpretation has varied. Samuel Schuman (1975:99–112) investigates a possible sexual meaning, especially of the ring;[67] yet one must still recall that the ruby, at least on the brooch "set was like an herte" (3.1371). A different interpretation develops when we are directed to Machaut's *Fontaine amoureuse* (a source of *The Book of the Duchess*), in which the narrator and prince fall asleep by the Fountain of Love, and the prince dreams of Venus and his lady. When the lover awakes, he discovers the lady's gift of a ruby ring on his finger. When the two texts are looked at without pressure or prejudice, suggestive interpretations evolve; the ruby may well have been an accepted symbol of accepted love.

I have taken the liberty of this brief digression to note, however minimally, the uses and the range of ascription and allusion. What becomes starkly apparent is that the posited Dante ascription is without verbal, contextual, or poetic confirmation. To force Chaucer into a comparison, to insist on a particular source (in this instance, Dante) may cause us to palliate or even lose what seems to be a piece of conscious artistry on Chaucer's part.

Bethel: "599–603: Juno's anger against the Theban blood; phraseology influenced by *Inf.* XXX, 1–4, 22f."

"...Now, blisful lord, so cruel thow ne be
Unto the blood of Troie, I preye the,
As Juno was unto the blood Thebane,
For which the folk of Thebes caughte hire bane."

[For *Inf.* 30.1–4, see *TC* 4.1538–40.]

Ma né di Tebe furie né troiane
    si vider mäi in alcun tanto crude,
[...quant' io vidi in due ombre smorte e
    nude]

But no fury of Thebes or of Troy was ever seen so cruel against any, [...as were two pallid shades that I saw]. [*Inf.*, p. 317]

While there is obviously an analogy here, the question of influence is more debatable, depending on the term *sangue tebano* in *Inf.* 30.2. The anger of Juno is, of course, the motivation of the *Aeneid*, as Virgil makes clear from the start,[68] and Chaucer's earlier reference in *The House of Fame* (lines 198–201) to the "Troianysshe blood" most likely came from *Aen.* 1.19: "Yet in truth she had heard that a race was springing from Trojan blood" (Virgil 1918:1.243), which is explaining the causes for Juno's anger. But a source for this is hardly necessary. Juno's anger is found in Ovid,[69] Statius,[70] and Boccaccio[71] and is, as Robinson says (p. 672), "repeatedly referred to." There is, therefore, the central motivation of Juno's anger that links the stories of the fall of Thebes and of Troy, so that it is not unusual for Dante (in *Inf.* 30.22f., above) to put the two together or for Chaucer to weave the one into the other, with methods so subtle—as here, or in the instance of the

---

[67] But see also Ross 1971–72. While Schuman sees the ring as the female genitals, he seems at a loss when faced with (Troilus's) ruby; one could spin out the image by recalling that Priapus (the phallic god found at the center of the temple in *The House of Fame*) was also known as *ruber* and *rubicundus*. But this is to become a "joyles juelere" indeed.

[68] *Aen.* 1.4: "through cruel Juno's unforgiving wrath" (Virgil 1918:1.241).

[69] *Met.* 3.253–315, 4.416–562, the story of Athamas.

[70] Wise (1911:22): "In the *Thebaid*, Juno is always inimical to Thebes." Cf. *Thebaid* 1.2, 10.74, 126, 162, 282.

[71] *Teseida* 3.1; 4.14, 16, 17; 5.56, 58; 9.44; 10.39, 94; 12.26.

"romaunce" which Criseyde reads in book 2 or in Cassandra's interpretation of the dream in book 5—that they might serve as examples of masterful poetic control of one's subject.

Therefore, while there is a certain verbal parallelism that might serve as a basis for comparison in the present citation, there is no reason to connect Chaucer's other references to Juno's anger (as is done most frequently with *KnT* A 1329)[72] to the opening lines of *Inf.* 30 because of their use of the term "the blood of Thebes." *Sanguis* in Latin and "blood" in English are commonly used for a race of people or lineal descendants. The present citation from Dante is in the literary tradition of Juno's anger against Thebes and Troy, but there is no positive indication that it influenced these lines from *Troilus.*

Bethel: "744–49: allusion to Prudence and her three eyes shows influence of *Purg.* XXIX, 132, and, probably, *Conv.* IV, xxvii, 5."

"To late is now to speke of that matere. Prudence, allas, oon of thyne eyen thre Me lakked alwey, er that I come here! On tyme ypassed wel remembred me, And present tyme ek koud ich wel ise, But future tyme, er I was in the snare, Koude I nat sen; that causeth now my care...."

d'una di lor, ch'avea tre occhi in testa [*Purg.,* 29.132]

Conviensi adunque essere prudente, cioè savio: e a ciò essere si richiede buona memoria de le vedute cose, buona conoscenza de le presenti e buona provedenza de le future. E, sì come dice lo Filosofo nel sesto de l' Etica, "impossibile è essere savio chi non è buono", e però non è da dire savio chi con sottratti e con inganni procede, ma è da chiamare astuto; chè sì come nullo dicerebbe savio quelli che si sapesse bene trarre de la punta d'uno coltello ne la pupilla de l' occhio, così non è da dire savio quelli che ben sa una malvagia cosa fare, la quale facendo, prima sè sempre che altrui offende. [*Conv.* 4.27.5]

one of them that had three eyes in her head [*Purg.,* p. 323]

It is meet, therefore, that a man should be prudent, that is wise; and for becoming wise there are required good memory of things that have been seen, good apprehension of things present, and good foresight of things future. And as the Philosopher says in the sixth book of the *Ethics,* "it is impossible for a man to be wise unless he is good"; and therefore a man who proceeds with subterfuge and deceit is not to be called wise but astute; for just as no one would call a man wise who knew how to hit the pupil of an eye with a dagger, so a man is not to be called wise who knows well how to commit a bad action, by doing which he always wrongs himself before he wrongs another. [Pp. 287–88]

In all probability this was a reasonably common symbol for Prudence. At least Dante does not feel called upon to identify "d'una di lor, ch'avea tre occhi in testa," even though there was evidently a great deal of argument about whether she belonged among the moral or

---

[72] Other references are *KnT* A 1543, 1559; *Anel.* 51; *HF* 198.

the intellectual virtues.[73] Nor was there any question in the minds of the earliest commentators from Benevenuto da Imola on, that this half line (which for Dante is most scantily worked out) ever referred to anything other than Prudence.

As one would suspect, a whole tradition leads to this symbol directly. Cicero, in the *De inventione*,[74] divides Prudence into three parts: "Memory, intelligence, foresight. Memory is that by which the soul brings back those things which were; intelligence, that by which it perceives those things which are; foresight, that by which anything that will be is seen before it happens." There is, likewise, the discussion in the Pseudo-Seneca (Robinson, p. 833) and, perhaps more important, the extensive comment of Saint Thomas.[75] Since this concept of Prudence as dependent on the past, present, and future was so widely held, it would seem that the three-eyed image would be a natural and fairly common iconographic symbol.[76] Until direct evidence to that effect is brought to light, however, we must accept Dante as a likely source. Bethel adds (p. 196): ". . . in view of the fact of our knowledge of Chaucer's acquaintance with the *Convivio*, especially with the fourth book, it is quite likely that Chaucer derived his information from it." This explanation is entirely plausible, and the two sources cited above would serve to connect the symbol and its meaning in Chaucer's mind if that connection had not been made before.

Bethel: "1541–45: thought and phrasing show influence of Dante's discussion of Fortune, *Inf*. VII, 67–96."

Fortune, which that permutacioun
Of thynges hath, as it is hire comitted
Thorugh purveyaunce and disposicioun
Of heighe Jove, as regnes shal be flitted
Fro folk in folk, or when they shal be
    smytted,
[Gan pulle awey the fetheres brighte of
    Troie
Fro day to day, til they ben bare of joie.]

[See citation *in extenso* under the poem *Fortuna*.]

An excellent explanation of this passage and all that it implies is that given by Kellogg (1954). Taking Eccles. 10.8[77] and Dan. 2.21, Kellogg—while citing Dante as the source of

---

[73] "Even in the *Convito* (iv, 17) where Dante follows Aristotle (in whose system Prudence is an intellectual virtue), he feels constrained to say: 'By many, Prudence, that is Wisdom, is well asserted to be a moral virtue; but Aristotle numbers that amongst the intellectual virtues, although it is the guide of the moral, and points out the way by which they are formed, and without which they cannot be.' Dante 1944a:369 n.18 (Carlyle-Wicksteed translation).

[74] Cited in Root's comments on these lines (1945:541).

[75] In the *Summa theologica*, part 2, Prima Secundae, q. 57, art. 6; q. 58, art. 4; q. 60, art 1; q. 64, art. 3; q. 65, art. 2; q. 66, art. 3; part 3, q. 11, art 1; q. 85, art. 3. Also *Comm. Ethic* 1. 6, lect. 7ff; Saint Ambrose, *De officiis*, 1.27. Cf. notes of Robinson, Root, Grandgent,, Busnelli and Vandelli, and Scartazzini to the appropriate lines.

[76] There are many examples of a tripartite Prudence and (in keeping with the confusion that Dante remarks on in n.74 above) of a three-headed Philosophy. A literary example of Prudence with two heads and the third reflected in a mirror is found in Francisco Imperial's *Dezir a las syete virtudes*, written in 1396 (see Woodford 1953:522, 524). Representations of Prudence in art range from the carvings of Andrea Pisano through fifteenth-century "gravures" and follow very closely Imperial's description (cf. van Marle 1931–32:2.22, fig. 24; 2.50, fig. 54). Philosophy was frequently shown with three heads, from as early as the twelfth until at least the beginning of the sixteenth century (cf. van Marle, 1.206, fig. 231; 2.240, fig. 268), though this is probably due to the division of philosophy into three branches.

[77] A brief but excellent survey of medieval historians' use of the biblical passage for substantiation of the idea of *translatio* is given by Curtius, pp. 28–29.

the *Troilus* passage—shows that the biblical, Dantean, and Chaucerian passages are all strictly within the sphere of a rigid providential interpretation of history. By illustrations and citations from such works as the *De mutabilitate mundi*, Kellogg not only stresses the relationship that existed in the medieval Englishman's mind between himself and the Trojans but also posits the concept that, in the mind of the historian of the time, the history of England began with Jason and led directly and ineluctably to the foundation of the European (and English) culture. In reply to his own rhetorical question why Fortune first consummated and then broke the love affair in Chaucer's poem, Kellogg points out the importance of Troilus to the defense of Troy and the fact that with his fall (as a result, that is, of his personal misfortunes) Troy fell. Within the framework of the rigid and providential interpretation of history, this fall led to the birth of the Western world, with the colonizations of Aeneas in Italy, Gallus in France, and Brutus in England. For the moment I will only point out that, in the Boethian and the Thomistic division, this would be an illustration of "purveyaunce" ruling the "destynye" of the characters concerned.

There is no doubt that Dante is a possible source for the lines from *Troilus* cited above, for, although the thought of lines 1541–45 is essentially Boethian (see discussion under *Fortune*), lines 1544–45 also echo Dante's "Di gente in gente" (line 80), and the "Permutacioun / Of thinges" can be found in juxtaposition as "permutasse...li ben vani" (line 79). Chaucer, however, is speaking of "regnes" and not "li ben vani"; we are therefore forced to consider that, though the phrasing might come from lines 79–80, the thought is more dependent on line 82: "per ch'una gente impera, e l'altra langue."

It would be strange, however, if Chaucer had based his entire philosophical and historical approach on twenty-nine lines of an Italian poem. If Kellogg is correct in the extent to which the rigid and providential interpretation of history was accepted, one would expect other possible sources or a terminology that was common knowledge. Not only is the Dantesque source by itself too limited to supply an entire philosophical and historical structure, but, to be applicable in the present case, it demands a combination of the phrase of one thought with the thought of another phrase.

Direct discussion of "regnes," "disposicioun," and the transfer "fro folk in folk" is found with a surprising similarity of construction and words in the much fuller discussion in Thomas Aquinas's *Contra gentiles* 3.80, which was most likely Dante's source as well. There the question of the relationship of *providentia* and *fortuna* to history is given the following explanation: "...in human affairs there is a common good, namely the good of the city or nation, and this apparently belongs to the order of *Principalities*...and *thus the government of kingdoms and the change of supremacy from one nation to another* must belong to the ministry of this order" (second italics mine). Saint Thomas had already established (3.74) that "divine providence does not take away fortune and chance from things" (Aquinas 1956:3.1.246) and that, "therefore, the order of divine providence requires that there be chance and fortune in reality" (3.1.248).[78] Saint Thomas's discussion in *Contra gentiles* 3.80 not only is closer to Chaucer's words but, more important, is dealing with the same topic[79] in a full, formal explication that would have supplied Chaucer with a firm basis on which to found his own historical and philosophical doctrine.

---

[78] For a full discussion of Dante's views in the *Commedia* and *Convivio* (4.11), see Dante 1934:2, app. 4, pp. 376–77. The Thomistic basis is there discussed in full.

[79] That is, *dispositio regnorum* as opposed to *li ben vani*. Saint Thomas had discussed fortune as the agent in charge of distribution and acquisition of riches in *Summa*, part 1, q. 21, arts. 1, 4.

While this Thomistic source does not totally deny the possibility of Chaucer's use of the passage in Dante, it does in part negate the overwhelming importance with which those lines had to be viewed in the past. The Dantean passage should be considered, therefore, as a confirmation, perhaps even a reminder, for Chaucer of a widely held and fully approved historiography. Such a reassessment seems to me to give a far more solid basis for investigation of Chaucer's historical and philosophical concepts.

Bethel: "1791f.: list of poets; cf. *Inf.* IV, 86–93 – doubtful."

And kis the steppes, where as thow
     seest pace
Virgile, Ovide, Omer, Lucan, and
     Stace.

"Mira colui con quella spada in mano,
     che vien dinanzi ai tre sì come sire.
quelli è Omero poeta sovrano;
     l'altro è Orazio satiro che vene;
     Ovidio è 'l terzo, e l'ultimo Lucano.
Però che ciascun meco si convene
     nel nome che sonò la voce sola,
     fannomi onore, e di ciò fanno bene."

"Note him there with sword in hand who comes before the other three as their lord. He is Homer, sovereign poet; next is Horace, satirist; Ovid comes third, and Lucan last. Since each shares with me the name the single voice has uttered, they do me honor, and in that they do well." [*Inf.*, p. 41]

Robinson (p. 837) summarizes the scholarship as follows:

The envoi in the Filocolo (II, 376–78) seems most likely to have influenced him [Chaucer]. Boccaccio there mentions Virgil, Lucan, Statius, Ovid, and Dante, for the last of whom Chaucer may have deliberately substituted Homer as more appropriate to a tale of Troy. But too much significance should not be attached to the similarity of the lists. The same poets, with the addition of Claudian, are represented in *HF* 1455 ff. and they correspond also, with the single exception of Statius (who takes the place of Horace) to the group whom Dante joined in Limbo (Inf. iv, 82 ff.).

Only two remarks should be added: first, that Dante used the same list in *Vita nuova* 25 as he does in the *Commedia*, and, second, that Root (1945:559), who points out the parallel names in Boccaccio, wisely concludes that "Too much weight must not be attached to the fact that Boccaccio here names four of the five poets mentioned by Chaucer; they are the great names of narrative verse."

Clark (1951:1–10): compares the Epilogue with *Par.* 14.25–30 and *Par.* 22.128–54.

Qual si lamenta perché qui si moia
     per viver colà sù, non vide quive
     lo refrigerio de l'etterna ploia.
Quell' uno e due e tre che sempre vive
     e regna sempre in tre e 'n due e 'n uno,
     non circunscritto, e tutto circunscrive

["... e però, prima che tu più t'inlei,]
     rimira in giù, e vedi quanto mondo
     sotto li piedi già esser ti fei;

sì che 'l tuo cor, quantunque può, giocondo
  s'appresenti a la turba trïunfante
  che lieta vien per questo etera tondo."
Col viso ritornai per tutte quante
  le sette spere, e vidi questo globo
  tal, ch'io sorrisi del suo vil sembiante;
e quel consiglio per migliore approbo
  che l'ha per meno; e chi ad altro pensa
  chiamar si puote veramente probo.
Vidi la figlia di Latona incensa
  sanza quell' ombra che mi fu cagione
  per che già la credetti rara e densa.
L' aspetto del tuo nato, Iperïone,
  quivi sostenni, e vidi com' si move
  circa e vicino a lui Maia e Dïone.
Quindi m' apparve il temperar di Giove
  tra 'l padre e 'l figlio; e quindi mi fu chiaro
  il varïar che fanno di lor dove;
e tutti e sette mi si dimostraro
  quanto son grandi e quanto son veloci
  e come sono in distante riparo.
L'aiuola che ci fa tanto feroci,
  volgendom' io con li etterni Gemelli,
  tutta m'apparve da' colli a le foci;
poscia rivolsi li occhi a li occhi belli.

Whoso laments because we die here to live there on high has not seen there the refreshment of the eternal rain.

That One and Two and Three which ever lives, and ever reigns in Three and Two and One, uncircumscribed, and circumscribing all things [*Par.*, p. 155]

["...And therefore, before you enter farther into it,][80] look back downward and behold how great a world I have already set beneath your feet, in order that your heart may present itself, joyous to its utmost, to the triumphant throng which comes glad through this round ether."

With my sight I returned through all and each of the seven spheres, and saw this globe such that I smiled at its paltry semblance; and that counsel I approve as best which holds it for least, and he whose thought is turned elsewhere may be called truly upright. I saw the daughter of Latona glowing without that shade for which I once believed her rare and dense. The aspect of your son, Hyperion, I there endured, and saw how Maia and Dione move around and near him. Then appeared to me the tempering of Jove between his father and his son, and then was clear to me the varying they make in their position. And all the seven were displayed to me, how great they are and swift, and how distant each from other in location. The little threshing-floor which makes us so fierce was all revealed to me from hills to river-mouths, as I circled with the eternal Twins. Then to the beauteous eyes I turned my eyes again. [*Par.*, p. 253, 255]

---

[80] Dante is on the point of entering the eighth sphere.

Undoubtedly *Par.* 14.28–30 is the source for *TC* 5.1863–65, as has long been recognized (see following entry), and *Par.* 22.128–54 may well have been in Chaucer's mind as he translated *Teseida* 11.1–3, but all the details that could suggest a parallel in Dante were already in Boccaccio's three stanzas. Root seems eminently just in attributing the Epilogue's primary sources to Boccaccio and to his original, the *Somnium Scipionis*.[81]

Clark's contention that Chaucer first thought of Dante and then was reminded of Boccaccio seems to be based on a number of posited assumptions that only present needless obstacles to an otherwise straightforward borrowing. The primary suggestion that *Par.* 14.25–27 and 22.136–38 represent the outstanding examples of the contrast of earthly and heavenly love in the *Commedia* seems debatable, since this is one of the fundamental subjects of at least the *Purgatorio* and the *Paradiso* which reflects, in turn, one of the most discussed topics of patristic writing.[82] Clark, however, feels that Chaucer first thought of these two passages (particularly in relation to *TC* 5.1835–41) and then, reading on in *Par.* 22.139–54, was struck by the mythological names of the planets which suggested to his mind the idea of "payens corsed olde rites." Even granted those assumptions which are posited at the opening of the article, the connection here seems to be of the most tenuous sort. Clark believes that Chaucer then read back through *Par.* 22 and found the passage (lines 128–35) where Beatrice tells Dante to look down at the earth below them. Chaucer would certainly seem to be closer to the Teseida passage, however.[83] Indeed, the article seems to offer no valid reason for not accepting the more obvious suggestion of direct relationship between Boccaccio's *Filostrato* and his *Teseida*.

In attempting to show that there is some difference between Chaucer and Boccaccio, it is suggested that Boccaccio was thinking of the lunar sphere when he put Troilo in the *cielo ottava* and that Chaucer—at the moment "full of the Divine Comedy" (Clark 1952:7) but not wanting to "differ plainly with any of his predecessors" (Clark, p. 7)[84]—purposely left the situation vague in *Troilus*. Clark stresses that Troilo "Quindi si volse in giù a rimirare. . . il poco terreno," after having viewed the rest of the heavens, but whether one locates the eighth sphere at the level of the moon or of the fixed stars, Troilo would have to turn his gaze backward, since the last thing he had looked at was *la somma bellezza*, which is certainly God. While Boccaccio's source, the *Somnium Scipionis*, does indeed count the spheres in reverse order, "it must be remembered that, in Cicero, Scipio takes his stand in the Milky Way (Cap. 16)" (Root 1945:562).[85] That Boccaccio emphasizes that his hero passes through the four elements does not mean that Troilo consequently stops at the

---

[81] Briefly, Root (1945:559–65) attributes lines 1807–27 to *Teseida* 12.1–3, 11, and lines 1800–1806, 1828–48 to *Filostrato* 7.27–29. The only ascription to Dante is, of course, lines 1863–65.

[82] See Makarewicz 1953, *passim*, esp. pp. 93–146.

[83] The *Teseida* passage is given for convenience of comparison (McCoy, p. 289):

"When Arcites had finished naming her whom he had loved more than anyone else in this world, his weightless spirit went soaring toward the concavity of the eighth heaven as it left the convex elements behind. Here he gazed in awe at the fixed stars, their order and their sublime beauty and he listened to their music replete with all sweetness.

"Then he turned to look back down on the things he had left behind, and he saw this small terrestrial sphere encircled by the sea and the air and the fire above, and every other thing that counts for little compared to heaven. But then his eyes came to rest, as he turned back, on the spot where he had left his body.

"And he laughed to himself at the plaintive laments of the Lernean people, and he severely censured the vanity of humankind, which pursues false beauty of the world, neglecting heaven out of the clouded madness and darksome blindness of their minds. Then he went to the place that Mercury had chosen for him."

[84] That Chaucer counted the spheres from the moon outward seems clearly indicated by his description of Venus as "the thridde heven faire" (*TC* 3.2).

[85] Root's point in favor of the lunar sphere, namely, that "Troilus, though able to see the planets 'with ful avysement,' is near enough to Earth to distinguish the spot 'ther he was slayn,' which he could hardly do from the eminence of the outermost sphere" (p. 561), seems to confuse Troilus's earthly and heavenly powers of sight.

lunar sphere but rather indicates that he has been translated above the earthly and into the heavenly realm.[86] Root's resolution seems admirable, for, after citing the instances in which Chaucer states that the eighth sphere is that of the Galaxy, he concludes (p. 562) that, while there is the possibility that Boccaccio may have been thinking of the lunar sphere, "Chaucer understood it to be that of the fixed stars."

There would thus seem to be no reason to abandon the more probable and accepted view that the primary source of the Epilogue is to be found in Boccaccio, though Chaucer, in speaking of the heavens, undoubtedly had the *Commedia* (as well as many other classical and medieval visions of the upper regions) in his mind as he wrote.

Bethel: "1863–65: address to the Trinity; closely modelled on *Par.* XIV, 28–32."

Thow oon, and two, and thre, eterne on lyve,	Quell' uno e due e tre che sempre vive,
That regnest ay in thre, and two, and oon,	e regna sempre in tre e 'n due e 'n uno,
Uncircumscript, and al maist circumscrive	non circunscritto, e tutto circunscrive,
	tre volte era cantato da ciascuno
	di quelli spiriti con tal melodia

> That One and Two and Three which ever lives, and ever reigns in Three and Two and One, uncircumscribed, and circumscribing all things, was thrice sung by each of those spirits with such a melody [*Par.*, p. 155]

While the last two verses Bethel cites from Dante do not seem to apply in the present case, Chaucer's three lines are an extremely close translation of Dante's tercet. Not only has Chaucer used the corresponding forms of "uncircumscript" (*non circunscritto*) and "circumscrive" (*circunscrive*), but there also seems to be a more fundamental parallel that is not at once apparent. Austin (1923:140–48) has pointed out Dante's tendency toward reversal of ordinary procedure (thus the tree with its roots on top, snow going upward, and so on) and remarks that *Par.* 14, 23, and 28 reverse the order of the Trinity. This is foreshadowed, among other places, in *Par.* 14: "... each of the souls in the Sun three times sings the praises of 'Quell' *uno e due e tre* che sempre vive / e regna sempre in *tre e 'n due e 'n uno*, / non circunscritto, e tutto circunscrive" (ll. 28–30) — a formula that reverses the Trinity most effectively and simply" (Austin, p. 145).[87] In other words, Chaucer was following Dante so closely that he did not correct the lines to their normal canonical order.

It is difficult to say with certainty whether Chaucer was consulting the *Commedia* directly or had committed Dante's tercet to memory; the faithfulness of the translation would seem to suggest either. It is perhaps not out of place here to broaden the discussion to point out that the situation in *Troilus* resembles what is found in the *Commedia*, where the souls sing of the love, the ardor, the vision that shall sustain them at the Resurrection. Significantly, the preceding lines are:

---

[86] Root (1945:561) notes that Dante hears the celestial harmony upon entering the lunar sphere. However, the music of the heavens, emanating from the friction of one sphere against the other (and thus beginning with the Primum Mobile's action on the eighth sphere) is able to be heard equally throughout the upper regions, according to Cicero.

[87] A. Wheeler has kindly shown me her article on Dante and the ending of *Troilus*. Her reading of lines 1083–85 seems to me both subtle and illuminating.

Qual si lamenta perché qui si moia
per viver colà sù, non vide quive
lo refrigerio de l'etterna ploia.

[Whoso laments because we die here to live there on high has not seen there the refreshment of the eternal rain.]

For *Troilus*, a poem profoundly informed by the widespread image of the *scala amoris*, these lines from Dante seem to epitomize all that Troilus has now discovered. In the course of the poem Troilus has climbed the ladder one rung at a time, which means that each preceding rung is necessary, and necessarily left, if understanding is to rise.[88] The upper end of the *scala* disappears into heaven, in the kind of *o altitudo* that Troilus experiences and that causes him to look back and reject through new understanding.

Whether or not we implicate the preceding lines from the *Paradiso*, it is noteworthy that this final borrowing for *Troilus* comes, in Chaucer as in Dante, in a passage of lyric prayer. This use of Dante's religious lyricism will be found to occur again in Chaucer's writing and in a more extensive, if not purer, form.

---

[88] By this reading the earthly tragedy in *Troilus* is that Criseyde, despite all reasons and excuses, is unable to keep up with Troilus's ever-mounting comprehension of love, recalling Pandarus's observation, "Women ben wise in short avysement" (4.936, and cf. Troilus's "ful avysement" at 5.1811). A not dissimilar reading can be found in Dronke 1964:47–52, esp. p. 49.

CHAPTER 6

The Legend of Good Women

SIDE FROM one or two very probable borrowings from the *Commedia* in the legends themselves, Chaucer's most significant use of Dante in *The Legend of Good Women* is found in the Prologue, where he twice draws upon tractate 4 of the *Convivio*. In both cases he continues the practice, begun in *Troilus and Criseyde*, of adapting to his discussion the ideas as well as the words. Thus in one instance he takes over Dante's summary and comment on Aristotle's *Nicomachean Ethics* and the discussion there of virtue as the mean. In the other instance Dante's view on true nobility is borrowed and molded to fit Alceste's speech on the perfect earthly ruler. Because Chaucer, in the latter instance, has so totally converted Dante's argument to his own poetic purpose, it has been suggested that he was, consequently, "passing his satiric judgment upon the nobility of his age."[1] An interpretation such as this, however, seems to lose sight of the manner in which the borrowings are made. Chaucer did not necessarily accept totally the concepts of the sources upon which he drew; rather, he took from them what he needed and molded it to suit the poem on which he was working. It is, indeed, this ability to assimilate and transform that gives such richness to his poetry and makes determination of sources (on no matter how broad a scope) so difficult.

All of Chaucer's undoubted borrowings from the *Convivio* are found in Tractate 4, and, as a result, there is a great temptation to think that he had read, or at least had available, only this one section of the work. That all the direct translations and uniquely Dantean ideas are from this tractate is countered, however, by the parallels and analogues which, although they can be attributed to other sources as well, are present in the first three sections.

The nature of the closer adaptations of tractate 4 would seem to indicate that Chaucer looked to Dante, among others, for concepts of nobility, whether in matters of *gentilesse* or good government. It is difficult, however, to say how much was accepted of Dante's philosophy by Chaucer the man (as opposed, that is, to the Chaucerian character who quotes Dante or to Chaucer the writer). Even if we were to consider that Chaucer is speaking personally through every character that cites the *Commedia* or the *Convivio*, we would be hard pressed to find a consistent view of Dante. It seems far more likely that Chaucer, rather than presenting in his writing a Dantean philosophical system, made use of his source as the particular poem demanded. Perhaps it is not too rash to recall here one of the differences that was suggested at the opening of this book as fundamentally

---

[1] A more extensive discussion of this point is given in the entry for lines 373–90, below.

separating the work of Dante and Chaucer: Dante was propounding a reasonably unified philosophy through the medium of his writing. Chaucer, generally speaking, was not trying either to indoctrinate or to pass judgment; his primary interest was to engage the reader and, having engaged him, to cause him to consider. This does not mean that he was indifferent or amoral but simply that his view of the function and end of poetry was not Dante's. If this suggestion is valid, we should not be surprised that Chaucer's use of Dante varies with the poem that he is writing; nor should we expect to be able to impose Dante's fiercely held doctrine on Chaucer's poetry. In the Chaucer-Dante relationship the direction almost always seems clear: it was Chaucer who made use of Dante.

The Legend of Good Women

Bethel: "F 165f.: reference to Etik and remark attributed thereto probably due to Conv. IV, canz. iii, 85–87."

for vertu is the mene, As Etik seith; in swich maner I mene.	[vertute, dico, che fa l' uom felice in sua operazione.] Questo è, secondo che l' Etica dice, un abito eligente lo qual dimora in mezzo solamente, [e tai parole pone.]

[. . .virtue, I mean, which maketh a man happy in all his doing.] This root (as the Ethics affirm) is a habit of choice, which resideth only in the mean; [and such words the book setteth down.] [P. 192]

If we can assume that Chaucer had not read Aristotle elsewhere in some form or other, this passage from Dante, along with the more precise explication of the reference to l'Etica dice in Convivio 4.17, is in all probability Chaucer's source; if he had read Aristotle, this passage would have served as a reminder, if one were necessary.

"The mene" here mentioned is the basis of Aristotle's view of virtues and, indeed, of a good part of the thinking of the Nicomachean Ethics. That Chaucer is referring to the Ethics seems obvious not only from the use of the term itself but also from the meaning of the preceding and subsequent phrases. What is difficult to understand is Robinson's note (p. 842):

Etik (or Etike) here might refer either to a book or to a person. The term is several times applied to Horace by John of Salisbury, who, in Policraticus, viii, 13. . .introduces a quotation from the Satires (i, 2, 24) and a paraphrase from the Epistles (i, 18, 9) with "ut enim ait ethicus." Chaucer's quotation doubtless comes, directly or indirectly from the latter passage. The version in Dante's Convivio, Canz., iii, 81 ff., may also have been in his mind. See further Lowes, MLN, XXV, 87–89.

In omitting any reference to Aristotle, Robinson is evidently basing himself totally on Lowes's article, in which the Policraticus source is propounded. In a later article, "Chaucer and Dante's Convivio," Lowes (1915:33) rejects the "interesting parallel in the canzone" on rather questionable grounds. His evidence for rejection is only the statement (1915:33):

"But as I have pointed out elsewhere,[2] there is a similar passage in John of Salisbury, and as between the two, honors seem easy." To this somewhat ambiguous remark, there is added in a footnote (p. 33): "The *context* in the *Convivio*, however is closer than in the *Polycraticus* to the context in the Legend" (Lowes's italics). Lowes does not, however, refer to *Convivio* 4.17, in which Dante has an extensive explication of the passage (cited above) from the canzone, repeating twice the phrase *l'Etica dice*, and taking up fully Aristotle's comments in the *Nicomachean Ethics*.

Now Lowes, in the conclusion of his article on John of Salisbury's *Policraticus* (1910:89), written several years before his article on the *Convivio*, had contradicted the opinions of Lounsbury and Skeat on the meaning of "Etik" in rather unequivocal and uncompromising terms: "The one thing that seems at present to be clear is the fact that Chaucer's "Etik" is not Aristotle but Horace." Had Lowes met with *Convivio* 4.xvii at the time of his article on the *Convivio*, he would undoubtedly have had to revise, if not retract in full, his previous absolute statement. Since, however, Lowes preferred the source in the *Policraticus* to the fuller and more direct source in *Convivio* 4.17, it might be well to review his argument for the ascription to Horace.

In speaking of John of Salisbury's descriptive appellations of writers cited in the *Policraticus*, Lowes (1910:88) gives varying adjectival nicknames and then says:

> Most striking of all, however, is John of Salisbury's use of the term *ethicus*. He applies it to Juvenal, Persius, Ovid and Dionysius Cato. But the writer whose designation it seems peculiarly to be, is Horace—the Horace, with perhaps one exception of the *Satires* and the *Epistles*. And four times one finds, with reference to him, precisely Chaucer's phrase, "As Etik saith": *ut ait ethicus*.

Lowes must now (p. 88) bring in the methodology of the "linked atom" to show that there is some connection in meaning:

> But that is not all. For in one of these four instances John of Salisbury ascribes to *Ethicus* the very doctrine which Chaucer attributes to *Etik*. The lines in Chaucer run as follows:

> > But I ne clepe nat innocence folye,
> > Ne fals pitee, for vertu is the mene,
> > As Etik seith; in swich maner I mene.
> > And thus thise foweles, voide of al malice,
> > Acordeden to love, and laften vice
> > Of hate, and songen alle of oon acord

The passage in John of Salisbury is this:

> "Nempe indoctorum haec opinio est; *ut enim ait ethicus*: Dum vitant stulti vitia in contraria currunt, *recedentes a medio vitiorum, quae regio virtutis est*.[3] [For, as the moralist writes, "The foolish, while avoiding vice, rush on / And fall into its opposite." They withdraw from the mean between vices, which is the field of virtue. (John of Salisbury 1938:374)]

But did he also have before him (or in memory) Horace's very phrase? The last eight words from the *Policraticus* are obviously a paraphrase of the ninth line of the eighteenth epistle (Ad Lollium) of the first book:

[2] "*MLN*, XXV (March, 1910), 87–89" (Lowes's note).
[3] "Lib. 8, c. 13 (762c). The 'dum vitant' line is Sat. I. 2. 24" (Lowes's note).

Virtus est medium vitiorum et utrinque reductum. And Chaucer's "vertu is the mene" is a translation not of the paraphrase, but of the original itself.

In other words, the *Policraticus* is not a source in itself but, according to Lowes's hypothesis, only one of the "atoms" which either sent Chaucer to a postulated Horatian source or recalled to his memory "the ninth line of the eighteenth epistle (Ad Lollium) of the first book." Lowes (p. 89) then comes to an expansive and absolute conclusion: "The point bears directly upon the question of Chaucer's knowledge of Horace, and indirectly upon the Lollius problem. . . . The one thing that seems at present to be clear is the fact that Chaucer's 'Etik' is not Aristotle but Horace." If Chaucer knew Horace as well as Lowes implies—so well, that is, that he either had a manuscript of his works or could give a particular line from memory—it is odd indeed that he never once mentions the Latin poet by name or makes any other reference to him in his works. Chaucer, it need hardly be remarked, was not one to shun "auctoritee."

On the other hand, in the later article, "Chaucer and Dante's *Convivio*," the passages from the *Convivio* which Lowes does *not* give make a strong argument for the more direct, traditional approach of Skeat and Lounsbury. The relevant portions of 4.17 might well be worth quoting here at length, since they indicate not only the basis for the ascription but also show how much of Aristotle's argument Chaucer could get at second hand:

> Appresso che vedute sone quelle due cose che parevano utili a vedere prima che sopra lo testo si procedesse, ad esso esponere è da procedere. E dice e comincia adunque: *Dico ch'ogni vertù principalmente Vien da una radice; Vertute, dico, che fa l'uom felice In sua operazione.* E soggiungo: *Questo è, secondo che l'Etica dice, Un abito eligente,* ponendo tutta la diffinizione de la morale virtù, secondo che nel secondo de l'Etica è per lo Filosofo diffinito. In che due cose principalmente s' intende: l'una è che ogni vertù vegna d'uno principio; l'altra sì è che queste *ogni vertù* siano le vertù morali, di cui si parla; e ciò si manifesta quando dice: *Questo è, secondo che l'Etica dice.*

> [Now that these two points have been examined, which it seemed helpful to examine before proceeding to deal with the text, we must go on to explain this. Now the text begins with saying, "I affirm that every virtue primarily cometh from one root, virtue I mean which maketh a man happy in all his doing," and it adds, "this root (as the *Ethics* affirm) is a habit of choice," laying down the whole definition of moral virtue, as it is propounded by the Philosopher in the second book of the *Ethics*. In this stress is laid chiefly on two points; the first is, that every virtue comes from a single principle; the second, that this expression "every virtue" refers to the moral virtues which are our theme; and this is plain when the text says, "This root (as the *Ethics* affirm)." (Jackson, p. 253)]

After again paying tribute to *la divina sentenza d'Aristotile*, Dante lists and briefly describes the eleven virtues—Courage, Temperance, Liberality, Magnificence, High-Mindedness, Love of Honor, Good Temper, Affability, Truthfulness, Pleasantry, and Justice—that Aristotle had given, *secondo la sua sentenza*, in accordance with his judgment. The explication continues:

> E ciascuna di queste vertudi ha due inimici collaterali, cioè vizii, uno in troppo e un altro in poco; e queste tutte sono li mezzi intra quelli, e nascono tutte da uno principio, cioè da l'abito de la nostra buona elezione: onde generalmente si può dicere di tutte che siano abito elettivo consistente nel mezzo. E queste sono

quelle che fanno l'uomo beato, o vero felice, ne la loro operazione, sì come dice lo Filosofo nel primo de l'Etica quando diffinisce la Felicitade, dicendo che "Felicitade è operazione secondo virtude in vita perfetta."

[And each of these virtues has two enemies, that is, vices, one on the side of excess, the other on the side of defect. And the virtues are the mean states between these; and they all spring from one principle, that is, from our habit of right choice. It may, therefore, be said generally that they are "a habit of choice residing in the mean." And these are they which make a man blest, or happy in their exercise, as the Philosopher says in the first book of the *Ethics* when he defines Happiness by saying that Happiness is "activity in accordance with virtue in a perfect life."] [p. 254]

This seems to me to make evident the reference to "Etik" for, in addition to the stricter contextual parallelism, there is in the canzone the parenthetical construction *secondo che l'Etica dice*, which parallels Chaucer's equally parenthetical "as Etik seith," and there is also, of course, "in swich maner I mene," which follows Dante's *vertute dico*.

These two parts of the *Convivio*—the canzone and its explication—can certainly serve as a highly probable source for Chaucer's lines. The complex allusion to Horace that must be traced through the medium of John of Salisbury does not seem warranted in the face of a simpler and more concrete explication.

Bethel: "F 252f.: *Marcia Catoun* as an example of a model wife; suggested very probably by Dante's account of her in *Conv.* IV, xxviii, 13ff."

[Hyd, Absolon, thy gilte tresses clere;
Ester, ley thou thy meknesse al adown;
Hyd, Jonathas, al thy frendly manere;]
Penalopee and Marcia Catoun,
Make of youre wifhod no comparysoun;
[Hyde ye youre beautes, Ysoude and
    Eleyne:
My lady cometh, that al this may
    disteyne.]

Dante's explication of Marcia's life is worked out in its full allegorical significance and might well have served as a reminder of the virtuous woman. Dante mentions her also in *Inf.* 4.128, and *Purg.* 1.78–81, 84–90. However, as Robinson indicates (p. 843), Marcia was also mentioned in Geoffrey of Vinsauf's *Poetria nova*...and Lucan's *Pharsalia*, "which gives some account of her." The mention of Marcia in Chaucer is so brief that it is difficult to find enough evidence on which to ascribe a source. Dante cites Lucan as his authority, but the only information that we can gather for Chaucer is negative; that is, first, Dante nowhere uses a form equivalent to Marcia Catoun, and, second, Dante uses merely the name Marcia. Even when he gives her name for the first time in the listing in *Inf.* 4, he does not go on to identify her, which tends to indicate that he expected her to be well enough known that his readers would require no other information. Marcia, in other words, might well have been a stock type, a "character" of wifely obedience for the writers of the time.

Such, at least, is the conclusion of Hamilton (1932–33:361–64), who—citing the references to "Marcia Catonis" in the *Pharsalia* (2.236–39), in Matthew of Vendôme's *Ars versificatoria* (1.55), in Geoffrey of Vinsauf's *Poetria nova* (line 1775) and his more extensive use of the *Pharsalia* verses as an example of determination in the *Documentatum de arte versificandi* (2.3.49–50)—feels that the constant references to her as a devoted and upright wife "indicates that during the Middle Ages Cato's wife was proverbial for virtue" (p. 362).[4] One must recognize, therefore, that, while Dante is a very plausible source, there is no real basis for the suggestion that the original is more likely to have come from the *Convivio* than from common knowledge or from any of the other possible references cited by Robinson and Hamilton.

Bethel: "358–60 Dante named (360); the lines are closely modelled on *Inf.* XIII, 64–66."

Envie ys lavendere of the court alway,
For she ne parteth, neither nyght ne
    day,
Out of the hous of Cesar; thus seith
    Dante

La meretrice che mai da l'ospizio
    di Cesare non torse li occhi putti,
    morte comune e de le corti vizio

> The harlot that never turned her whorish eyes from Caesar's household—the common death and vice of courts [*Inf.*, p. 133]

This "sententious remark" (Whiting 1934:44) undoubtedly has its source in Dante. "Lavendere" is, of course, an excellent, though very colloquial, translation of *meretrice*.

Ruggiers (1950:445–48): F 373–90: compared to *Convivio* IV, xx, 3–5.

This shoolde a ryghtwis lord have in
    his thoght,
And nat be lyk tirauntz of Lumbardye,
That han no reward but at tyrannye.
For he that kynge or lord ys naturel,
Hym oghte nat be tiraunt ne crewel,
As is a fermour, to doon the harm he
    kan.
He moste thinke yt is his lige man,
And is his tresour, and his gold in
    cofre.
This is the sentence of the philosophre,
A kyng to kepe his liges in justice;
Withouten doute, that is his office.
Al wol he kepe his lordes hire degree,
As it ys ryght and skilful that they bee
Enhaunced and honoured, and most
    dere—
For they ben half-goddes in this world
    here—
Yit mot he doon bothe ryght, to poore
    and ryche,
Al be that hire estaat be nat yliche,
And han of poore folk compassyoun.

[Poi appresso argomenta per quello che detto è, che nessuno, per poter dire: 'Io sono di cotale schiatta', non dee credere essere con essa, se questi frutti non sono in lui. E rende incontanente ragione, dicendo che] quelli che hanno questa *grazia*, cioè questa divina cosa, sono *quasi* come *dei*, sanza macula di vizio; e ciò dare non può se non Iddio solo, appo cui non è scelta di persone, sì come le divine Scritture manifestano. E non paia troppo alto dire ad alcuno, quando si dice: *Ch' elli son quasi dei*; chè, sì come di sopra nel settimo capitolo del terzo trattato si ragiona, così come uomini sono vilissimi e bestiali, così uomini sono nobilissimi e divini, e ciò pruova Aristotile nel settimo de l' Etica per lo testo d'Omero poeta. Sì che non dica quelli di li Uberti di Fiorenza, nè quelli de li Visconti da Melano: 'Perch' io sono di cotale schiatta, io sono nobile'; chè 'l divino seme non cade in ischiatta, cioè in istirpe, ma cade ne le singulari persone, e sì come di sotto si proverà, la stirpe non fa le singulari persone nobili, ma le singulari persone fanno nobile la stirpe.

---

[4] Hamilton's closing remark is: "Whatever the source of the tradition, its growth would explain why Dante portrays Marcia as a symbol of the noble soul, and why Chaucer couples her name with Penelope's" (p. 364).

[In the next place the Canzone argues from what has been said that no one, because he is able to say, "I am of such or such a stock," is entitled to believe that he is possessed of nobility, if these fruits are not in him. And it immediately supplies a reason, saying that] those who have this "grace," that is, this divine thing, are wellnigh like gods, free from all stain of vice. And none can confer this gift save God alone, with whom there is no respect of persons, as the divine Scriptures declare. And let it not seem too lofty a speech to be addressed to any one when the text affirms, "that they are wellnigh gods," for, as we have remarked above in the seventh chapter of the third Tractate, just as there are men who are vilest and most bestial, so also there are men who are noblest and most divine. And Aristotle proves this in the seventh book of the *Ethics* by a passage from the poet Homer. Therefore, let not any scion of the Uberti of Florence or of the Visconti of Milan say, "Because I am of such a race I am noble," for the divine seed does not fall upon a race, that is, a stock, but on the several individuals; and, as will be proved below, the stock does not make the several individuals noble, but the individuals ennoble the stock. [P. 261]

The passage in the *Convivio* is very probably the source of Alceste's advice to the god of love on the duties of the good ruler, particularly in light of Chaucer's use of *Convivio* 4.xvii in *LGW* 165. The lines from the canzone that are being explicated (109–20) are in the stanza following the one containing the *secondo che l'Etica dice* phrase and follow the general tone of Alceste's remarks:

> Dunque verrà, come dal nero il perso,
> ciascheduna vertute da costei,
> o vero il gener lor, ch' io misi avanti.
> Però nessun si vanti
> dicendo; 'Per ischiatta io son con lei',
> ch' elli son quasi dei
> quei c' han tal grazia fuor di tutti rei;
> chè solo Iddio a l'anima la dona
> che vede in sua persona
> perfettamente star: sì ch' ad alquanti
> che seme di felicità sia costa,
> messo da Dio ne l'anima ben posta.

[Therefore as perse from black so from nobility will each several virtue come, or the genus thereof which I have set down above. Therefore let no man boast himself, saying "By race am I her fellow." For they are wellnigh gods, they who have this grace apart from all sinners. For God alone endoweth that soul with it, whom He seeth in her own person stand perfect, so that with some few the seed of happiness doth join company, dispatched by God to the soul that is happily placed. (Jackson, p. 192)]

Ruggiers's argument (p. 447) is, in general, acceptable:

In both these passages, that from Dante and that from Chaucer, may be noted three points of similarity: the reference to despots of Milan, the dependence upon the authority of a philosopher qualified to give advice on political matters, and the insistence upon divinity in certain kinds of men, these last in Dante being men of inherently noble natures and dispositions, and in Chaucer lords of high station, precisely what Dante did *not* mean.

It is not entirely certain that Chaucer is being "ironic" or that "with gently mocking tone (he) passes his satiric judgment upon the nobility of his age" (Ruggiers, p. 447). We have seen instances throughout this study where Chaucer adapted lines from Dante to his own poetic purposes, and, if the poem was occasional,[5] there is no reason why Chaucer would not have converted the lines of the *Convivio* to a description of the ideal earthly noble. Certainly, the suggested irony would not have been caught by Chaucer's audience, who in all probability would have taken his lines at face value. And, just as surely, if the poem was occasional, Chaucer would not have indulged in such tactless satire, however gentle, if he expected the allusion to be understood. This is not to imply that Chaucer did not understand what he read, but it would be a mistake, one feels, to consider that Chaucer accepted totally all the sources that he used. More probably he assimilated his reading with his own beliefs or molded it to the exigencies of his poem. Tractate 4 of the *Convivio* became one of Chaucer's constant sources for concepts of nobility, but, whether used in *The Legend of Good Women* or in *The Wife of Bath's Tale*, it is shaped to fit the context in which it appears.

Bethel: "503: close adaptation of *Inf.* V, 100."

But pite renneth soone in gentil herte   [See under *TC* 1.894–96]

Bethel: "525f.: allusion to, and spelling of, Agaton; cf. *Purg.*, XXII, 106–08."

No wonder ys thogh Jove hire stellyfye, As telleth Agaton, for hire goodnesse!	Euripide v'è nosco e Antifonte, Simonide, Agatone e altri piùe Greci che già di lauro ornar la fronte.

    Euripides is with us there, and Antiphon, Simonides, Agathon, and many other Greeks who once decked their brows with laurel. [*Purg.*, p. 241]

There is no verbal or contextual parallel other than the name. Robinson (p. 846) summarizes as follows:

> *Agaton*, apparently Agatho, an Athenian tragic poet and friend of Plato. The reason for his association with Alcestis may be that Plato's Symposium, which tells her story, was known as Agatho's Feast. (It is called Agathonis Convivium by Macrobius, Saturnalia, ii, 1. See Hales, MLQ, I 5 ff.) The direct source of Chaucer's information is unknown. His spelling, Agaton, suggests an Italian original, and instances of the occurrence of the name in Dante, . . . and Boccaccio (Amorosa Visione, v, 50) have been pointed out; yet neither of these passages would have led Chaucer to associate Agatho with Alcestis.

The question of the spelling is an interesting one. The usual spelling in English is Agathon, though Robinson himself prefers to stress the alternate form Agatho. As might be suspected (and this is confirmed at once by the title that Macrobius uses), the name is a third-declension Greek noun, which in Latin has the alternate forms that are found in English. The most common example of this is, of course, Plato and Platon; the English use the -*o* form despite the contrary tradition elsewhere (cf. French Platon, Italian Platone). In addition, there seems to have been a confusion—whether orthographic, phonetic, or

---

[5] See Galway 1938.

both, is hard to tell—between *t* and *th*. This is apparent throughout Chaucer. Thus Thisbe is usually spelled Tesbe, though it appears once (*PF* 289) as Thisbe; Telephus becomes Thelophus (*SqT* F 238); Phlegethon, as we have seen (*TC* 3.1600), becomes Flegitoun; Ptolemy is spelled at least as Tholome, though more often than not *P* is the initial letter; Pythagoras can be Pithagores, Pictagoras, or Pittagoras. The list could be extended considerably, but the main purpose is to show, first, that where there is such variation, the *t*, *th* difference must not be stressed too heavily as a basis for ascription, and, second, that the *-o* or *-o(u)n* ending was almost equally flexible and is therefore equally inconclusive as a means of ascription (in the last case, cf. Phidoun for Phido (*FranT* F 1369) and Chaucer's use—though there is only a single instance of it—*HF* 251—of Platon for Plato.)

In any event, parallelism based on spelling is extremely hazardous when one tries to impose a sense of modern lexicographical exactness on a language that had little or no means to determine (let alone impose) such exactness.

Bethel: "547: Klaeber (*Das Bild bei Ch.*, 80, 345) suggests that the words "Thy litel wit was thilke tyme a-slepe" depend on *Purg*. XXXIII, 64; this seems to me doubtful."

The line in Dante is "Dorme lo 'ngegno tuo" ("Your wit sleeps," *Purg*., p. 367), but the contexts are so entirely different and the idea would appear to be so common that Bethel's evaluation seems amply justified.

The Legend of Cleopatra

Bethel: "582, 601, 604: the forms *Cleopatras*, *Cleopataras* show Dantean influence; cf. *Inf*. V, 63."

> poi è Cleopatràs lussurïosa
>
> next is wanton Cleopatra [*Inf*., p. 51]

Dantean influence here is highly doubtful. First, it should be noted that this is not the only way that Chaucer spells the name; in the four other instances of its use (*PF* 291; *LGW* 259, 566, 669), it appears as Cleopatre. This last spelling evolves evidently from the Latin form of the name. The Latin, however, seemed to have presented a homonymous confusion, resulting in uncertainty of declension; that is, was the word to be declined as a feminine first (i.e., *-patra*) or, by analogy, as a word that "originally" ended in *-pater*? Evidence of this confusion in the Latin can be seen at the beginning and end of this particular tale, which has, instead of Cleopatrae, "Incipit legenda Cleopatrie" and "Explicit Legenda Cleopatre."

As for the examples cited by Bethel, only one, that at line 604, follows the spelling in Dante.[6] The spelling is not, however, unique to Dante. As Grandgent (Dante 1933:50, n. to line 4) explains: "in mediaeval schools, Greek proper names, in the nominative, were very commonly stressed on the last syllable, this having been apparently regarded as the regular accentuation. . . . For some reason, *Cleopatras*, with an *s*, seems to have been considered the correct form" (Grandgent's italics). Chaucer used the Cleopat(a)ras form when he needed it for rhyme or meter and cut back to the more Latinate Cleopatre when

---

[6] According to the *Concordance to. . .Chaucer*, p. 145, all three examples are spelled Cleopatras.

such exigencies did not have to be met. This same technique is used with the English and Latin forms Antony and Antonius.

The Legend of Dido

Bethel: "924–26: allusion to Virgil as the lantern-bearer, from *Purg*. I, 43."

Glorye and honour, Virgil Mantoan,	["Chi siete voi che contro al cieco fiume
Be to thy name! and I shal, as I can,	fuggita avete la pregione etterna?"
Folwe thy lanterne, as thow gost	diss' el, movendo quelle oneste piume.]
byforn,	"Chi v'ha guidati, o che vi fu lucerna,
[How Eneas to Dido was forsworn.	[uscendo fuor de la profonda notte
In Naso and Eneydos wol I take	che sempre nera fa la valle inferna?...."]
The tenor, and the grete effectes	
make.]	

["Who are you that, against the blind stream, have fled the eternal prison?" said he, moving those venerable plumes.] "Who has guided you, or what was a lamp to you [issuing forth from the deep night that ever makes the infernal valley black?"] [*Purg.*, p. 5]

There is no definite connection here.[7] Verbal and contextual parallels are lacking—though this statement needs some explanation. In the context Dante and Virgil are coming out of the darkness of the Inferno into the light of day. While light imagery is to be emphasized henceforth, it was the darkness of hell itself, as well as its inhabitants, that had been stressed through the entire previous *cantica*. Cato's first question (cited above) emphasizes this imagery of darkness and light, and his subsequent question is on the guiding light that must have been present to lead the way through the terrors of the *profonda notte*. Cato is most likely referring to an angel or to divine grace,[8] both of which are always accompanied by or metaphorically expressed as light in the *Commedia*.

Dante is certainly not referring to Virgil either by name or by implication in the line "Chi v'ha guidati, o che vi fu lucerna...?" This statement is proved by the form that is used by Cato. He is addressing *both* Virgil and Dante, as is seen not only by the fact that Virgil answers him but more specifically by Cato's use of the plural *voi siete* and *avete*. This is not a question of *politesse* in Dante, for Cato, when he answers Virgil directly, just as when Virgil answers him, uses the *tu* form (lines 91 and 55, respectively). Nor is it *politesse* on the part of Dante as author, since he uses the *tu* form to Virgil from the very start.[9] It seems evident, therefore, that Cato is addressing both the men and is asking Virgil as well as Dante about the light that had brought them through the Inferno.

The reference to Virgil that Chaucer uses is a common enough image[10] so far as the

---

[7] Pratt 1946:263 n.18) considers lines 924–1367 as a reworking of *HF* 140–382 and 427–65.

[8] Dante's change, however, from *chi* to *che* seems to indicate a change from *who* to *what*, though I have no other basis for this remark than the change in wording. Cf. the Parson's use of light imagery (*ParsT* I 180–85): "...Job clepeth helle the lond of derknesse...; 'derk,' for he that is in helle hath defaute of light material. For certes, the derke light that shal come out of the fyr that evere shal brenne...sheweth him the horrible develes that hym tormenten. 'Covered with the derknesse of deeth,' that is to seyn, that he that is in helle shal have defaute of the sighte of God; for certes, the sighte of God is the lyf perdurable."

[9] *Inf.* 1.85–86: "'Tu se' lo mio maestro e 'l mio autore, / Tu se' solo colui...."

[10] Cf. the image in the Invocation in Boccaccio's *Amorosa visione* (1943?:2.15–17): "...menami tu colà ov'io ir voglio: / acciò che' passi miei che van per pace, / seguendo il raggio della tua stella..." ("...lead me there where I wish to go so that my steps may go in peace, following the ray of your star..."). Also see n.11, below, and the suggestion in the text of another possible parallel in *Inf.* 1.

master poet's being a light is concerned, and the change from guiding light to "lanterne" (in the sense of the linkboy) is natural, since Chaucer is acknowledging his source, the poet who has already gone over this subject. In short, if Chaucer were dependent on this passage in *Purg.* 1 for a not-unusual image, he would have had badly to mistake the meaning of the entire passage.

The inapplicability of the context is emphasized also by Chapman (1952:565), who, in offering another possible source,[11] remarks that Cato was addressing both Virgil and Dante and that "Chaucer, after all, was not emerging from hell; he, like Statius, was acknowledging the leadership of Virgil in poetry." Chapman's suggestion seems far more logical than that of *Purg.* 1, which demands so radical a misreading in order to begin to be relevant. It is odd that no one has yet offered as a parallel the classical lines in praise of Virgil in *Inf.* 1.82–87:

> "O de li altri poeti onore e lume,
>   vagliami 'l lungo studio e 'l grande amore
>   che m'ha fatto cercar lo tuo volume.
> Tu se' lo mio maestro e 'l mio autore,
>   tu se' solo colui da cu' io tolsi
>   lo bello stilo che m'ha fatto onore."

> ["O glory and light of other poets, may the long study and the great love that have made me search your volume avail me! You are my master and my author. You alone are he from whom I took the fair style that has done me honor." (*Inf.*, p. 9)]

It would seem, then, that Chaucer probably had some (or, perhaps, all) of Dante's eulogies in mind but that the common image of the mentor as a guiding light was present too.

Bethel: "930f.: allusion to Sinon, from *Inf.* XXX, 98."

Whan Troye brought was to destruccioun	[See under *HF* 152.]
By Grekes sleyghte, and namely by Synoun	

Bethel: "1005: form Sitheo may be due to *Inf.* V, 62."

That whilom was the wif of Sytheo	e ruppe fede al cener di Sicheo

and broke faith to the ashes of Sichaeus [*Inf.*, p. 51]

As Robinson remarks (p. 848), "The confusion of *c* and *t* is common in MSS." He then goes on to suggest that the *-o* ending may be due to Italian influence and cites the passage in the *Inferno* that is given above. Of course, without this presupposition of manuscript confusion, there is no relationship to these forms as they stand here; moreover, even with a manuscript variation, there is no direct evidence for Dante as the "Italian influence."

---

[11] Chapman suggests "the words of the poet Statius addressed to Virgil alone" (*Purg.* 22.64–69): "Ed elli a lui: 'Tu prima m'invïasti, / verso Parnaso a ber ne le sue grotte, / e prima appresso Dio m'alluminasti. / Facesti come quei che va di notte, / che porta il lume dietro e sè non giova, / ma dopo sè fa le persone dotte...'" ("And he to him: 'You it was who first sent me towards Parnassus to drink of its caves, and you who first did light me on to God. You were like one who goes by night and carries the light behind him and profits not himself, but makes those wise who follow him...'" [*Purg.*, p. 239]).

Moreover, Chaucer could very well have been using the line "non servata fides cineri promissa Sichaeo" in the *Aeneid* (4.552), which is just as good a source as far as spelling and ending are concerned.[12]

Bethel: "1104: 'swolow of helle'; phrase from *Purg.* XXI, 31f."

[This Eneas is come to paradys]
Out of the swolow of helle, and thus in
    joye
[Remembreth hym of his estat in
    Troye.]

Ond' io fui tratto fuor de l'ampia gola
    d'inferno per mostrarli, e mosterrolli
[oltre, quanto 'l potrà menar mia scola.]

> Wherefore I was brought forth from Hell's wide jaws to guide him, and I will guide him [onward as far as my school can lead him.] [*Purg.*, p. 227]

So far as context is concerned, Chaucer is using the figure "to contrast Aeneas' entertainment by Dido with his past misfortunes" (Spencer 1927:180). Past attempts by Skeat[13] to connect Chaucer's line with Dante's "tristo buco" (*Inf.* 32.2) and "de la valle d'abisso dolorosa" (*Inf.* 4.8)[14] have been successfully countered by Spencer's demonstration of how common the idea of hell as a pit or hole was in the Middle Ages. Bethel's suggested source has, at least on the surface, more plausibility than those previously offered. Although in both Chaucer and Dante there is the mention of coming out of hell, in the Italian it is strictly literal, while in the English it is totally figurative. The image that Chaucer is using for Aeneas is, of course, very common as an expression of extremes,[15] so we must certainly not assume that going from hell to paradise is an unusual idea or that Chaucer was in any way dependent on Dante for it.

While the verbal similarity to Dante is certainly striking enough to suggest a parallel, and possibly a source, for Chaucer's line, we must be somewhat cautious, since the entrance to the infernal regions was regularly configured as a flaming mouth in the form of a huge monster's head with widespread jaws and a cavernous throat down which the fiends are prodding the damned souls.[16] What makes the passage in *Purg.* 21 a likely source is (as Bethel has aptly noted) the precise image of the "gola / D'inferno."

The Legend of Hypsipyle and Medea

Bethel: "1371–73, 1603–08: references to Jason; descriptive details from *Inf.* XVIII, 83–92."

---

[12] As for the -*o* ending, one is tempted to think that Chaucer was rather hard pressed to find a rhyme to Dido and would not have been at all averse to seizing upon, or composing, this one despite the fact that it may not have been in the nominative form.

[13] See Skeat's note to this line.

[14] Spencer's note has incorrectly given for the first citation 33.2. For the Satan-Adam-Limbo tradition see the discussion of *MkT* B 3189–3204 in Pace 1963:25–35.

[15] The situations in which the image is used vary widely and show how ready a phrase it was. Cf. *MerT* E 1963–64 ("How that he wroghte, I dar nat to yow telle; / Or wheither hire thoughte it paradys or helle"); there is the Parson's more literal contrast which is the basis of his sermon "in consideracioun of the peynes of helle and the joyes of hevene" (*ParsT* I 735–40); *TC* 4.712–14 ("Remembryng hir, fro heven into which helle / She fallen was, syn she forgoth the syghte / Of Troilus"); *LGW* F 1–2 ("A thousand tymes have I herd men telle / That ther ys joy in hevene and peyne in helle"); *RR* 3621–22 ("Now am I raysed, at my devys, / Fro helle unto Paradys").

[16] See, for example, Twining 1885:172–76, plates 79–81; see also van Marle 1931–32:2.118, fig. 135. Cf. in Chaucer, *ParsT* I 855–60.

Thow madest thy recleymyng and thy
　　lures
To ladyes of thy statly aparaunce,
And of thy wordes, farced with
　　plesaunce

Now was Jason a semely man withalle,
And lyk a lord, and hadde a gret
　　renoun,
And of his lok as real as a leoun,
And goodly of his speche, and familer,
And coude of love al the art and craft
　　pleyner
Withoute bok, with everych
　　observaunce.

mi disse: "Guarda quel grande che vene,
e per dolor non par lagrime spanda:
quanto aspetto reale ancor ritene!
　　Quelli è Iasón, che per cuore e per senno
li Colchi del monton privati féne.
Ello passò per l'isola di Lenno
　　poi che l'ardite femmine spietate
tutti li maschi loro a morte dienno.
Ivi con segni e con parole ornate
　　Isifile ingannò, la giovinetta
　　[che prima avea tutte l'altre ingannate.
Lasciolla quivi, gravida, soletta;
　　tal colpa a tal martiro lui condanna;
e anche di Medea si fa vendetta."]

...said to me, "Look at that great one who comes, and seems to shed no tear
for pain. What a regal aspect he yet retains! That is Jason, who by courage and
by craft despoiled the Colchians of the ram. He passed by the isle of Lemnos
when the bold and pitiless women had given all their males to death. There,
with tokens and with fair words, he deceived the young Hypsipyle [who first
had deceived all the rest. He left her there pregnant and forlorn: such guilt
condemns him to such torment; and Medea too is avenged."] [*Inf.*, p. 189]

Lowes (1917a:714) italicizes "*Quanto aspetto reale ancor ritiene!*" and "*Ivi con seno e con parole
ornate*" in Dante, and the phrases "*...thy lures...of the statly apparaunce,...thy wordes,
farced with plesaunce*" in the first selection from Chaucer and "*And of his loke as real* as a
leoun, / And goodly of his speche, and famulere*" in the second. Among these extracts, the
relevant portions of the *Inferno* are the phrases *aspetto reale* and *parole ornate*."[17] It is, of
course, possible that if Chaucer needed a source for Jason's bearing and looks Dante could
have supplied the term *reale*,[18] but the major portion of the description can be found
elsewhere, as I shall indicate shortly.

Chaucer most surely did not follow Dante insofar as the version of the Jason myth was
concerned, for Dante follows that tradition that states that the hero "ingannò con parole
ornate" and then "lasciolla gravida soletta." On the contrary, Chaucer, like Ovid, has
Jason lawfully wedded to Hypsipyle, by whom he has two children before he leaves for
Colchos. In all except the precise word *reale*, Ovid supplies the basic background description for this passage. In *Met*. 7.5, Jason is pictured as an "illustrious leader" (Ovid
1940:3.343), and Medea goes on to speak of him as follows (lines 25-27): "Who that is not
heartless would not be moved by Jason's youth, his noble birth, his manhood? Who,

---

[17] *Senno* probably should not be included since it seems to refer not to promises but to actual physical gifts.
This interpretation seems borne out by the partial contrast of the word with "parole ornate"; that is, Jason
presented every outward appearance of a courtly lover by his fair words and by the love tokens which he gave.

[18] Jason was, of course, both the son and nephew of a king and later a king in his own right. The connection of
the lion (king of beasts) with royalty, and with the aspect of a king, is not unusual and can be found, for example,
in Chaucer, in his description of "the grete Emetreus, the kyng of Inde" (*KnT* A 2156), "And as a leon he his
lookyng caste" (lnie 2171), and in Theseus's earlier remarks (lines 1773-75): "Fy / Upon a lord that wol have no
mercy, / But been a leon, bothe in word and dede, / To hem that been in repentaunce and drede...." The idea is
ridiculed in Chaucer's description of Chauntecleer (*NPT* B² 3176, 3179): "Real he was, he was namoore
aferd... / He looketh as it were a grym leoun...." These examples, however, are not meant to deny Dante's
possible influence on this particular point. See the final remarks in this entry.

though the rest were lacking, would not be touched by his beauty? Certainly he has touched my heart" (Ovid 1940:3.345). Soon after, she brings up his *nobilitas* (lines 43–45): "But no: his look, his loftiness of soul, his grace of form are not such that I need fear deceit" (Ovid 1940:3.345). As in Chaucer, Fortune (here *cas*) plays its part in getting Medea to fall in love (lines 84–85): "It chanced that the son of Aeson was more beautiful than usual that day: you could pardon her for loving him" (Ovid 1940:3.349), though no little credit is given to Jason's rhetorical techniques at this critical point: "But when the stranger began to speak, grasped her right hand, and in low tones asked for her aid and promised marriage in return, she burst into tears and said, 'I see what I am about to do'" (Ovid 1940:3.349), and his oath (lines 94–97)[19] is most certainly an example of his being "goodly of his speche."

There is, however, one aspect of the description of Jason throughout the *Legend* that is not found in Ovid's *Metamorphoses* or in Dante, and that is the constant reference to Jason in terms of the courtly lover. This element, as well as much of the detail found in the passage above, could very well come from the interpolations and translations of the author of the *Ovide moralisé*.[20] The interpolated description of Jason is worth quoting at length:[21]

> Un neveu ot li riches rois (Peleus),
> Moult preux, moult sages, moult cortois.
> Moult debonaire, moult proisie,
> Moult apert et moult envoisie.
> Humbles estoit et serviçables.
> Debonaires et amiables.
> Li damoisiaux ot non Jason.
> Niez fu Pelie et Filz Heson.
> Moult estoit biaux à grant merveille.
> Nature ot mise et cure et veille
> En le former, ce m'est avis.
> Biau le fist de cors et de vis.
> En tous endrois biau le forma.
> En sor que tout si le forma
> De bones teches et de mours,
> Que s'il fust loiaus vers amours,
> En tout le monde n' eüst té,
> Mes moult petite leauté

---

[19] "Per sacra triformis / Illa deae, lucoque foret quod numen in illo. / Perque patrem soceri cernentem cuncta futuri, / Eventusque suos, per tanta pericula jurat" ("He swore he would be true by the sacred rites of the threefold goddess, by whatever divinity might be in that grove, by the all-beholding father of his father-in-law who was to be, by his own successes and his mighty perils" [Ovid 1940:3349]).

[20] Chaucer's version of the Jason story is actually a compilation of the various versions of the tale that he had encountered directly in reading Guido's *Historia Troiae* (bk. 2), Ovid's *Heroides* (epistles 6 and 12), and *Metamorphoses* (7), Benoit's *Roman de Troie* (lines 715–2062), but most particularly the *Ovide moralisé* (7.1–689), which combines (as does Chaucer) Ovid's accounts with the later medieval versions and converts Jason into a completely courtly lover. Chaucer seems to follow the *Ovide moralisé* not only in narrative emphasis but in the direct use of certain lines. Thus, to give some examples from the first 260 lines of the *Ovide moralisé*, OM 12–13 can be compared to *LGW* 1396, OM 41 to *LGW* 1409, OM 64–77 to *LGW* 1414–21, OM 93–95 to *LGW* 1423–25, OM 141–45 to *LGW* 1454–57, OM 252 to *LGW* 1462, OM 253–54 to *LGW* 1493–96, OM 255 to *LGW* 1463, OM 259–60 to *LGW* 1464–65 (Chaucer's phrasing in this last citation from the OM is one of the instances of direct translation and can be found again in *LGW* 2423–24). There are specific indications of the use of the other sources as well.

[21] *Ovide moralisé* 7.15–40. This is not meant to imply that Chaucer could have gotten his ideas on courtly love only from the *Ovide moralisé*, merely that the characterization of the hero that he found there (and in Benoit also) is unlike that given in Dante or Ovid.

Ot vers amours en son aäge,
Si l'en avint deulz et damage,
Si com porrez ou conte oïr.
Saciez que nulz ne puet joïr
A la parfin d' amours boisier.
Moult fist li valles à proisier.
Plus fu amez por sa proesce
Que Pelies pour sa richesse.

[A nephew had the rich king (Peleus), very bold, very shrewd, very courteous, very good-natured, very worthy, very open and very gay. Humble he was and obliging, good-natured and friendly. This young knight was called Jason; he was nephew of Peleus and son of Heson. He was wondrously handsome. Nature had devoted both care and watchfulness in shaping him, in my opinion, made him handsome in body and face, in every respect formed him handsome, so that she so formed him wholly of good points and manners, so that if he had been faithful in love, in all the world he would have been perfect. But he had very little honesty in love in his age, thus sorrows and ruin came to him because of it, as you will be able to hear in the story. Know that no deceiver is able to enjoy love to the very last. Much made the young man to be prized. He was loved more for his prowess than Peleus for his riches.]

Even the relevant lines from Ovid seem to have closer application to Chaucer in their French translation; thus, lines 25–28 become (lines 369–77):

Dur cuer et pautonner avroit
Cui de lui pitié ne mouvroit,
Car trop est de noble lignage,
Jones et de grant vasselage.
En sor que tout, a mon avis
Tant est biaux de cors et de vis,
Qu'il n'a dame deça la mer,
Qui bien ne deüst amer,
S'il estoit or filz d'un vilain.

[She would have a hard and craven heart who would not be moved by pity for him, because he is of noble lineage, young and of high nobility. So that, in my opinion, he is so handsome in body and face that there isn't a lady on this side of the sea who wouldn't really love even if he were now the son of a peasant.]

Medea's intuitive trust is expressed as (lines 403–406):

Tant a douz cuer et debonaire
Et tant a simple le viaire,
Tant est cortois et jentis hom,
Qu'l ne feroit point traïson

though the element of chance disappears entirely from the next passage of Ovid (lines 84–85), becoming merely (lines 494–95):

A cele hore fu, ce m'est vis,
Jason plus biaux c'onc mais ne fu.

Finally, Jason's appeal to Medea is translated as (lines 509–14):

> Jason le prent par la main nue.
> Debonairement la salue.
> A basse voix humble li prie
> Par amour qu'el li face aïe,
> Si li promet qu'il la prendra
> A feme et o soi l'enmenra.

Chaucer's emphasis on the courtly-love aspect, while it may well have been brought into the tale by Chaucer himself, very definitely follows the tone of the legend as given in the *Ovide moralisé*. Chaucer, then, used a great many sources[22] for the narrative and characterization of his double legend. Although Jason's royalty was common knowledge, and although Chaucer uses the complete idea of the phrase "real as a leoun" elsewhere, there is nonetheless the coincidence of Jason's name and the simpler *aspetto reale* in *LGW* 1605. For the rest, however, other sources seem more probable.

Bethel: "1383: adapted from *Inf.* XIX, 5."

Have at thee, Jason! now thyn horn is   or convien che per voi suoni la tromba
    blowe!

now must the trumpet sound for you [*Inf.*, p. 193]

Referring to Lowes's remark (1917*a*:714), Robinson states (p. 849) in his note to this line: "The figure of the horn possibly comes from Inf. xix, 5, where it refers to the public crying of the misdeeds of condemned criminals. But the phrase *Have at thee* suggests that Chaucer had in mind rather the hunter's horn, sounded to start the pursuit of the game." Exception must be taken to Robinson's interpretation. The preceding lines (1381–82) make fairly evident the meaning of the phrase. Chaucer, condemning Jason's falseness, says:

> Yif that I live, thy name shal be shove
> In English that thy sekte shal be knowe!

In other words, Chaucer is going to do all that he can to make known or proclaim abroad Jason's "sekte"—a term that will be dealt with shortly. This declaration is, of course, in keeping with the promise Chaucer had made to the God of Love and with the tone of light seriousness of the Prologue. Chaucer is here the champion of Love and, having proclaimed his purpose, formally issues his legalistic challenge in the following line. "'Have at thee' is almost equivalent to 'en garde' and announces the speaker's intention to get at or attack. . . . To go at or get at, esp. in a hostile way; to have a stroke at, make an attempt at."[23] In short, this line of Chaucer's means simply: "Prepare yourself for an attack, Jason, for you have now been exposed as a criminal."

This interpretation is borne out by one of the definitions of *horn*, which in Chaucer's time was "the wind instrument as used in a legal process, e.g., in the Scotch ceremony of proclaiming an outlaw, when three blasts were blown on a horn by the king's messenger,"[24] thus giving the phrases "to put [denounce] to the horn," that is, to proclaim an outlaw (or "to be at the horn") to be out of the protection of the law, i.e., proclaimed an

---

[22] See above, n.19.
[23] *Shorter Oxford English Dictionary*, sub have, III.5.
[24] *Oxford English Dictionary*, sub horn, III.14.

outlaw. The references, then, show that the procedure existed in Scotch and Italian law,[25] and, while Chaucer may have heard of it in the one case or seen it in the other, there is the question whether or not there was a specific English equivalent.

Outlawry was invoked against an absent party as the extreme punishment that could be applied. According to Pollock and Maitland (1895:2.578) the criminal "is not entitled to any 'law'[26] not even to that sort of 'law' which we allow to noble beasts of the chase." Or, to use the rather grim legal expression, "*Caput gerat lupinum*—in these words the courts decreed outlawry" (Pollock and Maitland, p. 447).[27] The procedure in the fourteenth century was in the form of a formal public proclamation made in four successive courts: "If the appellee did not appear, the ceremony of 'exacting' or 'interrogating'[28] him was performed in four successive county courts, that is to say, a proclamation was made bidding him 'come into the king's peace,' and if he came not, then the dread punishment was pronounced" (Pollock and Maitland, p. 579). The criminal, however,

> could not be prosecuted to outlawry in this way, unless a person stood forth to make the suit, who could speak *de visu et auditu* that the party had fled; and who would call upon him to return in the king's peace, or require that he might, at the proper time, be outlawed; and then he was to state the crime, as if the party was present, and the appeal was going to be heard; and he was to add, that should he appear, he would repeat the charge he had made. Thus not only *suit*, but the *appeal* was actually to be made, before the fugitive could be outlawed. [Reeves 1830:2.279]

Now in all likelihood formal public proclamations were made to the sounding of a trumpet,[29] and it is also very likely that this procedure, plus Chaucer's formal presentation of his suit against the absent Jason, was in his mind in the lines under discussion here.

If it is not outlawry that is being declared against Jason, it might very well be the next similar legal action: the formal declaration of "hue and cry." Again, such action was taken against a person who had absented himself (as Jason had deserted Hypsipyle and Medea) after the fact:

> ...the process was to raise *hutesium*, or hue and cry, and a *secta* or suit was made after them from town to town till they were taken, otherwise the township, where the fact happened, would be in *misericordia*. This hue and cry suit was made in a different way, according to the custom of different places. The suit was to be carried further than the search from town to town, for the offender was to be proclaimed in the county; a method which had been adopted in mercy to the absent fugitive, who, it should seem by the old law was considered as an outlaw upon his flight merely, without being proclaimed with this formality in the county court. [Reeves, 2.279][30]

---

[25] It seems almost unnecessary to point out that, even were we to grant Chaucer's dependence on the *Commedia* here, the lines would have been meaningless to him if he were not already familiar with the procedure. For a thorough and fascinating study of outlawry etc. (though not of its procedure), see Goebel 1937.

[26] "Ass. Clarend. c. 12: 'non habeat legem'" (Pollock and Maitland's note).

[27] "Select Pleas of the Crown (Selden Soc.), p. 47. Y. B. 20–1 Edw. I, p. 237: 'crie *Wolveseved*'" (Pollock and Maitland's note).

[28] "In out records *interrogetur = exigatur* = let him be demanded" (Pollock and Maitland's note).

[29] I am indebted to G. L. Haskins, of the University of Pennsylvania School of Law, for advice and help in this rather technical matter.

[30] Citations are given to "Bracton, 124 and 125." This is an explanation of the procedure involved in the formal hue and cry. For the hue and cry in its extracurial operation, see n.31 below.

For purposes of interpreting Chaucer's lines, let us keep in mind, for a moment, the importance of the *secta*, as well as the formality of the legal action. Indeed, a very specific procedure was to be followed in making the hue and cry [Pollock and Maitland, 2.576–77]:

> When a felony is committed, the hue and cry (*hutesium* et *clamor*) should be raised. If, for example, one comes upon a dead body and omits to raise the hue, one commits an amerciable offence, besides laying oneself open to ugly suspicions. Possibly the proper cry is "Out!" and therefore it is *uthesium* or *hutesium*.[31] The neighbours should turn out with bows, arrows, knives, that they are bound to keep[32] and, besides much shouting, there will be horn-blowing; the "hue" will be "horned" from vill to vill.[33]

There is, then, the specific procedure in which "tunc *cornaverunt* hutes."[34] With this detail of the procedure, let us join the previously noted emphasis on the *secta* and the formality of a legally proclaimed hue and cry and look once more at Chaucer's lines:

> Yif that I live, thy name shal be shove
> In English that thy sekte shal be knowe!
> Have at thee, Jason! now thyn horn is blowe!

The passage from Chaucer seems perfectly clear if we interpret it by the legal phraseology of the fourteenth century. Chaucer (perhaps as Love's advocate) is raising a formal hue and cry against Jason, who has committed a felony by deserting (and causing the death of) Hypsipyle and Medea. Chaucer vows that his "name shal be shove In English" and that his "sekte" shall be made known everywhere. He then issues his legalistic challenge and declares Jason an outlaw, to be put to the horn, to be, in the terms of the legal historians, "'horned' from vill to vill." It would seem that in the terms of both the process of outlawry and that of hue and cry Chaucer's lines have relevance. Jason's desertion and absence are being made a heinous crime, and Chaucer is following the accepted legal procedure in bringing formal charges against him, albeit more *de auditu* than *de visu*. On the basis of either legal procedure, therefore, it would appear that the phrase and custom of "putting to the horn" were as common in England as it was in Italy or Scotland.[35]

Dante, in *Inf.* 19.5, is speaking not about Jason but rather about the simoniac popes. This is another subject than Jason, with other lines and other characters intervening, and to suggest (as it has been suggested) that Chaucer's "linked atoms" worked by juxtapositions when there was no common subject matter[36] is to give still wider berth to the ignoring of literary and historical plausibility. Thus, in the present instance, though Chaucer may have seen, while abroad, the process of putting someone to the horn, it

---

[31] "See Brunner, D. R. G. ii, 482, for the various cries used for this purpose. The famous Norman *Haro* seems to mean *Hither*. See also Viollet, Etablissements, i. 189. However, Dr. Murray tells us that more probably uthesium, a latinization of O. E. *ut-haes*, merely means out-cry, not crying 'Out.' French scribes mix up this word with *huer*, to hoot" (Pollock and Maitland's note).

[32] "See the Writ of 1252 in Select Charters" (Pollock and Maitland's note).

[33] "Select Pleas of the Crown, p. 69: 'et tunc cornaverunt hutes'" (Pollock and Maitland's note).

[34] See preceding footnote. The italics are mine.

[35] Haskins (n.29 above) mentioned to me the very close parallel of Scotch and English law. One reason for the hesitation in the present instance is that (unlike the Scotch records) there would seem to be no readily available case to cite as precedent in English law besides that given immediately above; another is that the history of the process of proclamation and of "putting to the horn" has not been previously investigated.

[36] The suggestion would seem to be that Chaucer, writing of Jason, recalled Dante's reference to Jason in *Inf.*, 18, which is less than sixty lines away from the reference to the simoniac popes in *Inf.* 19, which Chaucer thereupon recalled.

would appear that he did not have to make a long, complex journey—either physical or literary—to discover what he might well have observed in any law court or public square of the realm.

The Legend of Ariadne

Bethel: "1886f.: Allusion to Minos as the judge of damned souls probably due to *Inf.* V, 1–15 (esp. 4–6), at least in part."

Juge infernal, Mynos, of Crete kyng, Now cometh thy lot, now comestow on the ryng.	Così discesi del cerchio primaio giù nel secondo, che men loco cinghia e tanto più dolor, che punge a guaio. Stavvi Minòs orribilmente, e ringhia: essamina le colpe ne l'intrata; giudica e manda secondo ch'avvinghia. Dico che quando l'anima mal nata li vien dinanzi, tutta si confessa; e quel conoscitor de le peccata vede qual loco d'inferno è da essa; cignesi con la coda tante volte quantunque gradi vuol che giù sia messa. Sempre dinanzi a lui ne stanno molte: vanno a vicenda ciascuna al giudizio, dicono e odono e poi son giù volte.

Thus I descended from the first circle into the second, which girds less space, and so much greater woe that it goads to wailing. There stands Minos, horrible and snarling: upon the entrance he examines their offenses, and judges and dispatches them according as he entwines. I mean that when the ill-begotten soul comes before him, it confesses all; and that discerner of sins sees which shall be its place in Hell, then girds himself with his tail as many times as the grades he wills that it be sent down. Always before him stands a crowd of them; they go, each in his turn, to the judgment; they tell, and hear, and then are hurled below. [*Inf.*, p. 47]

The allusion is Bethel's claim, for a source seems nonexistent.[37] In his text Bethel says (p. 191): "In the case of the mention of Minos in the *Legend of Ariadne*, however, the Dantesque influence is insufficient to account for everything." He cites the lines from Chaucer given above, admitting that they "might have come from the classical authors" (p. 191), though he persists in claiming that the "juge infernal" is Dantesque. Finally, in what seems a sort of desperation, he adds (pp. 191–92):

in the reference to "the ring" it may not be too fantastic to note the possibility of a rather clever juggling of words on Chaucer's part. Dante has

> Stavvi Minòs orribilmente e *ringhia;*
>   Essamina le colpe ne l' entrata,
>   Giudica e manda secondo c' *avvinghia.*

[37] See *TC* 4.118–88 for the rejection of Dante's Minos as a source of Chaucer's.

Now Dante's *ringhia* does not, of course, have any connection with "ring" but *avvinghia* means "he entwines, i.e., rings himself;" could Chaucer have been associating the spelling of one word with the meaning of another to form a play upon the latter? The supposition is at least entertaining and I think perfectly possible. [Bethel's italics]

This suggestion seems to very little help in explaining what is evidently an idiomatic expression somewhat analogous to the phrase in the first half of line 1887.

As for the "juge infernal" being dependent on Dante, see the previously noted discussion under *TC* 4.1187–88. The overemphasis on the adjective in this phrase does not deny the whole array of classical writers on the subject nor the medieval tradition that blended the Christian and pagan underworlds. The Christian word *inferno* might have given some small basis of argument for a Dantesque source, but the traditional adjective *infernal* denies even this and puts the phrase in the realm of common knowledge.

The Legend of Hypermnestra

Bethel: "2638: 'For al the gode under the colde mone'; the possibility that this line is adopted from *Inf.* VII, 64: 'tutto l'oro ch'è sotto la luna', has been suggested by Cary and Toynbee (*Dante in Eng. Lit.*, I, 10), but any indebtedness here seems doubtful."

There is no indebtedness here whatever. The word *gode* is not the word *gold*, and the expression "under the mone" was common enough to lead, in the next century, to the formation of the word *sublunary* for anything earthly. There is not, of course, a contextual parallel. Bethel's rejection seems totally justifiable.

CHAPTER 7

The Canterbury Tales

HE DEVELOPMENT of Chaucer's use of Dante in *The Canterbury Tales* cannot be treated in any way as a unit, of course, since the individual tales were undoubtedly composed, as Robinson has pointed out, over a period of at least twenty years. It is perhaps noteworthy that two of the longest Chaucerian passages based directly on the *Divina Commedia* – the "Hugelino" episode in *The Monk's Tale* and the *Invocacio ad Mariam* in *The Second Nun's Prologue* – are considered by Robinson among the earliest material incorporated into the work, and their date of composition is set at about 1373-74. These two passages, along with the discussion of "gentilesse" in *The Wife of Bath's Tale*, have, in fact, certain unique features insofar as the present study is concerned. Obvious at once are both their length and their closeness to the Dantean source; but, in addition, there is the nature of the passages themselves, the one being Chaucer's only use of a narrative from Dante, the second being a religious lyric of Marian adoration, and the third being Chaucer's clearest use of a philosophical doctrine of Dante's. Further, the first two, in their source, exist as separable verses, that is to say, as units capable of being removed from their context, which, considering the high degree of integration of Dante's work, makes them per se somewhat outstanding.

The conversion of Dante's Ugolino to Chaucer's Hugolino is probably one of the best illustrations that this study can offer of the differences between the two writers concerning the nature and function of their verses. As well, if we keep in mind the narrator of these exempla "De Casibus Virorum Illustrium" – and one suspects that his personality is not quite in line with the view of the Monk that we get in *The General Prologue* – we can perhaps observe the poetic intention that has governed the direction of the change from the terrifying account that Dante burns into the reader's mind to the moral illustration in support of the cleric's theme.

If the Monk's version of the Ugolino episode represents Chaucer totally converting Dante to his poetic purpose, the *Invocacio* in *The Second Nun's Prologue* represents his blending of Dante with other elements to form a new and enlarged lyric of no little merit. The use of Dante in such cases has already been seen in *Troilus* and is found again in *The Prioress's Tale* in a shorter but no less poetic form. Although precise evidence is lacking, there seems no reason to doubt the generally held opinion that the *Invocacio* was composed early in the so-called Italian period (Robinson 1957:756), and, indeed, this would appear to lend support to the suggestion, more fully discussed below (under *PrT* B² 1664-70) that a question of memorization might well be involved. In any event, the passage serves as an excellent example of Chaucer's ability to interweave verbal borrowings from many sources around the central Dantean lyric and achieve a sense of lyric unity.

The discussion of "gentilesse" by the loathly lady in *The Wife of Bath's Tale* represents Chaucer's most explicit use of one of Dante's doctrines. For this, Chaucer turned once more to tractate 4 of the *Convivio*, and, while this borrowing might well be as much as twenty years after the *Invocacio*,[1] the essential method of interweaving found in the verbal synthesis of the Second Nun's Marian prayer is found here in the synthesis of concepts drawn from many sources, but centering principally on Dante, Boethius, and the interpolations in *The Romaunt of the Rose*. With so explicit a reference to Dante it is tempting indeed to think that the basis of Chaucer's view of "gentilesse" at this time was governed by the discussion in tractate 4, but a close analysis of the passage would seem to indicate that, while Dante was the source for the important "antica richezza" tenet, the Boethian concept (among others) held a place of at least equal importance. To attribute almost exclusively to Dante's influence so common a theme as "gentilesse" seems to ignore the prevalence of the subject in the general poetry of the period.[2]

In *The Canterbury Tales*, "gentilesse" and fortune are the two major thematic borrowings that have been attributed to Dante's influence. Of the first we have already suggested that the dependence seems to be limited to one specific, though important, part of Chaucer's view. Of the second it would seem that, while there are definite and strong echoes of Dante's discussion in the *Commedia*, Chaucer's position is almost completely Boethian.[3] Confirmation of this position might well have come from Dante, who also based his interpretation of Fortune on Boethius, but Dante carried the discussion to a then-unique conclusion that Chaucer, at least in his writing, does not seem to have followed.

The outstanding examples of borrowings from Dante would seem to be those mentioned above in *The Monk's Tale*, the Second Nun's *Invocacio*, and *The Wife of Bath's Tale*, but we should not forget that there was a continued use of Dante's verse for the visual image (albeit at times radically changed to fit Chaucer's poetic needs) throughout *The Canterbury Tales*, though probably to a lesser degree than previously. It is difficult to say whether this change is due to a greater emphasis on narrative than descriptive development (though there is no use of Dante in *The General Prologue*), whether it is due to the actuality of Chaucer's subject, or whether it is merely emphasized by the presence of the longer borrowings already noted. *The Canterbury Tales* does, however, seem to indicate that Chaucer, besides borrowing from Dante a wide variety of phrases and images, turned to the *Commedia* for religious lyrics and to the *Convivio* for discussions of *gentilezza*. Many other sources were combined with these, but the continued use of the *Paradiso* in the one case and tractate 4 in the other would seem to show a point of view on Chaucer's part. Finally, we should not forget that there might be a more general influence of Dante in the living characters that inhabit *The Canterbury Tales*. Just how far Dante's *êtres vivants* influenced Chaucer's characterization of real or realistic persons is almost impossible to determine precisely, since it depends to such a large extent on our inividual interpretation of the work as a whole. To me this appears to be one of the deepest influences of Dante, for it would have given Chaucer confirmation of a poetic technique that, as *The Book of the Duchess* shows, was an inherent part of his literary style. If due allowance is made for the generalization, we might more briefly say that in this poetic view Dante confirmed what

---

[1] Robinson (p. 698) suggests that the probable date of *WBT* was about 1393–94.

[2] See also the discussions under *TC* 1.891 and the general remarks on *The Squire's Tale*, *The Franklin's Tale*, and *Gentilesse*.

[3] The problem is more generally discussed under the poem *Fortune* in order to have a central point for the investigation, but relevant comments have been offered (as in *Troilus*) at the individual entries in *The Canterbury Tales*.

Chaucer already knew. No matter how far they differ on the question of the purpose of the art, for both men poetry existed in the world of affairs and not in the world of stylized conventions.

The General Prologue

Bethel: "884: see under *Troil*. I, 568f."

The Knight's Tale

Bethel: "*920f.: influenced by the Dantesque conception of gentillesse."

> Som drope of pitee, thurgh thy gentillesse,
> Upon us wrecched wommen lat thou falle.

There would seem to be little basis for this remark. *Gentilezza* and the code of courtly love are such common knowledge of the period that only the most precise parallels should be offered as influences. See further discussions under *Gentilesse, TC* 1.894–96, *The Wife of Bath's Tale, The Franklin's Tale*, and *The Squire's Tale.*

Bethel: "1074: see under *Troil*. I, 568f."

Bethel: "1251–54: attitude towards Fortune shows Dante's influence; *Inf.* VII, 67–96."

> Allas, why pleynen folk so in commune
> On purveiaunce of God, or of Fortune,
> That yeveth hem ful ofte in many a gyse
> Wel bettre than they kan hemself
>   devyse?

[See citation and discussion under *Fortune*; see also *TC* 3.617–20, 5.744–49.]

As Jefferson (1917:142) remarks, "this is the point that [Boethius in] 4.p6 establishes." Boethius, to extract but one example, states:

> The whiche God, whan he hath byholden from the hye tour of his purveaunce, he knoweth what is covenable to every wight, and lenyth hem that he woot that is covenable to hem. Lo, herof comyth and herof is don this noble miracle of the ordre destynal whan God, that al knoweth, dooth swich thing, of which thing unknowynge folk ben astonyd.

It is also in this prosa that Boethius establishes the difference between the "purveiaunce of God" and the "ordre destynal." In addition, the illustrations used by Chaucer in lines 1255–64 are also those found in Boethius. The particular elements that make up Dante's own view of Fortune, as pointed out in the discussions cited above, are not involved in any way in the present citation. Chaucer's statements here are far more in the mainstream of medieval thinking on the problem. The idea, for example, can be found in Saint Thomas, *Summa contra gentiles*, 3.64:

> Moreover, that natural bodies are moved and made to operate for an end, even though they do not know their end, was proved by the fact that what happens to them is always, or often, for the best; and, if their workings resulted from art,

they would not be done differently. But it is impossible for things that do not know their end to work for that end, and to reach that end in an orderly way, unless they are moved by someone possessing knowledge of the end.... Therefore, God governs the world by His providence [Aquinas 1956:211]

This is extended in 3.92.

In short, the question of Fortune is one of the most popular areas of medieval philosophical inquiry. To claim ascription under such conditions, one must have evidence much more definite than merely a discussion of the same general topic.

Bethel: "1328–31: allusion to Juno; verbal influence of *Inf.* XXX, 1–4, 22f."

But I moot been in prisoun thurgh Saturne,
And eek thurgh Juno, jalous and eek wood,
That hath destroyed wel ny al the blood
Of Thebes with his waste walles wyde

[See citation and discussion under *TC* 5.599–602.]

Bethel: "*1431: same as 920f."

He was so gentil of condicioun

There is definitely no basis of comparison here. To use merely the word "gentil" as the basis for a suggested Dantesque allusion or source seems definitely open to question. See discussions under *Gentilesse*, *TC* 1.894–96, *The Franklin's Tale*, and *The Squire's Tale*.

Bethel: "1465: see under *Troil* I 568f."

Bethel: "1493: description of sunrise closely modelled on *Purg.* I, 19f."

And firy Phebus riseth up so bright
That al the orient laugheth of the light

Lo bel pianeto che d'amar conforta
faceva tutto rider l'oriente,
[velando i Pesci ch'erano in sua scorta.]

The fair planet that prompts to love was making the whole East smile, [veiling the Fishes that were in her train.] [*Purg.*, p. 5]

There is certainly a striking parallel here, though Chaucer is speaking of the sun, and Dante of Venus. This point has also been noted by J. A. W. Bennett (1953:114), who adds that:

it is the hour before, not after, sunrise that Dante is describing (cf. *Purgatorio* XXVII 94–96). To follow the process of Chaucer's adaptation [that is, from Dante] we must turn to Boccaccio, on whose *Teseida* the Knight's Tale is based. Boccaccio has no such description as the fateful morning..., but to the spring morning of two or three years before...(III 5–8), he devotes three stanzas, beginning with astronomical allusions to

Febo, salendo con li suoi cavalli...

[Phoebus sallying forth with his steeds...]

and to Venus:

> Venus facea de' passi con che sale,
> per che il cielo rideva tutto quanto
> d'Amon, che'n Pisce dimorava intanto,

[Venus stepped forth with him and . . . for this reason all the heaven of Ammon smiled, as he dallied for a time in Pisces]

and giving a bright picture of the branches decked in green, the birds "giulivi e gai" ["jubilant and merry"], and the "giovenetti lieti, che ad amare eran disposti" ["happy youths, ripe for love"]. [Translations from McCoy, p. 78]

Boccaccio's lines are so obviously based on Dante's that the connection must have been evident at once. Chaucer chose the more concise "rider l'oriente," as "the orient laugheth" shows, though he kept close to the *Teseida* otherwise.

Bethel: "1543–46: same as 1328–31."

How longe, Juno, thurgh thy crueltee,	[See citation and discussion under *TC*
Woltow werreyen Thebes the citee?	5.599–602]
Allas ybroght is to confusioun	
The blood roial of Cadme and	
Amphioun	

There would seem to be no basis for assigning the lines to Dante on grounds of context when so many other sources are possible. Nor can there be any ascription on the basis of "blood roial," a phrase found in *CT* A 1018, B 657, B² 3341, I 765–70; *Anel* 65; and *TC* 3.1800. The word, in its meaning of "lineage," is used by Chaucer too often to need citation in proof.

Bethel: "1638–43: description of wild-beast hunt; possible partial influence of *Inf.* XII, 112–doubtful." (Should read *Inf.* XIII.)

[This Arcite and this Palamon ben met.	[. . . noi fummo d'un romor sorpresi,]
Tho chaungen gan the colour in hir	similemente a colui che venire
face,]	sente 'l porco e la caccia a la sua posta,
Right as the hunters in the regne of	ch'ode le bestie, e le frasche stormire.
Trace,	
That stondeth at the gappe with a spere,	
Whan hunted is the leon or the bere,	
And hereth hym come russhyng in the	
greves,	
And breketh bothe bowes and the leves	

. . . when like one aware of the wild boar and the chase approaching his post, who hears the beasts and the branches crashing, [we were surprised by an uproar.] [*Inf.*, p. 137]

In his text Bethel follows Klaeber's attribution to *Teseida* 7.106, 107, coming in turn from Statius *Thebaid* 4.494ff.; and also the "weaker link" with *Teseida* 7.119. This ascription in the *Inferno*, notes Bethel (p. 18, n.1), "seems adequate as far as the possibility of Dantesque influence goes," but, of course, there is grave doubt in the first place that any basis for Dantesque influence exists.

Bethel: "1663–64: both thought and expression show influence of Dante's conception of Fortune, *Inf.* VII, 67–96."

The destinee, ministre general,   [See citation under *Fortune*.]
That executeth in the world over al
The purveiaunce that God hath seyn
    biforn,
So strong it is that, though the world
    had sworn
The contrarie of a thyng by ye or nay,
Yet somtyme it shal fallen on a day
That fallen nat eft withinne a thousand
    yeer.

The parallel here is obvious. It should be remarked, however, that, as far as source is concerned, the thought is strongly Boethian and Thomistic, and the term "ministre" is found also in Saint Thomas *Contra Gentiles* 3.80: "et sic dispositio regnorem et mutatio dominationis a gente ad ministerium huius ordinis pertinere oportet" ["and so, the arrangement of kingdoms and the changing of domination from one people to another ought to belong to the ministry of this order" (Aquinas 1956:269)]. See further discussion under *Fortune* and *TC* 3.617–20, 5.744–49.

Bethel: "1976–78: description of forest; modelled on *Inf.* XIII, 2–8. *1979f.: the same; modelled on *Inf.* IX, 64–70 (cf. XIII, 115–17)."

[I give Bethel's ascription with his italics and his reversal of the order of the *canti*. The added stanzas are to set the description in proper context.]

[Al peynted was the wal, in lengthe and
    brede,
Lyk to the estres of the grisly place
That highte the grete temple of Mars in
    Trace,
In thilke colde, frosty regioun
Ther as Mars hath his sovereyn
    mansioun.
First on the wal was peynted a forest,]
In which ther dwelleth *neither man ne
    best*,
With *knotty, knarry*, bareyne trees olde,
Of *stubbes sharpe* and hidouse to
    biholde,
In which *ther ran a rumbel in a swough,
As though a storm sholde bresten every
    bough.*
[And dounward from an hille, under a
    bente,
Ther stood the temple of Mars
    armypotente]

[quando noi ci mettemmo per] un bosco
che *da neun sentiero era segnato.*
Non fronda verde, ma di color fosco;
    non rami schietti, ma nodosi e 'nvolti;
    non pomi v'eran, ma stecchi con tòsco.
Non han sì *aspri sterpi* né sì folti
    quelle fiere selvagge che 'n odio hanno
    [tra Cecina e Corneto i luoghi cólti] [*Inf.*
    13.2–8][4]

E già *venìa* su per le torbide onde
    un fracasso d'un suon pien di spavento,
    per cui tremavano amendue le sponde;
Non altrimenti fatto che d'un vento
    impetüoso per li avversi ardori,
    che fier la selva, e sanz' alcun rattento
li rami schianta, abbatte e porta fori. [*Inf.*
    9.64–70]

Ed ecco due da la sinistra costa,
    nudi e graffiati, fuggendo sì forte
    che de la selva *rompieno ogne rosta*. [*Inf.*
    13.115–17][5]

[4] Bethel's text reads *sempri* for *aspri* in line 7.
[5] The *due* (line 115), however, refers not to any storm but to the spendthrifts Jacopo da Santo Andrea and Lano di Siena, who are running through the woods.

when we moved forward through a wood which was not marked by any path. No green leaves, but of dusky hue; no smooth boughs, but gnarled and warped; no fruits were there, but thorns with poison. Those wild beasts that hate tilled alnds between Cecina and Corneto do not have thickets so rough or dense. [*Inf.*, p. 129]

And now there came over the turbid waves a crash of fearful sound, at which both shores trembled: a sound as of a wind, violent from conflicting heats, which strikes the forest and with unchecked course shatters the branches, beats them down and sweeps them away. [*Inf.*, p. 93]

And behold, two on the left hand, naked and torn, fleeing so hard that they were breaking every tangle of the wood. [*Inf.*, p. 137]

Concerning the lines in Chaucer, Bethel begins by saying (p. 221): "Now this passage, it seems to me, combines elements from three places in the *Inferno*; I quote the lines from which it seems likely Chaucer drew most of the phrases he uses here." After citing the passages, he continues with the following line of argument: "If these passages are read in this order and the parts italicized noted, it will be observed that they account not only for every idea in Chaucer's description but for practically all of its wording."

In comparing the passages from Chaucer and Dante, first, we should recognize that there is no contextual parallel. Second, the pastiche form of parallel passage, with a word here and a phrase there, seems open to question because of the arbitrary selection and the consequent suggestive juxtapositions that have (whether consciously or not) been presented. Third, I feel justified here in once more paraphrasing Lounsbury: it was not necessary for Chaucer to go to Italy to be reminded of the particular kind of noise occasioned by an approaching storm in a darkening woods. Finally, Bethel offers in support of this ascription *KT* A 1638–43, on the basis of the possible coincidence of location. He states (pp. 221–22) that "it is interesting to note that two of these passages occur in the same canto [*Inf.* 13] as Dante's description of the hunter waiting in ambush for his game, the possible connexion of which with another section of the *Knight's Tale* I have just discussed." It will be recalled, however, that Bethel, in his discussion of lines 1638–43 on page 218 of his text, all but totally dismissed Dante as a source.

Were such a method of selection to be considered valid, the following "source" (Tolkien and Gordon 1952) could be offered with a sense of high seriousness rather than academic jest. Not even being as selective, the description given here is equally relevant to, if not more relevant than, that offered above:

> Þay boȝen bi bonkkeȝ þer boȝeȝ ar bare,
> Þay clomben bi clyffeȝ þer clengeȝ þe colde.
> . . . þe wyȝe in þe wod wendeȝ his brydel,
> . . . and leueȝ þe knyȝt þere
>   al one . . .
> [He] Showueȝ in bi a schore at a schaȝe syde,
> Rideȝ þurȝ þe roȝe bonk ryȝt to þe dale;
> And þenne he wayted hym aboute, and wylde hit hym þoȝt,
> And seȝe no syngne of resette bisydeȝ nowhere,
> Bot hyȝe bonkkeȝ and brent vpon boþe halue,
> and ruȝe knokled knarreȝ with knorned stoneȝ;
>   . . . at a lynde [he]tacheȝ
> Þe rayne and his riche with a roȝe braunche. . . .

"Now iwysse," quoþ Wowayn, "wysty is here; . . ."
Þene herde he of þat hyȝe hil, in a harde roche
Biȝonde þe broke, in a bonk, a wonder breme noyse. . . .
What! hit rusched and ronge, rawþe to here.[6]

and

Mo nyȝteȝ þen innoghe in naked rokkeȝ,
Þer as claterande fro þe crest þe colde borne renneȝ
And henged heȝe ouer his hede in hard iisse-ikkles,
         . . . he rydes
Into a forest ful dep, þat ferly watȝ wylde,
Hiȝe hilleȝ on vche a halue, and holtwodeȝ vnder
Of hore okeȝ ful hoge a hundreth togeder;
Þe hasel and þe haȝþorne were harled al samen,
With roȝe raged mosse rayled aywhere,
With mony bryddeȝ vnblyþe vpon bare twyges,
Þat pitously þer piped for pyne of þe colde.[7]

Bethel: "2337–40: simile of wet sticks burning; closely modelled on *Inf.* XIII, 40–44."

And as it queynte it made a
   whistelynge,
As doon thise wete brondes in hir
   brennynge,
And at the brondes ende out ran anon
As it were blody dropes many oon;
[For which so soore agast was Emelye
That she was wel ny mad, and gan to
   crye,
For she ne wiste what it signyfied]
	Come d'un stizzo verde ch'arso sia
	   da l'un de' capi, che da l'altro geme
	   e cigola per vento che va via,
	sì de la scheggia rotta usciva insieme
	   parole e sangue; [ond' io lasciai la cima
	   cadere, e stetti come l'uom che teme.]

    As from a green brand that is burning at one end, and drips from the other, hissing with the escaping air, so from that broken twig came out words and blood together; [whereon I let fall the tip, and stood like one who is afraid.] [*Inf.*, p. 131]

Dante definitely has the same image, though whether or not he is Chaucer's source is more difficult to say. The concept of the bleeding twigs, as Robinson points out in his note (p. 679), is found in *Teseida* 7.92, Chaucer's source for the story. Dante's use of the souls embodied in trees and the breaking of branches causing bleeding come almost certainly from a similar incident with the Heliades in Ovid's *Metamorphoses* (2.357–59). The chief difference between Chaucer and Dante lies in the contexts: in Dante there is the description of the metamorphosed souls in the woods of the suicides; in Chaucer there is the description of Emily's prayers at the altar and the omens that she receives there. A good deal closer, in context only, is the passage in the *Aeneid* (3.19–33) describing the rites and prayers of Aeneas at the altar, where the bleeding branches serve as omens presaging the appearance of Polydorus.

---

[6] *Sir Gawain and the Green Knight* 2077–78, 2152, 2154–55, 2161–66, 2176–77, 2189, 2199–2200, 2204.
[7] Ibid., lines 730–32, 740–47.

The idea as a whole is strongly suggested by Boccaccio in the *Teseida*. Emilia goes to the temple of Diana and lights two fires, representative of Palamon and Arcite, whereupon (7.91.4–8 – 7.92.1–3):

> She was not standing there long when one flame went out and then lit up again by itself. The other changed color and became sulphurous, with the flame tips bending here and there and murmuring aloud.
> The enkindled brands seemed like blood, and their spent heads wept such tears that they extinguished the coals. [McCoy, p. 184]

Even though the image is the same, Dante seems unnecessary as a source. Chaucer's Emelye (*KnT* 2334–38) had also seen

> . . .oon of the fyres queynte,
> And quyked agayn, and after that anon
> That oother fyr was queynt and al agon;
> And as it queynte it made a whistelynge,
> As doon thise wete brondes in hir brennynge

Paralleling Chaucer's Emelye, Boccaccio's Emilia is also disturbed by the omen (*Teseida* 7.93): "So she returned to her room as uncertain as she had been when she came out. . . . She passed that night in anguish until every star had fled" (McCoy, p. 184). In structure Chaucer is closer to Boccaccio in that most of his passage is narration, telling that the fire went out and that the drops of blood appeared. The structure of Dante's passage lies almost totally in the metaphor itself. Strictly, too, Dante is speaking of green wood, while Chaucer is speaking of wet wood; Dante's logs can talk, Chaucer's are content to burn. In the final analysis, however, Chaucer's departure from a strict translation of Boccaccio's lines, no matter how close the context might be, must be ascribed either to his creative ability or to his recollection of Dante's image.

Bethel: "2684f.: possible verbal influence of Dante's account of the Furies, *Inf.* IX, 34–51."

Out of the ground a furie infernal sterte,   [See citation and discussion under *TC*
From Pluto sent at requeste of Saturne   1.6–14.]

There is neither verbal nor contextual parallel here. References to the furies as being infernal are too numerous to mention, and certainly we have no indication of any source in these lines.

Bethel: "2779: 'Allone, withouten any companye'; cf. *Inf.* XXIII, 1; 'Taciti, soli, sanza compagnia' – (Longfellow's note). Indebtedness here seems doubtful."

Robinson's note (p. 681) conclusively disposes of this proposed allusion:

> The phrase which recurs in *MillT*, I, 3204, and *Mel*, VII, 1560, was a regular formula in both French and English. To the examples collected by Miss Hammond, English Verse Between Chaucer and Surrey, p. 471, may be added "soule sens compaignon," in the pastourelle of the Lamb and the Wolf. . .; "toz seus sanz compaignie," Gautier d' Aupais. . .; Jugement d' Amour, l. 44 in Fabliaux et Contes.

No doubt more have been turned up since Robinson's note.

Bethel: "*3012-15: this idea seems due to Dante; cf. *Inf.* VII, 78-90; *Par.* VIII, 133-35."

[Thanne may men by this ordre[8] wel
    discerne
That thilke Moevere stable is and
    eterne.
Wel may men knowe, but it be a fool,
That every part dirryveth from his hool;
For nature hath nat taken his bigynnyng
Of no partie or cantel of a thyng,
But of a thyng that parfit is and stable,
Descendynge so til it be corrumpable.
And therfore, of his wise purveiaunce,]
He hath so wel biset his ordinaunce,
That speces of thynges and
    progressiouns
Shullen enduren by successiouns,
And nat eterne, withouten any lye.

[For *Inf.* 7.78-90, see citation and discussion
under *Fortune*; see also *TC* 3.617-20,
5.1541-45.]

Natura generata il suo cammino
    simil farebbe sempre a' generanti,
    se non vincesse il proveder divino.

> The begotten nature would always make its course like its begetters, did not
> Divine provision overrule. [*Par.*, p. 91]

There does not seem to be any basis for comparison. In the first citation Dante is discussing the function of Fortune and the movement of goods, and in the second, the particular inclinations of a person that come from the influence of the stars at the time of birth. Chaucer, on the other hand, is discussing the relation of God's eternity and eternal plan to man's mortality. Robinson suggests, more properly, Boethius, *De cons.* 2, m. 8; 4, pr. 6; 3, pr. 10. He adds (p. 682): "For the figure of the chain or bond, cf. also RR, 16785-88. It goes back ultimately to the story of Homer. (Iliad, viii, 19)." I might also add, Saint Thomas *Summa theologica* 1, q. 3, art. 7; 1, q. 9, art. 2; 1, q. 10, art. 3; and *Summa contra gentiles* 3 passim. One could cite innumerable other instances since this is one of the fundamental tenets of the Thomistic doctrine.

The Man of Law's Tale

Bethel: "358f.: reference to Semiramis as "sowdanesse" due to *Inf.* V, 60."

O sowdanesse, roote of iniquitee!
Virago, thou Semyrame the secounde!
[O serpent under femynynytee,
Lik to the serpent depe in helle
    ybounde!
O feyned womman, al that may
    confounde
Vertu and innocence, thurgh thy
    malice,
Is bred in thee, as nest of every vice!]

["[Ella] fu imperadrice di molte favelle.
A vizio di lussuria fu sì rotta
    che libito fé licito in sua legge,
    per torre il biasmo in che era condotta.
Ell' è Semiramìs, di cui si legge
    che succedette a Nino e fu sua sposa:]
    tenne la terra che 'l Soldan corregge...."

---

[8] I.e., the "cheyne of love."

["(She) was empress of many tongues. She was so given to lechery that she made lust licit in her law, to take away the blame she had incurred. She is Semiramis, of whom we read that she succeeded Ninus and had been his wife:] she held the land the Sultan rules. . . ." [*Inf.*, p. 51]

The principal difficulty with Bethel's remark is that Chaucer seems to apply the term "sowdanesse" not to Semiramis (as it would appear when the lines are taken out of context) but to the actual "sowdanesse" of *The Man of Law's Tale* (i.e., Donegild), as can be seen by referring to the person speaking in the previous line and by the use of the same term again in line 372 ("This Sowdanesse, whom I thus blame and warye"), where Chaucer states plainly enough who his subject has been. If line 358, above, applied to Semiramis, it would have the same construction as line 365 ("O Sathan, envious syn thilke day"), where Satan is addressed; i.e., it would read, "O Semiramis, . . ." etc. Certainly the person addressed is Donegild, the villainess of this part of *The Man of Law's Tale*, as can be seen by lines 360 and 362. In addition, Chaucer would probably not break off his story for an entire, and mostly irrelevant, stanza, which this would be if it were addressed to Semiramis as "sowdanesse."

In the passage in the *Inferno*, it is evident that the reference to Semiramis as a "sowdanesse" can only be derived indirectly from line 60, while her more conventional title is specifically given at the opening of the description: "Fu *imperadrice* di molte favelle." Indeed, if the Chaucerian stanza is read as addressed to Donegild (as has been suggested here), Semiramis would seem to be brought in as a stock example of a "virago" and perhaps by juxtaposition a "roote of iniquitee" (cf. the use of "Marcia Catoun" as the symbol of wifely virtue in *LGW* 252). Such an interpretation seems borne out by Irene Samuel's study of Semiramis in the Middle Ages (1944). Having traced the symbolic development of the empress through Diodorus Siculus, Virgil, Orosius, Justinus, Eusebius, Jerome, Augustine, Conrad of Fabaria, Giovanni Villani, Dante, and Boccaccio,[9] she continues (pp. 41–42):

> And Chaucer, seeking a type of inhuman cruelty, addressed the mother-in-law of fair Constance:
>
> > O sowdanesse, roote of iniquitee!
> > Virago, thou Semyrame the secounde!
>
> But as the mediaeval mind turned the heroine of antiquity who, according to pagan Justinus, had done 'great things,' into the 'harlot,' the 'most cruel and dissolute woman in the world,' so with the dawn of the Renaissance the treatment of Semiramis changed. For Dante there was no question that she was thoroughly damned. But Chaucer wavered. When he wrote a mediaeval *exemplum* for his Man of Law, he used the mediaeval judgment of Semiramis. When he wrote an Ovidian *Legend of Thisbe*, he merely called her the builder of Babylon.[10]

[9] This is a partial list of names up to Chaucer; the study, however, continues on through Spenser.

[10] Samuel's note here reads: "Chaucer simply translated the reference in Ovid, *Metam.*, IV, 57–58, for his *LGW*, 706–09, Robinson, p. 585. Cf. Gower's reference in *Confessio Amantis*, iii, 1332–33." Briefly, the medieval version is based on the idea that Semiramis founded Babylon at the time of the founding of the seed of Abraham. This city of Baal was contrasted with Augustine's City of God, and thus the fundamental Christian opposition enhanced the already lurid tales of Semiramis. Not all the classical writers viewed her as a doer of "great things." Cf. Juvenal, who, in castigating the Roman nobles for their homosexuality in the *Second Satire*, lashes out at their civil and personal atrocities as those "quod nec in Assyrio pharetrata Semiramis orbe" ("that were not even in the Assyrian world of quiver-bearing Semiramis") (line 108). The tradition of the symbolic Semiramis was evidently well established in classical times, as Samuel's bibliography of studies would indicate.

Chaucer undoubtedly used the accompanying line, *Inf.* 5.58, at another section of *The Canterbury Tales* in reference to Nero, but there would appear to be no clear indication that at any of the three points at which he mentions Semiramis he made use of Dante's dramatic description. In *The Parliament of Fowls*, line 279 (cf. Samuel, p. 42), he is following Boccaccio; in the Legend of Thisbe he is following Ovid, and here he would seem to be using Semiramis's name as a commonly accepted symbol of the virago.

Bethel: "*448: influence of Dante's attitude toward Fortune, *Inf.* VII, 67ff."

He that is lord of Fortune be thy steere!   [See citation and discussion under *Fortune*; see also *TC* 3.617–20, 5.1541–45.]

There would seem to be no relevance here whatsoever. God and Fortune are always in relationship to each other according to Christian doctrine.

Bethel: "479–83: the unfathomable nature of God's plan; cf. *Conv.* IV, v, 1 f., 9."

Crist, which that is to every harm
   triacle,
By certeine meenes ofte, as knowen
   clerkis,
Dooth thyng for certein ende that ful
   derk is
To mannes wit, that for oure ignorance
Ne konne noght knowe his prudent
   purveiance.

[See citation at the end of the discussion of *Fortune*: cf. also *TC* 3.617–20, 5.1541–45; and *KnT* A 1251–54.]

There are no verbal parallels, and the thought involved in these verses was a generally held theological view of the times. The same thought is found, for example, in Boethius *De cons.* 4, pr. 6, and expressed in Saint Thomas *Contra gentiles*, 3.75, 91, 94:

> The fact that we are not able to think out, ahead of time, the order of all particular events in regard to matters to be arranged by us stems from the deficiency of our knowledge, which cannot embrace all singular things.... Moreover, divine providence must consist in the highest perfection, since He is absolutely and universally perfect.... So, in the function of providential foresight, by means of the sempiternal meditative act of His wisdom, He orders all things, no matter how detailed they may appear. [Aquinas 1956:3.2, 53–54]

or Saint Augustine, in *De civitate Dei* 5.21:

> We have already said something on this matter, so far as he has willed to make it plain to us. But to examine the secrets of men's hearts and to decide with clear judgement on the varying merits of human kingdoms – this would be a heavy task for us men, a task indeed far beyond our powers. [Augustine 1972:215]

Of course, finally, the theme of God's unfathomable plan is a constant motif of the Old Testament.

In view of the frequency with which this theme was expounded, any attempt at ascription must be founded on the most concise and concrete parallels.

Bethel: "641f.: reference to St. Anne possibly due to *Par.* XXXII, 133–35."

Marie I meene, doghter to Seint Anne,	Di contr' a Pietro vedi sedere Anna,
Bifore whos child angeles synge Osanne	tanto contenta di mirar sua figlia,
	che non move occhio per cantare osanna.

> Opposite Peter you see Anna sitting, so content to gaze upon her daughter
> that she moves not her eyes as she sings Hosannah. [*Par.*, p. 367]

The main basis for comparison, as Robinson points out (p. 695), is the rhyme, which is "reminiscent" of the lines in the *Paradiso*. Chaucer's verses refer, of course, to the Hosannas sung to Christ; Dante's to those sung to Mary. There is no contextual parallel. Undoubtedly the possibility of a parallel exists, but one wonders whether Chaucer, who took a certain amount of pride in "rymyng craftily," would need to borrow in this case not for context or fact but merely for rhyme words.

The same situation exists in the case of the *Prologue* to *The Second Nun's Tale* (G 69–70):

> Theras withouten ende is songe "Osanne,"
> Thow Cristes mooder, doghter deere of Anne!

But one couplet seems so definitely to be taken from the other that the problem can be handled as a single unit. If Chaucer were following the lines from the *Commedia*, it seems odd that he would not have followed Dante in having the Hosannas sung to Mary, since in both instances cited above from *The Canterbury Tales* we have prayers to the Virgin in glory. In other words, we would have to assume that Chaucer intentionally changed the appropriateness of Dante's lines rather than maintain their original application to the Virgin. There is no denying that the coincidence of rhyme is striking.

Bethel: "660: close adaptation of *Inf.* V, 100."

As gentil herte is fulfild of pitee	Amor, ch'al cor gentil ratto s'apprende

This "adaptation" presupposes the absolute equivalence and interchangeability of "love" and "pity" (see discussion above, *TC* 1.894–96). Not only is this somewhat questionable, but it cannot be claimed here on the grounds of courtly love (on which it had previously been offered), since the pity that is being spoken of here is rather what a later age would have termed "sensibility." The context shows how far we are from Dante's line:

> This Alla kyng hath swich compassioun,
> As gentil herte is fulfild of pitee,
> That from his eyen ran the water doun.

Bethel: "778–84: the belief that souls of traitors often go to Hell, while their bodies remain alive and are put in charge of a Devil; from *Inf.* XXXIII, 121–32."

O Donegild, I ne have noon Englissh digne	"Oh," diss' io lui, "Or se' tu ancor morto?"
Unto thy malice and thy tirannye!	Ed elli a me: "Come 'l mio corpo stea
And therfore to the feend I thee resigne;	nel mondo sù, nulla scïenza porto.
Lat hym enditen of thy traitorie!	Cotal vantaggio ha questa Tolomea,
Fy, mannysh, fy!—o nay, by God, I lye—	che spesse volte l'anima ci cade
	innanzi ch'Atropòs mossa le dea.
	E perché tu più volontier mi rade

Fy, feendlych spirit, for I dar wel telle,
Thogh thou heere walke, thy spirit is in
    helle!

le 'nvetrïate lagrime dal volto,
  sappie che, tosto che l'anima trade
come fec' ïo, il corpo suo l' è tolto
  da un demonio, che poscia il governa
mentre che 'l tempo suo tutto sia
    vòlto. . . ."

"Oh," I said to him, "are you then dead already?"

And he said to me, "How my body may fare in the world above I have no knowledge. Such vantage has this Ptolomea that oftentimes the soul falls down here before Atropos sends it forth; and that you may more willingly scrape the glazen tears from my face, know that as soon as the soul betrays as I did, its body is taken from it by a devil who thereafter rules it until its time has all revolved. . . ." [*Inf.*, p. 357]

Tatlock (1914*b*:97) first suggested the connection of these two passages. The idea, however, seems to have been a fairly familiar one. As Robinson notes (p. 695):

. . .a similar conception underlies LGW, 2066 ff. Cf. John of Salisbury, Policraticus, iii, 8. . .[cf. Tatlock 1914*a*:92]; A. Graf, Miti, Leggende e Superstizioni del Medio Evo. . .II, 99f; Lives of Saints from the Book of Lismore. . .p. 161; Caesarius Heisterbacensis, Dialogus Miraculorum, cii, 4. . .II, 317 f.; also the vision of the monk of Wenlock, related in a letter of Boniface, in Jaffe, Monumenta Moguntina. . .59 f. Biblical authority was found in John, ciii, 27, and Ps. 54, 15.

A fairly good case, therefore, can be made for a common tradition—if not the tradition of hell, at least the tradition of demonology—which was operating on both poets.[11] There is neither verbal nor contextual parallel here that would definitely indicate Dante as the source for the Chaucerian passage. This does not deny Dante as a possible source, but definite evidence must be presented before we can think of him as the sole source. We can in any event consider Chaucer's lines as closely analogous to the passage from the *Inferno*. The suggested parallelism should be limited, however, to line 784, or, at most, to lines 783–84, with the former line added on the basis of the word "feendlych."

The Wife of Bath's Tale

Bethel: "868: 'As thikke as motes in the sonne-beem'; possibly suggested by *Par.* XIV, 112ff. (see Cary's note)—doubtful."

Così si veggion qui diritte e torte,
  veloci e tarde, rinovando vista,
le minuzie d'i corpi, lunghe e corte,
moversi per lo raggio onde si lista
  talvolta l'ombra che, per sua difesa,
  la gente con ingegno e arte acquista.

---

[11] There is extensive discussion in the *Speculum maius*. See the fine dissertation of Pauline Aiken, "The Influence of Vincent of Beauvais" (Yale University, 1935).

. . . so we see here, straight and athwart, swift and slow, changing appearance, the motes of bodies, long and short, moving through the ray that sometimes streaks the shade which men with skill and art contrive for their defense. [*Par.*, p. 161]

The image of the mote in the beam is familiar enough. With reference to Dante's use of the image, Grandgent (Dante 1933) states (p. 787): "The moving lights in the cross are compared to bits of dust dancing in a ray of sunshine in a dark room. Cf. Lucretius II, 115–121. Cf. also Lactantius, also Seneca, *Quaestiones Naturales*, V, a close parallel; also Albertus Magnus, XXXVI, p. 681 (here allegorized)." More important, however, is the fact that Whiting (1934:168) lists the phrase as proverbial. In addition, it should be recognized that the Wife of Bath is using the phrase to emphasize the number of "lymytours and other holy freres" that there are, while Dante is using it for the visual description it gives of the souls that flash through and compose the cross in the sphere of Mars.

Bethel: "1109–1164: This whole discussion of *gentillesse* is thoroughly Dantesque. Besides mentioning Dante twice by name and adapting three lines from the *Purgatorio*, Chaucer shows his thorough acquaintance with the ideas of the fourth tractate of the *Convivio*. As far as it seems possible to do so I have given specific references to parts of Dante's work which Chaucer has taken over."

In his text Bethel is far more judicious than the statement here would imply. There can be no doubt that the passage is very strongly influenced by Dante and in particular by tractate 4 of the *Convivio*, but, as Bethel shows, there are certain elements that are accounted for by Boethius; certain other possibilities will be offered in the course of the discussion. It is probably best to take the passage part by part, as offered by Bethel, to see how this fusion of sources is obtained and how much of the phrasing of these fifty-five lines is based directly on Dante.[12]

Bethel: "1109–12: *Conv.* IV, canz. iii, 21–37; *Purg. XI, 61f."

But, for ye speken of swich gentillesse	Tale imperò che gentilezza volse,
As is descended out of old richesse,	secondo 'l suo parere,
That therfore sholden ye be gentil men,	che fosse antica possession d'avere
Swich arrogance is nat worth an hen.	con reggimenti belli;
	e altri fu di più lieve savere,
	che tal detto rivolse,
	e l' ultima particula ne tolse,
	chè non l' avea fors' elli!
	Di retro da costui van tutti quelli
	che fan gentile per ischiatta altrui
	che lungiamente in gran ricchezza è stata;
	ed è tanto durata
	la così falsa oppinion tra nui,
	che l' uom chiama colui

[12] I mark "Schless" those entries dealing with lines which Bethel has *not* treated but which I believe should be discussed to gain a complete picture of this passage. A discussion of the passages as a whole follows the entry for lines 1163–64. For other suggestions on Chaucer's use of the topic, see Baker 1962:631–40.

omo gentil che può dicere; 'Io fui
nepote, o figlio, di cotal valente',
benchè sia da niente.

[*Convivio* 4.3.21–37]

L'antico sangue e l'opere leggiadre
d'i miei maggior mi fer sì arrogante,
[che, non pensando a la comune madre,
ogn' uomo ebbi in despetto tanto avante,
ch'io ne mori', come i Sanesi sanno,
e sallo in Campagnatico ogne fante.]

[*Purg.* 11.61–66]

There was an Emperor who deemed that nobility, according to his thinking, consisted in possession of ancestral wealth coupled with manners fine. And some one else there was of slighter wisdom who pondered again this saying, and took the last part away, perhaps because he had it not. In his wake follow all those who deem a man gentle by reason of his stock, which long hath been possessed of great riches: and so ingrained hath become this false opinion among us that a man calleth him noble who can say "I was grandson or son of such a man of worth", though he himself be good for naught. [P. 190]

The ancient blood and the gallant deeds of my ancestors made me so arrogant [that, not thinking of our common mother, I held all men in such exceeding scorn that it was the death of me, as the Sienese know and every child in Campagnatico knows.] [*Purg.*, p. 113]

We can dismiss from the start the possibility that the two lines from the *Purgatorio* have any influence on the Chaucerian passage. At best there is only a weak analogy, since Dante is describing an inhabitant of the level of Pride on the mount of Purgatory and not in any way discussing the aspects of *gentilezza*, *antica possession d'avere*, or any other of the matters dealt with by the loathly lady. There is only the verbal coincidence of the words "arrogance" and *arrogante*.

So far as the citation from the canzone is concerned, although it is in line with Lowes's suggestion (1915:21) it would seem to apply far better to lines 1146–47. Chaucer does not follow the context of the canzone here but rather is closer to the explication of the lines in, for instance, 4.3.6–7, which, like Chaucer, is far more precise, using directly the phrase *antica ricchezza* rather than the *antica possession d' avere* that is found in the poem itself.[13] Chaucer, it should be noted, does not discuss the *reggimenti belli* here but concentrates on that portion which Dante stresses not only in cap. 3 but also, in all its varying aspects, in cap. 10[14] – to the exclusion of the *reggimenti belli*. It seems far more likely, therefore, that Chaucer was basing himself at this point not so much on the poem as on the explication of the one phrase in it that forms a definite philosophical basis for Dante's "negative treatment" (Lowes 1915:24) of *gentilezza*.

Bethel: "1110, 1118: the phrase old richesse: *Conv.* IV, iii, 6f.; x, 2, 5."

As is descended out of old richesse

[Frederic of Suabia says that *gentilezza* is] antica ricchezza e belli costumi. E dico che

---

[13] For the text of the relevant explications, see the following entry.
[14] See the citation from *Convivio* 4.10.1–2 in the following entry.

Nat of oure eldres for hire old richesse

altri fu di più lieve savere: che, pensando e rivolgendo questa diffinizione in ogni parte, levò via l'ultima particula, cioè li belli costumi, e tennesi a la prima, cioè a l'antica ricchezza; e, secondo che lo testo pare dubitare, forse per non avere li belli costumi non volendo perdere lo nome di gentilezza, diffinio quella secondo che per lui facea, cioè possessione d'antica ricchezza. [4.3.6–7]

[E però è da sapere che l'oppinione de lo Imperadore – avvegna che *con difetto* quella ponga – ne l'una particula, cioè là dove disse *belli costumi*, toccò de li costumi di nobilitade, e però in quella parte riprovare non s'intende.] L'altra particula, che di natura di nobilitade è del tutto diversa, s'intende riprovare; la quale due cose pare dicere quando dice *antica ricchezza*, cioè tempo e divizie, le quali a nobilitade sono del tutto diverse, come detto è e come di sotto si mostrerà. . . . [4.10.1–2]

. . .Poi dico similemente lui errare, che puose de la nobilitade falso subietto, cioè 'antica ricchezza'. . . . [4.10.5]

. . ."ancestral wealth and fine manners." And I say that "there was some one else of slighter wisdom" who, pondering and thinking over this definition in all its aspects, struck out the last portion, namely, "fine manners" and retained the first namely, "ancestral wealth." And as the text seems to suggest, "because perhaps he had not fine manners" he did not wish to forfeit his title to nobility, and defined it by the condition which suited himself, viz. "possession of ancestral wealth." [P. 201]

[Nevertheless, we must know that the opinion of the Emperor (although his statement of it is defective) did in one particular, I mean where he speaks of "fine manners," apply to the manners that belong to nobility. This portion of his opinion, therefore, I do not intend to refute.] The other particular which is altogether foreign to the nature of nobility, I propose to refute. This, when it speaks of ancestral wealth, appears to imply two things, viz. time and wealth, which are altogether foreign of nobility, as has been said, and as will be demonstrated below. [P. 226]

. . .Afterwards I say that he "likewise went astray" because he wrongly assumed "ancestral wealth" as the subject matter of nobility. . . . [P. 227]

Any one or all of these could serve as the source for Chaucer's phrase and for his ideas that are based upon it. There are other works in which such a phrase is used,[15] but all seem unlikely as sources for Chaucer.

---

[15] See the notes of Busnelli and Vandelli to these passages in the *Convivio* (Dante 1934).

Schless: Lines 1113–16:

Looke who that is moost vertuous
      alway,
Pryvee and apert, and moost entendeth
      ay
To do the gentil dedes that he kan;
Taak hym for the grettest gentil man.

While lines 1109–12 are rather obviously based on Dante's idea, they have no direct verbal parallel. Lines 1113–16 are even more indefinite so far as direct source is concerned. They could be based, in fact, on any one of the discussions of "gentilesse."

Schless: Lines 1117–24: For lines 1118–24, Robinson cites *RR* 18620–34 but does not include what seems to be the more obvious citation in Boethius, *De cons.* 3, pr. 6, m. 6, which is based on the religious aspect found also in line 1117. Boethius's passages are cited *in extenso* not only to establish this point but also to show what the conventional, Boethian interpretation of "gentilesse" was as far as Chaucer was concerned.

Crist wole we clayme of hym our
      gentillesse,
Nat of oure eldres for hire old richesse.
For thogh they yeve us al hir heritage,
For which we clayme to been of heigh
      parage,
Yet may they nat biquethe, for no
      thyng,
To noon of us hir vertuous lyvyng,
That made hem gentil men ycalled be,
And bad us folwen hem in swich
      degree.

But now, of this name of gentilesse, what man is it that ne may wele seen how veyn and how flyttynge a thyng it es? For yif the name of gentilesse be referred to renoun and cleernesse of lynage, thanne is gentil name but a foreyn thyng (*that is to seyn, to hem that gloryfien hem of hir lynage.*) For it semeth that gentilesse be a maner preisynge that cometh of the dessertes of auncestres; and yif preisynge make gentilesse, thanne mote they nedes ben gentil that been preysed. For which thing it folweth that yif thou ne have no gentilesse of thiself (*that is to seyn, prys that cometh of thy desert*), foreyn gentilesse ne maketh the nat gentil. But certes yif ther be ony good in gentilesse, I trowe it be al only this, that it semeth as that a maner necessite be imposed to gentil men for that thei ne schulde nat owtrayen or forlyven fro the vertus of hir noble kynrede.

Alle the lynage of men that ben in erthe ben of semblable byrthe. On allone is fadir of thynges; On allone mynystreth alle thynges.... He encloseth with membres the soules that comen from his heye sete. Thanne comen alle mortel folk of noble seed. Why noysen ye or bosten of your eldres? For yif thow loke youre bygynnyng, and God your auctour and yowr makere, thanne nis ther non forlyved wyght or ongentil, but if he noryssche his corage unto vices and forlete his propre byrthe.

Bethel: "1125–27: Dante named twice."

Wel kan the wise poete of Florence,
That highte Dant, speken in this
        sentence.
Lo, in swich maner rym is Dantes tale

These lines obviously have no source.

Bethel: "1128–30: close adaptation of *Purg.* VII, 121–23."

"Ful selde up riseth by his branches smale	rade volte risurge per li rami l'umana probitate; e questo vole
Prowesse of man, for God, of his goodnesse,	quei che la dà, perché da lui si chiami.
Wole that of hym we clayme oure gentilesse"	

Rarely does human worth rise through the branches, and this He wills who gives it ["better heritage" in previous tercet], in order that it may be asked from Him. [*Purg.*, p. 75]

Chaucer gives Dante as his source, and there is no doubt about the lines here. Note that Chaucer has welded on the idea of "gentilesse," which is not Dante's argument in the *Purgatorio* passage but which may very well come from Boethius. See further discussion under lines 1159–62 below.

Bethel: "1131f.: epitomizes thought of *Conv.* IV, xi–xiii, *passim*."

For of oure eldres may we no thyng
        clayme
But temporel thyng, that man may
        hurte and mayme

The idea is found in Dante's discussion of the temporal aspect of *antica* in the phrase *antica ricchezza*.

Bethel: "1133–38: *Conv.* IV, xiv, 3 f; xv, 3f.; *Pa.* VIII, 133–35."

Eek every wight woot this as wel as I,	Se nobilitade non si genera di nuovo, sì come
If gentillesse were planted natureelly	più volte è detto che la loro oppinione vuole
Unto a certeyn lynage doun the lyne,	(non generandosi di vile uomo in lui
Pryvee and apert, thanne wolde they nevere fyne	medesimo, nè di vile padre in figlio) sempre è l'uomo tale quale nasce, e tale nasce quale è
To doon of gentillesse the faire office;	lo padre; e così questo processo d'una
They myghte do no vileynye or vice	condizione è venuto infino dal primo parente: per che tale quale fu lo primo generante, cioè Adamo, conviene essere tutta l'umana generazione, chè da lui a li moderni non si puote trovare per quella ragione alcuna transmutanza. Dunque, se esso

Adamo fu nobile, tutti siamo nobili, e se esso
fu vile, tutti siamo vili; che non è altro che
torre via la distinzione di queste condizioni, e
così è torre via quelle. [*Convivio* 4.15.3–4]

Natura generata il suo cammino
   simil farebbe sempre a' generanti,
      se non vincesse il proveder divino. [*Par.*
8.133–35]

If nobility cannot be generated for the first time, as we have often affirmed
their opinion to imply, since they do not allow nobility to be generated by a
base man in himself, or by a base father in his son, then a man always remains
such as he is born. And he is born such as his father was, and so this
continuance of a single condition has come down all the way from our first
parent, because all the race of men must needs be such as was our first
progenitor, namely Adam, for this reasoning does not enable us to discover
any change of condition from the time of Adam to the men of the present day.
Therefore, if Adam was noble, we are all noble; and if Adam was base, we are
all base; and this is as good as to abolish the distinction between these conditions themselves. [P. 246]

The begotten nature would always make its course like its begetters, did not
Divine provision overrule. [*Par.*, p. 91]

The suggestion from the *Paradiso* epitomizes the idea in the passages from tractate 4 and in
this sense is a parallel, but the argument that Dante presents in the *Convivio* is almost
certainly the source for Chaucer's thought in these lines. This thought is also expressed in
Boethius's metrum 6 of book 3, but the line of argument that Chaucer has adapted from
Dante is not given there.

Schless: Lines 1139–45:

Taak fyr, and ber it in the derkeste hous
Bitwix this and the mount of
      Kaukasous,
And lat men shette the dores and go
      thenne;
Yet wole the fyr as faire lye and brenne
As twenty thousand men myghte it
      biholde;
His office natureel ay wol it holde,
Up peril of my lyf, til that it dye.

This is not from Dante. As Robinson notes (p. 704), "This comparison with fire is made, in
general terms, in Boethius, iii, pr. 4." The comparison is so general, however, as to be
almost worthless. Chaucer, in line 1145, mentions "the mount of Kaukasous," which is
mentioned also in Boethius *De cons.* 2, pr. 9, but the parallel here is again slight and
certainly not contextual. Robinson, continuing with the sources of the fire image, states
(p. 704): "It also occurs in Macrobius (Comm. in Somn. Scip., II xvi, 6) and in Servius
(Comm. in Vergilii Carmina, . . . II, 101, ll. 15–21) and certain detailed correspondences
make it appear probable that Chaucer used Servius, or perhaps his source. (See Lowes,
MP, XV, 199.)"

Schless: Lines 1146–47: Very possibly influenced by canz. 3.21–23. In any event, the idea is that presented by Dante throughout his discussion.

Heere may ye se wel how that genterye   [See under lines 1109–12, above.]
Is nat annexed to possessioun

Schless: Lines 1148–49: Not from Dante. A continuation of the fire image. See lines 1139–45 above.

Sith folk ne doon hir operacioun
Alwey, as dooth the fyr, lo, in his
          kynde.

Schless: Lines 1150–51: These lines are not based on Dante, but they are, nevertheless,
     closely allied to the subsequent idea (for discussion of which see next entry).

For God it woot, men may wel often
          fynde
A lordes sone do shame and vileynye

Bethel: "1152–58: *Conv.* IV, vii, 9; canz. iii, 34–37."

And he that wole han pris of his
          gentrye,
For he was boren of a gentil hous,
And hadde his eldres noble and
          vertuous,
And nel hymselven do no gentil dedis,
Ne folwen his gentil auncestre that deed
          is,
He nys nat gentil, be he duc or erl;
For vileyns synful dedes make a cherl.

E così quelli che dal padre o d'alcuno suo
maggiore [buono è disceso ed è malvagio],
non solamente è vile, ma vilissimo, e degno
d'ogni dispetto e vituperio più che altro
villano. E perchè l'uomo da questa infima
viltade si guardi, comanda Salomone a colui
che 'l valente antecessore hae avuto, nel
vigesimo secondo capitolo de li Proverbi:
"Non trapasserai li termini antichi che
puosero li padri tuoi"; e dinanzi dice, nel
quarto capitolo del detto libro: "La via de'
giusti", cioè de' valenti, "quasi luce
splendiente procede, e quella de li malvagi è
oscura. Elli non sanno dove rovinano."

[For canz. 3.34–37 see under lines 1109–12
above.]

And so he who is of noble stock through his father or any of his ancestors, if he does not persevere in nobleness is not only vile but vilest, and deserves more contempt and reproach than any churl. And in order that a man may keep himself from this lowest depth of vileness, Solomon in the twenty-second chapter of *Proverbs* enjoins on him who has had a man of worth for his ancestor, "Thou shalt not transgress the ancient bounds which thy fathers have set," and he says before in the fourth chapter of the said book, "The way of the just," that is, of the man of worth, "goeth forth as a shining light, and the way of the wicked is dark, and they know not to what ruin they go." [P. 216]

Although the *Convivio* contains in part the idea found in Chaucer, the same thought is to be found in Boethius as well. Most interesting, however, is the way in which Chaucer weaves in certain ideas from *The Romaunt of the Rose,* lines 2181–2202, particularly 2181–82, 2189–90, and 2200–2202:

> For vilanye makith vilayn,
> And by his dedis a cherl is seyn.
> Thise vilayns arn withouten pitee,
> Frendshipe, love, and all bounte.
> I nyl resseyve unto my servise
> Hem that ben vilayns of emprise.
> But undirstonde in thyn entent
> That this is not myn entendement,
> To clepe no wight in noo ages
> Oonly gentill for his lynages.
> But whoso is vertuous,
> And in his port nought outrageous,
> Whanne sich oon thou seest thee biforn,
> Though he be not gentill born,
> Thou maist well seyn, this is in soth,
> That he is gentil by cause he doth
> As longeth to a gentilman;
> Of hem noon other deme I can.
> For certeynly, withouten drede,
> A cherl is demed by his dede,
> Of hie or lowe, as we may see,
> Or of what kynrede that he bee.

There would seem to be in *WBT* 1152–58 an almost total fusion of Dante, Boethius (see the citation in the following entry), and the lines in the passage from *The Romaunt of the Rose* that have already been pointed out.

Schless: Lines 1159–62: These lines seem definitely from Boethius, though the thought can be found to a certain extent in Dante (Canz. iii, 112–20).

For gentillesse nys but renomee Of thyne auncestres, for hire heigh bountee, Which is a strange thyng to thy persone. Thy gentillesse cometh fro God allone.[16]	For yif the name of gentilesse be referred to renoun and cleernesse of lynage, thanne is gentil name but a foreyn thyng.... For it semeth that gentilesse be a maner preisynge that cometh of the dessertes of auncestres;...foreyn gentilesse ne maketh the nat gentil. [3, pr. 6]

Dempster (1942:173–76) confirms the ascription to the *De Consolatione* showing that lines 1159–62 make sense only if we recognize that Boethius's *tu,* translated by Chaucer's "thou," has its usual force of indefinite *you,* i.e., "anyone," and is so employed here by the loathly lady who elsewhere does not employ the second-person singular. If the pronoun were being used in any sense other than "anyone," it would be considered fairly insulting.

---

[16] Cf. Kenyon 1939:133–37. Kenyon's argument is summarized as follows: The Wife's statement "For gentilesse nys but renomee of thyn ancestres" runs contrary to the main argument of the passage and is directly contradicted by her following words: "Thy gentilesse cometh fro God alone." If "For gentilesse" and "Thy gentilesse" are transposed, it becomes clear and consistent. Lines 1159–60 then refer to the Knight's false "gentilesse" and maintain that true "gentilesse" is not this kind but comes from God alone.

Line 1162 reflects, of course, on the source of lines 1129–30. Now line 1162 can have three possible sources: (1) it can naturally evolve from the Boethian lines (1159–61) that precede it; see under lines 1117–24 above; (2) it can be a repetition of the idea found in lines 1129–30, or (3) it can come from canzone 3.116: "chè solo Iddio a l'anima la [tal grazia] dona." I tend to think that it serves as a summary of the preceding lines rather than as an introductory remark on the lines to come because, first, the indefinite second-person singular found in the former lines is found here and, second, the line from Dante is referring not to *gentilezza* but to *grazia*. On the other hand, reading line 1162 as an introductory remark connects it to lines 1163–64, which are more definitely in line with Dante's concept of *gentilezza*. Bethel groups lines 1159–64 together and thus chooses the completely Dantesque interpretation, for which there are certainly ample grounds. The interlocking of ideas here is that complex that the choice of one reading or the other depends almost wholly on the viewpoint of the individual scholar.

Bethel: "1163f.; 1173–76: *gentillesse* a gift of *grace*: *Conv.* IV, xx 6f."

Thanne comth oure verray gentillesse of
grace;
It was no thyng biquethe us with oure
place.

Poi, quando dice: *Chè solo Iddio a l' anima la dona*, ragione è del suscettivo, cioè del subietto dove questo divino dono discende: ch' è bene divino dono, secondo la parola de l' Apostolo: "Ogni ottimo dato e ogni dono perfetto di suso viene, discendendo dal Padre de'lumi". Dice adunque che Dio solo porge questa grazia a l' anima di quelli cui vede stare perfettamente ne la sua persona, acconcio e disposto a questo divino atto ricevere. Chè, secondo dice lo Filosofo nel secondo de l'Anima, "le cose convengono essere disposte a li loro agenti, e a ricevere li loro atti"; onde se l'anima è imperfettamente posta, non è disposta a ricevere questa benedetta e divina infusione: sì come se una pietra margarita è male disposta, o vero imperfetta, la vertù celestiale ricever non può, sì come disse quel nobile Guido Guinizelli in una sua canzone: *Al cor gentil ripara sempre Amore*.

Afterwards, when the text says "for God alone endoweth that soul with it," reference is made to that which is receptive, namely the subject on whom this divine gift descends, for it is truly a divine gift, according to the words of the Apostle, "Every good gift and every perfect gift cometh down from above, from the Father of lights." It affirms, therefore, that God alone extends this grace to the soul of that man whom He sees standing perfectly adapted and prepared in his own person for the reception of this divine act. For as the Philosopher says in the second book *On the Soul*, "Things must be adapted for the agents if they are to be receptive of their acts." Therefore, if the attitude of the soul is defective, it is not adapted to receive this blessed and divine infusion; just as a pearl if it be ill adapted, or defective, cannot receive the heavenly virtue, as that noble Guido Guinicelli remarks in a Canzone of his which begins, "to the gentle heart Love ever repaireth." [Pp. 261–62]

The idea of true nobility being a gift of grace (line 1163) is found, or at least strongly implied, in Boethius and, as Dante remarks, in Guinizelli, among other places. But the source seems certainly the one that Lowes has pointed out. The idea that "gentilesse" could not be inherited (line 1164) is, of course, a common one that Dante, among others, has discussed, though not so much here as in the explications of the *antica ricchezza* phrase.

In conclusion it should be pointed out that, while this long passage is based to a very great degree on the discussion in the first two-thirds of tractate 4 of the *Convivio*, it cannot be taken as an "untrammeled adaptation."[17] Many sources and many ideas are at work in this discussion of "gentilesse." Undoubtedly the most important in this particular case is Dante, but "gentilesse," as Robinson remarks (p. 704), "was a commonplace of Christian literature and in no sense an evidence of radical or advanced opinion on the part of Chaucer." "Gentilesse," it seems, was as fluid a term as, let us say, "democracy" is today, and it is a grave error to assume that every time Chaucer speaks of "gentilesse" he has the same aspect of it in mind or even that he has a rigid concept of the doctrine based on one particular source. "Gentilesse" can vary from a formalistic and hypocritical courtliness to a religious doctrine of the most eclectic sort. Nor is it a question of *entweder/oder*, black or white; "gentilesse" can often designate any one of the aspects that lies between these extremes and often assumes, albeit illogically, more than one at the same time. Whether found as a "complaint" in the tradition of courtly love or as an invocation in the tradition of Mariolatry, the one certainty is that it is too widely diffused an idea to be tied down to any one source by anything other than the strictest verbal or contextual similarities.

The position that Dante assumes on the worldly aspects of *gentilezza* is not in any way radically original, though he did make some definite contributions to the tradition. The "esoteric and highly sophisticated as well as erotic" rules of courtly love had been codified by Andreas Capellanus in the *De amore* about 1170. As seen by Andreas, courtly love "included only feudal aristocracy, and emphasized [the concept's] most undemocratic aspects.... Its most essential incongruity in this respect was the attempt of its cult to incorporate the doctrine of true gentility into its rationale" (Coffman 1945:44). Andreas, speaking to an aristocratic audience, outlines the following as

> the basis for the tradition of gentilesse in courtly love.... "Since all of us human beings are derived from the same stock and all naturally claim the same ancestor..., excellence of character alone... first made a distinction of nobility among men and led to the difference of class. Many... who trace their descent from these same first nobles... have degenerated.... The converse of the proposition is likewise true." (*Id.*, 9).... In the debate between a man of middle class and a woman of nobility, he says: "But if I have cultivated a character excellent through and through, I think that puts me inside the walls of nobility and gives me a true virtue of rank, and so my character puts me among the nobles." (*Id.*, 25). His final argument in their extended exchange is: "I cannot see any reason why if a man of middle class excels a nobleman in the excellence of his character, he might not receive a greater reward, since we are both descended from a common ancester [*sic*], Adam." [Coffman, p. 48][18]

[17] Of the 55 lines of this passage, only 19 are clearly ascribable to Dante, and in this count I am following Bethel rather closely. The lines would be 1109–12 (though not to the source that he gives), the phrase in line 1118, and lines 1128–30, 1131–38, 1146–47 (which Bethel does not give), and 1163–64.

[18] Coffman is citing the *Andreae Capellani regii francorum de amore*, bk. 3, ed. Amadeo Pages (Castellon de la Plana, 1929), the translation of which has been done by J. J. Parry as *The Art of Courtly Love*, no. 33 in Records of Civilization (New York: Columbia University Press, 1941).

It will be noticed at once that all of Dante's, and Chaucer's arguments — even to the citation of Adam — are found here.

Dante's principal contribution was the change of emphasis from nobility to nobleness; that is to say, his resolution of the "essential incongruity" (see Coffman's remark above) was simply to drop one of the two opposing elements, namely, the appeal to the aristocracy. That Chaucer follows the same resolution of this problem, never mentioning the aristocratic sine qua non of Andreas, is perhaps the most distinguishing feature of his debt to Dante on the subject of "gentilesse." Yet there can be little doubt that Chaucer was well aware of Andreas's arguments, as can be seen in the ballade *Gentilesse*. In the two instances where he might have used this basis of aristocracy — that is, in the case of the Knight and the case of the Squire — Chaucer avoids the issue by having the Knight "gentil" by virtue of his character and by making the Squire a courtly lover and therefore "gentil" only in the more outmoded sense of the word. This last is the sense which the kindly but rural Franklin would understand, and this is the sense which the more urbane Harry Bailey exclaims against with "Straw for youre gentillesse" (*SqT* F 695).

Bethel: "1192–94: the quotation from Juvenal may have been derived through *Conv.* IV, xiii, 11–12 (see Lowes, *Mod. Phil.*, XIII, 26) or through Boethius, *Cons. Phil.*, II, p. v, 96–98 (see Jefferson, *Ch. and the Cons. Phil.*, 146) whence Dante probably got his informatioin (see Moore, *Studies*, 1 S., 257, 356; 2 S. 378). Neither place, however, is in itself sufficient to account for all of Chaucer's references."

[Verray poverte, it syngeth proprely;]
Juvenal seith of poverte myrily:
'The povre man, whan he goth by the
   weye,
Bifore the theves he may synge and
   pleye.'

Thow thanne, that so bysy dredest now the swerd and the spere, yif thou haddest entred in the path of this lif a voyde weyfarynge man, thanne woldestow syngen byfor the theef. (*As who seith, a pore man that bereth no rychesse on hym by the weie may boldely synge byforn theves, for he hath nat whereof to be robbed.*) [Boethius, *De cons.* 2, p. 5, and Chaucer's gloss thereto]

Ben lo sanno li miseri mercatanti che per lo mondo vanno, che le foglie che 'l vento fa menare, li fa tremare, quando seco ricchezze portano; e quando sanza esse sono, pieni di sicurtade, cantando e sollazzando fanno loro cammino più brieve. E però dice lo Savio: "Se voto camminatore entrasse ne lo cammino, dinanzi a li ladroni canterebbe." [*Convivio* 4.13.11–12]

The wretched merchants who go about the world know this full well. The leaves which quiver in the wind make them tremble when they carry riches with them; and when they are without them they are filled with the sense of security, and shorten their journey with song and discourse. And therefore the wise man says that "if the traveller entered on his journey empty-handed, he would sing in the presence of the robber." [P. 240]

The passage from Boethius, with its gloss, seems closer to Chaucer than does the *Convivio*. First, so far as context is concerned, both the *De consolatione* and the Wife of Bath are talking about a poor man, while the *Convivio* is speaking of a rich merchant who happens not to have his goods with him. Likewise, the phrasing is far closer in the *De consolatione*, as Chaucer translates and glosses it. Note, for example: (1) "The povre man, whan he goth by the way" (line 1193) compared with "A pore man that bereth no rychesse by the weie," and "yif thou haddest entred in the path of this lif a voyde weyfaringe man," where the *Convivio* has *li miseri mercatanti* and *Se voto camminatore entrasse ne lo cammino*; (2) the fact that Boethius's remark is in the conditional, the mood which Dante follows, as does Chaucer (though not in his gloss); thus *The Wife of Bath's Tale* has "Bifore the theves he may synge," and, though Chaucer's gloss has "may boldely synge byforn theves," his text carefully follows Boethius's mood ("thanne woldestow syngen byfor the theef"), as does Dante, with *dinanzi a li ladroni canterebbe*.[19] Both syntactically and verbally the lines from *The Wife of Bath's Tale* seem somewhat closer to Chaucer's gloss of Boethius than to Dante. Dante, however, uses the phrase *cantando e sollazzando*, where WBT 1194 has "singe and pleye" and the Boethius passage uses only "syngen." As well, the loathly lady has already made extensive use of tractate 4. Neither Dante nor Boethius, however, mentions his source, and, in final analysis, Bethel's remark that neither place is in itself sufficient seems by far the best judgment.

The Friar's Tale

Bethel: "1515–20: Dante named and the *Inferno* alluded to."

Thou shalt herafterward, my brother
    deere,
Come there thee nedeth nat of me to
    leere.
For thou shalt, by thyn owene
    experience,
Konne in a chayer rede of this sentence
Bet than Virgile, while he was on lyve,
Or Dant also.

The Summoner's Tale

Bethel: "*1687f.: comparison of Satan's tail to the sail of a boat probably suggested by *Inf.* XXXIV, 46–48."

"And now hath Sathanas," seith he, "a   Sotto ciascuna uscivan due grand' ali,
    tayl   quanto si convenia a tanto uccello:
Brodder than of a carryk is the sayl. . . ."   vele di mar non vid' io mai cotali.

> From under each there came forth two mighty wings, of size befitting such a bird — sails at sea I never saw so broad. [*Inf.*, p. 363]

As Bethel says (p. 197), "The simile is of course a common one, but [he adds] the application to the same personage is perhaps more than mere coincidence." Since Bethel

---

[19] Busnelli and Vandelli point out the importance of the conditional mood when trying to determine whether Dante is following Boethius's quotation or Juvenal directly. Cf. Dante 1934:161n.

asterisks this entry, he evidently missed the previous scholarship on the description. Commenting on an earlier comparison, Spencer (1927:197 n.1) notes that Skeat considered these lines (1687–88) "reminiscent of Dante's description of Satan's *wings*. . . . But this is very doubtful" (Spencer's italics).

The difference between Dante's awesome picture of the gnawing icebound Satan and Chaucer's Rabelaisian view of the unholy resting place of errant "freres" is great indeed, and were the breadth of the wings of Satan (whose huge size was a commonplace) the only basis of comparison, the allusion would be comparatively weak. There is, however, additional evidence that Chaucer might have been thinking of Dante's Satan here. Curry (1923*b*:253) has observed that Virgil and Dante, on leaving the Inferno, climb down, then up, the body of Satan. He continues:

> Dante, also inverted, is surprised to find that Lucifer's legs are now held upward:
>
> > e s'io divenni allora travagliato,
> > la gente grossa il pensi, che non vede
> > qual è quel punto ch'io avea passato.
>
> This turning point is, of course, the center of the universe; but it seems quite likely that Chaucer — in the person of the Somnour — is for the time being one of the "grosser sort" who associates the curious "point," the lowest Hell, with that part of Satan's body which figures in the Somnour's joke.[20]

While Dante's *gente grossa* might very well refer to those people who are too slow to realize that he was inverted because he had passed the earth's center of gravity, the interpretation that Curry has given the passage is certainly natural enough. If we accept his reading and his suggested source, it would seem that Skeat's original comparison is more likely valid. If the passage from the *Inferno* is not the source, it is at least a recognizable analogy.

The Clerk's Tale

Bethel: "*155–61: true nobility; Dantesque influence is here mingled with Petrarchan (cf. *Conv.* IV, 121ff.; *Purg.* VII, 121–23)."

For God it woot, that children ofte been
Unlyk hir worthy eldres hem bifore;
Bountee comth al of God, nat of the streen
Of which they been engendred and ybore.
I truste in Goddes bountee, and therfore
My mariage and myn estaat and reste
I hym bitake; he may doon as hym leste.
	L'anima cui adorna esta bontate
	   non la si tiene ascosa,
	   chè dal principio ch' al corpo si sposa
	   la mostra infin la morte.
	
	[For *Purg.* 7.121–23 see *WBT* D 1128–30.]

> The soul whom this goodness doth adorn keepeth it not to herself close hid. For from the first, when to the body she is espoused, she displayeth it until death. [P. 192]

---

[20] *Inf.* 34.91–93. The Singleton translation reads: ". . . and if I became perplexed then, let the dull crowd judge who do not see what is the point that I had passed" (*Inf.*, p. 367).

Contextually these passages have nothing in common. The last lines in the Chaucerian stanza refer to Walter's tactics of delay, which involve turning over the choice of a prospective bride to God's, rather than his nobles', choice. In Dante the espousal is the common one between body and soul, the marriage image being one used innumerable times in the religious writing of the Middle Ages (cf. the bride of Christ theme, among others). As well, the citation from the *Purgatorio*, with its reference to *umana probitate* being dependent on God, has less relevance here than, perhaps, Chaucer's version of the line in *The Wife of Bath's Tale*, though even there it is "gentilesse" which derives from God. To the degree that this passage can be ascribed to Dante, the ascription should be not to the *Commedia* but to *Convivio* 4, as the discussion under *WBT* 1163f. indicates.

Bethel has a strong tendency to use "gentilesse" as a sort of *aqua regis* which will dissolve within itself any concept whatever. At one point "pitee" and "gentilesse" are completely interchangeable;[21] at another point, an attempt is made to strengthen a proposed Dantesque source of false felicity by looking at its opposite, true felicity, which is arbitrarily equated with true nobility, which in turn is allied to "gentilesse."[22] Likewise, here, lines 155–59 (the limitations which Bethel sets in his text) are speaking of "bountee," not "gentilesse," and it is questionable whether the substitution is allowable. Many things come from God, but that does not make them equivalent. Petrarch's Latin text, which is the source of the tale, gives ample basis for Chaucer's lines, and reads: "saepe filii dissimili sunt parentum. Quicquid in homine boni est, non ab alio, quam a Deo est" ("often sons are dissimilar from their parents. Whatever is good in man comes not from another person but from God").

Bethel (p. 324) goes on to add—whether as proof or as extension of his argument is not certain—lines from *The Merchant's Tale* (E 1917–19) which seem to have no connection whatever with Dante. They run:

> That of his bountee and his gentilesse,
> He wolde so conforten in siknesse
> His squyer, for it was a gentil dede.

If Chaucer believed as deeply in Dante's conception of *gentilezza* as has been suggested, he might hesitate to apply this description (so charged as, and though, it is with irony) to the garrulous, pathetic, and slightly passé January, who is soon to be cuckolded by the very squire toward whom he is being so "gentil."

Bethel: "*813: see under *Troil.* I, 568f."

The Merchant's Tale

Bethel: "1732: a phrase from *Inf.* XXV, 94ff."

Hoold thou thy pees, thou poete Marcian	Taccia Lucano omai là dov' e' tocca del misero Sabello e di Nasidio, e attenda a udir quel ch'or si scocca.

---

[21] See Bethel's many citations of *Inf.* 5.100 and the discussion under *TC* 1.894–96.
[22] See Bethel, pp. 296–99, 302–03. For Bethel, Dante's *gentilezza* is founded on virtue (not "virtu"), but the connection with true felicity is not the same as that which is established with true nobility.

> Taccia di Cadmo e d'Aretusa Ovidio,
>   ché se quello in serpente e quella in fonte
>   converte poetando, io non lo 'nvidio

Let Lucan now be silent, where he tells of the wretched Sabellus and of Nasidius, and let him wait to hear what now comes forth. Concerning Cadmus and Arethusa let Ovid be silent, for if he, poetizing, converts the one into a serpent and the other into a fountain, I envy him not. [*Inf.*, p. 265]

See the discussion at the close of the following entry.

Bethel: "*1732–41: the similarity both of the device of certain phrases indicates Dantesque influence; cf. *Inf.* XXXIV, 22–27; *Par.* XIX, 7–9."

Hoold thou thy pees, thou poete Marcian,	Com' io divenni allor gelato e fioco,
That writest us that ilke weddyng murie	nol dimandar, lettor, ch'i' non lo scrivo,
Of hire Philologie and hym Mercurie,	però ch'ogne parlar sarebbe poco.
And of the songes that the Muses songe!	Io non mori' e non rimasi vivo;
To smal is bothe thy penne, and eek thy tonge,	pensa oggimai per te, s'hai fior d'ingegno,
For to descryven of this mariage.	qual io divenni, d'uno e d'altro privo.
Whan tendre youthe hath wedded stoupyng age,	E quel che mi convien ritrar testeso,
Ther is swich myrthe that it may nat be writen.	non portò voce mai, né scrisse incostro,
Assayeth it youreself, thanne may ye witen	né fu per fantasia già mai compreso
If that I lye or noon in this matiere.	

How frozen and faint I then became, ask it not, reader, for I do not write it, because all words would fail. I did not die and I did not remain alive: now think for yourself, if you have any wit, what I became, deprived alike of death and of life! [*Inf.*, p. 363]

And that which I must now tell, never did voice report nor ink record, nor was it ever comprised by phantasy. [*Par.*, p. 209]

For the literary convention of the poet's inability to describe his subject fully, see *TC* 3.1688–89, 1693–94. The "certain phrases" to which Bethel refers, with two exceptions, evolve from lines in this convention. Of these two exceptions one is a comparison of "assayeth it yourself" to *pensa oggimai per te*, but the parallel is not very close and is, of course, inevitable in a style that uses the tradition of direct address. Thus in Juvenal, for example, there is the constant command to the reader to "see," "think," and so on. Dante is obviously addressing his reader, but Chaucer might well be addressing the "poete Marcian" throughout the entire citation, since all the other second-person pronouns apply to him, and there is no reason why the last two lines (as seems to be implied) should suddenly change their subject and be addressed to the reader. In any event, the device of direct address, used so frequently in Chaucer, is a technique that hardly needs a source. Finally, it should be noted that there is no possible contextual parallel in any of these citations and that in the cases so far discussed the poetic device is not an extraordinary one by any means.

Quite different is the case of the first citation of line 1732, one which Klaeber pointed out in *Das Bild bei Chaucer*.[23] Here it is possible that Chaucer might have obtained from Dante the rhetorical pattern of silencing a former poet by trying to record an event of greater magnitude than the one that made him famous. The rhetorical device seems rather rare and, combined with the verbal equivalence, would appear to confirm a source in Dante.

Bethel: "*1917–19: general influence of Dante's conception of nobility."

See the discussion under *The Clerk's Tale*, lines 155–61.

Bethel: "1967–69: see under *Troil.* I, 568."

Bethel: "1986: closely modelled on *Inf.* V, 100.

See the citation and discussion under *TC* 1.894–96.

The Squire's Tale

Bethel: "The general influence of Dante is discernible in the tone of the tale, particularly in the frequent references to *gentilesse*...."

As has been previously suggested, the Squire's type of "gentilesse" ought not to be confused with what Dante, and probably Chaucer, considered "gentilesse." The Squire evidently has claims, though certainly not to the "blood royal" of an Eleanor of Aquitaine or Marie de France, at least to a lower order of nobility to which such a man as the Franklin would look with admiration and pride. The Squire is, above all, a courtly lover, and it is in this sense, I believe, that he makes his references to "gentilesse." The Squire, however, like his father, the Knight, represents a way of thinking that must have been fast disappearing, an old order that, even in the Franklin's youth, must have been rapidly dying. Says Coffman (1945:45):

> ...by the second half of the fourteenth century in England, the social order for which courtly love had been an artificial game was fast becoming as obsolete as the knightly armor had been at Crécy. The War of the Roses gave this order its *coup de grace*. Ten Brink's statement that Chaucer wrote in the Indian summer of chivalry applies with special emphasis to the literary convention of courtly love. And he is, in the "Wife of Bath's Tale," I believe, the Meredithian Comic Spirit presenting and observing its incongruities.

This seems a particularly apt summation of the background against which the Squire's version of "gentilesse" is operating, and the only change that one might make here is the addition of *The Squire's Tale* to that of the Wife of Bath. Let us note here that over two hundred years had passed since "the rules of the game as codified by Andreas and as preserved in tradition as part of Chaucer's heritage" (Coffman, p. 45) had first appeared in

---

[23] "166, 348, 407" (Bethel's note).

the *De amore*, and we cannot be reminded too frequently of the fact that two hundred years for the fourteenth century took just as long to pass as two hundred years do now for the twentieth century. Slower communications and a still comparatively rigid social system in the fourteenth century undoubtedly held back change to a great degree, but not to so great a degree that courtly love would not long since have passed out of the realm of the aristocrats and filtered down first to their inferiors in the lower nobility and then (having become outmoded even there) been taken up by the rich bourgeois landowners (cf. Gerould 1952:33–54).

Does such a view hold up in the text? The Franklin's comments on the Squire's tale seem to bear it out. The Franklin himself has been made almost the personification of merry old England by many a critic. His hospitality, his groaning board, his heartiness and kind-liness all make him a sort of Squire Western or Sir Roger of his time. And his views, like Sir Roger's or Squire Western's, though not his good-heartedness, are slightly outmoded and held up for more or less gentle laughter. The Franklin's praise of the Squire is lavish but sincere, for the Squire represents to him all that the older man thinks should be the standards of the younger generation – that is to say, those which he had been taught to admire in his youth. The Squire has quit himself well and "gentilly," though this "gen-tilesse" certainly has no reference to Dante's concepts but seems merely an adverb meaning "gracefully" or "graciously." The Franklin, then, praises the Squire's "wit . . . considerynge thy yowthe" on the basis, first, of the feeling with which the young man has spoken and, second, of the eloquence which he has exhibited.

Does the Squire's tale actually merit such praise, or is the Franklin judging rather by the standards of a stylized genre? The Franklin has been taken by the unparalleled eloquence (and this after having heard such masters as the Clerk and the Man of Laws), that is, by the social graces of "thy speche [for which] I have greet deyntee," (line 681). Chaucer's gentle chiding of the well-landed Franklin becomes steadily more obvious. The Franklin's reason for admiring the Squire's good manners is, of course, because his own son does not seem to want to take social advantage of all that his father can afford to give him. Says the wealthy landowner (lines 683–86):

> "I hadde levere than twenty pound worth lond,
> Though it right now were fallen in myn hond,
> He were a man of swich discrecioun
> As that ye been!"

And, as if to underline how little he knows of true "gentilesse," Chaucer brings in the inherent problem of courtly love and "gentilesse," though now it is seen by the Franklin as a tension not between aristocracy and true grace but rather between financial position and true graciousness. Speaking for the Squire's benefit, the financially successful Franklin can follow his vow of "twenty pound worth lond" with "'Fy on possessioun, / But if a man be vertuous withal!'" (lines 686–87).[24] But "possessioun" is not any further from the Franklin's mind than aristocracy has been from Andreas's. It is exactly for this reason that the Franklin has "snybbed" his son, for whom "to playe at dees, and to despende / And lese al that he hath, is his usage" (lines 690–91). Nor is the worthy Franklin as democratic in his view of who might be "gentil" as one might at first expect. His son, despite all the advantages his father can give him as an eminently successful member of the squirearchy,

---

[24] For the relationship of *antica possession d'avere* and *antica richezza* with "gentilesse," see the discussion under *The Wife of Bath's Tale* above.

"hath levere talken with a page / Thanne to comune with any gentil wight / Where he myghte lerne gentillesse aright" (lines 692–94).

But here we have the crux of the matter. True "gentilesse" "cometh fro God allone." Even Alison knew that, but then Alison had traveled a great deal more in her day than had the rural Franklin. The main point is, of course, that no "gentilesse"—at least not Dante's or Chaucer's versions of "gentilesse"—can possibly be attained by an individual through communing "with any gentil wight / Where he myghte lerne gentillesse aright." And the same thing is true of Vertu, whether you "listeth nat entende" (line 689) or whether you do; for Dante virtue is an act of grace.

The Franklin's words are not totally meaningless, however. It is only that we must change our definition of "gentilesse" when he uses it. For the Franklin, who is eminent enough in his shire to have represented it in Parliament, "gentilesse" implies the social graces, the courtly niceties which can, as he states, be learned through association with what today would be termed the "right kind of people." To the Franklin "gentilesse" was not to be found in the Dantesque discussions of Dame Alison or in the exemplary life of a simple parson; rather it was exemplified in "A lovyere and a lusty bacheler, / With lokkes crulle as they were leyd in presse. / Of twenty yeer of age." (lines 80–82). For the Franklin, then, "gentilesse" meant the good breeding and manners exemplified in the courtly squire which he, as a member of the gentry, would have liked to see in his own son. Such attributes were not to be learned from any "page," in the opinion of the white-bearded vavasor, and it is undoubtedly this remark and the general idea that good manners (or what the Franklin considers good manners) are not to be found in the "lower" classes that rile the usually jovial Harry Bailey into snapping at the older man, "Straw for youre gentilesse!" (line 695).[25]

One should not make the mistake of underestimating Chaucer's creative ability. Subjects such as "gentilesse" do not remain static in Chaucer; they are subtly changed and colored by the personality of the character who is speaking.

Bethel: "The general influence of Dante is discernible in the tone of the tale, particularly in the frequent references to *gentillesse*: cf. e.g. 483–87, 505, 517, etc. Specific borrowings follow."

For gentil herte kitheth gentillesse.
I se wel that ye han of my distresse
Compassion, my faire Canacee,
Of verray wommanly benignytee
That Nature in youre principles hath
    set. [F 483–87]

[Tho dwelte a tercelet me faste by,]
That semed welle of alle gentillesse;
[Al were he ful of treson and falsnesse]
    [F 504–506]

[And kepeth in semblaunt alle his
    observaunces]
That sownen into gentillesse of love.
    [F 516–17]

---

[25] To the degree that such a reading is feasible, the pronoun *youre* would receive emphasis.

These are instances of "gentilesse" used in its most general sense. It is this same idea that pervades *The Romaunt of the Rose* (cf., for example, lines 2597–2612) and the courtly love lyrics.[26] The squire is using, of course, all the terms of the "game" which would be expected of him if he were "In hope to stonden in his lady grace" (*GP* A 88). There is certainly nothing here of Dante's concepts of the divinity that shapes our "gentilesse."

Bethel: "156–65: verbal influence of *Inf.* XXXI, 1–6 (see ll. F. 236–42 below)."

This naked swerd, that hangeth by my
    syde,
Swich vertu hath that, what man so ye
    smyte,
Thurgh out his armure it wole kerve
    and byte,
Were it as thikke as is a branched ook;
And what man that is wounded with
    the strook
Shal never be hool til that yow list, of
    grace,
To stroke hym with the plat in thilke
    place
Ther he is hurt; this is as muche to seyn,
Ye moote with the platte swerd ageyn
Stroke hym in the wounde, and it wol
    close.

[See discussion under *TC* 4.925–27.]

Bethel: "*209f: allusion to Sinon; verbal influence of *Inf.* XXX, 98."

Or elles it was the Grekes hors Synon,
That broghte Troie to destruccion,
[As men moun in thise olde geestes
    rede.]

See the previous discussion under *HF* 1.152. Chaucer is giving his sources, e.g., the *Aeneid* (2.15.195), Benoit, and Guido. The *Commedia* could not possibly be classed as one of "thise olde geestes."

Bethel: "236–42: reference to the spear of Achilles; cf. *Inf.* XXXI, 1–6."

And oother folk han wondred on the
    swerd
That wolde percen thurghout every
    thyng;
And fille in speche of Thelophus the
    kyng,
And of Achilles with his queynte spere,
For he koude with it bothe heele and
    dere,

---

[26] Cf. Robbins 1952:200, no. 198, beginning: "Exemplye sendynge to you, rowte of gentylnes, / Bothe true and trusty stok of all nature. . . ."

Right in swich wise as men may with
    the swerd
Of which right now ye han youreselven
    herd.

In his text (p. 155) Bethel recognizes that "Chaucer could easily have derived his reference to Achilles' spear immediately from a Latin source" and that "there is, too, the further argument that Dante's wording does not explicitly state that the spear 'coude bothe hele and dere,'" but he sees the implications when lines 1, 3, and 6 are put into a relationship. He continues (p. 155): "If then it can be shown that Chaucer had already made use of the Dantean passage the probability that he had Dante in mind here—perhaps in conjunction with some other source—will appear." In other words, since the reference in *The Squire's Tale* to Achilles' spear is relatively insignificant and could come from any one of a number of sources, it must be shown that Chaucer had already used it and considered it in some way an important passage. As proof of this, Pandarus's remark in *TC* 4.925-27 is noted (see discussion under these lines), but, in proof of a Dantesque source for this *Troilus* passage, the use here in *The Squire's Tale* had been offered. In the final analysis, then, no real proof has been given. Likewise, it will be noted that the argument, to be valid, assumes that (1) there can be no other source for the image of Achilles' spear than Dante and (2) no other source could have come between the writing of the *Troilus* passage and that of *The Squire's Tale*. If either of these assumptions is not accepted, then the entire dependence falls apart. The idea of Achilles' spear is, of course, classical and, as has been already stated, can be found in Ovid in a number of places; moreover, the conjunction of Thelophus's name seems a strong indication that Chaucer knew the classical source quite well. The implication, from the passage that has been cited from *The Squire's Tale* and that above at lines 156-65, would seem to be that this entire section of the oriental tale of Canacee is based on a suggestion that Chaucer had picked up from Dante's brief allusion to Achilles. Not only would such a suggestion be extravagant, but no convincing proof has been given for a negation of the classical source or an affirmation of the Dantesque.

It is interesting to note that Chaucer at one time refers to the "flat [and]...egge," evidently of a sword, and at another time to Achilles' "queynte spere," while in the Canacee story itself he is again referring to a sword. It is almost impossible to reconcile these divergences on what is, after all, a very minor reference in Dante. The source in Ovid where Thelophus is mentioned (*Met.* 12.112) is short: "...and when Telephus twice felt the weight of my spear" (Ovid 1940:4.189). And in the following book (13.171-72) it is hardly longer, being only: "'Twas I who conquered the warring Telephus with my spear and healed him, vanquished and begging aid" (Ovid 1940:4.241). However, in the *Ovide moralisé* (12.1840-46) the first, briefer reference is extended considerably to "Telephon I would have killed with this spear of mine that covered him with wounds, but because he begged mercy of me, he appeased me, so I saved him with the very weapon with which I had struck him fatally. I wounded him; I cured him." This is not, of course, being offered as a strictly verbal source for Chaucer's passages, but it does serve, it would seem, as a better explanation than the brief reference in Dante.

Bethel: "*448: verbal influence of Dante's description of the Furies, *Inf.* IX, 34-51."

["What is the cause, if it be for to telle,]   [See citation and discussion under *Pity* 92.]
That ye be in this furial pyne of helle?"
[Quod Canacee unto this hauk above.
"Is this for sorwe of deeth or los of
    love?..."]

Bethel: "479: closely modelled on *Inf.* V, 100."

[See under *TC* 1.894–95.]

Bethel: "*568: closely modelled on *Purg.* XXXIII, 130f."

[And shortly, so ferforth this thyng is went]	Come anima gentil, che non fa scusa,
That my wyl was his willes instrument;	ma fa sua voglia de la voglia altrui
[This is to seyn, my wyl obeyed his wyl	[tosto che è per segno fuor dischiusa;
In alle thyng, as fer as reson fil,	così, poi che da essa preso fui,
Kepynge the boundes of my worshipe evere.]	la bella donna mossesi]

> As a gentle spirit that makes no excuse, but makes its will of another's will, as soon as that is disclosed by outward sign, so the fair lady, after I was taken by her, moved on. [*Purg.*, p. 371]

There is undoubted verbal similarity here, reinforced perhaps by the fact that the peregrine falcon is to be considered an *anima gentil*. The context is strikingly different, however. The female peregrine is describing her unfortunate affair with the tercelet and his eventual betrayal of her. Dante, on the other hand, is telling how Beatrice's request becomes Matilda's will, and the passage is but one more example of Dante's description of the beatitude that is summed up in Piccarda's ". . . in la sua volontade è nostra pace." The line in Chaucer marks the submission of the female peregrine to a very faithless and very earthly lover; the line in the *Commedia* emphasizes the willingness that Dante finds among the beatified spirits when he enters the realms of "l'amor che move il sole e l'altre stelle." Nor, in Dante, is one will made the instrument of another; the *Divina Commedia* ends on this very note that Dante has been stressing throughout the entire last *cantica*: ". . . il . . . disio e 'l velle" become one and the same under God's beatitude and plan. It is perhaps this vast difference in the contexts of the two passages that has led Robinson to omit any notation of possible source. Nevertheless, the verbal equivalences that do exist should be noted.

The Franklin's Tale

Bethel: "As is the case with the *Squire's Tale*, the whole tone of the *Franklin's Tale* owes much to Dante. The story illustrates the negative side of the Dantesque discussion of true nobility, and emphasizes the fact that *gentillesse* and birth are not intimately related. Though it is not easy to cite specific borrowings in this connexion, attention should be called to the frequent mention of gentillesse. . . ."

It is not at all strange that the Franklin, whose character we have somewhat investigated in the introductory remarks to *The Squire's Tale*, should follow with a story that stresses that "*gentillesse* and birth are not intimately related." The Franklin, although an eminent member of the gentry himself, is not a member of the inherited nobility to which Andreas's concepts of an aristocratic and inherent "gentilesse" applied. As well, this view would seem to be supported by a home truth for the Franklin, who, having just heard the "gentil" Squire, is painfully aware that he has a son who has certainly not inherited what his father considers "gentilesse." The Franklin, then, would seem to have ample reason for recognizing that "gentilesse" and birth are not intimately related.

The negative aspect of "gentilesse" is far from being uniquely or typically Dantesque, however. We have already seen that Boethius, for one, takes this same position.[27] On the other hand, it seems eminently just to say that to Dante "the Boethian doctrine of the vanity of nobility of blood was...but the starting-point for a loftier treatment which relates *gentilezza*, the direct gift of God, to ultimate and perfect felicity." (Bethel, p. 329). But is this last the type of *gentilezza* or "gentilesse" that we find in the Franklin's tale? Is not the Franklin using the older idea of "gentilesse"—that which *The Romaunt of the Rose* explains first in the negative terms of "vilanye" and then in the positive terms of "gentilesse"? It is worth requoting the passage here for its relevance (*Rom* 2181–2202):

> For vilanye makith vilayn,
> And by his dedis a cherl is seyn.
> Thise vilayns arn withouten pitee,
> Frendshipe, love, and all bounte.
> I nyl resseyve unto my servise
> Hem that ben vilayns of emprise.
> But undirstonde in thyn entent
> That this is not myn entendement,
> To clepe no wight in noo ages
> Oonly gentill for his lynages.
> But whoso is vertuous,
> And in his port nought outrageous,
> Whanne sich oon thou seest thee biforn,
> Though he be not gentill born,
> Thou maist well seyn, this is in soth,
> That he is gentil by cause he doth
> As longeth to a gentilman;
> Of hem noon other deme I can.
> For certeynly, withouten drede,
> A cherl is demed by his dede,
> Of hie or lowe, as we may see,
> Or of what kynrede that he bee.

It is this type of "gentilesse," or something very close to it, that is the motif of *The Franklin's Tale*. "Gentilesse," for the Franklin, ordinarily centers on a social graciousness that at its highest point becomes magnanimity, but it is never the mark of divine grace, as it is for Dante. All the characters of the Franklin's tale have human virtues almost to the point of sinfulness. Arveragus almost becomes a wittol, Dorigen an adulteress, Aurelius an adulterer, and the magician a pander. Is it *gentilezza* that leads to this situation, or is it an overweening regard for honoring one's agreement that threatens to turn the virtue to a fault? It is shame that leads Aurelius to break his part of the contract, and if the deeds that follow are "gentil," they are so only in the sense that they are acts of graciousness or largesse. This is far from the "sublime view" (to use Bethel's phrase) with which Dante saw *gentilezza*, but it is, I believe, a view emanating directly from the personality of the Franklin.

We may, therefore, suggest that the negative view of "gentilesse," as Chaucer expresses it, is found in far more similar passages in *The Romaunt of the Rose*, Boethius, and Andreas[28]

[27] Cf. under *WBT* D 1117–24, citation of Boethius *De cons.* pr. 6, m. 6.
[28] See citation and discussion under *WBT* 1163f.

and that it was probably, so well accepted as to be traditional. Likewise, the consequent positive view is dealing not with *gentilezza* as the divine manifestation that it was under Dante but rather with the *gentilesse* of inherent honor, good breeding, and "stedfastnesse." It is not *gentilezza* but rather the almost incredible sense of honor and the "stedfastnesse" of Arveragus and Dorigen that shame the basically "ryght vertuous" Aurelius and recall to the "lusty squier" his own former standards of behavior.

Bethel: ". . . Though it is not easy to cite specific borrowings in this connexion, attention should be called to the frequent mention of *gentillesse*; cf. e.g. F 686–94; 1522–27; 1543f.; 1607–12; etc."

Individual treatment of these citations will be given in order. For discussion of *SqT* F 686–94, see introductory remarks to *The Squire's Tale*.

[And in his (Aurelius's) herte he
    caughte of this greet routhe,
Considerynge the beste on every syde,]
That fro his lust yet were hym levere
    abyde
Than doon so heigh a cherlyssh
    wrecchednesse
Agayns franchise and alle gentillesse;
For which in fewe wordes seyde he
    thus:
"Madame, seyth to youre lord
    Arveragus,
That sith I se his grete gentillesse
To yow, and eek I se wel youre
    distresse,
[That him were levere han shame (and
    that were routhe)
Than ye to me sholde breke thus youre
    trouthe,
I have wel levere evere to suffre wo
Than I departe the love bitwix yow
    two.] [*FranT* F 1520–31]

Aurelius's self-estimation is based almost directly on the standards that are set up in the passage from *The Romaunt of the Rose* cited above. An applicable definition for the second use of "gentilesse" in this passage is more difficult to determine; "graciousness" seems in many ways to fit the context in which the word appears. In any event, there is certainly nothing specifically of Dante here.

". . . Thus kan a squier doon a gentil
    dede
As wel as kan a knyght, withouten
    drede." [*FranT* F 1543–44]

This purely social approach is again close to the *Romaunt* and the *débat* set forth by Andreas and, indirectly, to Boethius. Dante's particular discussion centers on *antica ricchezza*, not on social differences. This last element seems to be illustrating the character of the person telling the story. There is nothing positively Dantesque here; everything can be accounted for better by the traditional arguments found in Jean de Meun and Andreas, among others.

This philosophre answerde, "Leeve
    brother,
Everich of yow dide gentilly til oother.
Thou art a squier, and he is a knyght;
But God forbede, for his blisful myght,
But if a clerk koude doon a gentil dede
As wel as any of yow, it is no drede!"
    [FranT 1607–12]

See the preceding citation for discussion of the social element.

Bethel: "*950: verbal influence of Dante's description of the Furies, *Inf.* IX, 34–51."

But langwissheth as a furye dooth in   [See discussion under *Pity* 92.]
    helle

Bethel: "*1077: the suggestions for this promise to Apollo may have come from *Par.* I, 25f."

Thy temple in Delphos wol I barefoot   vedra'mi al piè del tuo diletto legno
    seke.   venire, e coronarmi de le foglie
                                               [che la materia e tu mi farai degno.]

    . . . you shall see me come to your beloved tree and crown me with those leaves
    [of which the matter and you shall make me worthy.] [*Par.*, p. 5]

The citation from the *Commedia* is part of Dante's invocation to Apollo at the beginning of the *Paradiso*. Aside from the fact that Phebus (or rather "Lord Phebus") is mentioned by Chaucer and that some sort of movement is implied in both (i.e., walking), there is apparently neither verbal nor contextual parallel of any sort.

Bethel: "*1101: same as 950."

In langour and in torment furyus   [See discussion under *Pity* 92.]

There is, of course, no reason at all to connect the adjective "furyus" with Dante. Any comparison here only illustrates the dangers of using the single-source approach to an author.

Bethel: "1508: see under *Troil.* I, 568f.,"

The Prioress's Tale

Bethel: "1664–70 [VII, 474–80]: address to the Virgin; modelled on *Par.* XXXIII, 16–21."

Lady, thy bountee, thy magnificence,   La tua benignità non pur soccorre
Thy vertu, and thy grete humylitee,   a chi domanda, ma molte fïate

Ther may no tonge expresse in no
 science;
For somtyme, Lady, er men praye to
 thee,
Thou goost biforn of thy benyngnytee,
And getest us the lyght, of thy preyere,
To gyden us unto thy Sone so deere.

liberamente al dimandar precorre.
In te misericordia, in te pietate,
 in te magnificenza, in te s'aduna
quantunque in creatura è di bontate.

> Thy loving-kindness not only succors him who asks, but oftentimes freely
> foreruns the asking. In thee is mercy, in thee pity, in thee munificence, in thee
> is found whatever of goodness is in any creature. [*Par.*, pp. 371, 373]

Dante's lyric jewel, the prayer to the Virgin, is definitely the original source for Chaucer's Prioress's address. As in the conclusion of *Troilus*, Chaucer here turned to the Marian exultations of the *Commedia* when he was attempting to re-create the lyric intensity of religious adoration. Indeed, Chaucer seems to emphasize the ineffability through the slight departure of line 476 ("Ther may no tonge expresse in no science"), which seems, with consummate skill, to take the prayer from a saint in paradise and give it to a human being in adoration.

Pratt's suggestion (1946:259–61) that Chaucer was borrowing from his own *Invocacio* in *The Second Nun's Prologue* is as sensitive as it is persuasive, but he seems to come even closer to the heart of the matter when he notes (p. 261, n.7) that "it is conceivable that lines 36–70 of the Invocacio had become for Chaucer a personal prayer which he knew by heart." It is not perhaps too rash to suggest that the main literary source of that prayer in Dante might also have been memorized, for it would seem that the closeness of the lines in *The Prioress's Tale* to both the words and the feelings of Saint Bernard's magnificent Marian prayer can hardly be denied. What is being suggested here is not so much a question of which passage preceded the other but rather the possibility that there are two separate borrowings from *Par.* 33, one affected by the precedence of the other. The similarities which Pratt points out in Chaucer's two passages would seem to indicate that the Second Nun's *Invocacio* in all probability did precede the Prioress's prayer, but (as Pratt himself notes with admirable objectivity) certain direct relationships of the Prioress's lines to the *Paradiso* would seem to be demonstrated by the similarity of the expressions "bountee" and *bontate* and by the opening "Lady" in Chaucer's stanza as compared with the beginning of Saint Bernard's preceding tercet: "'Donna, se' tanto grande e tanto vali.'" As well as these two examples, the final purpose of the Prioress's prayer (lines 479–80) is reasonably close to the purpose and wording of Saint Bernard's request that Dante be permitted to see (line 43) "l' etterno lume" (*Par.* 33.31–33):

> Perché tu ogne nube li disleghi
> di sua mortalità co' prieghi tuoi,
>   sì che 'l sommo piacer li si dispieghi.[29]

These more direct relationships with Dante would seem to be accounted for if we were to suppose that the religious lyric from the *Paradiso* had been firmly fixed in Chaucer's mind and was present, *along with* the Second Nun's *Invocacio*, as he composed the Prioress's prayer to the Virgin. Indeed, one might equally observe that Chaucer's longest Marian prayer, *An ABC*, likewise stayed with him and formed yet another element. Thus the Prioress's stanza as a whole can be compared with *ABC* 65–70:

---

[29] The Singleton translation reads: "...that with thy prayers thou wouldst dispel for him every cloud of his mortality, so that the Supreme Pleasure may be disclosed to him" (*Par.*, p. 373).

> I wot it wel, thou wolt ben oure socour,
> Thou art so ful of bowntee, in certeyn.
> For, whan a soule falleth in errour,
> Thi pitee goth and haleth him ayein.
> Thanne makest thou his pees with his sovereyn,
> And bringest him out of the crooked strete.

It would be difficult to say definitely whether *An ABC* was directly recalled, let alone whether it affords any evidence of precedence in the passages being discussed. Finally, while it may be true that Chaucer had no "other source material than his own text of the Invocacio" (Pratt 1946:261) when composing the Prioress's prayer, we should not omit the possibilities that he had memorized Dante's lyric or that he could directly recall his own poem on a similar theme.

The Tale of Sir Thopas

Kellogg (1960:119–20): Kellogg finds the source of B² 1885–87 in *Purg.* 19.40–53.

. . ."What man artow?" quod he; "Thou lookest as thou woldest fynde an hare, For evere upon the ground I se thee stare. . . ."	Seguendo lui, portava la mia fronte come colui che l'ha di pensier carca, che fa di sé un mezzo arco di ponte; quand'io udi' "Venite; qui si varca" parlare in modo soave e benigno, qual non si sente in questa mortal marca. Con l'ali aperte, che parean di cigno, volseci in sù colui che sì parlonne tra due pareti del duro macigno. Mosse le penne poi e ventilonne, *"Qui lugent"* affermando esser beati, ch'avran di consolar l'anime donne. "Che hai che pur inver' la terra guati?" la guida mia incominciò a dirmi, [poco amendue da l'angel sormontati.]

Following him, I was bearing my brow like one that has it burdened with thought, who makes of himself a half-arch of a bridge, when I heard, "Come, here is the passage," spoken in a tone gentle and kind, such as is not heard in this mortal region. With open wings that seemed like a swan's he who thus had spoken to us turned us upward between the two walls of hard rock, then moved his feathers and fanned us, declaring *"Qui lugent"* to be blessed, for they shall have their souls possessed of consolation.

"What ails you that you keep gazing on the ground?" my guide began to say to me, [when we had both climbed a little above the angel.] [*Purg.*, pp. 203, 205]

The comparison should be, at most, with lines 40–42 and 52. Kellogg (p. 119) states that

Dante, weighed down by his vision of the "femina balba," takes on the appearance of "un mezzo arco di ponte" (42). Virgil, here as elsewhere, described by the term "guida" (53), comments, as does Harry Bailly, upon this singular posture:

> "Che hai che pur inver la terra guati?" (52)

> If one removes the "hare" amplification from Harry Bailly's remarks, the words
> of the two guides to their respective poets have become virtually identical.

Kellogg's assertions seem difficult to justify. First, the contexts are quite different, and to equate Harry Bailly with Virgil the teacher and psychopomp (*il mio maestro*) is to invite a categorization that obliterates distinction—unless, that is, one has decided that *The Canterbury Tales* is a *Commedia* writ light. Nor should one compare quite so facilely the "respective poets," for in the narrative fiction of *The Canterbury Tales* the "I" figure is (carefully, I would suggest) never identified as a poet.

Again, it seems significant that Dante's striking image (*un mezzo arco di ponte*) is *not* present; Chaucer uses the equally arresting but totally different image of a "hare"—a difference that is so striking that Kellogg "removes" it in order to press his comparison.

Finally, since "What man artow?" and "Che hai?" ("What ails you?") can be compared only in the most nebulous way (especially considering the respective motivations), we are left with two "I" characters looking at the ground in the conventional attitude of someone "in a studie."

What seems really to have impressed Kellogg (p. 119) is that "if one compares, in the broadest terms, the artistic methods of Dante and Chaucer, one is struck by their remarkably similar use of what might be called the dual first-person singular." That Fergusson pointed to Dante the pilgrim[30] and Donaldson to Chaucer the pilgrim[31] seems to have led Kellogg to a concluding equation open to serious question (p. 120):

> Chaucer is, I think, showing himself to us as the artist, the withdrawn intelligence which does not exist from moment to moment, but encompasses the whole fabric of its work. Hence in choosing a model for his final self-portrait, he chose that figure of Dante which most fully suggested to him the distancing and objectification great art requires.

The Monk's Tale

Bethel: "*3335 [VII 2145]: the form Nabugodonosor is possibly Dantesque; cf. *Par.* IV, 14."

That hadde the kyng Nabugodonosor   Nabuccodonosor levando d'ira

when he lifted Nebuchadnezzar out of the wrath [*Par.*, p. 37]

There is no basis for verbal or contextual comparison here. The present form of the name in Romance languages (cf. Modern French, Nabuchodonosor) suggests that the most obvious source—the source common to the whole of the Middle Ages—gave the spelling. If we check the Vulgate at, let us say, Daniel 2.1, we find the spelling Nebuchodonosor. This spelling seems to have been retained in all Latin versions not affected by later English spellings. A source as common as Jerome's Vulgate totally negates any demonstrable dependence on Dante. Chaucer would probably not have known any other form than the one he used.

Bethel: "3597–3652 [VII 2407–62]: the story of Ugolino is retold from Dante's account in *Inf.* XXXIII, 13–75. In B. 3651 Dante is named."

---

[30] "Francis Fergusson, *Dante's Drama of the Mind*, Princeton, 1953, pp. 9–10" (Kellogg's note).
[31] "E. T. Donaldson, 'Chaucer the Pilgrim,' *PMLA* LXIX (1954), pp. 928–36" (Kellogg's note).

The Ugolino passage in Dante is one of the finest dramatic narratives in the *Commedia*, as Grandgent says, "second only to that of Francesca da Rimini in its appeal to popular sympathy"[32] and similar to the earlier episode in that in both "we find the same exclusion of all detail that might blur the one overwhelming impression to be produced on the reader" (Dante 1933:294). Chaucer's Hugelino passage, as Spencer (1934:295–30) has shown,[33] carefully shifts the emphasis away from the concentrated terror of Dante's description to the sympathetic, one might almost say sentimental, description of the death of Hugelino's innocent children. After their deaths the account of Hugelino becomes scarcely more than a rapid fulfillment of the Monk's primary moral, the adversity of Fortune and the downfall of princes. The direction of the transformation is faithful to the general tone of *The Monk's Tale*, for what is stressed throughout the series of exempla

> is the emotion of pathos. And this is just what we find in Chaucer's account of Ugolino.

> > Off the Erl Hugelyn of Pyze the langour
> > Ther may no tonge telle for pitee.

> Even if we remember that *langour* had a stronger meaning ("slow starvation") to Chaucer than to us, the word pitee at once sets the tone of pathos. And if we think of Dante's *disperato dolor*, we are immediately aware that Chaucer's emphasis will be very different from Dante's. [Spencer, p. 296]

While Chaucer's principal addition is epitomized by the narrator's interjection (*MkT* B² 3603–3604):

> > Allas, Fortune! it was greet crueltee
> > Swiche briddes for to putte in swich a cage!

his principal *change* — and it can hardly be less than intentional, considering that it transforms the very essence of Dante's account — can be seen in Hugelino's tempered grief and Christian submission to the death of his first child (lines 3635–36):

> > "Allas, Fortune, and weylaway!
> > Thy false wheel my wo al may I wyte."

Against this we may set the raw terror that is sustained from the very opening of *Inf.* 33:

> > La bocca sollevò dal fiero pasto
> > quel peccator, forbendola a' capelli
> > del capo ch'elli avea di retro guasto.

> [From his savage repast the sinner raised his mouth, wiping it on the hair of the head he had spoiled behind. (*Inf.*, p. 349)]

or the horrifying ambiguity that closes the account:

> > Poscia, più che 'l dolor, potè 'l digiuno.[34]

---

[32] To me the fact that Chaucer never made use of the Francesca story from *Inf.* 5 is one of the most striking problems of the Chaucer-Dante relationship.

[33] Spencer's excellent article gives a searching analysis of the shift in narrative emphasis and moral judgment, and it is difficult to avoid mere paraphrasing of his critique. The comments given here are directed toward a view of the relevance of the Chaucerian version to the narrator.

[34] *Inf.* 33.75; cf. *MkT* B 3645: "Hymself, despeired, eek for hunger starf." Chaucer's reemphasis has been regularly noted, but nowhere so cogently as in the generally excellent article of Boitani (1976:50–69): "[Chaucer] has transformed 'dolor' in its despair and 'digiuno' (fasting) into hunger. The verb 'potè,' which is the key to Dante's ambiguity, has been replaced by 'starf.'. . . Chaucer achieves poetic intensity with means exactly opposite to those which Dante uses" (pp. 62–63).

[Then fasting did more than grief had done. (*Inf.*, p. 353)]

Not only is the stark brutality excised for a more Monk-like sense of submission, but Chaucer has simplified the story to the point of melodrama. Like his children, Hugelino is an innocent victim (B² 3605–3607):

> Dampned was he to dyen in that prisoun,
> For Roger, which that bisshop was of Pize,
> Hadde on hym maad a fals suggestioun.

Fortune is, of course, the real villainess of the piece, and both Bishop Roger and the people are merely pale agents of her turning wheel. Nowhere in Chaucer is there the hint of Ugelino's treachery; nowhere is there the indication that

> horrible as his experience in life has been, we are not for a moment to forget that his memory of it is part of his punishment for a sin equally horrible, the sin of treachery, and that if we pity him, our pity is to be only a passing emotion. . . . The terror, in the Aristotelian sense of the word, which we felt during the recital of his narrative, is mingled with the moral terror of Dante, and it is the combination of the two that shakes us so profoundly. [Spencer 1934:296]

For Dante, poetry was a medium for the expression of a unified doctrine, and Ugelino's guilt in deserting the Ghibeline faction to join the Tuscan Guelfs against Pisa[35] was as much a part of the purpose of the passage as the frightful story itself. Probably nowhere else in the Chaucer-Dante relationship are the fundamental differences between the two writers so clearly stressed.

With extraordinary care Boitani (p. 56) analyzes the nature of this transformation: "In Chaucer, the delicate balance of history and meta-history[36] is altered; meta-history disappears because it is the Monk who tells the Tale and because he stresses the historical situation in which Hugelyn's death took place (*MkT* 2416–19)." The specifics are enlightening (Boitani, p. 58):

> Now, in changing the tone of the episode from horror to pathos, Chaucer has adopted a new technique. The first thing to disappear in his version is indirectness. Everything is pointed out with precision and in due order. . . . Time becomes irrelevant, vague, loose. . . . The Hugelyn episode relies on matter-of-fact details to produce pathos. Historical and topographical notations, the quality of the temporal dimension, the directness of the language contribute to this prosaic dimension.

There follows an analysis which at times threatens to overwhelm the poetry and its sentiment but which never loses its essentially right direction (p. 63):

> The Hugelyn version does not simply, as F. N. Robinson says,[37] "differ in some details from its source." It can be defined as a total *twisting* of Dante's text. Only five lines (*MkT* 2444, 2447–48, 2450–51) have been translated by Chaucer, but in any case set in different context. The structure, the register, the imagery, the semantic level, the setting, the theme are different. [Boitani's italics]

These decisions, in turn, affect the decision about whether the episode in the *Monk's Tale* was composed from memory or from text, for one feels almost certain that the result

---

[35] See Singleton's summary and references, *Inf.*, Commentary, esp. pp. 606–12.

[36] For Boitani, meta-history constitutes "the inner experience" and those "episodes unknown to all but the sinner himself" (p. 55).

[37] "*The Works of Geoffrey Chaucer*, p. 749, n. 2407" (Boitani's note).

would have been almost the same, that Chaucer, while he would have been quick to see the intensely dramatic situation of Dante's Ugelino and convert it to moral melodrama, would never—even with the text before him—have brought in the political doctrine, the scorching judgment, or the uncompromising brutality that makes Dante's story "perhaps the most intensely shocking in literature" (Spencer, p. 296).[38] Moreover, the direction which Chaucer gave the episode is so foreign to the tone and purpose of Dante's account that, no matter what the absolute date was, the version that we have in *The Monk's Tale* must have been made at a time when Chaucer was thinking in terms of a series of exempla on Fortune's "adversitee" and the Christian's submission thereto.

Bethel: "3667 [VII 2477]: the words here applied to Nero, Dante applies to Semiramis in *Inf.* V, 56."

His lustes were al lawe in his decree   che libito fé licito in sua legge

    She made lust licit in her law. [*Inf.*, p. 51]

Very likely the source for Chaucer's line is this verse from *Inf.* 5, for Dante's expression is unlike that which is almost always found in his source, Orosius's *Adversum paganos*. Moore (1896:280–81) explains this variation on the basis of a posited error in Dante's manuscript:

> No one can doubt the direct imitation, almost amounting to actual quotation, of this passage in Inf. v. 52–59, respecting Ninus and Semiramis. The words speak for themselves. "Huic (Nino) mortuo Semiramis uxor successit (confirming the certainly correct reading *succedette* in l. 59). . . . Haec libidine ardens (l. 55). . . privatem ignominiam publico scelere obtexit: praecepit enim ut inter parentes et filios nulla delata reverentia naturae de coniugiis adpetendis, ut cuique libitum esset liberum fieret (ll. 56, 57)." Though "liberum" is the reading generally adopted, I find there was an old reading "licitum" which was probably that in the MS. used by Dante. One Bodleian MS. reads "libero" for "licito" at Inf. v. 56. This looks like a correction made by a scribe who had verified the reference.[39]

Chaucer follows Dante more precisely than the *Adversum paganos*, which he could have read in Vincent of Beauvais's *Speculum historiale* (2.103). There one finds a detailed account of Semiramis compiled from Justinus, Valerius Maximus, and Orosius, but the relevant section shows little significant variation, reading "cui libitum esset liberum fieret." Unless we assume the very unlikely possibility that Chaucer and Dante were both working from similarly faulty manuscripts, it seems conclusive that Chaucer followed Dante's phrase in preference to—or, perhaps, through ignorance of—the original wording of Orosius.

---

[38] I feel strongly that Chaucer was working with the text close at hand rather than from memory; not only are the specific lines translated (see above), but no matter how impressed Chaucer may have been by Dante, as I have said earlier, in the Chaucer-Dante relationship the direction almost always seems clear: it was Chaucer who made use of Dante.

[39] Singleton (*Inf.*, Commentary, p. 78) supports the ascription to Dante but believes that Dante's words are "an exact translation" of the phrase as normally found in Orosius. Raymond's translation of the passage quoted by Moore reads as follows: "His wife Semiramis succeeded him on the throne. . . . Burning with lust, . . . [she] covered her private disgrace with a public crime. For she prescribed that between parents and children no reverence for nature in the conjugal act was to be observed, but that each should be free to do as he pleased" (Orosius 1936:49–50).

The Nun's Priest's Tale

Bethel: "4189 [VII 2999]: see under *Troil.*, I, 568f."

Guerin (1973:313–15): Guerin compares B² 4388–4403 [VII 3198–3213] with *Inf.* 5.112–42 (the Paolo and Francesca episode).

Guerin's suggestion seems based principally on the reference to "the book of Launcelot de Lake" (line 4402), which Paolo and Francesca had been reading (5.127–28), and to a posited ironic relationship of Chauntecleer and Pertelote to Paolo and Francesca. The reference comes more likely from common knowledge, and the relationship seems to me ingenious but unlikely.

Hamm (1954:394–95), B² 4405–08 [VII 3215–18]: Hamm compares Chaucer's "heigh ymaginacioun" to *Purg.* 17.25 and *Par.* 33.142.

A col-fox, ful of sly iniquitee,	Poi piovve dentro a l'alta fantasia
That in the grove hadde woned yeres three,	[un crucifisso, dispettoso e fero ne la sua vista, e cotal si moria.]
By heigh ymaginacioun forncast,	
The same nyght thurghout the hegges brast	A l'alta fantasia qui mancò possa;
	[ma già volgeva il mio disio e 'l velle, sì come rota ch'igualmente è mossa, l'amor che move il sole e l'altre stelle.]

Then rained down within the high fantasy [one crucified, scornful and fierce in his mien, and so was he dying.] [*Purg.*, p. 181]

Here power failed the lofty phantasy; [but already my desire and my will were revolved, like a wheel that is evenly moved, by the Love which moves the sun and the other stars.] [*Par.*, p. 381]

In speaking of the Platonic background to prophetic power arriving in sleep or in madness—a power that reaches its highest point in Dante's writing, Hamm (p. 395) mentions the coincidence of terms in Chaucer and the *Commedia*: "It is particularly interesting, therefore, to note that in that dream vision which is the *Divina Commedia*, Dante uses the very phrase "alta fantasia," the exact equivalent of Chaucer's 'heigh ymaginacioun.'" Hamm's statement is certainly correct in modern terms, but Chaucer had a more nearly exact cognate in "fantasye," a word which he uses twenty or thirty times. There is an even closer verbal and thematic use of the phrase *alta fantasia* in *The Merchant's Tale* (lines 1577–81):

> Heigh fantasye and curious bisynesse
> Fro day to day gan in the soule impresse
> Of Januarie aboute his mariage.
> Many fair shap and many a fair visage
> Ther passeth thurgh his herte nyght by nyght.

The question whether these lines are based on *Par.* 33 is not as quickly answered as the verbal similarity would lead us to suppose. The problem of the powers of "fantasye" is discussed at some length by Dante in *Convivio* 3.4, but the topic was one that engaged the minds of the great philosophers of the age and it is discussed fully by Saint Augustine,

Saint Thomas, Albertus Magnus, and Boethius, among others.

Chauntecleer's extensive explanation of the prophetic powers of the mind show that Chaucer was well read on this subject, but the discussion, despite its fullness, does not help us determine definitely the origin of line 4407. Whether the source is in Dante or in one of the scholastic philosophers, Hamm's interpretation seems to clear up the meaning of a troublesome line. It would appear that the line does not refer directly to divine foreknowledge but rather is a parenthetical remark by Chaucer (who had just forced himself to "torne agayne to my sentence") and is equivalent to "as forecast by Chauntecleer's prophetic imagination."

The philosophical concept in both Dante and Chaucer (here and in *The Merchant's Tale*) stems from the same general philosophical discussion, but Chaucer's reading on this was so wide and the contexts are so radically different form the *Commedia* that it is admittedly difficult to determine the source. It seems certain, however, that there is a definite parallel.

Bethel: "[B²] 4418 f [vii 3228]: allusion to Sinon; verbal influence of *Inf*. XXX, 98."

False dissymulour, O Greek Synon,
That broghtest Troye al outrely to
    sorwe!

[See citation and discussion under *HF* 152 and *SqT* 209f.]

The Second Nun's Tale

Bethel: "30: the mention of St. Bernard may possibly be due to the fact that the prayer to the Virgin which forms the basis of the Second Nun's invocation was one which Dante had placed in the mouth of the same saint (*Par.*, XXXIII)."

[And thow that flour of virgines art
    alle,]
Of whom that Bernard list so wel to
    write,
[To thee at my bigynnyng first I calle]

The source of Chaucer's citation of Saint Bernard is almost indeterminable. Dante put the prayer into the mouth of the saint because his writings were devoted particularly to honoring Mary. The Second Nun (or, more exactly, Chaucer) would have been well aware of the tradition surrounding the saint and would have been well acquainted with his writings, but whether this citation of him was due to common knowledge or to the fact that Dante makes him his spokesman seems impossible to determine.

Bethel: "36–56: these verses, with the exception of ll. 45–49, are fairly closely modelled on *Par*. XXXIII, 1–21."

Thow Mayde and Mooder, doghter of
    thy Sone,
Thow welle of mercy, synful soules
    cure,
In whom that God for bountee chees to
    wone,
Thow humble, and heigh over every
    creature,

"Vergine Madre, figlia del tuo figlio,
    umile e alta più che creatura,
    termine fisso d'etterno consiglio,
tu se' colei che l'umana natura
    nobilitasti sì, che 'l suo fattore
    non disdegnò di farsi sua fattura.
Nel ventre tuo si raccese l'amore,
    per lo cui caldo ne l'etterna pace

Thow nobledest so forferth oure nature,
That no desdeyn the Makere hadde of
    kynde
His Sone in blood and flessh to clothe
    and wynde.

Withinne the cloistre blisful of thy sydis
Took mannes shap the eterneel love and
    pees,
That of the tryne compas lord and gyde
    is,
Whom erthe and see and hevene, out of
    relees,
Ay heryen; and thou, Virgine
    wemmelees,
Baar of thy body—and dweltest mayden
    pure—
The Creatour of every creature.

Assembled is in thee magnificence
With mercy, goodnesse, and with swich
    pitee
That thou, that art the sonne of
    excellence,
Nat oonly helpest hem that preyen
    thee,
But often tyme, of thy benygnytee,
Ful frely, er that men thyn help biseche,
Thou goost biforn, and art hir lyves
    leche.

così è germinato questo fiore.
Qui se' a noi meridïana face
    di caritate, e giuso, intra' mortali,
    se' di speranza fontana vivace.
Donna, se' tanto grande e tanto vali,
    che qual vuol grazia e a te non ricorre,
    sua disïanza vuol volar sanz' ali.
La tua benignità non pur soccorre
    a chi domanda, ma molte fïate
    liberamente al dimandar precorre.
In te misericordia, in te pietate,
    in te magnificenza, in te s'aduna
    quantunque in creatura è di bontate."

"Virgin Mother, daughter of thy Son, humble and exalted more than any
creature, fixed goal of the eternal counsel, thou art she who didst so ennoble
human nature that its Maker did not disdain to become its creature. In thy
womb was rekindled the Love under whose warmth this flower in the eternal
peace has thus unfolded. Here thou art for us the noonday torch of charity, and
below among mortals thou art the living fount of hope. Lady, thou art so great
and so availest, that whoso would have grace and has not recourse to thee, his
desire seeks to fly without wings. Thy loving–kindness not only succors him
who asks, but oftentimes freely foreruns the asking. In thee is mercy, in thee
pity, in thee munificence, in thee is found whatever of goodness is in any
creature." [*Par.*, pp. 371, 373]

Robinson's far more accurate ascription of these lines (p. 757) is worth giving *in extenso*:

These lines follow in general the prayer of St. Bernard in the *Paradiso*, xxxiii,
1 ff., as indicated by line numbers below:

l. 36.	Vergine Madre, figlia del tuo Figlio,
l. 39.	Umile ed alta più che creatura,
	Termine fisso d' eterno consiglio,
	Tu se' colei che l' umana natura
ll. 40, 41.	Nobilitasti sì che il suo Fattore
ll. 41, 42.	Non disdegnò di farsi sua fattura.

l. 43.   Nel ventre tuo si raccese l' amore,
l. 44.   Per lo cui caldo nell' eterna pace
             Così è germinato questo fiore.
             Qui sei a noi meridiana face
             Di caritate, e giuso intra i mortali
             Sei di speranza fontana vivace.
             Donna, sei tanto grande e tanto vali,
             Che qual vuol grazia ed a te non ricorre,
             Sua disianza vuol volar senz' ali.
ll. 53,54.   La tua benignità non pur soccorre
ll. 53, 54. A chi domanda, ma molte fiate
ll. 55, 56. Liberamente al domandar precorre.
l. 51.   In te misericordia, in te pietate,
l. 50.   In te magnificenza, in te s'aduna
             Quantunque in creatura è di bontate

On other passages reminiscences of which Chaucer apprently combined with these lines from Dante, see the introductory note above.

The introductory note relevant here (p. 756) reads:

> The *Invocatio ad Mariam* is a fabric made up of elements from the Paradiso of Dante, several Latin hymns, or anthems, the Anticlaudianus of Alanus de Insulis and the Commentary of Macrobius on the Somnium Scipionis. Stanzas 2, 3 and 4 are in large part translated from the address of St. Bernard to the Virgin. . . . But several lines and phrases from Alanus are interwoven with Dante. The fifth stanza is indebted to the Salve Regina, and lines 43–47 echo the Quem Terra (and perhaps also another canto of the Paradiso). Both these Latin hymns occur in the Hours of the Virgin, whence Chaucer probably derived the passages here used. The often repeated *motif* of ll. 47–49 occurs in the anthems for Evensong, Post Partum and Beata es Virgo.

Robinson completes his ascription as follows (p. 757):

> With ll. 37–38 cf. the Anticlaudianus, v, 9 (Migne, Pat. Lat., CCX, 538 ff.); ll. 13–14, 26; with l. 42, the same chapter, ll. 14–16; and with l. 56, perhaps l. 66, ibid. But some of these phrases were commonplaces of the Marian hymns. With ll. 45–49 cf. the opening lines of a hymn of Venantius Fortunatus . . . :

> > Quem terra, pontus, aethera,
> > Colunt, adorant, praedicant,
> > Trinam regentem machinam,
> > Claustrum Mariae bajulat.

> > [Whom earth and sea and air
> > Revere, adore, beseech,
> > The triune ruling system,
> > Bears up Mary's cloister.]

The *cloistre blisful* of l. 43 may be an echo of this passage as well as of the "beato chiostro" of *Paradiso*, xxv, 127.

It should be noted that, just as the Ugolino episode is a narrative vignette, so Saint Bernard's prayer is one of the very few lyric vignettes in Dante; that is, it is one of the few portions of poetry in the *Commedia* that can exist outside the highly organic work itself. Certainly this type of passage would be the kind most easily transferable, and Chaucer was no doubt quick to see this. For further discussion, see entry under *The Prioress's Tale*, lines 474–80.

Bethel: "*58: 'desert of galle'; the phrase may possibly be due to *Purg.* XI, 14. Doubtful."

Me, flemed wrecche, in this desert of galle	sanza la qual per questo aspro diserto [a retro va chi più di gir s'affanna.]

> . . . without which [that is, manna] he backward goes through this harsh desert [who most labors to advance.] [*Purg.*, p. 109.]

It is highly doubtful that Chaucer took the aforementioned phrase from the *Commedia*, where the only thing in common is the word *diserto* and the idea that a desert is *aspro*. Dante's paraphrase of the Lord's Prayer is emphasizing an entirely different aspect of a not-uncommon image. The comparison of this life to a wilderness (that is, a desert) can be seen, for example, in "vox clamantis in deserto."

Bethel: "68–70: the phrasing of the reference to St. Anne was possibly suggested by *Par.* XXXIII, 133–35."

Be myn advocat in that heighe place Theras withouten ende is songe "Osanne," Thow Cristes mooder, doghter deere of Anne!	[See discussion under *MLT* B^1 641f.]

Bethel: "71–74: a phrase or two may have been suggested by *Par.* XXXIII, 31–36."

And of thy light my soule in prison lighte, That troubled is by the contagioun Of my body, and also by the wighte Of erthely lust and fals affeccioun	perché tu ogne nube li disleghi di sua mortalità co' prieghi tuoi, sì che 'l sommo piacer li si dispieghi. Ancor ti priego, regina, che puoi ciò che tu vuoli, che conservi sani, dopo tanto veder, li affetti suoi.

> that with thy prayers thou wouldst dispel for him every cloud of his mortality, so that the Supreme Pleasure may be disclosed to him. Further I pray thee, Queen, who canst do whatsoever thou wilt, that thou preserve sound for him his affections, after so great a vision. [*Par.*, p. 373]

Noting the "general resemblance to the sense of Bernard's prayer," Robinson goes on to state (p. 757) that these lines "correspond much more closely to passages in the commentary of Macrobius on the Somnium Scipionis (i, 10, 9; 11, 2, 3; 8, 8, 9). This contains the figures of the prison, the contagion of the body, and the weight of earthly desire." Lowes (1917b:200–201) has pointed out several other possibilities in *Aen.* 6.730–34, Servius's commentary, and Albericus the Mythographer, where Servius and Macrobius are brought together.

The Parson's Tale

Bethel: "*574: see under *Troil.* I, 568f."

Bethel: "749: the only distinction between an idolater and an avaricious man is that the latter goes to greater extremes, for 'every florin in his cofre is mawmet.' Klaeber (*Das Bild bei Ch.*, 173) shows that this whole paragraph depends probably on *Inf.* XIX, 112ff. (cf. Miss Petersen, *Sources of Parson's Tale*, 67)."

What difference is bitwixe an ydolastre and an avaricious man, but that an ydolastre, per aventure, ne hath but o mawmet or two, and the avaricious man hath manye? For certes, every floryn in his cofre is his mawmet. / And certes the synne of mawmettrie is the firste thyng that God deffended in the ten comaundementz, as bereth witnesse in *Exodi capitulo vicesimo*.	Fatto v'avete dio d'oro e d'argento; e che altro è da voi a l'idolatre, se non ch'elli uno, e voi ne orate cento?

You have made you a god of gold and silver; and wherein do you differ from the idolators, save that they worship one, and you a hundred? [*Inf.*, p. 201]

The parallel here rests not on the comparison of the idolater to the avaricious man but, as Bethel points out, on the distinction of the one or two false gods of the latter.[40]

The basic idea of the avaricious man as an idolater is found throughout the Scriptures. Besides the story of the golden calf in Exodus, which the Parson cites, there are such phrases as "Avarus...est idolorum servitus" ("covetous person [which is the service of idols]") (Eph. 5.5, also cited by the Parson), "Avaritiam quae est simulacrorum servitus" ("covetousness, which is the service of idols") (Col. 3.5), "Argentum suum et aurum suum fecerunt sibi idola" ("of their silver and gold they have made idols to themselves") (Hos. 8.4), and "Simulacra gentium argentum et aurum" ("The idols of the Gentiles are silver and gold") (Ps. 113.4; King James, Ps. 115, ending "the work of men's hands"; translations Rheims-Douay Version).

Nor had these passages or the sin escaped notice. Tawney's investigations (1948)[41] show how much this question was in the foreground of ecclesiastical legislation:

> The high-water mark of the ecclesiastical attack on usury was probably reached in the legislation of the Councils of Lyons (1274) and of Vienne (1312). The former...virtually made the moneylender an outlaw. No individual or society, under pain of excommunication or interdict, was to let houses to usurers.... They were to be refused confession, absolution, and Christian burial, until they made restitution.... The legislation of the Council of Vienne was even more sweeping.... Any person obstinately declaring that usury is not a sin is to be punished as a heretic, and inquisitors are to proceed against him *tanquam contra diffamatos vel suspectos de haeresi* [as if against those accused by report, or suspected, of heresy]. [Tawney, p. 46][42]

---

[40] The Parson uses the "mawmet" image again in his sermon: "Certes, be it wyf, be it child, or any worldly thyng that he loveth biforn God, it is his mawmet, and he is an ydolastre" (lines 860–65).

[41] With reference to the problem here, see the section in Tawney entitled "The Sin of Avarice," pp. 36–55.

[42] Tawney's citation is from *Corpus juris canonici*, Clementinarum, lib. 5, tit. 5, cap. 1.

The numbers of sermons and tracts that lashed out at the avaricious man as an idolater must have been legion in the fourteenth century. One example among the patristic writers shows how close the Parson's argument was to the accepted thinking of the time:

> But hear what saying "a greedy man" has imparted, that is, it signifies one greedy for idols, whose God is money. Therefore avarice is equated with idolatry, since just as the idolater usurps the worship due to God and lays claim to it for himself, so the greedy man usurps and hides away from the poor the things of God which he wants to be kept.[43]

This is not to deny the very definite possibility that the Parson's distinction between an idolater and an avaricious man might have come from the passage in the *Inferno* but rather to show that such a distinction might well have been a common sermon image of the time. In any event, Klaeber's ascription certainly seems plausible.

Bethel: "*771–74: Chaucer's arguments here, that monarchy was ordained to maintain (1) the 'estaat or holy chirche,' (2) 'commune profit,' and (3) 'pees and reste on erthe,' echo Dante's discussion of monarchical necessity in chapter IV of the fourth tractate of the *Convivio*. Cf. esp. (1) *Conv*. IV, iv, 6; (2) *Conv*. IV, iv, 1; (3) *Conv*. IV, 4."

But certes, sith the time of grace cam, God ordeyned that som folk sholde be moore heigh in estaat and in degree, and som folk moore lough, and that everich sholde be served in his estaat and in his degree. / And therfore in somme contrees, ther they byen thralles, whan they han turned hem to the feith, they maken hire thralles free out of thraldom. And therfore, certes, the lord oweth to his man that the man oweth to his lord. / The Pope calleth hymself servant of the servantz of God; but for as muche as the estaat of hooly chirche ne myghte nat han be, ne the commune profit myghte nat han be kept, ne pees and rest in erthe, but if God hadde ordeyned that som men hadde hyer degree and som men lower, / therfore was sovereyntee ordeyned, to kepe and mayntene and deffenden hire underlynges or hire subgetz in resoun, as ferforth as it lith in hire power, and nat to destroyen hem ne confounde. /

Questo vedemo ne le religioni, ne li esserciti, in tutte quelle cose che sono, come detto è, a fine ordinate. Per che manifestamente vedere si può che a perfezione de la universale religione de la umana spezie conviene essere uno, quasi nocchiero, che, considerando le diverse condizioni del mondo, a li diversi e necessari offici ordinare abbia del tutto universale e inrepugnabile officio di comandare. [4.4.6]

La fondamento radicale de la imperiale maiestade, secondo lo vero, è la necessità de la umana civilitade, che a uno fine è ordinata, cioè a vita felice; a la quale nullo per sè è sufficiente a venire sanza l'aiutorio d'alcuno, con ciò sia cosa che l'uomo abbisogna di molte cose, a le quali uno solo satisfare non può. E però dice lo Filosofo che l'uomo naturalmente è compagnevole animale. [4.4.1]

Il perchè, a queste guerre e le loro cagioni torre via, conviene di necessitade tutta la terra, e quanto a l'umana generazione a possedere è dato, essere Monarchia, cioè uno solo principato, e uno prencipe avere; lo quale, tutto possedendo e più desiderare non possendo, li regi tegna contenti ne li termini de li regni, sì che pace intra loro sia, ne la quale si posino le cittadi, e in questa posa le vicinanze s'amino, in questo amore le case

---

[43] Petrus Lombardus, *Collectanea in Epist. de Pauli*, 5, in Migne, *Pat. Lat.* 117.209. Cited in Makarewicz 1953:174.

> prendano ogni loro bisogno, lo qual preso,
> l'uomo viva felicemente; che è quello per che
> esso è nato. [4.4.4]

We see an example of this in religious brotherhoods and in armies, and in everything which, as has been said, is adapted to some end. Wherefore we may see plainly that in order to make the universal brotherhood of the human species perfect, there must needs be one captain, as it were, who, studying the different conditions of the world, and arranging the various necessary offices, should have a universal and incontestable office of command over the whole. [P. 203]

The root and ground of the imperial majesty is, in truth, the necessity of man's social state, which is ordained for a single end, namely, a life of happiness; to which no one is able to attain by himself without the aid of some one else, inasmuch as man has need of many things for which a single individual cannot suffice. And therefore the Philosopher says that man is by nature a "companionable animal." [Pp. 201–202]

Wherefore, in order to do away with these wars and their causes, it is necessary that the whole earth, and all that is given to the race of man to possess, should be a monarchy, that is to say, a single princedom; and should have a single prince, who, possessing everything, and having nothing left to desire, should keep kings confined within the borders of their kingdoms, so that peace should reign between them, and townships should rest in peace, and while they so rest neighbourhoods should love each other, and in this mutual love families should satisfy all their wants; and when these are satisfied, a man should live happily, which is the end for which he is born. [P. 202]

There would seem to be very little basis for comparison here. In his discussion of avarice Chaucer is talking not of monarchy but of the hierarchical society in which he lived. The justification of the social structure is found throughout the philosophical literature of the Middle Ages. The question of order naturally led to the question of monarchy, which was supported by both the political and theological *Weltanschauungen* of the time. For his view of a universal *Roman* empire, Dante merely stressed nationalistic thinking in the specific arguments of Aristotle, as he read them in Aquinas.[44] The point that is being stressed here is, obviously, that the hierarchical concept of society, its divine sanction and the purpose of this "sovereyntee," were not only common knowledge but the very basis of medieval political and social thought.

Peace, prosperity, and the maintenance of Holy Church are certainly not unusual arguments to offer as *raisons d'être* for human government. Dante, here and in the *De monarchia*, offers these and many others, but the argument in tractate 4 has as its basic purpose the demonstration of the need not of social ranks as viewed in Chaucer but of a

---

[44] Cf. the sources given in *Convivio* (Dante 1934), which include "Aristotle, *Metaphysics*, 1, 12, cap. 10, and Aquinas, *Comment.*, lect. 12, n. 2661–63; Aquinas, *Contra Gent.*, lib. 3, cap. 64, 1; *Summa* 1, quest. 103, art. 3, and 1, 2, quest. 13, arts. 4–5; *Comment. Ethic.*, lib. 3, lect. 5, n. 444. Also Aristotle, *Politics*, lib. 1, lect. 3; Albertus Magnus, *Polit.*, lib. 1, cap. 3; Egidio Colonna, *De regimine principum*, lib. 3, p. 2, cap. 3, and lib. 1, cap. 2; and Aquinas, *Comment. Polit.*, lib. 3, lect. 3, as well as the beginning of the introduction of the *Comment. metaph.*" Dante was not, of course, original in his glorification of Rome. For this one can find authority in Saint Augustine *De civit. Dei* 5.1; Orosius *Hist. adversus paganos* 2.1; and *De regimine principum* 3.4, among other places.

world emperor and a world empire, both of which (according to Dante's interpretation of the Scriptures) God has ordained to be Italian. Indeed, in the first citation (4.4.6) Dante is speaking not of monarchy defending Holy Church but of the strict rank that is found in the religious orders. Likewise, the argument for the necessity of order to maintain peace hardly needs a source.[45] There are, then, no real parallels in the *Convivio*. In fact, Chaucer had no need for sources of the ideas as he presents them here; he merely had to be alive sometime before October 31, 1517, or perhaps July 14, 1789.

Bethel: "*773: see under *Troil*. I, 15; doubtful."

The Pope calleth hymself servant of the
servantz of God

TC 1.15 is the line "For I that God of Loves servantz serve," which Bethel had tried formerly to connect with *Inf*. 15.112, "Colui potei che dal servo de' servi." This citation of "the Pope calleth hymself servant of the servantz of God," a direct translation of *servus servorum Dei*, should totally negate even the most doubtful sort of ascription to the *Inferno*. To suggest that this use, in *The Parson's Tale*, unquestionable as its common source is, may be due in some way to Dante seems to point up again the inherent weakness of the single-source approach to an author.

---

[45] It permeates, of course, the patristic writings. Cf., for example, Aquinas *Contra gent*. 3.146, and also 89, 111, 128, 129.

CHAPTER 8

The Minor Poems

The Complaint unto Pity

Bethel: "This whole poem shows the influence of the *dolce stil nuovo*. 64–98: in general, the struggle between Pity and Cruelty and several other ideas seem to indicate Chaucer's use of one of Dante's "Pietra" poems. (Rima CII)."

From Bethel's discussion in chapter 4 of his thesis it would seem that he has confused the *dolce stil nuovo* and the French poems of courtly love. If we may speak in the broadest terms, the formality, style, personifications, and poetic techniques in this complaint are far more in keeping with the poetry of the school of *cortoisie* than of *dolce stil nuovo*. In fact, there seems little or nothing of the Italian school in the content of the poem, if Dante or Guinizelli is to be taken as a standard. There is none of the ethos of *gentilezza*, no adoration of the woman with that uniquely religious sense of Love, nothing like Dante's "Amor e 'l cor gentil sono una cosa" ("Love and the gentle heart are but one thing"), or "Tanto gentile e tanto onesta pare / La mia donna" ("So gracious and so decorous appears my lady"), or Guinizelli's "al cor gentil ripara sempre Amore" ("to the gentle heart Love repairs always"), or his "Foco d'amor in gentil cor s'apprende" ("The fire of love betakes itself to the gentle heart"). Pity is not dead in the *dolce stil nuovo* but is inherent in the *cor gentil* and is a manifestation of *gentilezza* just as cruelty cannot possibly be a part of someone who is "gentil e . . . onesta." Finally, one of the principal thematic differences can be pointed out here: where the poetry of courtly love had a tendency to use allegory, the *dolce stil nuovo* tended to stress the religious and at times even the anagogical; the one seems to stress human perfectability, the other divine perfection. Robinson's note (1957:855) emphasizes justly that this complaint is fully in the tradition of that genre of writing:

> The source, if Chaucer had one, is unknown. Skeat suggested the notion of personifying Pity came from Statius, and he compared the struggle between Pity and Cruelty in the Thebaid, xi. But the parallel is remote. In Statius Pietas checks the Furies in their attempt to bring on war; and in Chaucer Pity is concerned with the affairs of love. And a lady's Pity or Mercy toward her lover was commonly personified in allegorical verse of Chaucer's age. For instances where it is represented as destroyed or dead see Flügel in Angl. XXIII, 196. Professor Brusendorff (p. 270), on the evidence of rather dubious parallel passages, argued for the influence of Dante and Petrarch.

Bethel: "92: Herenus queene; the reference is probably due to Dante's description of the Furies, *Inf*. IX, 34–51, a passage upon which Chaucer draws on several occasions."[1]

First of all, it must be recognized that any interpretative suggestions for this line are highly dangerous because of textual difficulties. Robinson's textual note (p. 916) gives the following variant readings: "*herenus (heremus, herenius?)* β Th; *vertuous*(e) α; *serenous* Globe em." Robinson's comments on the line (p. 856) show, in part, the difficulties incurred:

> *Herenus*, which has the best MS. support, is usually taken to be an error or corruption for *Herines*, the Erinyes, the three Furies (cf. *Tr.*, iv, 22). Chaucer's reason for calling Pity the queen of the Furies is uncertain. Skeat took it to mean that she alone was supposed to be able to control them, and he referred again to the struggle between Pietas and Tisiphone in Statius. Professor Lowes (MP, XIV, 723) has sought an explanation in the Inferno, ix, 44 ff., where Proserpine is represented as the "queen of everlasting lamentation," and the Furies ("le feroci Erine") as her handmaids. In *Tr.*, iv, 789, he points out, the Elysian Fields are called the *feld of pite*, and Chaucer may thus have connected the figure of Pity with the queen of Elysium. The association of ideas is possible, though by no means obvious. Flügel (Angl., XXIII, 205) rejected *Herenus* altogether, and favored the emendation *my hertes quene*. The Globe edition reads *serenous*, Professor Liddell's emendation. Koch adopts the reading *vertuouse* (MSS. Harl. 78 and 7578, Add. 34360).

The first important point is that Herenus is not a clear reading; the second point is that, even if it were a clear reading and even if the emendation to Herines were authorized, Herines—as Robinson remarks—simply does not make sense within the context of the poem. Chaucer, who is trying to differentiate precisely between Cruelty and Pity, would not want to connect the two personifications by referring to Proserpine, nor (assuming Lowes's explanation for the moment) would he want to make the confusion of the two characters complete by referring to Proserpine in her capacity of queen of the Furies, the tormentors of man. Lowes's explanation seems overcomplex and seems, indeed, to forget the main poetic line which Chaucer is establishing. Finally, even granting a clear reading of Herenus, an emendation to Herines, and the reference to Proserpine that Lowes suggests, there is no definite indication of any use of Dante here. True, Spencer (1927:184) takes the stand that Proserpyne is in a region where one "compleyne(s) eternally" (*TC* 4.472–76, 785–87), and he points out more particularly in *The House of Fame* (lines 1511–12) she is "quene of the derke pyne." This is close, Spencer thinks, to *Inf*. 9.44, where the Furies are called "'le meschine / della regina dell'eterno pianto,' the handmaids of the queen of eternal lamentation" (p. 184).

But this complete mélange of the classical and the Christian was not uniquely Dantesque but of the Middle Ages. Proserpine was queen of the infernal regions by classical tradition; the infernal regions were places of eternal torment by Christian tradition; therefore, Proserpine is queen of eternal torment in medieval tradition. Spencer himself remarks (p. 199) that the inconclusiveness of source

> shows, for one thing, that in describing hell, Chaucer (as indeed we might have suspected) was entirely dependent on convention, and that his phraseology is

---

[1] For a full discussion of the passage from Dante, see *TC* 1.6–14 above.

derived from that convention; and it shows that this convention itself was (when expressed in literature) a changing one—shifting as occasion demanded, from a classical to a medieval outline, and back again.

Indeed, Spencer goes on to note this mélange more precisely (p. 199, n.1):

> An entertaining example of this Classical-Christian confusion may be seen in the 13th century poem, *Le Tournoiement d'Antecrist*, by Huge de Berti (cited in T. Wright, *St. Patrick's Purgatory*, London, 1844, p. 111 from *MS Harl* 4417) where Pluto and Proserpine appear as monarchs of hell, leading an army composed indiscriminately of Christian vices, classical deities, and the companions of Beelzebub. Cf. p. 183, n. 7.

In short, even ignoring the strong textual and poetic objections to the reading *Herenus* and the emendation *Herines*, there is every reason to suppose that Dante and Chaucer were both working from a common medieval tradition. This is far more likely than the supposition that the depiction of Proserpine was unique to Dante and that therefore Chaucer must have gained his concept of her from the Italian poet.

As a matter of fact, none of the objections mentioned so far has been met by commentators, and the citation (lines 34–51) which Bethel gives, is seen upon inspection to be exactly opposite to the carefully delineated picture of Pity that Chaucer is attempting to create.

I would suggest that a much more appropriate reading, one that is in line with the traditional poetic concepts of Pity and supporting Chaucer's description of her, would be "hevenes quene," which would bring in the whole tradition of Mariolatry and the medieval view of Mary as the one who has pity on mankind and intercedes with Christ on man's behalf. Not only would a manuscript misreading of *hevenes* be easily possible, but, once *hevenes* is accepted, there are no problems whatever of interpretation. In other words, Chaucer's lines, with this suggested reading, would maintain the conventional meaning and tone of the rest of the complaint.

A Complaint to His Lady

Bethel: "The fragments in *terza rima* (ll. 15–43) contain the first example of the use of this metre in English. The experiment with it was probably due to Chaucer's reading of the *Commedia*."

Bethel, in his text (p. 131), indicates the wider possible scope for ascription: "There is some doubt as to the immediate source of his inspiration. He might have been following Dante, Petrarch or Boccaccio, and although Dante seems his most likely source[2] one cannot be absolutely certain." If Chaucer had read through the *Commedia*, Dante would certainly have inspired, or at least strongly influenced, a metrical experiment of this sort. That the final rime of the last rime-royal stanza furnishes the initial rime of the first terza-rima section seems evident, but Skeat's suggestion (cf. Robinson, p. 916) that the last rime-royal line should be repeated verbatim, while it is interesting, is far more conjectural.

---

[2] "See Skeat, *Oxford Chaucer*, I, 76. Toynbee, *Dante in English Literature*, I, xv, and 2. Lowes *MP*, XIV, 722ff." (Bethel's note).

The Complaint of Mars

Bethel: "165f.: These lines seem to show Chaucer's assimilation of Dante's doctrine of the Intelligence; see esp. *Conv.*, II, iv, and viii, *passim*."

Once more, in dealing with any possible source here, we must attempt to understand the poetic intent and be aware of medieval tradition and thought. Bethel cites the possible source passages on the basis of Lowes's article (1915:31–32). The relevant lines from Chaucer are the opening of Mars's complaint, as given by the "foule" (lines 164–67):

> The firste tyme, alas! that I was wroght,
> And for certeyn effectes hider broght
> Be him that lordeth ech intelligence,
> I yaf my trewe servise. . . .

From the interpretative point of view it must be recognized that the entire poem would seem to be an extended pun, almost to the limits of what the seventeenth century would have called an elaborate conceit. The tone is light, a Valentine-bird poem, which soon launches, in a spirit almost equaling the high comedy that Pandarus first uses with Troilus, into a gentle mock praise of the mighty Mars (lines 43–46):

> Who regneth now in blysse but Venus,
> That hath thys worthy knyght in governaunce?
> Who syngeth now but Mars that serveth thus
> The faire Venus, causer of plesaunce?

In both matter and style the poem maintains an air of light though ingenious jesting. The subject is, on one level, the age-old comic situation the bedroom farce. It is through the verbal intricacies, however, that Chaucer achieves his tour de force. The whole poem is a play on astrological terminology. Mars is both the classical god and the planet, and Venus, Phoebus, and Cilenios also exist in dual capacities. Beneath this play, and changing it from ingenuity into true comedy, is the human application: the gallant lover, the flirtatious mistress, and the angry intruder returning to break up their affair. But Chaucer's technique saves the poem from being mere wordplay on the one hand or just another fabliau (though of nobles) on the other. Not only the characters but also the vocabulary of astrology is worked into the poem to transform it into an intricate joke of a highly comic nature. If, as has been asserted by commentators from Shirley to Brusendorff (cf. Robinson, pp. 856–57), *Mars* is a *poème à clef*, then there is an additional level of interplay possible, and we are faced with a poem at least as complex as, if not more complex than, *The Parliament of Fowls*. It must be added, of course, that "the astronomical data which underlie Chaucer's narrative have been carefully worked out by Skeat and Manly" (Robinson, p. 857).

Now what, in essence, is the connection that Lowes makes with the *Convivio*? Basically it is the connection between Love and the astrological idea of the intelligences that rule the third sphere, i.e., that of Venus. But we must be quick to recognize that the very human Venus of whom Chaucer is writing is far different from the abstract principality that Dante was outlining, and the courtly love that Chaucer would seem to be gently mocking is far different from the Divine Love to which Dante attempts to connect his adoration. Dante's address is to the Intelligences, the movers, of the outermost of those three spheres controlled by the Holy Spirit, i.e., Love (cf. *Convivio* 2.6), and this sphere, being the outermost, is nearest the Empyrean, where Beatrice, as the Blessed Love which will help Dante to his view of the Ultimate, resides. Where Dante is using the medieval science of astrology as a stepping-stone in the deification of his concept of love *ad maiorem Dei gloriam*, Chaucer is using the same science for the wordplay of a witty love poem.

As his first connection between the *Convivio* and *Mars*, Lowes points to *Convivio* 2.5.1–8, 20–25, 28–35, seizing on the words *Intelligenze* and *effeti*. Not only are these common terms of medieval astronomy and astrology but, for Dante, these *Intelligenze* are the Platonic concept of what "la volgare gente chiama Angeli" (*Convivio* 2.5.8), and neither the Mars nor the Venus that Chaucer portrays could be connected upward to this divine frame of reference. Rather, the word "intelligence" as used in *Mars* can connect only downward, i.e., from the astrological term to its ordinary meaning of human intellect. Dante is explaining, as exactly as his sources allow him, the structure of the universe, a theme that he is to take up once again in *Par.* 28–29. Despite the statement to the contrary, the *effeti* of the Intelligences are not stressed in *Convivio* 2.5 (or 2.4, depending on the edition used), at least insofar as I have been able to discover; rather the word is used in its usual non-technical sense of "no effect is greater than the cause" (cf. *Convivio* 2.4.12–14).[3]

Lowes's second citation (1915:31) is *Convivio* 2.9.22–27, 31–33:

> Portrebbe dire alcuno: conciossiacosachè amore sia *effetto di queste Intelligenze* (a cui io parlo), e quello di prima fosse amore così come questo di poi, perchè la loro virtù corrumpe l'uno, e l'altro genera?... A questa quistione si può leggiermente rispondere, che *lo effetto di costoro è amore*, come è detto. [Lowes's italics]

Jackson's translation (Dante 1924*b*:94) reads:

> Some might say, "Inasmuch as love is the effect of these Intelligences whom I address, and that the former feeling was love just as much as the latter, why does their virtue destroy the one and give birth to the other?..." To this question it may easily be answered that the effect of these Intelligences is love, as has been said.

Just as there seems to be a confusion in the words *Intelligenze* and *effeti* in *Convivio* 2.4, so here there seems to be an overemphasis on the verbal coincidence of *effetto*, *Intelligenze*, and *amore*, which, considering Dante's subject of God and the universe, was a juxtaposition which was sure to appear eventually. What Lowes fails to note, however, is the diametrically opposed meanings of *amore* in Dante's use, and "love" in Chaucer's very earthy sense of the word. The first three spheres—the moon, Mercury, and Venus—are those ruled by the Holy Ghost, i.e., that part of the Trinity which epitomizes Divine Love. On the basis of his sources Dante is demonstrating how the astrological and divine hierarchies coincide. In the section which Lowes omits, Dante goes on to show how these Intelligences have power only over a person within their reach (i.e., someone alive) and

---

[3] There would seem to be only two points at which the word occurs. Dante, in speaking of the angelic powers, discusses the superiority of the contemplative life to the civil or active (Dante 1924*b*:83–84): "And because this life is more divine, and the more divine a thing is the more it is like God, it is manifest that this life is more beloved by God; and if it is more beloved by Him its power of conferring bliss is more ample; and if this power has been made more ample, He has apportioned more living beings to this life than to the other. Wherefore it is concluded that the number of these creatures is much greater than is shown by the effects. And this does not contradict what Aristotle seems to say in the tenth book of the *Ethics*, namely, that the contemplative life befits separate substances, as the speculative life alone befits them. However the rotation of the heaven by which the world is steered follows the contemplation of certain beings, the world being as it were a civil order conceived in the contemplation of those who moved it. The second reason is that no effect is greater than its cause, because no cause can impart that which it does not possess. Wherefore, inasmuch as the divine Intellect is the cause of all things, especially of the human intellect, for the human intellect does not exceed but is immeasurably exceeded by the divine.

how, when that person dies—as Beatrice does—they move this power onto him who was involved in that love and is still living. This, of course, has little, if any relationship to the *Mars*, but the argument continues (Lowes 1915:31): "The emphasis on 'effect' is Dante's own: 'Dico *effetto*, in quanto,' etc." The "etc." unfortunately leaves out Dante's main thought. An accepted translation of this passage shows that the emphasis is by no means on "effect," since the passage reads (Dante 1924b:95): "I use the term 'effect' in so far as soul and body conjoined are the effect of the soul; for the soul which is departed lives on without break in a nature which is more than human. So this question is resolved." Lowes's partial citation and the italicization, "Dico *effetto*, in quanto, etc.," imply that Dante (1) is emphasizing *effetto*, (2) is (by virtue of the "etc.") going to enlarge on the *effetto*, and (3) is developing a relationship that was unique enough to lead Chaucer to use it in *Mars*. Actually, as can be seen from the translation of the text, (1) Dante is emphasizing not *effetto* but the concept of transferred divine love, (2) the term *effetto* is not enlarged upon, but rather the theological concept is carried to its conclusion, and (3) this theological concept has nothing whatever to do with *Mars*, the divinely moved *amore* of the one being separated from the courtly love of the other by a world of flesh and at least three spheres of spirit.

Lowes continues (1915:31–32) with an even more questionable explication:

> In Chaucer's lines, now, it must be remembered that it is *Mars*—that is, one of the Intelligences themselves—who is speaking, and as such he declares that he has been brought hither for "certeyn [i.e., fixed, determined] effectes." In other words, he was brought and set in his place for the *effetti* that belong to the Intelligences—"[e] lo effetto di costoro è amore." [Lowes's italics and brackets]

This interpretation would certainly seem open to question, even with its admixture of Chaucer and Dante. First of all, Mars is not within that group of planets (moon, Mercury, and Venus) ruled over by the Holy Ghost and consequently whose *effetto*...*è amore*. Actually, this planet is in the second group, composed of the sun, Mars, and Jupiter, and is ruled over by the Son, who embodies the concept of Wisdom. Mars thus belongs to a totally different grouping, just as the *amore* of which Dante is speaking belongs to a concept totally different from that of Chaucer. The inherent weaknesses of the argument are pointed out in an accompanying footnote (Lowes, p. 31, n.5), which supplies the following very pertinent information:

> Into Chaucer's variation from Dante in his use of "the third heaven" (l. 29) it is not necessary to go. Mars is not, strictly speaking, one of the intelligences *of the third heaven*. But Chaucer's whole conception in the poem is as far removed from that of Dante's canzone as the conception of the *House of Fame* is remote from that of the *Divine Comedy*, and his recollection of certain phrases must be treated, in the one case as in the other, independently of any idea that he is following in Dante's footsteps in his *plan*. It is only a single idea and its phraseology that is involved. [Lowes's italics]

The explication, however, continues (Lowes, p. 32):

> And the reference to "him that *lordeth* ech intelligence" is no less clear. The canzone is directly addressed, as we have seen, to the Intelligences, and in the address Dante names his "soave pensier," that went often "a piè del vostro Sire." In the comment this line receives its explanation: "...questro pensiero che se ne già spesse volte a' piè *del Sire di costoro a cui io parlo, ch' è Iddio*. [Lowes's italics]

(Jackson [Dante 1924b] translates the pertinent passages above as "A suave thought, who went oft-times to the feet of your Lord" [p. 71], and ". . . that thought which oft-times departed to the feet of the 'Lord' of those to whom I address myself, who is God" [p. 92].) Save for the fact that Dante could not possibly have had Mars in mind when addressing the Intelligences of the third sphere or, even more generally, when addressing the Intelligences who are within the realm of Love, the explanation of Dante can be accepted. There follows an unfortunate attempt (despite the footnote) to correlate the entire poem on a basically false premise (Lowes, p. 32):

> Chaucer's lines, accordingly, in the light of their sources, are clear. Mars complains that as one of the Intelligences he was created by his lord — "the god that sit so hye" (l. 218) — to fulfill the very end of his existence, which end was love. He *has* loved — has given to his lady his true service and his thought, and his love has ended in "misaventure." The cause of his complaint, on which he lays stress, lies therefore deep enough. [Lowes's italics]

It is to be noted, of course, that there is no clear statement that the end for which Mars was created[4] was love; certainly such a theory receives no support from the passages in Dante. But is there any justification for the gloss of "created"? If this is how we are to take "wroght," then the phrase "the *firste* tyme" (my italics) is vague. If, however, we read the line as being in the same tenor as the rest of the poem, that is, in the sense of astrological wordplay, then the line fits in with the meaning and tone of what precedes and what follows. Likewise, one should be extremely wary of trying to give the poem the depth of Dante's religious philosophy by connecting, through the word "lordeth," Dante's Iddio and Mars's "god that sit so hye." Dante would hardly have accused his *Sire* or claimed: "Hit semeth he hath to lovers enmyte" (line 236). But then Dante, it must be repeated, is talking of *l'amor che move il sole e l'altre stelle* (*Par.* 33.145),[5] which is far removed from Mars's complaint that "joy, for oght I can espye, / Ne lasteth not the twynkelyng of an ye" (lines 221–28). Indeed, on closer examination, we see that the complaint is a completely independent piece, done in the full tradition of the formalities of the genre and totally lacking organic connection with the rest of the poem.

Lowes's argument concludes (p. 32): "The fact that Dante's whole doctrine of the Intelligences is implicit in two lines is evidence again of Chaucer's power of assimilation. And his ability to "reject what cannot clear him" is no less striking. For what he takes from the *Convivio* (as well as how he takes it) and what he leaves are equally significant." Now, if there had been no other book available to Chaucer save the *Convivio*, there would perhaps be a temptation to make a connection, however, weak, between *Mars* and Dante, but the number of sources for astrological information was very large and stretches far back into antiquity (see, for example, Dreyer 1953). The concept of Intelligences can be taken as far back as the Platonic theory of Ideas, to which Dante refers directly at *Conv.* 2.5.21–34 and 4.15.55. As Moore (1896:163) notes, such a concept might have come from the *Timaeus*, but more probably would have come from Aristotle, Cicero,[6] Saint Augustine, or Saint Thomas (Moore, pp. 163, 377). We may safely assume that many of these

---

[4] If this reading is valid, then the act must be certainly by God, for who else in Chaucer's mind could create in this sense?

[5] It seems hardly necessary to add that the previous erotic passages can scarcely be considered as setting the stage for the high seriousness that Lowes suggests.

[6] "Orator, c. iii: 'Ut igitur in formis et figuris est aliquod perfectum et excellens cuius ad cogitatem speciem referentur ea quae sub oculos ipsa cadunt; &c. Has rerum formas apellat ideas. . . Plato, esque gigni negat, et ait semper esse, &c'" (Moore's note).

sources, in one form or another, would also have been available to Chaucer. Grandgent, in his edition of the *Commedia*, gives still another array of writers. He notes the "Neo-Platonic treatise... dealing with the heavens and Heavenly Intelligences" (Dante 1933:xxx) entitled

> *De Caelesti Hierarchia*, sometimes called the Pseudo-Dionysius. This work, attributed to St. Paul's disciple, "Dionysius the Areopagite," was translated into Latin in the 9th century by the Irish monk and mystic, Johannes Scotus Erigena; in the first half of the 12th century an elaborate commentary on this version was composed by Johannes Sarracenus, a friend of John of Salisbury. St. Thomas, in his *Summa Theologiae*, uses both versions and also, apparently, the original; in his commentary on Dionysius's *De Divinis Nominibus* he uses always the Sarracenus version. [Dante 1933:915]

These sources too were available to Chaucer, though in the final analysis, when we consider the extent to which he used astrology in *The Canterbury Tales* and *Troilus*, among other places, we would be hard pressed to find *the* source and would probably, once more, be safer in attributing such information to the general knowledge of Chaucer's world (cf. Harrison 1947:31, 34–36). "The nature and influence of the planets was discussed in innumerable treatises" (Bennett 1953:103), and it is not strange that the writer of one of the astrolabe should have a fairly close acquaintance with the astrological and astronomical concepts and terminology of his day.

It would seem, therefore, that we have no real evidence of overall indebtedness to Dante. Indeed, the two parts of *Mars* seem so unintegrated that even the most simple suggestion of a unifying Dantesque idea must be treated with extreme caution. There are, of course, other possible sources for the story and idea of the *Complaint*. The love affair of Mars and Venus is in Ovid's *Metamorphoses* (4.167–89) and the *Ovide moralisé* (4.1268–1371), though here it is Vulcan who interrupts the two and, chaining them, holds them up to ridicule. The concept of the story of the loves of Mars and Venus as an allusion to the nature of the planets and the influence that they exercise on each other can be found in the commentary on the above in the *Ovide moralisé* (4.1488–1537), while allegories, explications, and antiadultery statements run throughout the moralized portion from line 1488 to line 1755. Here again, however, we are dealing with one possible source among many, though this one does seem more relevant than the amorphous suggestion by which Lowes seeks to connect Chaucer and Dante.

The Former Age

Bethel: "7f: Skeat (*Oxf. Ch.*, I, 539f.) compares *Purg.*, XXII, 148f. In this stanza Chaucer is following Boethius (*Cons. Phil.*, II, m. V), but, as these lines are not exactly parallel in the *Cons.*, Dante may also have been in his mind."

They eten mast, hawes, and swich pounage, And dronken water of the colde welle.	Lo secol primo, quant' oro fu bello. fé savorose con fame le ghiande, e nettare con sete ogne ruscello

The first age was fair as gold: with hunger it made acorns savory, and with thirst made every streamlet nectar. [*Purg.*, p. 245]

In his notes to the poem Robinson (p. 859) is quick to point out that

> the tradition of the Golden Age has been familiar in literature since antiquity.... However many expressions of the doctrine Chaucer knew, his actual sources for the *Former Age* were apparently few. He drew chiefly upon Boethius, ii, m. 5, and made use also of Ovid's Met., i, 89–112; of RR, 8355ff.; and possibly of Virgil's Fourth Eclogue 32f.

The extended treatment which Chaucer gives the subject here would appear to preclude the brief mention in Dante. Indeed, the lines cited above have a close resemblance to Boethius, or to Boethius's more obvious source, Ovid, which Chaucer might have read in the *Ovide moralisé*. Comparison of the entire poem with the related portions of Boethius and Ovid—either in the original or in the moralised version—show how unnecessary Dante is for the lines which Bethel has cited. The Boethius metrum reads:

> Blisful was the firste age of men. They heelden hem apayed with the metes that the trewe feeldes broughten forth. They ne destroyeden ne desseyvede nat hemself with outrage. They weren wont lyghtly to slaken hir hungir at even with accornes of ookes. They ne coude nat medle the yift of Bachus to the cleer hony (*that is to seyn, they coude make no pyment or clarree*), ne they coude nat medle the bryghte fleeses of the contre of Seryens with the venym of Tyrie (*this is to seyn, thei coude nat deyen white fleeses of Syrien contre with the blood of a maner schellefyssch that men fynden in Tirie, with which blood men deyen purpre*). They slepen holsome slepes upon the gras, and dronken of the rennynge watres, and layen undir the schadwes of the heye pyn-trees. Ne no gest ne straunger ne karf yit the heye see with oores or with schipes; ne thei ne hadden seyn yit none newe stroondes to leden marchandise into diverse contrees. Tho weren the cruele clariouns ful hust and ful stille. Ne blood ischad by egre hate ne hadde nat deyed yit armures. For wherto or which woodnesse of enemys wolde first moeven armes, whan thei seyen cruele wowndes, ne none medes be of blood ishad? I wolde that our tymes shold torne ayen to the oolde maneris! But the anguysschous love of havynge brenneth in folk more cruely than the fyer of the mountaigne of Ethna that ay brenneth. Allas! what was he that first dalf up the gobbettes or the weyghtes of gold covered undir erthe and the precyous stones that wolden han be hydd? He dalf up precious periles. (*That is to seyn, that he that hem first up dalf, he dalf up a precious peril; for-why, for the preciousnesse of swich thyng hath many man ben in peril.*)

Ovid's description of the *aetas aurea* supplies practically all of Boethius's information (cf. *Met.* 1.89–112 and 127–43), and the *Ovide moralisé* (1.454–512, 944–91) would appear to supply whatever the other two did not. The lines which Bethel has pointed out as not being from Boethius—though he must mean in the sense of precise verbal source—are probably from *Met.* 1.105–107, and *Ovide moralisé* 1.492–98.[7] The close use of Ovid and the

---

[7] Cf. "[contenti] in duris haerentia mora rubetis, / Et, quae deciderant patula Jovis arbore, glandes. / Ver erat aeternum..." ("[Content with] berries hanging thick upon the prickly branble, and acorns fallen from the spreading tree of Jove. Then spring was everlasting..." [Ovid 1916:3.9]; and "Les boutons, les freses mengoient, / Cormes et mores et faïnes, / Et les glandes et les racines; / Sans arer estoient de blé / La terre et li champ tout comblé; / Adont corient les rivieres / Par la terre..." ("They ate buds, strawberries, cornfruit, cherries, beechnuts, acorns, and roots; without plowing, the land and the fields were covered with wheat; and the rivers ran through the land").

French version can be seen throughout; for example, line 9 ("Yit nas the ground nat wounded with the plough") is *Met.* 1.101–102:

> Ipsa quoque immunis rastroque intacta, ne ullis
> Saucia vomeribus per se dabat omnia tellus.

[The earth herself, without compulsion, untouched by hoe or plowshare, of herself gave all things needful. (Ovid 1916:1.101–102).]

and *Ovide moralisé* 1.488–90:

> La terre, sans cultiveüre
> De soich et de coultre donnoit
> A touz quanqu'il lor convenoit.

[The earth, without cultivation by plowshare or coulter, gave to all whatever they needed.]

Nor should one forget the evidence of *The Roman de la Rose* here and in other parts of the poem (Fansler 1914:55–56, 223), though Ovid is undoubtedly the largest influence, as line-for-line parallels can show. If there is any connection with Dante, it is only through a common source once more, this time the *Metamorphoses*, from which both poets drew, though Chaucer more heavily than Dante.

Bethel: "*59f: spelling of *Nembrot* possibly from Dante; cf. *Inf.* XXXI, 77; *Purg.* XII, 34; *Par.* XXVI, 126; – doubtful."

One can only agree with Bethel on the uncertainty of a dependence based on spelling, since it is hardly an exclusive feature of Dante.

Fortune

Bethel: "This poem contains evidences of the influence of Jean de Meun, Boethius, and Dante, in the treatment of the various attitudes towards the goddess Fortuna.
  "65–71: This stanza shows the influence of Dante's conception of Fortune, both in its thought and phraseology; cf. (1) *Inf.* VII, 67–96; *(2) *Conv.* IV, iv, 9; v, 1 f., & 9."

Lo, th'execucion of the majestee
That al purveyeth of his rightwysnesse,
That same thing "Fortune" clepen ye,
Ye blinde bestes, ful of lewednesse!
The hevene hath propretee of
  sikernesse,
This world hath ever resteles travayle;
Thy laste day is ende of myn intresse

"Maestro mio," diss' io, "or mi dì anche:
  questa fortuna di che tu mi tocche,
  che è, che i ben del mondo ha sì tra
    branche?"
E quelli a me: "Oh creature sciocche,
  quanta ignoranza è quella che v'offende!
  Or vo' che tu mia sentenza ne 'mbocche.
Colui lo cui saver tutto trascende,
  fece li cieli e diè lor chi conduce
  sì, ch'ogne parte ad ogne parte splende,
  distribuendo igualmente la luce.
    Similemente a li splendor mondani
    ordinò general ministra e duce
che permutasse a tempo li ben vani
  di gente in gente e d'uno in altro sangue,

oltre la difension d'i senni umani;
per ch'una gente impera e l'altra langue,
seguendo lo giudicio di costei,
che è occulto, come in erba l'angue.
Vostro saver non ha contasto a lei:
questa provede, giudica, e persegue
suo regno come il loro li altri dèi.
Le sue permutazion non hanno triegue:
necessità la fa esser veloce;
sì spesso vien chi vicenda consegue.
Quest' è colei ch'è tanto posta in croce
pur da color che le dovrien dar lode,
dandole biasmo a torto e mala voce;
ma ella s'è beata e ciò non ode:
con l'altre prime creature lieta
volve sua spera e beata si gode."

"Master," I said, "now tell me further: this Fortune which you touch on here, what is it, which has the goods of the world so in its clutches?"

And he to me, "O foolish creatures, how great is the ignorance that besets you! I would have you receive my judgment on this now. He whose wisdom transcends all, made the heavens and gave them guides, so that every part shines to every part, equally distributing the light. In like manner, for worldly splendors He ordained a general minister and guide who should in due time transfer the vain goods from race to race, and from one to another blood, beyond the prevention of human wit, so that one race rules and another languishes, pursuant to her judgment, which is hidden like the snake in the grass. Your wisdom cannot withstand her: she foresees, judges, and pursues her reign, as theirs the other gods. Her changes know no truce. Necessity compels her to be swift, so fast do men come to their turns. This is she who is much reviled even by those who ought to praise her, but do wrongfully blame her and defame her. But she is blest and does not hear it. Happy with the other primal creatures she turns her sphere and rejoices in her bliss. [*Inf.*, pp. 73, 75]

Now the queston is, What is in the Chaucer passage that "shows the influence of Dante's conception of Fortune"? What is here that makes it relate to Dante as opposed to other philosophers of the Middle Ages? Grandgent (Dante 1933:67) points out the distinctive quality of Dante in his Argument to this canto: "In many of his utterances about Fortune, Dante evidently follows Boethius, in whom, as later in Albertus Magnus, there appears not only the pagan but also a distinctly Christian conception of her as God's instrument; but her rank as an angelic intelligence is bestowed by Dante himself." Grandgent's remarks are based on Patch's excellent studies (1922) of the evolution of the goddess Fortuna, and his analysis of this specific passage in Dante is worth quoting at length (pp. 201–202):

The treatment [of Fortune] is a fusion of the old traits of the pagan goddess with Christian doctrine. Fortuna is pagan and Boethian in that she embodies the pagan whimsicality in outward manner and is yet subordinate to a greater Deity; she does not award necessarily according to merit, and yet her madness has method because she is obeying the decrees of a superior will. To give her official recognition as an angelic power with her own peculiar duties, was a step

Boethius and Albertus Magnus did not take. So far as Italy is concerned, this is an entirely new poetical conception, however much suggestive material Dante might have found in his predecessors. The most original touch is that of the martyrdom of the goddess ("Quest' è colei ch' è tanto posta in croce"); but we are told that she is quite serene about it, because, of course, she knows the heavenly plan ("beata si gode"). The picture is, like everything in Dante, sublime.

According to Patch, the three characteristics of Fortune that are peculiar to Dante—though there is a problem of translation with the second—are the following: (1) she is (in Grandgent's words) "a power similar to the celestial intelligences that move the heavens. She may be called the Angel of the Earth" (Dante 1933:67); (2) she is suffering martyrdom; [8] (3) she is serene because she is a part—no matter how distant from the center—of the divine plan. Here it should be remarked that Jefferson (1917:134–35) has listed the sources, predominantly from Boethius but also in part from the *Romaunt de la Rose* and from convention, of at least fifty-four lines of this balade, and he discusses the extent of the borrowing elsewhere (pp. 57–60). The source for lines 65–69 he gives as *De cons.* 5, met. 1.13–15, and 4, pr. 6.42–46; and, for line 71, *De cons.* 2, pr 3.58–61.

But before looking directly at other possible sources, let us compare those elements which are peculiar to Dante's conception of Fortune with the stanza from Chaucer:

1. Chaucer does not make an angelic intelligence of Fortune. True, she does execute the divine plan and is ruled by a higher power, but this is different from being made an intelligence which was the solution peculiar to Dante. Indeed, as I hope to show, Chaucer's was a conception that has other possible sources.

2. There are two possibilities for *posata in croce*": (a) if we take it to mean martyred, as Patch does, there is no parallel in Chaucer, and (b) if we take it to mean reviled, then we have as source almost every poem from the very start of the Fortuna cult.

3. Dante's Fortune "is in bliss," and, in fact, like the other *prime creature lieta* (i.e., like the other angels who control and are the intelligences of a sphere) she *volve sua spera, e beata si gode*. She is, in other words, apart from the world and ruling it only as a mechanical agent of the blessed paradise, like the other angels impersonal to all save the Divine Will. As a matter of fact, it is this very point that Dante's Virgil is making throughout his discourse; not only is Fortune not subject to mankind, but *ciò non ode*, she doesn't even hear them reviling her, or blaming her "with evil words." As a part of the divine plan, she is far above such mundane matters and this, in effect, is Dante's "complete Christian Fortuna" (Patch 1922:200), which takes her out of the world of man and puts her in the realm of the Divine; it is the answer, or at least the resolution, of the traditional Fortune of the Middle Ages. Fortune's turning wheel is replaced by Dante with a turning sphere. Now this concept of Fortune is exactly what Chaucer's is not. Chaucer's Fortune is the traditional one, not an angel but the defendant answering charges "countre le Pleintif" and very definitely listening to and hearing the blame which is being cast upon her.

On the other hand, Boethius's conception of Fortuna, which contains "the promise of practically every theme and formula that were used down through the Middle Ages" (Patch 1922:200), is parallel to Chaucer's. The lady Philosophy, appearing to the author, who has been unjustly imprisoned, "discourses on the ways in which he can accept

---

[8] Exception must be taken to this translation of *tanto posta in croce*, which, though literally meaning "placed on the cross," i.e., "crucified," is much more figurative and closer to Singleton's and to Carlyle-Wicksteed's translation, "reviled," or to Grandgent's notation, "cursed" or "vilified."

Fortuna, and . . . represents Fortuna as personally appearing to him and defending her-self" (Patch 1922:190). Perhaps now one can look at the philosophical "compromise," to use Patch's term, which Boethius and others worked out to incorporate Fortuna in a Christian *Weltanschauung*. Though this same idea that is expressed in Chaucer pervades the *De consolatione*, I shall try to limit myself, for convenience's sake, to 4, pr. 6, and 2, pr. 3, where the two aspects of Fortune are analyzed. Corresponding lines from Chaucer's *Fortune* appear in brackets:

> "The engendrynge of alle thinges," quod sche, "and alle the progressiouns of muable nature, and al that moeveth in any manere, taketh his causes, his ordre, and his formes, of the stablenesse of the devyne thought [cf. Chaucer's "The hevene hath propretee of sikernesse"]. And thilke devyne thought that is iset and put in the tour (*that is to seyn, in the heighte*) of the simplicite of God, stablissith many maner gises to thinges that ben to done; the whiche manere whan that men looken it in thilke pure clennesse of the devyne intelligence, it is ycleped purveaunce; but whanne thilke manere is referred by men to thinges that it moeveth and disponyth, than of olde men it was clepyd destyne. . . . For purveaunce is thilke devyne resoun that is establissed in the sovereyn prince of thinges, the whiche purveaunce disponith alle thinges [cf. Chaucer's "That al purveyeth of his rightwysnesse"]; but, certes, destyne is the disposicioun and ordenaunce clyvyng to moevable thinges, by the whiche disposicion the pur-veaunce knytteth alle thingis in hir ordres; for purveaunce enbraceth alle thinges to-hepe, althogh that thei ben diverse and although thei ben infinit. . . . Thanne, whethir that destyne be exercised outhir by some devyne spiritz, servantz to the devyne purveaunce, or elles by som soule, or elles by all nature servynge to God, or elles by the celestial moevynges of sterres, or elles by vertu of aungelis, or elles by divers subtilite of develis, or elles by any of hem, or elles by hem alle; the destinal ordenaunce is ywoven and acomplissid. . . . Thanne ryght swich comparysoun as is of . . . the cercle to the centre; ryght so is the ordre of moevable destyne to the stable symplicite of purveaunce. Thilke ordenaunce moveth the hevene and the sterres, and atemprith the elementz togidre amonges hemself, and transformeth hem by entrechaungeable muta-cioun. And thilke same ordre neweth ayein alle thinges growynge and fallynge adoun, by semblable progressions of sedes and of sexes (*that is to seyn, male and female*). And this like ordre constreyneth the fortunes and the dedes of men by a bond of causes nat able to ben unbownde; the whiche destynal causes, whan thei passen out fro the bygynnynges of the unmoevable purveaunce, it moot nedes be that thei be nat mutable. And thus ben thinges ful wel igoverned yif that the symplicite duellynge in the devyne thoght scheweth forth the ordre of causes unable to ben ibowed. And this ordre constreyneth by his propre stablete the moevable thingis, or elles thei scholden fleten folyly. For which it es that alle thingis semen to ben confus and trouble to us men, for we ne mowen nat considere thilke ordenaunce. . . .
>
> But thou mayst seyn, "What unreste may ben a worse confusioun than that gode men han somtyme adversite and somtyme prosperite . . . ?" [cf. Chaucer's "The world hath ever resteles travayle"]. [*Bo* 4, pr. 6]

For although that selde is ther any feith that fortunous thynges wollen dwellen, yet natheles the laste day of a mannes lif is a maner deth to Fortune, and also to thilke that hath dwelt. And therfore what wenestow thar rekke, yif

thow forleete hir in deyinge, or elles that sche, Fortune, forleete the in fleynge
awey [cf. Chaucer's "Thy laste day is ende of myn intresse"]. [*Bo* 2, pr. 3]

As Patch (1922) points out, the medieval writers had to annihilate Fortuna (pp. 180–90),[9]
to Christianize her totally as Dante and some of his followers had done (pp. 204–30) or to
reach the compromise that Boethius and others had logically deduced. If one is to include
both God and Fortuna in one system, the conclusion of Albertus Magnus–"Cum enim
prima causarum sit Deus, et omnium quorum causa est, ipse providentiam habeat"[10] ("For
if God be the first of the causes and of all things of which there is a cause, he must have
foresight")–is the only possible one. Above all, however, it must not be forgotten that, as
Patch says (p. 191), "the influence of Boethius on the Middle Ages can hardly receive full
estimate." Dante himself was deeply affected by Boethian philosophy, and the concept
expressed in the *Inferno* represents a change from his earlier view. As Scartazzini notes
(Dante 1921: note to *Inf.* 7.67–96):

> And through the mouth of V[ergil], he would appear to confute the opinion
> already expressed in the *Convivio*, where he had said (IV, 11) of the goods of
> this world "that their the perfection may be noted firstly in the lack of discrimi-
> nation in their advent, in which no distributive justice." [Jackson, p. 230]] Here
> [in the *Commedia*] Fortune is instead a celestial intelligence who is ordained by
> God to govern worldly goods and to assign them in the process now to this
> one, now to that, without caring about the accusations that men hurl against
> her. The difference between *Conv.* and *D.C.* comes through considering the
> nature and the vicissitudes of worldly goods; there [in *Convivio*], as these are
> perceived in fact by men; here [in the *Commedia*], objectively, in themselves.

Now this change of view might well have come from an extension of Boethian ideas. In the
final analysis, then, there is no idea in Chaucer's *Fortune* that is purely Dante's, while there
is much that is purely Boethius's, the latter probably being the common source to both
Chaucer and Dante.

There is also an inherent contradiction in this ascription. According to Bethel (p. 101), it
was the verbal and narrative imitation of Dante that forced Chaucer to break off from "the
hampering conventions" of French poetry.[11] Now the philosophy of *Fortune*, according to
Bethel, is Dante's, and yet, even if there were not in all probability a large disparity in
posited dates of composition, there can be no doubt that the form of the poem *Fortune* is in
the "hampering convention" of a French balade. Since the form is undeniable, it would
appear that Bethel's general critical and chronological view of the Dantesque influence
could only be maintained if he were willing to admit the possibility of no Dantesque
influence at all in the philosophy of the present poem. Since there seems to be an evident
debt to Boethius here, he must likewise put himself in the anomalous position of considering *Fortune* as being one of the "later poems," composed after *Troilus and Criseyde*.[12]

There is a great deal of evidence that suggests that Chaucer's position was the "compromise" of Boethius. The frequent "pagan" uses of Fortune as the arbitrary blind goddess are

---

[9] Patch gives examples of this from Lactantius, Saint Augustine, Saint Jerome, Saint Thomas, Hildebert of
Lavardin, and Alanus de Insulis.

[10] "*Physicorum*, lib. II, tr. ii, cap. xix (*Opera*, II 92)," cited by Patch, p. 198.

[11] Bethel, of course, is merely representative of a number of scholars (Tatlock, Lowes, etc.) discussed in the
opening chapters.

[12] For another aspect of Fortune which is frequently attributed to Dante, see *TC* 4.1541–45.

noted to some extent by Bethel himself, though he does not deal with them in his text.[13] These tend to show that (1) Chaucer had not given himself over to the philosophical Christian resolution of the problem that Dante had evolved and (2) Chaucer took the compromise position which Boethius assumed and which could incorporate both pagan and Christian viewpoints.

As for the suggested parallels in the *Convivio*, there seems to be little relevance to Chaucer. *Convivio* 4.4.9 has no connection, being Dante's famous attempt to show that monarchy, and particularly the Roman monarchy, has divine sanction. It reads (Dante 1924b:203–204):

> To this it is easy to reply that the choice of the highest officer must needs primarily emanate from that wisdom which provides for all men, namely, God; otherwise the choice would not have been made impartially for all, inasmuch as before the officer above named there was no one who paid heed to the good of all.

Convivio 4.5.1 is very vague, though there is a mention of Divine Providence (Dante 1924b:205):

> It is no wonder if divine Providence which utterly transcends the apprehension of angels and of men, often proceeds incomprehensibly to us, inasmuch as human actions often hide their tendencies from men themselves. We should rather marvel greatly if at any time the process by which the eternal counsels are fulfilled is so manifest as to be discerned by our reason.

Finally, *Convivio* 4.5.9 seems once more to have no relationship whatever to the passage from Chaucer (Dante 1924b:206):

> O inexpressible and incomprehensible wisdom of God, who at the same hour both yonder in Syria and here in Italy madest Thy preparations for Thy coming. And O ye most vile and silly brutes pasturing under the semblances of men who presume to talk against our faith, and fain would know, as ye spin and delve, what God with much foresight has ordained. Accursed be ye and your presumption and all those who give heed to you.

The one element that all three passages have in common is the dominance, mystery, and wisdom of God's plan; but if we try to connect this to Chaucer's statement in *Fortune* or see anything in this that might not crop up in almost any sermon, gloss, or tract of medieval religion, then we will have become totally out of touch with the philosophical and theological commonplaces of the later Middle Ages.

Gentilesse

Bethel: "The whole of this balade is based upon the third *canzone* of the *Convivio* and displays the Dantesque attitude towards true nobility. A hint or two came from Jean de Meun or Boethius but the influence of Dante is most prominent throughout."

---

[13] Bethel's list (p. 246, n.2) reads: "*Tr.*, I, 138–40, 837ff, 843ff; III, 1667, 1714f.; IV, 274f., 323f; V, 1774–77 (from Bocc., *Filos.* VIII, 25, 1–4); *Kt's T.*, I 915f., 925f., 1234f., 1242, 1489; *Sumn's T.*, III. 2020; *Clerk's T.*, IV. 68–70, 754–56; *Sq's T.*, V. 576–78; *Franklin's T.*, V. 1355f.; *LGW*, 589, 1609."

The previous discussions of "gentilesse" are highly pertinent to the present problem and should, but for limitations of space, be restated here. The principal discussions are to be found in the final remarks upon the passage on "gentilesse" (lines 1109–64) in *The Wife of Bath's Tale* and in the introductory comments on *The Squire's Tale* and *The Franklin's Tale*.

That there is the influence of Dante's *Convivio* here is hardly to be doubted – if for no other reason than that the phrase "old richesse" is an echo of Dante's heavily stressed *antica ricchezza* for which no substitute has yet been offered. Bethel seems to push his source far beyond its legitimate limits, however. Certainly there is more than "a hint or two . . . from Jean de Meun or Boethius." Robinson (p. 861) resets the emphasis as follows: "The ultimate source is Boethius, iii, pr. 6, m. 6. But . . . Chaucer was also influenced by Dante and the Roman de la Rose and it is hardly possible to determine what he took from each authority."

Now much of the phraseology in Chaucer's poem is highly conventional. The two following examples, though slightly later than Chaucer, show the degree to which the Christian "gentilesse" had been incorporated into courtly-love poetry. With respect to the stylization, Chaytor says of the first selection (Robbins 1952, no. 190, pp. 190–91) that "this poem . . . is interesting for the number of troubadour commonplaces which it contains; in particular, it repeats ideas from the love letter of Folquet de Romans" (Chaytor 1934:138; cited in Robbins, p. 286). The poem opens (lines 1–4, 12–14, 29–35):

> That pasaunte Goodnes, the Rote of all vertve,
>   which Rotide is in your femynete
> whos stepes glade to Ensue
>   ys eueri woman in their degre;
>
> . . . .
>
>   hit is my will to purches youre fauoure;
>   whiche wilde to Criste I myght atteyn
>   As ye of all floures Are my Souerayn.
>
> . . . .
>
> Nowe, lady myn, in Whome Vertus All
>   Ar Ioyned and also comprehendide,
> as ye of al women y call moste principall
>   lette my gref in youre herte be entendered,
>   And also my veri treueloue Rememberde;
>   And for my treueloue ayene me to loue
>   As welethe nature and god that setithe Above.

We are, of course, very close to the poetry of Mariolatry[14] – which is not strange, since "gentilesse" has both Christian and courtly aspects in its approach to the ideal woman. This can be seen again in the second example, a courtly epistle (Robbins, no. 198, pp. 200–201, lines 1–2, 9–10, 18–20, 26–29, 36–39):

> Exemplye sendynge to you, rowte of gentylnes,
>   Bothe true and trusty stok of all nature,
>
> . . . .
>
>   I recommand me and all my seruyse,
> To you , me lady soueraynne, & gronde of nature;
>
> . . . .

---

[14] Cf., for example, the anonymous "A Hymn to the Virgin," no. 9, *The Oxford Book of English Verse* (Oxford, 1948), p. 11.

I make you surans by that lord that borne was of [a mayde],
  though y shulde my lyf forthe wythe you forfethe,
  y shulde do for yoie, that y may youre plasauns for to g[ete].
. . . .

Now fayreste of stature formyd by nature,
  of beaute the merrour, and grond of gentylnes,
Most amyable, benyng, and constant creature,
  Stynter of stryfe, & causere of pesse —
. . . .

  the well Replet of gentylnys —
Vowchasafe ye now on myn hevynes,
  Sythyn ye be myn hert hole Reserthe,
  Sum drope of mercy to be my comforte.

The courtly and the Christian merged not because of a single poetic act (even though a Dante was one of its earliest spokesmen) but because the two were two images of the same medieval world picture. One may have begun in the court of Marie and the other in the cloister of Saint Bernard, but the fusion of the two was as inevitable as, let us say, the fusion of poetry and psychology is today. This discussion, of course, serves only as background to Chaucer's poem, but its purpose is to emphasize that by the beginning of the fifteenth century the Christian element of "gentilesse" was not dependent — if it ever had been — on any single writer. Dante, Boethius, Jean de Meun, or Andreas might supply phrases or even lines, but the idea had long been present. For this Christianizing theme Chaucer's balade is not primarily dependent on the third canzone of the *Convivio*, nor is it only "the Dantesque attitude towards nobility" that we find here. No single source has gone unchallenged because there is no single source; there is the common knowledge of the time — in a sense, the *Zeitgeist* — plus the introduction of an occasional phrase, be it Dante's *antica ricchezza*, Boethius's "on allone is fadir of thynges," Andreas's "character alone . . . first made a distinction of nobility," *The Romaunt of the Rose*'s "he is gentil by cause he doth / As longeth to a gentilman," or, indeed, any other work on the same subject in roughly the same period. In short, one could, with a little effort, make almost any author who dealt with the subject at that time a "basis" for such a poem as this.

Bethel, in addition to attempting to establish Dante as the primary source, is faced with the problem of reconciling two of his fundamental concepts which assert that: (1) Chaucer was under the strictures of French verse until the glories of Italian literature released him, and (2) Chaucer did not really understand Dante until later readings, being at first capable only of recognizing the brilliance of the mechanics and narrative. Taking the second statement first, Bethel (pp. 302–303, 319–20) sees this poem as an illustration of Chaucer's deep understanding of Dante's *gentilezza*, which is then connected to the concept of true felicity in a somewhat sudden enlarging of the subject. But the "influence of Dante the philosopher" does not come, according to Bethel (p. 102), until after *Troilus and Criseyde*, in the "later poems." This, according to Root's dating, would be sometime after 1385. Keeping this facts in mind, let us turn to the first statement, which expresses a belief in the "triplicity" (to use Kittredge's phrase) of Chaucer's development, with Italian poetry (and in this case Dante specifically) liberating him from the stylized formality of French traditions (Bethel, pp. 75–76). Despite some critics' attempts to make the date of Chaucer's reading of the *Commedia* as late as possible (the usual arguments being that he was too busy on his return with official duties and house moving), this date certainly cannot be set much past 1375 — on the assumption, that is, that Chaucer could not have read the *Commedia* before 1372. But even granting all the assumptions that are necessary for the date of 1375, if we accept Bethel's view, we are faced with the same problem that was presented with the *Fortune* poem, namely, that the form and the thought are in opposition as far as dating is concerned. For the balade is a fairly exacting form, with three stanzas rhyming *a b a b b c b c* and an envoy rhyming *b c b c*. Chaucer, however, does not use this "traditional" pattern as Villon had developed it.[15] Rather, in his deviations from the standard balade form he becomes, if anything, even more stylized. Thus *Fortune*, like *The Complaint of Venus*, is actually a triple balade with an envoy of varying length and complexity,[16] while the "moral balade" *Gentilesse*, like *Truth* and *Lak of Stedfastnesse*, is composed of three rhyme-royal stanzas, though it lacks the rhyme-royal envoy of these last two. It should be added that all the stanzas of *Gentilesse* are based on the same rhyme and end, as a balade should, with a refrain.

It would seem legitimate, therefore, to question either one or both of Bethel's critical assertions. For, following these statements to their logical conclusions, we find that (1) if we go on the assumption that Chaucer left French poetic conventions around 1375, we must then admit that he read and understood Dante at a comparatively early date, or (2) if we go on the assumption that Chaucer did not fully comprehend Dante's philosophy until the "later poems," we must then admit that his use of French forms might well have continued throughout his writing career. Finally, it must be remarked that underlying this entire rationale is the still unproved assertion that "the whole of this balade is based upon the third *canzone* of the *Convivio*." As a matter of fact, if we are to draw any conclusion from this fundamental conflict in tenets, we must reject, at least in part, both of the critical assertions and admit that Chaucer might have written these poems at almost any time after he learned Italian and that a date for them can only be set by evidence more specific than an a priori categorization of style. We must, therefore, examine the poem closely to see to just what extent we can accept the statement that "the whole of this balade is based upon the third *canzone* of the *Convivio*."

In his text Bethel is not nearly as dogmatic, for there he is willing to admit that the *Gentilesse* "shows the influence not only of Dante, but of Boethius and Jean de Meun as well" (p. 319). His claim for Dante as the primary source of the poem is based on the concept that Dante "is especially apparent in the general tone of the poem, particularly in the association, as in the *Wife of Bath's Tale*, of 'gentilesse' with Christ" (p. 320). There is, then, the general question whether Dante is Chaucer's source for such an association—a question that I touched on at the beginning of this discussion. There is, even more fundamentally, the question whether this association of Christ and "gentilesse" is mentioned in the balade at all.

For the answer to the latter question, we are dependent on a reading of the poem itself. The discussion naturally centers on an interpretation of the opening line that speaks of "the firste stok." Robinson (p. 862) says that the phrase "is surely to be taken (as by Scogan) as referring to Christ or God. Cf. *WBT*, III, 1117 ff. Professor Brusendorff (p. 257), on the evidence of a passage in Lydgate's *Thoroughfare of Woe*, applied the term to Adam and Eve." I agree with Robinson that the line does not refer to Adam and Eve, but if we assume that the reference is to Christ or God, some very peculiar readings evolve. First of all, the line which Robinson cites in *The Wife of Bath's Tale*—"Crist wole we clayme of him oure gentillesse"—refers to Christ neither as "the firste stok" nor as the "fader of gentilesse" but rather as the giver of such a virtuous characteristic.[17] So far as I have read,

---

[15] The closest he comes to it is in *Rosemounde*, which lacks an envoy.

[16] In the first case, *a b a b b c b*; in the second, *a a b a a b a a b*.

[17] *WBT* 1117; see citation and discussion of the line under that entry.

Christ is never referred to, even metaphorically, as "fader," a term which would, of course, have been close to a unitarian heresy. In addition, the phrase "firste stok" hardly seems applicable, even if we assume that Chaucer was ambiguously referring to God and Christ at one and the same time. For God created man; he was not—nor is he yet—considered as being a part of the same "stock, origin or race" (to give Robinson's glossorial meanings of the word). Following this phrase come instructions to "folwe his trace," to pursue virtue and flee vices, but one is to follow such a course not to attain the kingdom of heaven (which should logically come from an emulation of Christ or God) but because "unto vertu longeth dignitee / And noght the revers."

The second stanza refers again to "this firste stok," describing it in the past tense as having been

ful of rightwisnesse,
Trewe of his word, sobre, pitous, and free.

Now the description becomes distinctly awkward if it is Christ or God to whom Chaucer is referring. To say that God is "clene of his gost" is, to say the least, a pleonasm. And what would be the relevance of remarking that God or Christ "loved besinesse...in honestee," even though it is "ayeinst the vyce of slouthe"? And, again, if "his" refers to Christ or God, what is meant by "but his heir love vertu, as did he, / He is noght gentil, thogh he riche seme"? Now unless Chaucer is speaking of human lineage, the increasing confusion of these first two stanzas will become total when the third is reached. If Christ or God is meant in reference to the pronoun of "his heir" in line 12, then line 15—"Vyce may wel be heir to old richesse"—is totally meaningless.

It should be obvious, then, that the third stanza is speaking, first, of men, and, second, of the fact ("as men may wel see") that "ther may no man...bequethe his heire his vertuous noblesse," which is the property of ("appropred unto") no rank, status, or condition ("degree") but belongs to God. And it is God who chooses as heir to the *original* man of "vertuous noblesse" that successor who can serve Him (i.e., God). The confusion here is in the pronominal referents, but careful reading will show, I think, that "his heir," both in line 17 and in line 20, refers to the same person and that what is being passed on, through God's choice, is the first man's "vertuous noblesse," i.e., his "gentilesse."[18]

We are left with the problem of identifying the original man whose "vertuous noblesse" returns to God to be given again by him to someone worthy of it. A perfectly clear reading can be had if we take "the firste stok, fader of gentilesse" to refer not to Christ but to the first race of nobles, which is the "fader of gentilesse" in the same way that Chaucer is the father of English poetry. Such an interpretation is based on the traditional argument expressed in part in *Andreas* as "excellence of character alone...first made a distinction of nobility among men and led to the difference of class. Many...who trace their descent from these same first nobles...have degenerated.... The converse of the proposition is likewise true" (cited in Coffman 1945:48). No difficulty arises if we recognize that Chaucer's "firste stok" refers to the tradition of "these same first nobles," that he is recalling—as he does in *Lak of Stedfastnesse*—an age when

Somtyme the world was so stedfast and stable
That mannes word was obligacioun.[19]

---

[18] Line 20, it will be noted, is perfectly in keeping with the remark in *WBT* D 1117, since in both cases "gentillesse cometh fro God allone" (*WBT* D 1162), as does, let us say, grace.

[19] Cf. the negative listing of all these "gentil" qualities in stanza 3 of *Lak of Stedfastnesse*.

To prove "gentilesse," then, a man must follow the ways of the "firste stok," of those who were of the first, *l'âge d'or de la chevalerie*. This group was spiritually pure, honestly active and opposed to sloth, "sobre, pitous, free" and true to its—*his* in at least the first four lines of Stanza two is modern *its*—word. But the legitimate heir of such a noble can inherit only his material wealth, not his "gentilesse," which, like any other virtue, derives from God alone. Being subject to human laws, material wealth, no matter how long it has been in a family, may well come down to a person steeped in vice, but God's gift of "gentilesse" goes to him who is worthy of it—and here Chaucer gives a slight but brilliant twist to the refrain—*even though* that worthy person, that person who can serve God, wears a miter, crown, or diadem, i.e., is a bishop, king, or noble.

Considered thus, the poem, though it loses somewhat in religiosity, gains a unity and comprehension that are otherwise lacking. Admittedly, Chaucer is working much more with traditional ideas, but they seem at least to be consistent. Such an interpretation means, of course, that Dante's influence can be seen clearly in only one point, that of *antica ricchezza*, which, it seems to me, was the one original element that Chaucer added to his otherwise clear but conventional view of "gentilesse." And it is possible that by this late date—many decades after Dante's death—the theme of *antica ricchezza* might well have been a part of the conventional view itself.

Bethel: "5f.: both the idea and the phrasing are due partly to *Conv.* IV, *canz.* iii, 101-04."

For unto vertu longeth dignitee,	E gentilezza dovunqu' è vertute,
And noght the revers, saufly dar I deme	ma non vertute ov'ella;
	sì com' è 'l cielo dovunqu' è la stella,
	ma ciò non e converso.

Wherever virtue is, there is nobility. But virtue is not always there where nobility is; as there is sky wherever there is a star, but there is not always a star wherever there is sky. [P. 192]

The possible ascription refers, of course, only to lines 101–102. Noting the possibility of this Dantesque source, Jefferson (1917:100–101) summarizes the situation well as follows:

In the Consolation there are the following parallels:

And therfor it is thus, that *honour ne comth nat to vertu for cause of dignitee, but ayeinward honour comth to dignitee for cause of vertu.* 2. p. 6. 17–19. "Certes, *dignitees*," quod she, "*apertienen proprely to vertu*;" 3. p4. 35–36.

The decision here, if one is to decide whether Boethius or Dante had more influence in determining Chaucer's conception of gentilesse, seems to rest on whether to give more weight to *revers*, corresponding to Dante's *converso*, or to *dignitee*, corresponding to the *dignitee* of Chaucer's translation of Boethius. As a matter of fact, the influence of the two authors seems to be fused almost beyond separation. [Jefferson's italics]

Bethel: "15: the phrase *old richesse* is from Dante; cf. *Conv.* IV, iii, 6f; x, 2, 5."

Vyce may wel be heir to old richesse   [See under *WBT* 1110, 1118.]

In all probability, Dante is the source for this line.

The Envoy to Scogan

Bethel: "1: Skeat compare *Purg.* I, 47, 76 (*Oxf. Ch.* I, 556); and Klaeber compares *Purg.* I, 46 (*Das Bild bei Ch.*, 347); doubtful."

Tobroken been the statuz hye in hevene

Son le leggi d'abisso così rotte?
o è mutato in ciel novo consiglio [lines 46–47]

Non son li editti etterni per noi guasti [line 76]

Are the laws of the abyss thus broken? Or is some new counsel changed in Heaven [*Purg.*, p. 5]

The eternal edicts are not violated by us [*Purg.*, p. 7]

There would seem to be neither demonstrable verbal dependence nor contextual parallel here. The difference between broken laws and changed counsel seems evidence enough for rejection. That heaven's laws are violated is, unfortunately, not so unique a fact that its observation in two separate works indicates borrowing.

CHAPTER 9

Conclusion

I T HAS BEEN the endeavor of this book to investigate contextually the literary relationships between Chaucer and Dante. To this end the biographical problem of the time when Chaucer could have learned Italian or discovered Dante has been set against the relevant social background in relation not only to the general intercourse between the two countries but, more specifically, to a particular group—the Italian merchants—who would appear to have been a not-unimportant element of the court society in which Chaucer moved in the early 1370s. The result of this investigation has been to suggest that Chaucer might very well have acquired a knowledge of Italian and of the *Commedia* at some time before his 1372–73 journey to Italy, and this suggestion appears to find support in the discussion of the date of *The House of Fame*.

Naturally, such a hypothesis directly affects the critical view of the Chaucer-Dante relationship, for it would seem to militate against not only the view of the distinct "triplicity" of Chaucer's works but also the concept of Dante as the precise cause of an immediate and profound change in Chaucer. That a new direction resulted from Chaucer's exposure to Italian poetry seems virtually certain, but how radical that change was depends to a great degree on our opinion of his earliest datable work, *The Book of the Duchess*.[1] It appears to me that Chaucer at that time already showed poetic independence in his transformation of a love-vision poem into an extraordinarily delicate and mature poem of consolation. One is tempted, indeed, to think that Chaucer was never liberated by Italian poetry simply because he had never been enchained by the French. Certainly, of his minor balades, complaints, and envoys, few, if any, can be placed before the time he learned Italian. Being of such fundamental critical importance, the determination of Chaucer's relative position to these two "schools" of poetry needs a far more detailed study than the admittedly limited comparison that has been made here for purposes of investigating, with at least a semblance of literary context, the broader aspects of Chaucer's relationship to Dante.

The major emphasis of this book has been, of course, the literary relationships of the two writers. To determine the extent and degree of these relationships, and to avoid the

---

[1] The precise date remains uncertain. While Blanche died in September, 1369, Chaucer refers to the Black Knight (John of Gaunt) as "this king" (*BD* 1314). Gaunt, to counteract French successes in Spain, married Pedro's daughter and heiress, Constance, in 1371 and in 1372 assumed the title of king. It is perhaps a tribute to the poem's power that scholars generally refuse to consider its having been composed subsequent to Gaunt's remarriage; one should, however, point out that if a date of 1372 or later were to be accepted "the neat triplicity of Chaucer's work" to which I referred in chapter 1 would need even further reconsideration, as would our critical view of Chaucer and his poetry.

danger of unfounded generalizations, the suggested instances of indebtedness to Dante have been investigated individually. Here again the intention has been to look at the specific lines not only in the context of the passages from which they come but also (insofar as the confines of this book will allow) in the light of contemporary literature and thought. Aside from direct translation, or citation, a source can be offered on either a verbal or a contextual basis. Together these give an almost certain indication of either a very close parallelism or a direct borrowing; separately it would seem that they must be supported by some unique feature of thought or terminology in order not to be merely analogies. The encyclopedic nature of Dante's poetry and the assimilative quality of Chaucer's make particularly necessary a very cautious approach in evaluating source and influence.

To speak in the most general terms for the purposes of summary, Chaucer's literary indebtedness to Dante would seem to fall into two main categories: the few direct adaptations and translations made for purposes of their content and the many shorter images borrowed for their verbal and dramatic force. The first group would seem to divide chronologically into the early "translations" from the *Commedia* that make their appearance in the later poems and the adaptations (perhaps ten to fifteen years later) from tractate 4 of the *Convivio*. With the exception of the Ugolino episode, Chaucer seems to have returned to this material for certain specific topics: to tractate 4 for the philosophical discussion of nobility and to the *Paradiso* for the lyric expression of religious adoration. A statement of so general a nature as this must be accompanied by many reservations, and, indeed, it has been another of the purposes of this book to show how Chaucer turned to other sources as well, combining and molding the whole to fit the thematic purpose of the individual poem.

Far wider is Chaucer's borrowing of images of verbal or dramatic force (which I call the second group). While these may come from the whole of the *Commedia*, they are at first drawn chiefly from the opening and closing cantos of Dante's three *cantiche*, with particular emphasis on the opening of the *Inferno*. Such images may vary from the generally recalled scene of the eagle or the gates of the *Inferno* to the inclusion of a specific phrase, such as Dante's *rider l'oriente*. In almost all cases, however, these images, like the longer direct adaptations, are assimilated into the general material and shaped to fit Chaucer's poetic intent. Again, this summary leaves out a large number of borrowings for purposes of giving a more general view of the direction of the indebtedness, and with these exceptions in mind we can perhaps tentatively see an early use of short visual images from the *Commedia* which, while it continues throughout Chaucer's writing, is somewhat displaced by his later use of Dante for specific subjects.

Perhaps we can now venture certain views on the relationship as a whole. Chaucer, it would seem, remained always in control of his material. Poetically, he attempted neither to copy the complex structure of Dante's "four levels of meaning" nor, save for a few verses, to write in terza rima or the canzone. To judge from his works, poetry to Chaucer was primarily entertaining, moral, and undoctrinaire; to Dante, however, poetry was a medium for expressing, with even more concentrated power than prose, the fiercely held theological and political doctrines that he had formed into a philosophic whole. It seems incorrect to consider that Chaucer, when borrowing an image or even a passage from Dante, necessarily believed the entire doctrine that informed the borrowing. Not only does such a view in many cases seem contrary to the tone of the poem concerned, but it leads to a singleness of interpretation that turns the journey to the House of Fame into a spiritual autobiography and makes of Alceste's speech to the God of Love a scathing satire that is not borne out by the rest of *The Legend of Good Women*.

Chaucer drew on Dante not heavily but over a long period of time, and, while he was later to employ in part the ideas behind *Convivio* 4 and perhaps had early committed to memory the lyricism of Saint Bernard's Marian prayer from the close of the *Commedia*, his most extensive indebtedness would seem to lie in his use of the visual and dramatic images that help make Dante's poem the striking literary masterpiece that it is. Below this level of borrowing, one feels that Dante's most fundamental effect might well lie in the confirmation of a stylistic technique (inherent in almost all of Chaucer's poetry) based upon a primary regard for the actual world of living people, as opposed to the personified abstractions of the closed and conventional world of stylized verse. While both men sought their symbols in the "world of affairs," Chaucer remained a poet primarily interested in people and not doctrines; his is a full view of the life around him, and if he borrowed from Dante's universal vision, he took what helped him explain the world of men of which he was so much a part and of which he, himself, is so much a symbol.

One closes such a study as this with a sense of the many problems it has raised rather than the few that it has perhaps settled. No definitive date can yet be offered for the time Chaucer first read the *Commedia*; there is the question of his heavy use of the opening and closing cantos of the work, as well as his preference for tractate 4 of the *Convivio*; there is the matter of the precise opinion in fourteenth-century England of French, as opposed to Italian, poetry. Above all, there is the constant problem of looking at Chaucer in relation to an always painfully inadequate picture of the literary and historical context of his age. With all these problems — and perhaps, in part, by virtue of them — we can only conclude with the remark of an early editor, made in the Proem to his second (1484) edition of *The Canterbury Tales*:

> Great thanks, laud, and honour ought to be given unto the clerks, poets, and historiographs that have written many noble books of wisdom of the lives, passions, and miracles of holy saints, of histories of noble and famous acts and faites... among whom and in especial before all others, we ought to give a singular laud unto that noble and great philosopher Geoffrey Chaucer, the which for his ornate writing in our tongue may well have the name of a laureate poet.

Index of Comparisons

Note: Works are in alphabetical order, entered by poem, fragment, book, part, and/or line number. The number at the end of each entry is the page number of this book.

Dante

Commedia

Inferno

Purgatorio

Bibliography

Aetius 1879. *Philosophumena*. In *Doxographi greci*, edited by H. Diels. Berlin.

Albertus Magnus 1890. *De meteoris*. Vol. 4 of *Opera omnia*, edited by Auguste Borgnet, 38 vols. Paris.

Anderson, Melville Best 1944. See Dante.

Aquinas, Saint Thomas 1920. *Summa theologica*. 2d ed. Rome.

———— 1923. *The* Summa contra gentiles *of St. Thomas Aquinas*. Translated by the Fathers of the English Dominican Province. London.

———— 1927. *Summa contra gentiles*. Rome.

———— 1947. *The* Summa theologica *of St. Thomas Aquinas*. Translated by the Fathers of the English Dominican Province. 2d ed. 3 vols. New York. Reissue of London, 1922, printing.

———— 1956. *On the Truth of the Catholic Faith: Summa contra gentiles*. Translated by Vernon E. Bourke. 6 vols. Garden City, N.Y.

Augustine, Saint 1972. *Concerning the City of God Against the Pagans*. Translated by Henry Bettenson. Introduction by David Knowles. Harmondsworth, Middlesex.

Austin, H. D. 1923. Dante Notes. *MLN* 38:140–48.

Averroës 1530. *Aristote. Stagyrite meteorum libri quattuor Auer. cordubensis exactiss. commentariis denuo acutissime traductis*. Lugduni [Lyons].

Axon, W. E. A. 1900. Italian Influence on Chaucer. In *Chaucer Memorial Lectures, 1900*, edited by P. W. Ames, pp. 83–110. London.

Baker, Donald C. 1962. Chaucer's Clerk and the Wife of Bath on the Subject of *Gentilesse*. *SP* 59:631–40.

Battaglia, Salvatore 1938. See Boccaccio.

Baugh, A. C. 1948. *Literary History of England*. New York.

Beardwood, Alice 1931. *Alien Merchants in England, 1350 to 1377: Their Legal and Economic Position*. Cambridge, Mass.

Bennett, H. S. 1948. *Chaucer and the Fifteenth Century*. Oxford.

Bennett, J. A. W. 1953. Chaucer, Dante, and Boccaccio. *MÆ* 22:114–15.

———— 1957. *The Parlement of Foules: An Interpretation*. Oxford.

———— 1968. *Chaucer's Book of Fame*. Oxford.

Benoit de Sainte Maure 1904–12. *Le Roman de Troie*. Edited by Leopold Constans. 6 vols. Paris.

Bethel, J. P. 1927. The Influence of Dante on Chaucer's Thought and Expression. Ph.D. dissertation, Harvard University.

Bland, H. S. 1948. Chaucer and the Art of Narrative Verse. *English* 7:216–20.

Blenner-Hassett, Roland 1953. Autobiographical Aspects of Chaucer's Franklin. *Speculum* 28:791–800.

Block, E. A. 1954. Chaucer's Millers and Their Bagpipes. *Speculum* 29:239–43.

Bloomfield, M. W. 1953. Chaucer's Sense of History. *JEGP* 51:301–13.

Boccaccio, Giovanni 1831. *Il Filostrato.* In *Opera volgare de Giovanni Boccaccio,* vol. 13. Florence.

———— 1929. *The* Filostrato *of Giovanni Boccaccio.* Translated by Nathaniel Edward Griffin and Arthur Beckwith Myrick, with parallel text. Reprinted 1967. New York.

———— 1938. *Teseida.* Edited by Salvatore Battaglia. Florence.

———— [1943?]. *Amorosa visione.* Edited by Vittore Branca. Florence.

———— 1951. *Genealogie deorum gentilium libri.* Edited by Vincenzo Romano. Vol. 10 of Scrittori d'Italia *Opere* of Giovanni Boccaccio.

———— 1974. *The Book of Theseus.* Translated by Bernadette Marie McCoy. New York.

Boitani, Piero 1976. The *Monk's Tale*: Dante and Boccaccio. *MÆ* 45:50–69.

————, ed. 1983. *Chaucer and the Italian Trecento.* Cambridge.

Bond, E. A. 1840. Extracts from the Liberate Rolls, Relative to Loans Supplied by Italian Merchants to the Kings of England, in the Thirteenth and Fourteenth Centuries; with an Introductory Memoir. . . . *Archaeologia* 28:107–326.

Boughner, D. C. 1939. Elements of Epic Grandeur in the *Troilus. ELH* 6:200–10.

Boutemy, André, et al. 1946–47. La Version parisienne du Poème de Simon Chevre d'Or sur la guerre de Troie (MS. Lat. 8430). *Scriptorium* 1:267–88.

Braddy, Haldeen 1932. *Chaucer's* Parlement of Foules *in Its Relation to Contemporary Events.* Lancaster, Pa.

———— 1953. Chaucer's Comic Valentine. *MLH* 78:232–34.

Bronson, B. H. 1934. Chaucer's *Hous of Fame*: Another Hypothesis. *University of California Publications in English* 3:171–92.

Brusendorff, Aage 1925. *The Chaucer Tradition.* London.

Burlin, Robert B. 1977. *Chaucerian Fiction.* Princeton, N.J.

Caplan, Harry 1925. A Late Mediaeval Tractate on Preaching. In *Studies in Rhetoric and Public Speaking in Honor of J. A. Winans,* pp. 61–90. New York.

———— 1929. The Four Senses of Scriptural Interpretation and the Mediaeval Theory of Preaching. *Speculum* 4:282–90.

Chapman, C. O. 1952. Chaucer and Dante. *Times Literary Supplement* (London), August 29, 1952, p. 565.

———— 1953. Chaucer and the Gawain Poet: A Conjecture. *MLN* 68:521–24.

Chaucer, Geoffrey 1877. *The* Parlement of Foules *by Geoffrey Chaucer.* Edited by T. R. Lounsbury. Boston.

———— 1912. *The Complete Works of Geoffrey Chaucer.* Edited by W. W. Skeat. London.

———— 1945. *The* Book of Troilus and Criseyde *by Geoffrey Chaucer.* Edited by R. K. Root. Princeton, N.J.

———— 1957. *The Works of Geoffrey Chaucer.* Edited by F. N. Robinson. 2d ed. Boston.

Chaytor, H. J. 1934. *The Troubadours in England.* Cambridge.

———— 1945. *From Script to Print: An Introduction to Medieval Literature.* Cambridge.

Chiarini, Cino 1902. *Di una imitazione della Divina Commedia: La Casa della Fama di G. Chaucer.* Bari.

Clark, J. W. 1952. Dante and the Epilogue of *Troilus. JEGP* 50:1–10.

Claudian 1918. *Claudian.* Translated by Maurice Platnauer. 2 vols. New York. Reprinted Cambridge, Mass., 1940, 1976.

Clemen, Wolfgang 1963. *Chaucer's Early Poetry.* Translated by C. A. M. Sym. New York.

Clouston, W. A. 1889. *Magical Elements in the* Squire's Tale. London.

Coffman, G. R. 1945. Chaucer and Courtly Love Once More—*The Wife of Bath's Tale.* *Speculum* 20:43–50.

Coghill, Nevill 1949. *The Poet Chaucer.* London.

Cook, A. S. 1916*a*. The Historical Background of Chaucer's Knight. *Transactions of the Connecticut Academy of Arts and Sciences* 20 (February):161–240.

——— 1916*b*. The Last Months of Chaucer's Earliest Patron. *Transactions of the Connecticut Academy of Arts and Sciences* 21 (December):1–144.

——— 1919. Chaucerian Papers—I. *Transactions of the Connecticut Academy of Arts and Sciences* 23 (November):1–63.

Cope, J. I. 1952. Chaucer, Venus, and the Seventhe Spere. *MLN* 67:245–46.

Croce, Benedetto 1922. *The Poetry of Dante.* Translated by Douglas Ainslie. New York.

Cummings, H. M. 1916. *The Indebtedness of Chaucer's Works to the Italian Works of Boccaccio.* Menasha, Wis.

Curry, W. C. 1923*a*. Fortuna Maior. *MLN* 38:94–96.

——— 1923*b*. The Bottom of Hell. *MLN* 38:253.

——— 1926. *Chaucer and the Medieval Sciences.* New York.

Curtius, E. R. 1953. *European Literature and the Latin Middle Ages.* Translated by W. R. Trask. New York.

Dante Alighieri 1921. *La Divina Commedia.* Edited by G. Vandelli. Commentary by G. A. Scartazzini. 8th ed. Milan.

——— 1922. *La Vita Nuova di Dante Alighieri.* Edited by Kenneth McKenzie. Boston.

——— 1924*a*. *Le Opere di Dante Alighieri.* Revised by E. Moore from the edition of Paget Toynbee. 4th ed. Oxford.

——— 1924*b*. *Dante's Convivio.* Translated by W. W. Jackson. Oxford.

——— 1933. *La Divina Commedia di Dante Alighieri.* Edited by C. H. Grandgent. Boston.

——— 1934. *Il Convivio.* Edited by G. Busnelli and G. Vandelli. 2 vols. Florence.

——— 1944*a*. *The Divine Comedy of Dante Alighieri.* Translated by John Aitken Carlyle, Thomas Okey, and Philip Henry Wicksteed. Introduction by C. H. Grandgent. New York.

——— 1944*b*. *The Divine Comedy of Dante Alighieri.* Translated by Melville Best Anderson. Introduction by Arthur Livingston. New York.

——— 1970–75. *The Divine Comedy.* Translated by Charles S. Singleton. 6 vols. Princeton, N.J. Second printing, with corrections, 1977.

David, Alfred 1974. How Marcia Lost Her Skin: A Note on Chaucer's Mythology. In *The Learned and the Lewed,* edited by Larry A. Benson, pp. 19–29. Cambridge, Mass.

De Boer, C., ed. 1915–38. *Ovide Moralisé: Poème du commencement du quatorzieme siècle publié d'après tous les manuscrits connus.* (In series *Verhandelingen der Koninklijke Akademie van Wetenschappen,* Deele 15, 21, 30 no. 3, 37, 43.) Amsterdam.

Delany, Sheila 1972. *Chaucer's House of Fame: The Poetics of Skeptical Fideism.* Chicago.

Dempster, Germaine 1942. "Thy Gentilesse" in the *Wife of Bath's Tale,* D 1159–62. *MLN* 42:173–76.

Denomy, A. J. 1953. Courtly Love and Courtliness. *Speculum* 28:44–63.

Devlin, Sister Mary Aquinas 1929. An English Knight of the Garter in the Spanish Chapel in Florence. *Speculum* 4:270–281.

De Wulf, Maurice 1953. *Philosophy and Civilization in the Middle Ages.* New York. Reissue of the first edition of 1922.

Dilts, D. A. 1942. Observations on Dante and the *Hous of Fame.* *MLN* 57:26–28.

Dreyer, J. L. E. 1953. *A History of Astronomy from Thales to Kepler.* 2d ed. revised. New York.

Dronke, Peter 1964. The Conclusion of *Troilus and Criseyde*. *MÆ* 33:47–52.

Emerson, O. F. 1929. *Chaucer Essays and Studies*. Cleveland.

Eneas: Roman du xiie siècle. See Salverda de Grave, J.-J., ed.

Everett, Dorothy 1955. *Essays on Middle English Literature*. Edited by Patricia Kean. Oxford.

Fansler, D.S. 1914. *Chaucer and the* Roman de la rose. New York.

Francis, W. N. 1949. Chaucer's "Airish Beasts." *MLN* 44:339–41.

Friend, A. C. 1953. Chaucer's Version of the *Aeneid*. *Speculum* 28:317–23.

Furnivall, F. J. 1871. *Trial Forewords to My "Parallel-Text Edition of Chaucer's Minor Poems"*. . . . Chaucer Society, 2d ser., no. 6. London.

Fyler, John M. 1979. *Chaucer and Ovid*. New Haven, Conn.

Gabotto, Ferdinand 1890. *Il marito di Beatrice*. Bra.

Galway, Margaret 1938. Chaucer's Sovereign Lady: A Study of the Prologue to the *Legend* and Related Poems. *MLR* 33:145–99.

Gerould, G. H. 1952. *Chaucerian Essays*. Princeton, N.J.

Giamatti, A. Bartlett 1966. *The Earthly Paradise and the Renaissance Epic*. Princeton, N.J.

Gilson, Étienne 1939. *Dante et la philosophie*. Études de philosophie médiévale, no. 28. Paris. Translated by David Moore as *Dante and Philosophy*, New York, 1963.

———— 1955. *History of Christian Philosophy in the Middle Ages*. New York.

Goebel, Julius, Jr. 1937. *Felony and Misdemeanor: A Study in the History of Criminal Law*. Philadelphia. Reprinted 1976.

Grandgent 1933. See Dante.

Griffith, D. D. 1955. *Bibliography of Chaucer, 1908–1953*. University of Washington Publications in Language and Literature, no. 13. Seattle.

Guerin, Richard 1973. The Nun's Priest and Canto V of the *Inferno*. *ES* 54:313–15.

Guido de Columnis 1936. *Historia destructionis Troiae*. Edited by N. E. Griffin. Cambridge, Mass.

Hales, J. W. 1893. Dante in England. In *Folia Litteraria*. . . . Pp. 65–69. Originally appeared in *Bibliographer* 2 (1882):37–39.

Ham, E. B. 1950. Knight's Tale 38. *ELH* 17:252–61.

Hamilton, Marie 1932–33. Chaucer's "Marcia Catoun." *MP* 30:361–64.

Hamm, V. H. 1954. Chaucer: "Heigh Ymaginacioun." *MLN* 69:394–95.

Hammond, E. P. 1908. *Chaucer: A Bibliographical Manual*. New York.

———— 1916. Chaucer and Dante and Their Scribes. *MLN* 31:121

Harrison, Frederick 1947. *Medieval Man and His Notions*. London.

Honoré-Duvergé, Suzanne 1955. Chaucer en Espagne? (1366). In *Recueil de travaux offerts à M. Clovis Brunel*. 2 vols. Paris. Vol. 2, pp. 9–13.

Horace 1874–91. *Opera omnia*. . . . Edited by E. C. Wickham. 2 vols. Oxford.

———— 1918. *Horace: The Odes and the Epodes*. Translated by C. E. Bennett. New York. Reprinted Cambridge, Mass., 1940, 1976.

———— 1936. *Horace: Satires, Epistles, and* Ars poetica. Translated by H. Rushton Fairclough. New York. Reprinted Cambridge, Mass., 1940, 1976.

Howard, Donald R. 1976. *The Idea of the Canterbury Tales*. Berkeley, Calif.

Huizinga, J. 1924. *The Waning of the Middle Ages*. London. Reprinted 1950.

Hutson, A. E. 1954. Troilus's Confession. *MLN* 69:468–70.

Jack, A. A. 1920. *A Commentary on the Poetry of Chaucer and Spenser*. Glasgow.

Jefferson, B. L. 1917. *Chaucer and the* Consolation of Philosophy *of Boethius*. Princeton, N.J.

Joannes Januensis, ed. [1495]. *Catholicum, editum a fratre Joanne Januensi*. Venetus.

John of Salisbury 1938. *Policraticus*. In *Frivolities of Courtiers and Footprints of Philosophers*, edited, abridged, and translated by Joseph B. Pike. Minneapolis, Minn.

Jones, H. S. V. 1912. Parliament of Fowls 693f. *MLN* 27:95.

Juvenal 1903. *Saturarum*. Edited by H. L. Wilson. New York.

Kellett, E. E. 1921. Chaucer as a Critic of Dante. *London Mercury* 4:282–91.

Kellogg, A. L. 1951. An Augustinian Interpretation of Chaucer's Pardoner. *Speculum* 26:465–81.

———— 1954. *Troilus and Criseyde* and Ecclesiasticus x. 8. Paper delivered at the Chaucer Section of the Modern Language Association meeting, New York, December, 1954.

———— 1960. Chaucer's Self-Portrait and Dante's. *MÆ* 29:119–20.

Kenyon, J. S. 1939. Wife of Bath's Tale: 1159–62. *MLN* 54:133–37.

Kirby, T. A. 1940. *Chaucer's Troilus: A Study in Courtly Love*. Baton Rouge, La.

———— 1942. Note on the Irony in the Merchant's Tale. *PQ* 21:433–35.

Kirk, R. E. G. 1900. *Summary of the Life-Records of Chaucer*. Chaucer Society, 2d ser., no. 32. London.

Kissner, Alfons 1867. *Chaucer in seinem Beziehungen zur italienischen Literatur*. Bonn.

Kittredge, G. L. 1907. *The Date of Chaucer's* Troilus *and Other Chaucer Matters*. Chaucer Society, 2d ser., no. 42. London.

———— 1915. Chaucer's Troilus and Guillaume de Machaut. *MLN* 30:69.

———— 1951. *Chaucer and His Poetry*. 9th printing. Cambridge, Mass. First printing, 1915.

Koch, John 1923. Chaucers Belesenheit in den romischen Klassikern. *Englische Studien* 57:8 ff.

Koonce, B. G. 1966. *Chaucer and the Tradition of Fame*. Princeton, N.J.

Kuhl, E. P. 1947. Why Was Chaucer Sent to Milan in 1378? *MLN* 62:42–44.

Kuhns, O. 1904. *Dante and the English Poets from Chaucer to Tennyson*. New York.

Langhans, Viktor 1918. *Untersuchungen zu Chaucer*. Halle.

Layamon 1847. *Brut*. Edited by Sir Frederic Madden. 3 vols. London.

Legouis, Emile 1913. *Geoffrey Chaucer*. Translated by L. Lailavoix. New York.

Levy, M. L. 1943. "As myn auctor seyth." *MÆ* 12:25–39.

Looten, le Chanoine 1931. *Chaucer: ses modèles, ses sources, sa religion*. Memoires et travaux, fasc. 38. Lille.

Lorris, Guillaume de, and Jean de Meun 1914–24. *Le Roman de la rose*. Edited by Ernest Langlois. 5 vols. Société des anciens textes français. Paris.

———— 1962. *The Romance of the Rose*. Edited by Charles W. Dunn. Translated by Harry W. Robbins. New York.

Lounsbury, T. R., ed. 1877. *The* Parlement of Foules *by Geoffrey Chaucer*. Boston.

———— 1892. *Studies in Chaucer*. 3 vols. New York.

Lowes, J. L. 1905. The Prologue to the *Legend of Good Women* Considered in Its Chronological Implications. *PMLA* 20:749–864.

———— 1910. Chaucer's "Etik." *MLN* 25:87–89.

———— 1915. Chaucer and Dante's *Convivio*. *MP* 13:19–33.

———— 1917a. Chaucer and Dante. *MP* 14:705–35.

———— 1917b. the Second Nun's Prologue, Alanus, and Macrobius. *MP* 15:193–202.

———— 1918. Chaucer and the *Ovide moralisé*. *PMLA* 32:303–19.

———— 1930. *The Art of Geoffrey Chaucer*. Sir Israel Gollancz Memorial Lecture, British Academy. London.

———— 1934. *Geoffrey Chaucer and the Development of His Genius*. Boston.

Lumiansky, R. M. 1954. The Story of Troilus and Briseida According to Benoit and Guido. *Speculum* 29:727–33.

Lynch, J. J. 1942. The Prioress' Gems. *MLN* 57:440–41.

MacCracken, H. N. 1909. Dant in English: A Solution. *Nation* 79:276–77.

Machaut, Guillaume de 1908–11. *Oeuvres*. Edited by Ernest Hoepffner. 2 vols. Société des anciens textes français. Paris.

McKenzie 1922. See Dante.

Madeleva, Sister Mary 1951. *A Lost Language and Other Essays on Chaucer*. New York.

Makarewicz, Sister Mary Raynelda 1953. *The Patristic Influence on Chaucer*. Washington, D.C.

Malone, Kemp 1951. *Chapters on Chaucer*. Baltimore, Md.

Manly, J. M. 1913. What Is Chaucer's *Hous of Fame? Kittredge Anniversary Papers* 1913:73–81. Boston.

———— 1926a. *Chaucer and the Rhetoricians*. Warton Lecture on English Poetry, no. 17, read before the British Academy June 2, 1926. London.

———— 1926b. *Some New Light on Chaucer*. New York.

Mather, F. J. 1897. On the Asserted Meeting of Chaucer and Petrarca. *MLN* 12:1–11.

Maynard, Theodore 1934. *The Connection Between the Ballade, Chaucer's Modification of It, Rime Royal, and the Spenserian Stanza*. Washington, D.C.

Meech, S. B. 1930. Chaucer and the Italian Translation of the *Heroides. PMLA* 45:110–28.

———— 1931. Chaucer and the *Ovide moralisé* – A Further Study. *PMLA* 46:182–204.

Migne, J.-P., ed., 1855. *Dictionnaire des légendes du Christianisme*. In *Encyclopédie théologique*, ser. 3, vol. 14. Paris.

Miller, R. P. 1955. Chaucer's Pardoner, the Scriptural Eunuch, and the Pardoner's Tale. *Speculum* 30:180–99.

Moore, Edward 1896. *Studies in Dante, First Series: Scripture and Classical Authors*. Oxford.

Muscatine, Charles 1964. *Chaucer and the French Tradition*. Berkeley, Calif.

Olson, Paul A. 1961. The Merchant's Lombard Knight. *TSLL* 3:259–63.

Orosius, Paulus 1936. *Seven Books of History Against the Pagans: The Apology of Paulus Orosius*. Translated by Irving Woodworth Raymond. Columbia University Records of Civilization: Sources and Studies, no. 26. New York.

Osgood, C. G. 1930. *Boccaccio on Poetry*. Princeton, N.J.

Ovid 1790. *Metamorphoseon, libri xv cum versione anglica*. . . . Translated by John Clark. 8th ed. Gloucester.

———— 1825. *Opera*. 5 vols. Oxford.

———— 1916. *Metamorphoses*. Translated by Frank Justus Miller. 2 vols. New York. Reprinted Cambridge, Mass., 1940, 1976.

Ovide moralisé. See De Boer, C., ed.

Pace, George B. 1963. Adam's Hell. *PMLA* 73:25–35.

Patch, H. R. 1919. Chaucer's Desert. *MLN* 34:321–28.

———— 1922. The Tradition of the Goddess Fortuna in Medieval Philosophy and Literature. *Smith College Studies in Modern Language* 3, no. 4.

———— 1927. *The Goddess Fortuna in Medieval Literature*. Cambridge, Mass. Reprinted 1967, New York.

———— 1939. *On Rereading Chaucer*. Cambridge, Mass.

Patterson, Lee W. 1979. Ambiguity and Interpretation: A Fifteenth-Century Reading of *Troilus and Criseyde. Speculum* 54:297–330.

Petrarca, Francesco 1946. *Le Rime, di su gli originali*. . . . Edited with commentary by Giosue Carducci and Severino Ferrari. Florence.

Petrus Comestor [1500]. *Scholastica historia magistri Petri Comestoris*. . . .

Pickering, J. W. 1980. *Essays on Medieval German Literature and Iconography*. Cambridge, Mass.

Plumptre, E. H. 1881. Two Studies in Dante. *Contemporary Review* 40:843–64.

Pollard, A. W. 1931. *Chaucer*. London.

Pollock, Sir Frederick, and F. W. Maitland 1895. *The History of English Law before the Time of Edward I.* 2 vols. Cambridge.

Pratt, R. A. 1939. Chaucer and the Visconti Libraries. *ELH* 6:191–99.

——— 1946. Chaucer Borrowing from Himself. *MLQ* 7:259–64.

——— 1950*a*. A Note on Chaucer and the *Policraticus* of John of Salisbury. *MLN* 65:243–46.

——— 1950*b*. A Note on Chaucer's Lollius. *MLN* 65:183–87.

Preston, Raymond 1951. Chaucer and the Ballades Notées of Guillaume de Machaut. *Speculum* 26:615–23.

Purdy, R. R. 1951. Chaucer Scholarship in England and America. *Anglia* 70:345–81.

Rambeau, A. 1880. Chaucer's "House of Fame" in seinem Verhältniss zu Dante's "Divina Commedia." *Englische Studien* 3:209–68.

Rand, E. K. 1926. Chaucer in Error. *Speculum* 1:224.

Randi, Luigi 1892. *Il marito e i figluoli di Beatrice Portinari.* Florence.

Reeves, John 1880. *Reeves' History of the English Law from the Time of the Romans to the End of the Reign of Elizabeth.* New American edition, edited, with introduction and commentary, by W. F. Finlason. 5 vols. Philadelphia.

Renouard, Yves 1949. *Les Hommes d'affaires italiens du moyen age.* Paris.

Rhodes, W. E. 1902. The Italian Bankers in England and Their Loans to Edward I and Edward II. In *Historical Essays by Members of the Owens College, Manchester,* edited by T. F. Tout and James Tait, pp. 137–68. London.

Rickert, Edith 1928. Chaucer Abroad in 1368. *MP* 25:511–12.

Robbins, R. H., ed. 1952. *Secular Lyrics of the XIVth and XVth Centuries.* Oxford.

Robertson, D. W., Jr. 1951. The Doctrine of Charity in Mediaeval Literary Gardens: A Topical Approach through Symbolism and Allegory. *Speculum* 26:24–49.

——— 1954. Why the Devil Wears Green. *MLN* 69:470–72.

Robinson, F. N. 1903. Chaucer and Dante. *Journal of Comparative Literature* 1:292–97.

———, ed. 1957. *The Works of Geoffrey Chaucer.* Boston.

Root, R. K. 1909. Chaucer's Legend of Medea. *PMLA* 24:124–53.

——— 1922. *The Poetry of Chaucer: A Guide to Its Study and Appreciation.* Rev. ed. Boston.

———, ed. 1945. *The Book of Troilus and Criseyde. . . .* 3d printing. Princeton, N.J.

Ross, Thomas W. 1971–72. *Troilus and Criseyde,* II.582–587: A Note. *ChauR* 5.

Rossetti, M. F. 1881. *A Shadow of Dante.* Edinburgh.

Ruggiers, P. G. 1950. Tyrants of Lombardy in Chaucer and Dante. *PQ* 29:445–48.

——— 1953. The Unity of Chaucer's *House of Fame. SP* 50:16–29.

——— 1954. Words into Images in Chaucer's *House of Fame*: A Third Suggestion. *MLN* 69:34–36.

——— 1965. *The Art of The Canterbury Tales.* Madison, Wis.

——— 1968. Italian Influence on Chaucer. In *Companion to Chaucer Studies,* edited by Beryl Rowland, pp. 139–61. Oxford.

——— 1977. *Versions of Medieval Comedy.* Norman, Ok.

Saintsbury, George 1901. *A Short History of French Literature. . . .* 6th ed. Oxford.

Salverda de Grave, J.-J., ed. 1925–29. *Eneas: Roman du xiie siècle.* 2 vols. Les Classiques français du moyen age, nos. 44, 62. Paris.

Samuel, Irene 1944. Semiramis in the Middle Ages: The History of a Legend. *M&H* 2:32–44.

Sandras, E. G. 1859. *Étude sur Chaucer considéré comme imitateur des trouvères.* Paris.

Sapori, Armando 1926. *La Crisi delle compagnie mercantili dei Bardi e dei Peruzzi.* Biblioteca storica toscana, no. 3. Florence.

Scartazzini, G. A. 1921. See Dante 1921.

Schaar, Claes 1954. *Some Types of Narrative in Chaucer's Poetry*. Lund Studies in English, no. 25. Lund.

Schlauch, Margaret 1937. Chaucer's *Merchant's Tale* and Courtly Love. *ELH* 6:201–12.

Schless, Howard H. 1960. Chaucer and Dante. In *Critical Approaches to Medieval Literature*, edited by Dorothy Bethurum, pp. 134–54. New York.

———— 1974. Transformations: Chaucer's Use of Italian. In *Geoffrey Chaucer*, edited by Derek Brewer, pp. 184–223. London.

———— 1977. Dante: Comedy and Conversion. In *Versions of Medieval Comedy*, edited by Paul G. Ruggiers, pp. 135–149. Norman, Ok.

Schramm, W. L. 1933. The Cost of Books in Chaucer's Time. *MLN* 48:139–45.

Schuman, Samuel 1975. The Circle of Nature: Patterns of Imagery in Chaucer's *Troilus and Criseyde*. *ChauR* 10:99–112.

Seibert, Harriet 1916. Chaucer and Horace. *MLN* 31:304–306.

Sells, A. L. 1955. *The Italian Influence in English Literature from Chaucer to Southwell*. Bloomington, Ind.

Servianus 1946. *Servianorum in Vergilii carmina commentariorum editionis Harvardianae, vol. ii: quod in Aenidos libros i et ii explanationes continent*. Edited by E. K. Rand et al. Lancaster, Pa.

Shanley, J. L. 1939. The *Troilus* and Christian Love. *ELH* 6:271–81.

Shannon, E. F. 1929. *Chaucer and the Roman Poets*. Harvard Studies in Comparative Litrature, no. 7. Cambridge, Mass.

Shelly, P. V. D. 1940. *The Living Chaucer*. Philadelphia.

Skeat, W. W. 1912. See Chaucer.

Smyser, H. M. 1941. Chaucer's Two-Mile Pilgrimage. *MLN* 56:205–207.

Spencer, Theodore 1927. Chaucer's Hell. *Speculum* 2:177–200.

———— 1934. The Story of Ugolino in Dante and Chaucer. *Speculum* 9:295–301.

Spiers, John 1951. *Chaucer the Maker*. London.

———— 1954. A Survey of Middle English Verse. In *The Age of Chaucer*, edited by Boris Ford, pp. 17–67. London.

Steadman, John M. 1961. Chaucer's "Desert of Libye," Venus, and Jove (*The Hous of Fame*, 486–87). *MLN* 76:196–201.

Stilwell, Gardner 1940. Analogues to Chaucer's *Maunciple's Tale* in the *Ovide moralisé* and Machaut's *Voir-dit*. *PQ* 19:133–38.

Stroud, T. A. 1952. Boethius' Influence on Chaucer's *Troilus*. *MP* 49:1–9.

Sypherd, W. O. 1907. *Studies in Chaucer's* Hous of Fame. Chaucer Society 2d ser., no. 39. London.

———— 1915. The Completeness of Chaucer's *Hous of Fame*. *MLN* 30:65–68.

Tatlock, J. S. P. 1905. Chaucer and Dante. *MP* 3:367–72.

———— 1914*a*. Another Parallel to the First canto of the *Inferno*. *Romanic Review* 5:90–93.

———— 1914*b*. Notes on Chaucer: Earlier or Minor Poems. *MLN* 29:97–101.

———— 1920. Dante and Guinizelli in Chaucer's *Troilus*. *MLN* 35:443.

———— 1950. *The Mind and Art of Chaucer*. Syracuse, N.Y.

————, and A. G. Kennedy 1927. *A Concordance to the Complete Works of Geoffrey Chaucer and to the* Romaunt of the Rose. Washington, D.C.

Tawney, R. H. 1948. *Religion and the Rise of Capitalism*. London.

Ten Brink, Bernhard 1870. *Chaucer: Studien zur Geschichte seiner Entwicklung und zur Chronologie seiner Schriften*. Münster.

Thomas, M. E. 1950. *Medieval Skepticism and Chaucer*. New York.

Tolkien, J. R. R. and E. V. Gordon, eds. 1952. *Sir Gawain and the Green Knight*. Oxford.

Torraca, Francesco 1902. Un Passo oscuro di G. Chaucer. *Journal of Comparative Literature* 1:82–84.

Tout, T. F. 1929. Literature and Learning in the English Civil Service in the Fourteenth Century. *Speculum* 4:365–89.

—— 1934*a*. The English Civil Service in the Fourteenth Century. In *The Collected Papers of Thomas Frederick Tout* (Publications of the University of Manchester 231, Historical Series 66), vol. 3, pp. 191–221. Manchester.

—— 1934*b*. Some Conflicting Tendencies in English Administrative History during the Fourteenth Century. In *The Collected Papers of Thomas Frederick Tout* (Publications of the University of Manchester 231, Historical Series 66), vol. 3, pp. 223–47. Manchester.

Toynbee, Paget 1909. *Dante in English Literature from Chaucer to Cary.* 2 vols. London.

—— 1914. *Concise Dictionary of Proper Names and Notable Events in the Works of Dante.* Oxford.

Trigona, F. Prestifilippo 1923. *Chaucer: Imitatore del Boccaccio.* Catania.

Tupper, Frederick 1915. Chaucer's Bed's Head. *MLN* 30:5–12.

—— 1916. Chaucer and Trophee. *MLN* 31:11–14.

Tuve, Rosamond 1930. Guillaume's Pilgrim and the Hous of Fame. *MLN* 45:518–22.

Twining, Louisa 1885. *Symbols and Emblems of Early and Mediaeval Christian Art.* London.

Van Marle, Raimond 1931–32. *Iconographie de l'art profane au moyen-age et à la renaissance.* 2 vols. La Haye.

Vincent de Beauvais [1473]. *Speculum . historiale . fratris . Vincencii . ordinnis . predicatorum . impressum . per . Iohannem . Mentellin. . . .* 4 vols. Strasbourg.

—— [1481]. *Opuscula* [containing the *Liber gratias, Laudes Virginis Mariae, De Sancto Iohanne Euangelista,* and *Consolatio super morte amici*]. Basel.

—— [1485]. *Speculum naturale Uincentum beluacensis fratris ordinis predicatorum.* 3 vols. Nuremberg.

Virgil 1918. *Virgil.* Translated by H. Rushton Fairclough. 2 vols. New York. Reprinted Cambridge, Mass., 1940, 1976.

—— 1930. *The Aeneid.* Edited, with introduction and commentary, by J. W. Mackail. Oxford.

—— 1935. *The Bucolics of Vergil.* Edited by F. J. De Veau. New York.

—— 1952. *The Aeneid of Vergil.* Translated by C. Day Lewis. London.

Watson, M. R. 1953. Wyatt, Chaucer, and terza rima. *MLN* 68:124–25.

Whiting, B. J. 1934. *Chaucer's Use of Proverbs.* Harvard Studies in Comparative Literature, no. 11. Cambridge, Mass.

Whitwell, R. J. [1903]. Italian Bankers and the English Crown. *Transactions of the Royal Historical Society,* n.s., 6:175–233.

Wilkins, E. H. 1949. Cantus Troili. *ELH* 16:167–73.

Wilkinson, B. 1955. English Politics and Politicians of the Thirteenth and Fourteenth Centuries. *Speculum* 30:37–48.

Williams, Arnold 1953. Chaucer and the Friars. *Speculum* 28:499–513.

Williams, J. T. 1947. Words into Images in Chaucer's *House of Fame. MLN* 62:488–90.

Winny, James 1973. *Chaucer's Dream-Poems.* New York.

Wise, B. A. 1911. *The Influence of Statius upon Chaucer.* Baltimore.

Woodford, Archer 1953. Mediaeval Iconography of the Virtues: A Poetic Portraiture. *Speculum* 28:521–24.

Young, Karl 1913. The Plan of the Canterbury Tales. *Kittredge Anniversary Papers,* pp. 405–17. Boston.

—— 1944. Chaucer and Geoffrey of Vinsauf. *MP* 41:172–82.

Ziegler, Julian 1949. Two Notes on J. T. Williams' "Words into Images in Chaucer's *House of Fame." MLN* 64:73–76.

General Index

Aetius: 62.

"Agaton": 156.

Alanus de Insulis: 58, 60, 65, 216, 236.

Aiken, P.: 182.

Albericus: 217.

Albertus Magnus: 63, 120, 183, 214, 220, 233, 234, 236.

Alceste: 112, 149, 155, 246.

Aldgate: 40.

Aldhelm: 18.

Alecto: 103, 104, 129.

Alien Merchants: 6.

Alighieri:
  Jacopo: 9.
  Pietro: 6, 9.

Allegory: 15–20.

Amorosa Visione: 51, 52, 59, 69, 92, 124.

St. Ambrose: 141.

Anaxagoras: 61–63.

Andreas Capellanus: 12, 192, 198-99, 204-206, 239, 241.

Anelida and Arcite: Chapter III, passim. For individual entries see Index of Comparisons.

St. Anne: 217.

Apollo: 68–71, 80–83, 86, 132, 172, 206, 226.

Aquinas, St. Thomas: 18, 21, 56, 57, 63, 65, 67, 76, 94, 106, 127, 141, 142, 171–72, 174, 178, 180, 214, 220, 221, 229, 230, 236.

Ariadne, Legend of: 135, 167.

Aristotle: 61–63, 76, 115, 140, 149–155, 220, 227, 229.

Astrolabe, Treatise on: 21.

Athamas: 135, 136.

St. Augustine: 18, 19, 58, 60, 65, 107, 113, 114, 179, 180, 213, 220, 229, 236.

Austin, H. D.: 146.

Averroes: 63.

Avicenna: 61, 62.

Axon, W. E.: 130.

Ayenbite of Inwyt: 73.

Baker, D. C.: 183.

Bale, J.: 29, 30.

Bankers, royal: 7.

Bardi: 5–8.
  history of: 6–8.
  settlement: 5–6.
  de Bardi, Philip: 6.
  de Bardi, Walter: 6.
  de Bardi, Walter, king's moneyer: 6.
  dei Bardi, Simone: 6, 8.

Baugh, A. C.: 13, 23, 39.

Beardwood, Alice: 5–7.

Beatrice (see also Portinari, Beatrice): 21, 49, 50, 57, 58, 66, 145, 203, 226, 228.

Becker, E. J.: 136.

Bede: 18, 136.

Bennett, H. S.: 4, 11, 23, 106, 107.

Bennett, J. A. W.: 26, 30, 34, 45, 47, 49–50, 52, 54, 57, 69, 90–91, 97, 172, 230.

Benoit de Sainte-Maure: 162, 201.

St. Bernard of Clairvaux: 21, 101, 207, 214–217, 239, 247.

Bethel, J. P.: ix, 4, 13, 25, 42–50, 52–60, 64, 68, 70–74, 78, 87, 90–97, 99, 100, 102–41, 143, 146, 150, 153, 154, 156–60, 164, 167, 168, 171–84, 187, 189, 191–98, 200–206, 209, 212–14, 217–19, 221, 223–26, 230–32, 236, 237, 239, 240, 242.

Bianchi: 4.

Bible:
  Rev., IX, 7–11: 45.
  Rev., I, 17: 99, 54.
  Ezek., xvii, 3–4: 47
  2 Corinth. XII, 1–4: 64.
  Exod., XXXIII, 20: 65.
  Exod., XX: 218.
  Job: 136.
  Eccl., X, 8: 141.
  Daniel, II, 1: 209.
  Daniel, II, 21: 141
  John, CIII: 182
  Ps., LV, 15: 182.
  Ps., CXIII, 4: 218.
  Hosea, VIII, 4: 218.